THE BEST OF
McCall's

A Treasury of Favorite Recipes

THE BEST OF
McCall's

A Treasury of Favorite Recipes

By the
FOOD EDITORS OF McCALL'S

Edited by
ELAINE PRESCOTT WONSAVAGE

FIELDPUBLICATIONS

Design
Blackbirch Graphics, Inc.

Senior Writer/Copy Editor
Meg Beutel

Recipe Editor
Ruth Pomeroy

Senior Editorial Coordinator
Dorcas Comstock

Copyright © 1987 by
The McCall Publishing Company
230 Park Avenue
New York, NY 10169

Published by
Field Publications
4343 Equity Drive
Columbus, OH 43216

Printed in the
United States of America

ISBN 0-8374-1951-4

CONTENTS

Introduction

America has been blessed with an abundance of riches, and among the most treasured is our rich culinary heritage. From the American Indians who first taught the colonists to grow and cook the native foods, through the waves of immigrants who brought with them their own unique cultures, to contemporary cooks who create modern-day classics in step with today's life-styles, ours is a history of taste and diversity that spans the generations. Through it all, only the very best recipes and dishes have endured the test of time to become cherished classics.

This cookbook is our celebration of the very best of American cuisine. We looked into our own treasure trove of recipes and carefully selected our tried-and-true favorites to share with you. Here are our Star-Spangled classics, from juicy apple pie to the famous specialties of America's finest country inns and restaurants. Taste the fabulous international flavors that have become so much a part of our culture. Let us entertain you with our very best party recipes and menus for all occasions. Sit down to our favorite entrées, the exciting main attractions for elegant company dinners as well as everyday family meals.

Savor nature's bounty with our delightful fresh-from-the-garden vegetable dishes. And indulge in America's best-loved pies, tarts, cakes and yummy ice-cream creations.

Think of this book as a culinary diary of Americana, one we hope you'll treasure for years to come. It's a tribute to America's enduring tradition of fine cookery.

CHAPTER

1

AMERICA'S HERITAGE OF FOODS

★

Among this country's great natural resources is its rich tradition of fine cookery. From the time of the Pilgrims to the present, America's treasury of excellent cuisine has grown in diversity and size, as has our nation itself. With apple pie leading the way, many other classic dishes have made the journey from their different regions of origin to crisscross the country and eventually become an integral part of American cooking as we know it today.

This chapter pays tribute to our country's great culinary heritage, which has evolved over the past two centuries and which continues its own evolution in the world today.

Star-Spangled Favorites

★ ★ ★

Here is a glorious cornucopia of great American cookery—delectable cuisine that has been delighting us all for generations. On these pages is some of the best-loved fare that this country has to offer, beginning with the all-American favorite: apple pie—double crusted and filled with tangy green apples. Recipes start on page 18.

Above: This magnificent Pork Crown Roast is a feast for the eyes as well as the palate. It's topped with vegetables and fruits in a tangy brown-sugar-mustard sauce. *See recipes on page 18.*

From sea to shining sea, and anywhere in between, comes this taste-tempting trio: fresh boiled lobster with shrimp-and-scallop kabobs in a lemony garlic marinade; Pineapple Boats with succulent chunks of fresh fruit (perfect for dipping into honeyed poppy-seed sauce); and Layered Ham Salad—a spiral of crisp greens, tender peas, sharp Cheddar and more—that can stand overnight and appear the next day for a party. *Recipes begin on page 19.*

Left: In creative kitchens all across the land, wonderful home-made specialties like these are served with pride. The vegetable tray shows off scrumptious Potato Baskets with peas and pearl onions, Squash Boats smothered in a zesty tomato sauce and Stuffed Mushrooms. Fresh from the oven are gooey, nutty Sticky Buns, buttery Herb Bread spiraled with parsley and green onion and a moist Zucchini-Walnut Bread topped with cream cheese. *Recipes begin on page 20.*

Above: Two distinctive desserts to grace any table: a show-off Chocolate-Nut Torte elegantly adorned with chocolate butter-cream and dainty sugared violets and a delicate apple-glazed cream-puff ring filled with swirls of almond Chantilly, sprinkled with toasted almonds and served with lovely whole strawberries. *See recipes on pages 23 and 24.*

Regional
Favorites

Right: Chicken-And-Noodle Pot-pie, colorful with saffron and typically Pennsylvania Dutch, makes a hearty yet thrifty meal with extra-moist Potato Bread. *See recipes on pages 25 and 26.*

Below left: Iowa Corn Relish accompanies Stuffed Pork Chops brimming with a savory stuffing chock-full of apples and raisins. *See recipes on pages 25 and 28.*

Below right: Kentucky Bourbon Cake, with pecans, cherries and raisins, marinates in the native American whiskey for a spirited flavor. *See recipe on page 29.*

Left: Michigan Baked Beans are bacon-crusted and brown-sugared. Stuffed Whitefish bakes up delicious with a thyme-flavored bread stuffing. *See recipes on page 27.*

Below left: Cobb Salad, a California creation of avocados and chicken, is as healthful as it is attractive. *See recipe on page 29.*

Bottom left: Broiled Salmon Steak, basted with parsley-lemon butter, is an easy-to-make yet elegant entrée from Washington State. *See recipe on page 28.*

Bottom right: Southern Baked Ham from Tennessee tastes as good as it looks. The gourmet trick: a crusty glaze of brown sugar, mustard and sherry. *See recipe on page 26.*

Below right: A tumble of Parker House Rolls awaits New England Fish Chowder, a creamy soup stocked with bacon, potatoes and "Pilgrim's bread"—the old New England term for fish. *See recipes on page 28.*

Star-Spangled Favorites

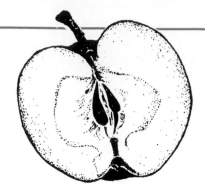

continued from page 11

All-American Apple Pie
(pictured)

1 **pkg (11 oz) piecrust mix**
1 **cup sugar**
2 **tablespoons all-purpose flour**
1 **teaspoon ground cinnamon**
⅛ **teaspoon ground nutmeg**
¼ **teaspoon salt**
7 **cups thinly sliced, pared, tart cooking apple—**
   greening, Northern Spy, McIntosh (2½ lb)
2 **tablespoons lemon juice**
2 **tablespoons butter or margarine**
   Ice cream or Cheddar cheese (optional)

1. Make pastry as package label directs. Handling gently, shape pastry into a ball. Divide in half; form each half into a round; then flatten each with palm of hand. On lightly floured pastry cloth, roll out half of pastry into a 12-inch circle. With a sharp knife, cut off and reserve pastry trimmings.
2. Fold rolled pastry in half; carefully transfer to 9-inch pie plate, making sure fold is in center of pie plate. Unfold pastry and fit carefully into pie plate, pressing gently with fingers, so pastry fits snugly all around. Do not stretch pastry. Refrigerate until ready to use.
3. Preheat oven to 425F. In small bowl, mix sugar, flour, cinnamon, nutmeg and salt. In a large bowl, toss apple with lemon juice. Add sugar mixture to apple; toss lightly to combine.
4. Roll out remaining pastry into a 12-inch circle. If necessary, trim circle to even edges. Reserve pastry trimmings. Fold in half. Turn apple mixture into pastry-lined pie plate, mounding high in center. Dot apple with butter.
5. Adjust folded pastry over filling. Moisten edge of bottom pastry with a little water. Fold top pastry under edge of bottom pastry. Press edges together to seal, so juices won't run out. Crimp edge. Make large slit in center for steam vent.
6. Bake 45 to 50 minutes, or until apple is fork-tender and crust is golden. Cool on wire rack. Serve warm; if desired, serve with ice cream or Cheddar cheese. *Makes 8 servings.*

Note: If desired, with sharp knife, cut out pastry apples from reserved trimmings; moisten one side and place on pie, as pictured, before baking.

Pork Crown Roast
(pictured)

6-**lb pork crown roast**
1 **teaspoon salt**
¼ **teaspoon pepper**
   Water
   Mustard-Glazed Mélange, recipe follows
   Ornamental pineapples or small bunches of
   seedless green grapes (optional)

1. Preheat oven to 400F. Rub pork well with salt and pepper. Place on rack in shallow roasting pan.
2. Roast pork, uncovered, 20 minutes. Reduce oven temperature to 325F. Pour 1 cup water into pan. Cover pork with foil. Roast 1 hour and 45 minutes longer. Add more water during roasting, if necessary, so that pan does not become dry. Remove foil; roast 45 to 55 minutes longer, or until meat thermometer inserted in the thickest part of the roast and not touching bone reaches 170F.
3. Meanwhile, prepare Mustard-Glazed Mélange. Place pork on heated platter; cover loosely with foil to keep warm. Garnish platter with ornamental pineapples or small bunches of green grapes. *Makes 10 servings.*

Mustard-Glazed Mélange

1 **can (1 lb) unpeeled apricot halves**
   Water
¼ **cup (½ stick) butter or margarine**
½ **cup firmly packed light-brown sugar**
2 **tablespoons prepared mustard**
2 **teaspoons dry mustard**
2 **large carrots, pared**
1 **large red pepper**
¼ **lb snow-pea pods, stemmed (1 cup)**
½ **lb seedless green grapes (1 cup)**

1. Drain apricots, pouring syrup into a 1-cup glass measuring cup; add water to make 1 cup. Reserve apricots.
2. In small saucepan, combine apricot syrup, butter, brown sugar and mustards; mix well. Bring to boiling; boil, uncovered, 5 minutes, or until slightly thickened.
3. Meanwhile, with a fluted cutter, slice carrots ¼ inch thick on the diagonal. In large skillet, bring 2 cups

Star-Spangled Favorites

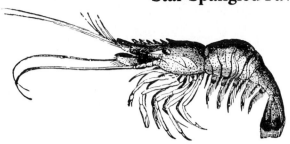

water to boiling; add carrot; cook, covered, 4 minutes. Meanwhile, remove and discard stem and seeds from pepper; cut in 1-inch pieces; add to carrot; boil, uncovered, 1 minute. Add pea pods to skillet; cook, uncovered, 1 minute longer. Thoroughly drain vegetables in colander; return to skillet.

4. Pour mustard glaze over vegetables in skillet; stir in grapes and reserved apricots; heat thoroughly—about 1 minute.

5. With slotted spoon, remove fruit and vegetables from glaze mixture; spoon half in center of roast; spoon remaining fruit and vegetables into serving dish.

6. Bring glaze to boiling; cook, uncovered, until thickened—about 5 minutes. Spoon some hot glaze over fruit-vegetable mixture in crown roast; spoon remaining glaze over fruit and vegetables in serving dish.

Marinated Scallops, Shrimp and Lobster
(pictured)

- **1 lb sea scallops**
- **1 lb fresh jumbo shrimp (about 22), shelled (leave last tail segment attached) and deveined**
- **1 medium onion, sliced**
- **1 bay leaf**
- **1 teaspoon salt**
- **½ teaspoon white pepper**
- **3 lemons**
- **1½- to 2-lb whole (live or cooked) lobster**
- **Lemon Marinade, recipe follows**
- **Cocktail skewers or long wooden picks**
- **6 to 8 cups crushed ice**
- **Parsley sprigs**

1. Day ahead: In large kettle (6- to 8-quart), combine scallops, shrimp, onion, bay leaf, salt and pepper. Cut 1 lemon in thin slices; add to kettle. Add 8 cups water, or to cover ingredients; bring to boiling. Remove kettle from heat; cover; let stand 5 minutes. With slotted spoon, remove scallops and shrimp to large shallow dish.

2. (If using cooked lobster, omit Steps 2 and 3.) Add 4 quarts water to kettle; return to boiling. With tongs, hold lobster by the body, claws away from you; place in boiling water; cover kettle and return to boiling. Reduce heat; simmer 12 minutes.

3. Remove lobster from kettle with tongs; place on its back on cutting board. With scissors, split body in half lengthwise, cutting through the undershell. Remove and discard dark vein and small sac 2 inches below the head.

4. Cut away and discard undershell of lobster tail. With mallet or cracker, crack large claws to let excess moisture drain off and facilitate eating. Arrange lobster on its back in shallow dish with shrimp and scallops. Let cool while making Lemon Marinade. Pour marinade over fish; cover tightly with plastic wrap or foil. Refrigerate overnight.

5. To serve: Thread shrimp and scallops on skewers or long wooden picks. Detach large claws from body of lobster; cut tail into four sections.

6. Line a large rimmed serving platter (preferably a fish platter with perforated draining insert plate) with crushed ice. Reassemble lobster, shell side up, in center of platter; surround with shrimp and scallop skewers. Replenish skewers as necessary. Cut 2 lemons in wedges. Use with parsley to garnish platter. *Makes about 40 appetizer servings.*

Lemon Marinade

- **¾ cup lemon juice**
- **¼ cup olive or salad oil**
- **2 teaspoons salt**
- **¾ teaspoon white pepper**
- **1 teaspoon dried tarragon leaves**
- **2 medium cloves garlic, finely minced or crushed**

In small bowl, combine all ingredients. Stir well to blend.

Ambrosia

- **1 ripe pineapple**
- **3 large navel oranges**
- **¼ cup orange juice**
- **¼ cup confectioners' sugar**
- **1 can (3½ oz) flaked coconut or 1 cup peeled and grated fresh coconut**

1. Peel pineapple; cut into rounds ¼ inch thick. Peel oranges; cut into crosswise slices ¼ inch thick.

2. On serving platter, arrange pineapple rings in a single

Star-Spangled Favorites

layer; top each with orange slices. Sprinkle with orange juice, then with confectioners' sugar.

3. Sprinkle with coconut. Refrigerate to chill well. *Makes 8 servings.*

Layered Ham Salad
(pictured)

 1   **pkg (10 oz) frozen peas**
½   **medium head iceberg lettuce, crisped**
 1   **cup shredded Cheddar cheese (4 oz)**
 1   **large red pepper, seeded and chopped**
 2   **containers (1-pint size) cherry tomatoes or 1 pint each red and yellow cherry tomatoes, halved**
 1   **large cucumber, scored and thinly sliced**
 1   **cup sliced green onion, with green tops**
 1   **lb unsliced boiled ham, cut into 2½-by-¼-inch strips**
1½   **cups mayonnaise**
½   **cup bottled oil-and-vinegar dressing**

1. Day ahead: Cook frozen peas as package label directs, omitting butter; drain. Tear lettuce into bite-size pieces. Reserve 2 tablespoons cheese.
2. In large salad bowl, layer, in order, lettuce, remaining cheese, red pepper, half of tomatoes, cucumber, remaining tomatoes and green onion. Arrange peas around edge of dish; place ham strips in center. Spoon on mayonnaise; spread to edge to cover entire surface of salad. Refrigerate, covered, overnight.
3. Just before serving: Pour bottled dressing over mayonnaise. Sprinkle with reserved cheese. To serve, do not toss; spoon down through layers. *Makes 10 servings.*

Fruited Pineapple Boats
(pictured)

 1   **large pineapple with top**
 2   **kiwi fruit**
 1   **small cantaloupe**
 1   **container (1 pint) fresh strawberries, hulled**
½   **lb fresh sweet cherries with stems (1 cup)**
     Poppy-Seed Dipping Sauce, recipe follows
     Decorative wooden picks

1. With large sharp knife, cut pineapple, with top, in half vertically. With small sharp knife, cut pineapple fruit from both halves, leaving two pineapple boats. Cut away and discard core from pineapple; cut pineapple into 1-inch chunks.
2. Pare kiwi; cut each into 8 wedges. Pare cantaloupe, and cut in half. Scoop out and discard seeds; cut fruit into 1-inch chunks.
3. Combine all fruit in large bowl; stir gently. Use half

to fill pineapple boats, dividing evenly. Cover and refrigerate remaining fruit; use to refill boats. Make Poppy-Seed Dipping Sauce.

4. To serve: Arrange filled pineapple boats on serving dish; stick about 15 decorative wooden picks into base of each frond, to use in spearing fruit. Serve with Poppy-Seed Dipping Sauce. *Makes 24 appetizer servings.*

Poppy-Seed Dipping Sauce
(pictured)

¾   **cup sugar**
 1   **teaspoon dry mustard**
 1   **teaspoon salt**
⅓   **cup cider vinegar**
 1   **tablespoon onion juice (or finely grated onion)**
 1   **cup salad oil**
1½   **tablespoons poppy seeds**

1. In medium bowl, combine sugar, mustard, salt, vinegar and onion juice.
2. Using portable electric mixer or rotary beater, gradually beat in oil until mixture is thick and smooth. (Or combine first 5 ingredients in blender or processor and gradually add oil, on low speed, through feed tube, until mixture is thickened.) Stir in poppy seeds.

Filled Potato Baskets
(pictured)

 1   **pkg (12 oz) frozen shredded hashed brown potatoes**
 1   **large egg**
 1   **teaspoon salt**
 2   **pkg (10-oz size) frozen peas and pearl onions**
 2   **tablespoons butter or margarine**
 2   **tablespoons chopped pimiento**
     Dash pepper

1. Thaw potatoes; pat dry with paper towels; crumble to separate shreds. In medium bowl, beat egg with salt; add potatoes and blend well.
2. Preheat oven to 400F. Butter six (6-ounce) custard cups; place on cookie sheet. Divide potato mixture evenly among cups; with fork, press potatoes over bottom and sides to form baskets. Bake 30 minutes, or until mixture is lightly browned on bottom and rim. Remove cookie sheet to wire rack; let stand 2 minutes. Loosen baskets around edges with small metal spatula; carefully lift out onto cookie sheet. Return to oven 5 minutes to dry slightly.
3. Meanwhile, prepare peas and onions as package label directs. Drain water from pan; toss vegetables with butter, pimiento and pepper. Fill baskets with vegetable mixture. *Makes 6 servings.*

Star-Spangled Favorites

Squash Boats With Fresh-Tomato Sauce
(pictured)

- 6 medium yellow squash (3 lb)
  Boiling water

Filling

- ¾ lb ground lamb or beef
- 2 tablespoons butter or margarine
- ½ cup chopped onion
- 1 medium clove garlic, crushed
- 1 tablespoon chopped fresh mint or 1 teaspoon dried mint leaves
- 1 tablespoon chopped parsley
- ¾ teaspoon salt
- ⅛ teaspoon pepper
- ½ cup canned tomato sauce
- 1 cup cooked white rice

  Fresh-Tomato Sauce, recipe follows

1. Preheat oven to 350F. Wash squash; cut off a thin, lengthwise slice from each (save slices for salads). With small spoon, scoop out and discard seeds from squash, leaving a shell ½ inch thick.
2. In baking dish, arrange squash shells; pour in enough boiling water to cover shells; bake 5 minutes. Remove pan from oven; pour off water; drain squash well.
3. Make Filling: In medium skillet, brown lamb in butter over medium heat. Add onion and garlic; sauté, stirring often, until onion is tender—5 minutes. Add mint, parsley, salt, pepper and canned tomato sauce; bring to boiling. Reduce heat; simmer 5 minutes to blend flavors; stir in rice.
4. With small spoon, fill squash shells with lamb mixture. Arrange in baking pan; pour ¼ cup boiling water in bottom of pan. Cover pan tightly with foil; bake 30 minutes. Meanwhile, make Fresh-Tomato Sauce. Arrange baked squash on a serving plate; spoon sauce over squash. *Makes 6 servings.*

★

Fresh-Tomato Sauce

- 1 cup chopped onion
- 1 medium clove garlic
- ¼ cup olive or salad oil
- 3 large tomatoes, peeled and chopped (1½ lb)
- ¼ cup canned tomato sauce
- 1 teaspoon salt
- ¼ teaspoon dried basil leaves
- ¼ teaspoon pepper

1. In medium saucepan, sauté onion and garlic over medium heat in hot oil until onion is golden—about 5 minutes.
2. Add tomato, tomato sauce, salt, basil and pepper. Simmer, covered, 10 minutes.

Stuffed Mushrooms
(pictured)

- 12 large fresh mushrooms
- ½ cup (1 stick) butter or margarine
- 2 tablespoons chopped green pepper
- 1 tablespoon chopped red pepper
- 3 tablespoons finely chopped onion
- 3 slices white bread
- ½ teaspoon salt
- ⅛ teaspoon pepper
  Dash ground red pepper

1. Preheat oven to 350F. Wipe mushrooms with damp cloth. Remove stems; chop stems finely; set aside.
2. In large skillet, sauté mushroom caps in 3 tablespoons butter (bottom side only) 2 to 3 minutes; remove. Arrange, rounded side down, in shallow baking pan.
3. In same skillet, sauté chopped stems, green and red peppers and onion in remaining butter until tender—about 5 minutes; remove from heat. Meanwhile, cut bread into ¼-inch cubes. Add to stem mixture with seasonings. Fill mushroom caps, mounding high in center. Bake 15 minutes. *Makes 4 servings.*

Spiral Herb Bread
(pictured)

- 7 to 7½ cups all-purpose flour
- 2 pkg fast-rising or regular dry yeast
- ¼ cup sugar
- 2 teaspoons salt
- 1½ cups milk
- ½ cup (1 stick) butter or margarine, cut in pieces
- ½ cup water
- 3 large eggs

Filling

- 1½ cups finely chopped parsley
- 1½ cups finely chopped green onion
- 2 tablespoons butter or margarine
- ¼ teaspoon salt
- ⅛ teaspoon pepper
  Dash hot red-pepper sauce
- 1 large egg, slightly beaten

- 1 large egg white, slightly beaten
- 2 tablespoons sesame seeds

1. In large bowl of electric mixer, combine 2½ cups flour, the yeast, sugar and 2 teaspoons salt; mix well. In saucepan, combine milk, ½ cup butter and the water; heat until hot (120 to 130F).
2. With mixer at medium speed, add hot milk mixture to flour mixture; beat until smooth—about 2 minutes. Add 3 eggs and 2½ cups flour; continue beating

Star-Spangled Favorites

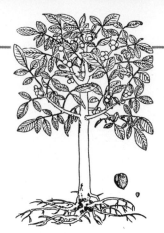

until smooth—about 2 minutes. With wooden spoon or hands, gradually add enough remaining flour to make dough stiff enough to leave side of bowl.

3. Turn dough out onto a lightly floured surface. Knead until smooth and elastic—5 to 10 minutes.
4. Place in lightly greased large bowl; turn dough over to bring up greased side. Cover with towel; let rise in warm place (85F), free from drafts, until double in bulk—1 to 1½ hours.
5. Make Filling: In saucepan, combine parsley, onion and butter. Over medium heat, sauté, stirring constantly, till soft but not browned—2 minutes. Remove from heat; cool 5 minutes. Add salt, pepper and red-pepper sauce. Reserve about 2 tablespoons beaten whole egg; add remaining egg to parsley mixture.
6. Turn dough out onto lightly floured surface. Divide in half. Roll out one half into 16-by-8-inch rectangle. Brush with 1 tablespoon reserved whole egg; spread with half of filling.
7. Starting at narrow end, roll up jelly-roll fashion. Pinch edges and ends together to seal. Tuck ends under. Place, seam side down, in greased 9-by-5-by-3-inch loaf pan. Cover with towel. Repeat with other half.
8. Let rise in warm place, free from drafts, until sides come to top of pan and tops are rounded—45 to 60 minutes. Lightly brush each loaf with beaten egg white; sprinkle each with 1 tablespoon sesame seeds. Place oven rack in middle of oven. Preheat oven to 350F. Bake 35 to 40 minutes—tops should be well browned. (If crust seems too brown after 25 minutes of baking, cover loosely with foil.) Loaf should sound hollow when tapped with knuckle.
9. Remove from pan immediately; cool completely on rack, away from drafts. *Makes 2 loaves.*

Savory Sliced Steak

3 lb top round steak, cut 1½ inches thick
⅓ cup soy sauce
¾ cup dry white wine
2 tablespoons dark rum
2 tablespoons salad oil
Watercress sprigs (optional)
1 bunch radishes with tops (optional)

1. Day ahead: Trim steak if necessary. Prick steak with fork on both sides. In dish slightly larger than steak, combine soy sauce, wine and rum. Place steak in soy-sauce mixture to marinate; cover with plastic wrap. Refrigerate overnight, turning occasionally.
2. Preheat broiler. Place steak on rack in broiler. Brush both sides lightly with oil. Broil steak, 6 inches from heat, 12 minutes; turn and brush with marinade. Broil 12 minutes, or until steak is of desired doneness.
3. Remove steak to board or platter. Slice on the diagonal into ⅛-inch-thick slices. Garnish with watercress sprigs and radishes. *Makes 8 to 10 servings.*

Zucchini-Walnut Bread
(pictured)

2½ cups all-purpose flour
2 teaspoons baking soda
1 teaspoon baking powder
1 teaspoon ground cinnamon
½ teaspoon ground cloves
½ teaspoon salt
1½ cups sugar
¾ cup salad oil
3 large eggs
2 cups grated unpeeled zucchini (1 lb)
1 cup finely chopped walnuts
1 teaspoon vanilla extract
Softened cream cheese (optional)
Walnut halves (optional)

1. Preheat oven to 350F. Grease well a 9-by-5-by-3-inch loaf pan. On waxed paper, mix flour, baking soda, baking powder, cinnamon, cloves and salt.
2. In large mixing bowl, with wooden spoon or electric mixer, combine sugar, oil and eggs; beat until smooth.
3. Add dry ingredients, mixing until smooth. Add zucchini, chopped nuts and vanilla; stir until well combined.
4. Pour batter into prepared pan. Bake 1 hour and 15 minutes, or till cake tester inserted in center comes out clean. Cool in pan 10 minutes. Remove from pan; cool completely on wire rack. To serve: Top with cream cheese; garnish with walnut halves. *Makes 1 loaf.*

Star-Spangled Favorites

Sticky Buns
(pictured)

2½ to 3 cups all-purpose flour
  1 pkg fast-rising or regular dry yeast
  ¼ cup granulated sugar
  ½ teaspoon salt
  ⅓ cup milk
  ¼ cup (½ stick) butter or margarine, cut in pieces
  ¼ cup water
  1 large egg

Filling
  ¾ cup (1½ sticks) butter or margarine, softened
  1 cup firmly packed light-brown sugar
  ½ cup pecan or walnut halves (optional)
  ½ cup chopped pecans or walnuts
  ½ cup chopped raisins
  ½ teaspoon ground cinnamon

1. In large bowl of electric mixer, combine 1½ cups flour, the yeast, granulated sugar and salt; mix well. In small saucepan, combine milk, ¼ cup butter and the water; heat until hot (120 to 130F).
2. With mixer at medium speed, add hot milk mixture to flour mixture; beat until smooth—about 2 minutes. Add egg and ½ cup flour; continue beating until smooth—about 2 minutes. With wooden spoon or hands, gradually add enough remaining flour to make dough stiff enough to leave side of bowl.
3. Turn out dough onto lightly floured surface. Knead until dough is smooth and elastic—about 5 minutes. Place in lightly greased large bowl; turn dough over to bring up greased side. Cover with towel; let rise in warm place (85F), free from drafts, until double in bulk—45 to 60 minutes.
4. Meanwhile, make Filling: In small bowl, with wooden spoon, cream ½ cup butter with ½ cup brown sugar. Spread on bottom and sides of 9-by-9-by-2-inch square baking pan. If desired, place pecan halves evenly over filling in pan.
5. On lightly floured surface, roll dough into a 16-by-12-inch rectangle. Spread with ¼ cup butter; sprinkle with remaining ½ cup brown sugar, the chopped pecans, raisins and cinnamon. Roll up from long side, jelly-roll fashion; pinch edge to seal. Cut crosswise into 12 equal pieces; place, cut side down, in prepared pan.
6. Let rise, covered, in warm place (85F), free from drafts, until doubled (rolls rise to top of pan)—45 to 60 minutes. Meanwhile, preheat oven to 375F. Bake 25 to 30 minutes, or until golden. Invert on board; let stand 1 minute; remove pan. Serve warm. *Makes 1 dozen sticky buns.*

Paris Brest
(pictured)

Cream-Puff Ring
  ½ cup (1 stick) butter or margarine
  1 cup water
  ¼ teaspoon salt
  1 cup all-purpose flour
  5 large eggs

Almond Chantilly
1½ cups heavy cream
  ⅓ cup confectioners' sugar
  2 teaspoons vanilla extract
  ¼ teaspoon almond extract

  ¼ cup apple jelly
  ¼ cup sliced blanched almonds, toasted (see Note)
    Whole strawberries (optional)

1. Make Cream-Puff Ring: In medium saucepan, combine butter, water and salt; bring to boiling; remove from heat. Immediately add flour all at once, beating with wooden spoon until smooth. Return to heat and continue beating until mixture forms a ball and leaves side of pan. Remove from heat. Add eggs, one at a time, beating well after each addition. After adding last egg, continue beating until mixture is shiny and breaks in strands.
2. Preheat oven to 400F. With handle of wooden spoon, trace a 9-inch circle on foil-lined 15½-by-12-inch cookie sheet. Trace a 4-inch circle in center of 9-inch circle. Spoon cream-puff batter into large pastry bag fitted with ½-inch star tip. Pipe cream-puff batter onto foil in rings to cover area between circles, forming a ½-inch-high base. Pipe remaining batter onto base to form ten 2-inch-wide mounds.
3. Bake about 50 minutes, or until ring is firm and deep golden-brown. Turn off heat; leave ring in oven 30 minutes more. Remove to wire rack to cool completely.

Star-Spangled Favorites

4. Meanwhile, make Almond Chantilly: In small bowl of electric mixer, beat cream with confectioners' sugar and extracts until stiff peaks form when beaters are slowly raised. Refrigerate.

5. In small saucepan, heat apple jelly, stirring just until melted; remove from heat; cool slightly. To assemble: With long serrated knife, split ring in half horizontally. Pull out and discard any filaments of soft dough. Brush jelly on top half of ring to glaze. Sprinkle almonds on top. Peel off and discard foil from bottom of ring; place ring on serving plate. Spoon Chantilly into large pastry bag fitted with large star tip. Just before serving, pipe Chantilly decoratively into bottom half of ring. Cover with top of ring. Arrange whole strawberries in center. *Makes 10 servings.*

Note: Toast almonds in 350F oven, stirring occasionally—about 10 minutes, or until lightly browned.

Chocolate-Nut Torte
(pictured)

Sugared Violets, recipe follows

Torte Layers
    7 large eggs
    1 cup granulated sugar
    1 teaspoon vanilla extract
 1¼ cups ground hazelnuts (about 4 oz)
 1¼ cups ground pecans (about 4 oz)
  ½ cup packaged dry bread crumbs
    1 teaspoon baking powder
  ½ teaspoon salt

Filling
    1 cup heavy cream, chilled (½ pint)
  ¼ cup confectioners' sugar
    1 teaspoon vanilla extract

Chocolate Butter-Cream
    1 pkg (8 oz) semisweet chocolate, chopped
  ¾ lb (3 sticks) unsalted butter, softened
    2 cups sifted confectioners' sugar
       Dash salt
    3 large egg yolks

  ¼ cup seedless raspberry jam (optional)

1. Day before: Make Sugared Violets; let dry overnight.
2. Make Torte Layers: Separate eggs, placing whites in large bowl of electric mixer and yolks in smaller bowl; let whites warm to room temperature—20 minutes.
3. Preheat oven to 375F. Line bottom of three (9-inch) round layer-cake pans with circles of waxed paper.

With mixer at high speed, beat egg whites until soft peaks form when beaters are slowly raised. Gradually beat in ½ cup granulated sugar, beating until stiff peaks form. With same beaters, beat egg yolks with remaining ½ cup granulated sugar until thick and light—about 3 minutes; beat in 1 teaspoon vanilla.

4. On waxed paper, combine ground nuts, bread crumbs, baking powder and ½ teaspoon salt. Add to yolk mixture; stir to mix. Add one-third of beaten egg-white mixture to yolk mixture, stirring until blended. With rubber spatula, using an over-and-under motion, fold yolk mixture into egg-white mixture until no white streaks remain. Pour into prepared pans, dividing evenly; smooth surfaces. Bake 20 minutes, or until surface is lightly browned and springs back when gently touched. To cool, invert pans on wire racks. Cool cakes completely in pans—about 1 hour.

5. Meanwhile, make Filling: In small bowl of electric mixer, beat cream with ¼ cup confectioners' sugar and the vanilla until stiff peaks form; spoon into another small bowl; refrigerate.

6. Make Chocolate Butter-Cream: In top of double boiler, over hot, not boiling, water, melt chocolate, stirring occasionally; remove from heat. (Or place chocolate in glass bowl; microwave on HIGH until melted—2 minutes, stirring after each minute.) Cool completely.

7. In small bowl of electric mixer, beat butter until light and fluffy. Add cooled chocolate and gradually beat in confectioners' sugar and salt. Add egg yolks, one at a time, beating well after each addition.

8. To assemble cake: Run small-bladed knife around side of each pan to loosen cake layers. Invert and tap each pan to release cake layers. Peel off and discard waxed paper. Place one cake layer on serving plate. With flat icing spatula, spread half of raspberry jam evenly on layer. Spoon half of filling onto cake layer, spread evenly. Place second cake layer on first; spread remaining jam and filling on layer. Place remaining layer on top. If necessary, use serrated knife to trim uneven side of cake.

9. Spoon one-third of butter-cream into pastry bag fitted with ¼-inch star tip; set aside. With icing spatula, spread remaining two-thirds of butter-cream to cover side and top of cake, running spatula over butter-cream to smooth surface. Pipe a shell border around bottom and top edges of cake. With tip of knife, lightly mark top edge of side of cake at eight even intervals. Beginning at top edge, pipe a shell swag onto side of cake from one mark to the next. Repeat to make eight swags. To garnish, press a sugared violet into icing at each junction of swags. Place additional violets and violet leaves around cake, if desired. *Makes 16 servings.*

Star-Spangled Favorites

Sugared Violets

(Sugared violets should be made day ahead to allow for drying.)

Fresh violets in assorted colors (see Note)
1 egg white, lightly beaten
Granulated sugar

1. Cut each violet with a 1-inch-long stem *just* before sugaring. Dip small craft paintbrush into egg white and brush underside, then top side, of petals until coated. Using small spoon, holding violet over bowl, lightly sprinkle both sides of petals with sugar, shaking off excess and reserving sugar in bowl to use again.
2. Set sugared violets on wire rack placed over waxed-paper-covered tray to dry. When violets are completely dried, store in single layer in airtight container (sugared violets will keep indefinitely if properly stored).

   Note: Many nontoxic flowers, such as pansies, cosmos and wild roses, can be substituted for violets. Select flowers with only a few petals, since they are easier to coat and dry. (Flowers from florists may have been sprayed with insecticide and should not be eaten.)

Baked Stuffed Pork Chops
(pictured)

6 rib pork chops, cut 1½ inches thick, each with a pocket

Savory Stuffing
¼ cup (½ stick) butter or margarine
½ cup finely chopped onion
½ cup chopped celery
2 cups soft bread cubes
½ cup dark raisins
2 tablespoons chopped parsley
½ teaspoon salt
⅛ teaspoon pepper
1 teaspoon dried marjoram leaves
¼ cup apple juice

½ teaspoon salt
Apple juice
Glazed Apple Rings, recipe follows

1. Preheat oven to 350F. Wipe pork chops well with damp paper towels.
2. Make Savory Stuffing: In hot butter in skillet, cook onion and celery until tender—about 5 minutes. Add bread cubes and brown slightly. Remove from heat.
3. Add raisins, parsley, ½ teaspoon salt, the pepper, marjoram and ¼ cup apple juice; toss mixture lightly to combine.

4. Fill pockets in chops with stuffing. Stand chops on rib bones in a shallow roasting pan; sprinkle with ½ teaspoon salt. Pour apple juice to ¼-inch depth in roasting pan. Cover chops and pan with foil.
5. Bake chops 45 minutes. Remove foil; bake, uncovered, 45 to 55 minutes longer, or until chops are tender and brown. Garnish with Glazed Apple Rings. *Makes 6 servings.*

Glazed Apple Rings

2 lb red cooking apples (6 apples)
¼ cup lemon juice

Glaze
½ cup (1 stick) butter or margarine
½ cup sugar
2 tablespoons light corn syrup
½ cup water

1. Wash apples; do not peel. Core; cut into slices about ¾ inch thick.
2. In medium bowl, toss apple slices with lemon juice.
3. Make Glaze: In large skillet, combine butter, sugar, corn syrup and water. Cook over medium heat, stirring, until sugar melts.
4. Layer apple slices in skillet. Add any lemon juice remaining in bowl. Cook over medium heat, turning once, 5 to 7 minutes, or until glazed and tender but not mushy. *Makes 8 servings.*

Potato Bread
(pictured)

1 medium potato, pared and cubed (8 oz)
Boiling water
2 pkg active dry yeast
1½ teaspoons salt
2 tablespoons sugar
2 tablespoons butter or margarine
7 cups all-purpose flour
2 tablespoons butter, melted

1. Cook potato, covered, in 2½ cups boiling water 15 minutes, or until tender. Drain, reserving liquid.
2. Mash potato; there should be 1 cup.
3. In large bowl, sprinkle yeast over ½ cup potato liquid, cooled to 105-115F; stir until dissolved.
4. To remaining potato liquid, add water, if necessary, to make 2 cups; add salt, sugar, the 2 tablespoons butter and mashed potato; stir until butter is melted; cool to 105-115F.
5. To yeast mixture, add mashed-potato mixture and

Star-Spangled Favorites

3½ cups flour; with electric mixer at medium speed, beat until smooth—about 2 minutes.

6. Gradually add remaining flour, mixing with hands until dough is smooth and stiff enough to leave side of bowl.

7. Turn out dough onto lightly floured board. Knead until dough is smooth and elastic and small blisters appear on the surface—about 10 minutes.

8. Place in lightly greased large bowl; turn dough to bring up greased side. Cover with towel; let rise in warm place (85F), free from drafts, until double in bulk—about 1 hour.

9. Turn out dough onto lightly floured pastry cloth or board. Divide in half. Roll out one-half into a 16-by-8-inch rectangle; roll up, starting at one end. Press ends even; pinch to seal; tuck under loaf.

10. Place, seam side down, in greased 9-by-5-by-3-inch loaf pan. Brush surface lightly with some of the melted butter. Repeat with other half of dough.

11. Let loaves rise in warm place (85F), free from drafts, until sides come to top of pan and tops are rounded. Set oven rack at lowest level. Preheat oven to 400F.

12. Bake 30 to 40 minutes, or until crust is deep golden-brown and loaves sound hollow when tapped. If crust becomes too brown while baking, cover with a piece of aluminum foil.

13. Turn out of pans onto racks. Cool completely. Brush tops lightly with flour, if desired. *Makes 2 loaves.*

Southern Baked Ham
(pictured)

10- to 12-lb fully cooked bone-in ham
1 pkg (1 lb) light-brown sugar
1 tablespoon prepared brown mustard
¼ cup sherry or orange-juice concentrate
   Whole cloves

1. Preheat oven to 325F. Wipe ham with damp paper towels. Place ham, fat side up, in shallow roasting pan lined with foil.

2. Bake, uncovered, 2 hours. Meanwhile, in small bowl, combine brown sugar, mustard and sherry; mix to a paste consistency.

3. Remove ham from roasting pan; pour off all fat and drippings.

4. With sharp knife, carefully remove any skin. To score, make diagonal cuts in fat (be careful not to cut into meat) ¼ inch deep and 1¼ inches apart, using ruler, to form diamond pattern.

5. Stud center of each diamond shape with a whole clove. To glaze ham, spread surface with brown-sugar mixture. Return to oven.

6. Bake 1 hour, or until meat thermometer registers 140F.

7. Remove from oven. For easier slicing, let ham stand 20 minutes. *Makes 16 to 18 servings.*

Chicken-And-Noodle Potpie
(pictured)

5 - lb roasting chicken, cut up
6 cups water
1 celery stalk, cut in 1½-inch pieces
6 black peppercorns
1½ teaspoons salt
¼ teaspoon crumbled saffron threads
4 medium potatoes, pared and sliced ¼ inch thick (2 lb)
3 carrots, pared and cut in 1-inch pieces
1 cup sliced onion

Noodles

1 cup all-purpose flour
1 tablespoon butter or margarine
1 teaspoon salt
1 egg
2 tablespoons water

   Chopped parsley

1. Wipe chicken pieces with damp paper towels. Place in 6-quart Dutch oven with 6 cups water. Add celery, peppercorns, 1½ teaspoons salt and the saffron.

2. Bring to boiling; reduce heat and simmer, covered, 60 minutes, or until tender. Remove chicken pieces from broth; reserve broth.

3. Remove chicken meat from bones in large pieces; discard skin and bones.

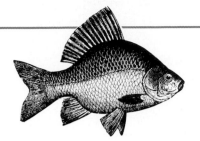

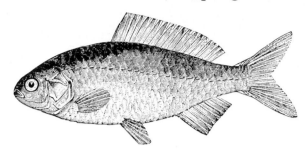

Star-Spangled Favorites

4. To broth, add potato, carrot and onion. Bring to boiling; simmer, covered, until potato and carrot are tender—15 minutes. Remove from broth with slotted utensil.
5. Meanwhile, make Noodles: In medium bowl, combine flour, butter and salt; mix with fork. Make well in center. Add egg and water; beat with fork until combined.
6. On lightly floured pastry cloth or surface, roll dough ⅛ inch thick.
7. With sharp knife or pastry wheel, cut into strips 4 inches long and 2 inches wide. Cut in half to make 2-inch squares.
8. To boiling broth, add noodle squares; return to boiling. Boil, uncovered and stirring occasionally, until tender—about 15 minutes.
9. To serve: Add reserved chicken pieces and vegetables to broth. Simmer, uncovered, 5 minutes. Sprinkle with chopped parsley. *Makes 8 servings.*

Baked Stuffed Whitefish
(pictured)

2½- to 3-lb whole whitefish

Stuffing
- ¼ cup (½ stick) butter or margarine
- ½ cup chopped onion
- ½ cup chopped celery
- 2 tablespoons chopped parsley
- ¼ teaspoon salt
- ⅛ teaspoon pepper
- ½ teaspoon dried thyme leaves
- 1 cup fresh bread cubes (2 slices)

- 2 tablespoons melted butter or margarine
- 6 lemon wedges
  Parsley sprigs

1. Wash fish inside and out under cold running water. Drain well; pat dry with paper towels.
2. Make Stuffing: In hot butter in medium skillet, sauté onion and celery until tender—about 5 minutes. Add chopped parsley, the salt, pepper, thyme and bread cubes; toss to mix well.

3. Preheat oven to 400F.
4. Spoon stuffing into cavity of fish. Place fish in large, greased roasting pan. Brush with melted butter.
5. Bake 30 to 35 minutes, or until fish flakes easily when tested with a fork.
6. To serve: Remove fish to heated platter. Garnish with lemon and parsley. *Makes 6 servings.*

Michigan Baked Beans
(pictured)

- 1 lb mixed dried navy, pinto and kidney beans or
  1 lb dried navy beans
- 2 quarts water
- 4 slices bacon
- 1½ cups chopped onion
- 1 clove garlic, crushed
- ¾ cup catsup
- ¼ cup firmly packed light-brown sugar
- ¼ cup cider vinegar
- 1 teaspoon dry mustard
- ½ teaspoon salt
- ¼ teaspoon pepper

1. Day ahead: Wash beans, discarding imperfect ones. Cover beans with 2 quarts cold water; refrigerate, covered, overnight.
2. Next day, turn beans and water into 5-quart kettle. Bring to boiling; reduce heat and simmer, covered, 1 hour, or until beans are tender.
3. Meanwhile, sauté bacon until just crisp; remove and set aside. In bacon drippings, sauté onion and garlic until onion is transparent; remove from heat. Stir in catsup, brown sugar, vinegar, mustard, salt and pepper; mix well.
4. Drain beans, reserving liquid. Turn beans into a 2-quart baking dish. Preheat oven to 350F. Heat reserved bean liquid to boiling. Add 1 cup bean liquid to catsup mixture; pour over beans. Add enough bean liquid just to cover beans.
5. Bake, covered, 30 minutes. Remove from oven; place bacon slices on top of beans; bake 45 minutes longer. *Makes 8 servings.*

Star-Spangled Favorites

Iowa Corn Relish
(pictured)

15 ears sweet corn or 6 cans (12-oz size) whole-kernel corn, undrained
 2 cups water
 1 cup chopped green pepper
 1 cup chopped sweet red pepper or 2 cans (4-oz size) pimientos, drained and chopped
1¼ cups chopped onion
 1 cup chopped celery
1½ cups sugar
1½ teaspoons mustard seed
 1 tablespoon salt
 1 teaspoon celery seed
 ½ teaspoon ground turmeric
2⅔ cups white vinegar

1. Sterilize six pint jars with lids.
2. Boil fresh corn for 5 minutes; drain. Plunge into cold water; let stand until cool enough to handle. Cut kernels from cobs; measure—you should have 2½ quarts.
3. In a 6-quart Dutch oven, combine corn, 2 cups water and all remaining ingredients. Bring to boiling; reduce heat, and simmer, uncovered, 20 minutes.
4. Bring to a full boil. Pack, boiling hot, into sterilized jar, leaving ⅛-inch headspace. Seal. *Makes 6 pints.*

Broiled Salmon Steaks
With Parsley-Lemon Butter
(pictured)

 4 salmon or swordfish steaks, ½ inch thick
¼ cup (½ stick) butter or margarine, melted
½ teaspoon salt

Parsley-Lemon Butter
¼ cup (½ stick) butter or margarine
 2 tablespoons lemon juice
 2 tablespoons chopped parsley

1. Rinse salmon well under cold running water; drain; pat dry with paper towels.
2. Place salmon on rack of broiler pan. Brush with 2 tablespoons melted butter; sprinkle with ¼ teaspoon salt.
3. Broil, 4 inches from heat, 5 to 10 minutes. Turn salmon; brush with remaining melted butter and sprinkle with rest of salt. Broil 5 to 8 minutes longer, or until fish flakes easily when tested with a fork.
4. Meanwhile, make Parsley-Lemon Butter: Melt butter in small saucepan. Stir in lemon juice and parsley. Keep warm.
5. Remove salmon to heated serving platter. Pour Parsley-Lemon Butter over salmon. *Makes 4 servings.*

New England Fish Chowder
(pictured)

 2 lb halibut fillets
 2 cups water
 2 teaspoons salt
 3 cups cut-up pared potato
 6 bacon slices, chopped
 1 cup chopped onion
 2 cups milk
 2 cups light cream or half-and-half
¼ teaspoon pepper

1. Place halibut, with 2 cups water, in large saucepan; bring to boiling.
2. Reduce heat; simmer, covered, 10 minutes, or until fish flakes easily with fork. Remove fish; set aside.
3. To fish broth, add 1 teaspoon salt and the potato; boil, covered, about 8 minutes, or until potato is almost tender.
4. Meanwhile, sauté bacon until crisp; remove and drain on paper towels.
5. Sauté onion in bacon fat until tender—about 5 minutes.
6. Flake fish. Add, along with bacon, onion, remaining salt and rest of ingredients, to broth and potato; slowly bring to boiling.
7. Reduce heat; simmer, uncovered, 15 minutes. *Makes 3 quarts, 8 large servings.*

Parker House Rolls
(pictured)

¾ cup milk
¼ cup sugar
 2 teaspoons salt
½ cup (1 stick) butter or margarine
½ cup warm water (105 to 115F)
 1 pkg active dry yeast
 2 eggs, beaten
4½ cups all-purpose flour
½ cup (1 stick) melted butter or margarine

1. Heat milk just until bubbles form. Add sugar, salt and ½ cup butter; stir to dissolve sugar and melt butter. Cool to lukewarm.
2. If possible, check temperature of warm water, in large bowl, with thermometer. Sprinkle yeast over water and stir to dissolve.
3. With a wooden spoon, stir in milk mixture, beaten eggs and 2 cups flour; beat until smooth—about 2 minutes.
4. Gradually add rest of the flour, beating until dough is stiff and smooth enough to leave side of bowl. Turn dough onto lightly floured board. Knead until smooth and elastic—about 5 minutes.

5. Place dough in lightly greased bowl; turn dough to bring up greased side. Cover with towel; let rise in warm place (85F), free from drafts, about 1 hour, or until double in bulk.
6. Punch down dough. Turn out onto lightly floured pastry cloth; divide in half. Roll out one-half to ¼-inch thickness. Cut with 2½-inch biscuit cutter. With dull edge of knife, press a crease just off center of each round. Brush lightly with melted butter. Fold over, so larger part just touches edge of the smaller; press folded edge. Repeat with remaining dough.
7. Place rolls, 1 inch apart, on greased cookie sheet. Brush rolls lightly with melted butter. Cover with towel; let rise in warm place, free from drafts, until almost double in bulk—about 1 hour.
8. Meanwhile, preheat oven to 375F. Bake 12 to 15 minutes, or until golden-brown. Serve hot. *Makes 30 rolls.*

Kentucky Bourbon Cake
(pictured)

2 **cups chopped walnuts or pecans**
1 **cup candied red cherries, halved**
2 **cups light or dark raisins**
1 **cup bourbon**
3¼ **cups all-purpose flour**
1½ **teaspoons baking powder**
½ **teaspoon salt**
1 **teaspoon ground nutmeg**
1½ **cups (3 sticks) butter or margarine, softened**
2 **cups sugar**
1 **teaspoon vanilla extract**
7 **eggs**

1. Grease and flour well a 10-inch kuchen, Bundt or tube pan. In large bowl, combine walnuts, cherries and raisins with ½ cup bourbon; mix well. Let stand at room temperature several hours—liquid will be absorbed.
2. On sheet of waxed paper, sift flour with baking powder, salt and nutmeg.
3. Preheat oven to 350F. In large bowl of electric mixer, at medium speed, beat butter, sugar and vanilla until smooth, light and fluffy. Add eggs, one at a time, beating well after each addition. Continue beating at medium speed 4 minutes, occasionally scraping side of bowl and guiding batter into beaters with rubber spatula. Batter will become thick and fluffy and lighter in color. At low speed, gradually beat in flour mixture until smooth.
4. Add to fruit; mix with wooden spoon to combine well. Turn into prepared pan; smooth top with spatula.

5. Bake in center of oven 1 hour and 20 minutes in kuchen pan, 1 hour and 15 minutes in Bundt pan, or 1 hour and 10 minutes in tube pan. Cake tester inserted in center should come out clean.
6. Cool in pan on wire rack 20 minutes. Use small spatula to loosen cake around inside; invert on rack; cool completely.
7. In small bowl, soak a large piece of cheesecloth in ½ cup bourbon. Stretch cheesecloth on large piece of foil. Place cake in center. Wrap cake in cheesecloth; then wrap in foil. Refrigerate several days to mellow. (Will keep several weeks in refrigerator.)
8. To serve, slice thinly; let warm to room temperature. *Makes 25 servings.*

Cobb Salad
(pictured)

2 **cups crisp iceberg lettuce, in bite-size pieces**
2 **cups crisp romaine, in bite-size pieces**
2 **cups crisp chicory, in bite-size pieces**
2 **medium tomatoes, cut in eighths**
2 **medium avocados, peeled and sliced**
3 **cups slivered cooked chicken, chilled**
6 **crisp-cooked slices bacon, cut in ½-inch pieces**
1 **hard-cooked large egg**
2 **tablespoons snipped chives**
Watercress
Russian Dressing, recipe follows

1. Just before serving, assemble salad: Place lettuce, romaine and chicory in salad bowl. Arrange tomato and avocado around edge of bowl. Mound chicken in center; sprinkle with bacon. Chop egg white and yolk separately; sprinkle, with chives, on top of salad. Garnish with watercress.
2. To serve: At the table, pour half of dressing over salad; toss well. Pass remaining dressing. *Makes 8 to 10 servings.*

Russian Dressing

½ **cup mayonnaise**
2 **tablespoons milk**
2 **tablespoons lemon juice**
2 **tablespoons finely chopped stuffed olives**
1 **tablespoon finely chopped onion**
1 **tablespoon finely chopped green pepper**
1 **tablespoon chili sauce**
1 **tablespoon prepared horseradish**
¼ **teaspoon salt**

In small bowl, blend all ingredients; mix well. Refrigerate, covered.

Bounty From The Land And Sea

This country has truly been blessed with a fantastic abundance and variety of foods. Since before Colonial times, the fertile land has burst forth with an unceasing harvest of fruits, vegetables, nuts and grains, while the teeming waters have yielded fishes of every kind. With such a wealth of foods available, it's no wonder that we have developed such a rich and treasured heritage of recipes. And the fascination and challenge of creating new classics are still very much alive today all across the country. This section offers both traditional and contemporary recipes, each one a delicious celebration of the bounty of America. Recipes begin on page 41.

Left: In New England, hearty fare, simply prepared, has been the style for centuries. New England's specialty: the great traditional clambake in which clams, lobsters, corn and sometimes chicken are steamed ceremonially on hot rocks in a covered pit, with plenty of seaweed. But if you don't have a pit, an oversize kettle on the stove will do nicely. *See recipe on page 41.*

Autumn is apple season, but this fruit's versatility and taste make it a favorite all year long. Whether you like your apples fresh off the tree, baked with brown sugar or swirled into apple-sauce, you're sure to find these four unique desserts lusciously appealing. **At top,** Swedish Apple Meringue Cake; **below,** flaky Apple Crumble Pie. **Opposite, at top,** apricot-glazed Apple Kuchen; **below,** Frosted Apple Pie with walnuts. *Recipes begin on page 45.*

To every county fair and festival the best of country cooking comes to be sampled, judged and—it is hoped— awarded the coveted blue ribbon. These luscious treats are all winners: Taste and judge for yourself. **Top row, left to right:** Burnt-Sugar Cake With Caramel Frosting, Amber Citrus Marmalade, Spiced Peaches, our Chocolate Spice Cake with Seven-Minute Allegretti Frosting. **Center row:** Tomato-Soup Spice Cake With Cream-Cheese Frosting, Coconut-Custard Pie. **Bottom row:** Fresh Berry Pie, Old-Fashioned Potato Bread. *Recipes begin on page 41.*

As the leaves begin to fall, crowds of pumpkins make their yearly appearance at roadside farm stands and in markets across the country. In various shapes, sizes and intensities of orange, they seem to herald the beginning of the holiday season. This year, discover the possibilities of pumpkins that go beyond the Halloween jack-o'-lantern and the classic Thanksgiving pie. For instance, a hollowed-out pumpkin makes a sensational serving bowl for Hot Mulled Cider. *See recipe on page 47.*

Pumpkin adds pizzazz to a crunchy-topped upside-down cake, a layered Mexican casserole and chewy oatmeal bars with raisins and nuts. *Recipes begin on page 47. Turn the page for more dazzling pumpkin treats.*

Glazed Pumpkin Cookies are soft morsels chock-full of raisins and nuts and spread with a lightly sweetened lemon glaze. *See recipe on page 48.*

Peach-Pumpkin Upside-Down Cake pairs two great tastes in a moist, delicately spiced batter adorned with glazed peach halves and pecans. *See recipe on page 49.*

Sliced-Pumpkin Tart swirls with cooked pumpkin, sliced thinly and set in a translucent cinnamon-apricot sauce. *See recipe on page 49.*

38

Left: Pumpkin-Rum Mousse is a creamy, spirited spectacular that will rise to the demands of any elegant celebration. *See recipe on page 49.*

Below: The South is famous for many things, but perhaps none more delight-ful than the divine pecan. Here the pe-can displays its tasteful talents in a meaty casserole of sausage and cheese and in a delicately rich Butter-Pecan Cheesecake. *See recipes on pages 50 and 51.*

From the time the Indians first shared them with the Pilgrims, cranberries have been a much-favored, versatile fruit. As a saucy ice-cream topping, in a warming grog or layered in a cream-cheese torte, the cranberry's blushing color and characteristic tangy flavor shine through. *Recipes begin on page 51.*

Peanuts are just about as American as apple pie. (Where would kids be without peanut butter?) And here are two recipes that every member of the peanut gallery will cheer: crunchy Gold Coast Stew and rich Peanut-Butter-Fudge Cake. *See recipes on page 53.*

Unearthing great potato recipes is no problem, especially in the Midwest where the spuds are so plentiful. For a hearty beginning or an end to a long day, these Potato-Rye Rolls, laced with molasses, caraway seeds and cheese, are downright delicious. *See recipe on page 52.*

Bounty from the Land and Sea

continued from page 31

New England Clambake
(pictured)

2 dozen clams in the shell
4 ears corn
2 (2½-lb size) broiler-fryers, quartered
½ lb (2 sticks) butter or margarine, melted
4 small baking potatoes, sweet potatoes or yams, scrubbed
4 small onions, peeled and washed
   Rockweed or corn husks
2 (1-lb size) live lobsters (optional, see Note)
   Lemon wedges

1. Under cold running water, scrub clam shells with stiff brush to remove sand.
2. Trim tops of ears of corn with scissors. Turn back husks; remove silk; pull back husks as they were. Remove outer husks from ears; reserve. Soak ears and reserved husks in lightly salted water until cooking time.
3. In large skillet, sauté chicken in 2 tablespoons butter until golden—about 10 minutes on each side—adding more butter as needed.
4. Place wire rack in bottom of a very large kettle (at least 4-gallon) with tight-fitting cover. Pour in 2 cups water. Arrange potatoes and onions on rack; cover with a layer of rockweed or reserved corn husks. Add corn and another layer of rockweed or corn husks. Then add chicken and/or lobster. Top with clams; cover with rockweed or any remaining husks.
5. Steam, covered, over medium heat 1 hour and 15 minutes, or until potatoes, onions and corn are tender. (Check corn at this point to see if it is done.) Remove clams to large bowl and remainder of clambake to large platter. Pour broth from bottom of kettle into four (8-ounce) cups or bowls and serve to dip seafood, meat and vegetables in for flavor.
6. Serve with lemon wedges and melted butter. *Makes 4 servings.* (To serve 8, make a second batch in a separate kettle.)

   Note: Since lobster is difficult to find in some areas, you may omit lobster and serve chicken. Or, if available, serve both lobster and chicken to each person.

   To kill lobster before adding to kettle: Lay each lobster on wooden board. To sever spinal cord, insert point of knife through back shell where body and tail of lobster come together. Turn lobster over. With sharp knife, split body of lobster down middle, cutting through thin undershell just to back shell and leaving back shell intact. Discard dark intestinal vein running down center of lobster; also discard small sac below head. Crack large claws.

Burnt-Sugar Cake
With Caramel Frosting
(pictured)

Caramel Syrup
½ cup sugar
⅔ cup boiling water

2 cups sifted cake flour
¾ teaspoon baking powder
½ teaspoon baking soda
¼ teaspoon salt
½ cup (1 stick) butter or margarine, softened
1 cup sugar
2 eggs
1 teaspoon vanilla extract
⅔ cup milk

   Caramel Frosting, recipe follows
   Walnut halves

1. Make Caramel Syrup: Melt ½ cup sugar in 8-inch heavy skillet over medium heat. Shake pan slightly as sugar melts and turns golden. Continue heating until it turns dark amber color. Remove from heat.
2. Gradually add boiling water, stirring constantly. Return to heat; boil rapidly, uncovered, 10 minutes, or until slightly thickened. Pour into 1-cup measure. Set aside to cool completely.
3. Preheat oven to 375F. Grease well and flour two 8-by-1½-inch round layer-cake pans. On waxed paper, sift flour with baking powder, soda and salt. Set aside.
4. In large bowl, with electric mixer at medium speed, cream butter until soft. Gradually beat in sugar; continue beating until light and fluffy. Add eggs, one at a time, beating well after each addition.
5. At medium speed, beat in cooled Caramel Syrup and vanilla. Then beat in flour mixture (in fourths) alternately with milk (in thirds), beginning and ending with flour mixture. Pour into prepared pans.
6. Bake 25 to 30 minutes, or until top springs back when gently pressed with fingertip.
7. Cool in pans 10 minutes. Remove from pans; cool completely on wire racks.
8. Spread half of Caramel Frosting between layers. Spread rest on top, letting it run unevenly down side. Decorate top with walnuts. *Makes 8 servings.*

Caramel Frosting

2 cups firmly packed light-brown sugar
½ cup (1 stick) butter or margarine
5 tablespoons light cream or half-and-half
½ teaspoon vanilla extract
½ teaspoon baking powder

Bounty from the Land and Sea

1. In medium saucepan, combine sugar, butter and cream; bring to boiling over medium heat, stirring constantly. Boil gently, stirring, 2 minutes. Remove from heat.
2. Add vanilla and baking powder. With electric mixer, beat until smooth and creamy—about 5 minutes. *Makes enough to frost tops of 2 (8-inch) cake layers.*

Amber Citrus Marmalade
(pictured)

1 **grapefruit**
1 **orange**
1 **lemon**
1½ **quarts water**
   Sugar (about 7 cups)

   Paraffin for sealing

1. Wash fruit. Cut grapefruit into 8 wedges, orange and lemon into 4 wedges. Then cut wedges crosswise into thin slices; save juice.
2. In 6-quart kettle, combine all fruit, fruit juice and the 1½ quarts water. Bring to boiling; boil rapidly, uncovered, 30 minutes, or until peel is tender.
3. Measure fruit mixture; return to kettle. Add 1 cup sugar for each cup of fruit mixture; bring to boiling, stirring until sugar is dissolved. Boil rapidly, stirring frequently, 30 minutes, or until mixture is thick and reaches jellying point. (See Note.) (Be careful not to overcook; marmalade would become too dark and taste scorched.)
4. Meanwhile, sterilize eight 8-oz jelly glasses by boiling 20 minutes. Keep in hot water until ready to fill. Lift out with tongs.
5. Remove marmalade from heat. Ladle immediately into hot, sterilized glasses, filling to within ½ inch of top. Cover immediately with about ⅛-inch hot paraffin. Let glasses stand overnight or until cool. Cover glasses with metal lids. *Makes seven or eight 8-oz glasses.*

Note: Test for jellying point: Dip a large metal spoon into boiling syrup; tilt spoon so syrup runs off edge. Syrup is at jellying point when it doesn't flow but divides into two drops that run together and sheet from the spoon.

Spiced Peaches
(pictured)

4 **lb peaches**
4½ **cups sugar**
1½ **cups cider vinegar**
¾ **cup water**
1 **tablespoon whole allspice**
2 **(3-inch) cinnamon sticks**

1. Peel peaches, placing them as they are peeled in slightly salted water to prevent discoloring.
2. In 5-quart kettle, combine sugar, vinegar, ¾ cup water and spices tied in a cheesecloth bag.
3. Bring to boiling. Add peaches; return to boiling; reduce heat; simmer 10 minutes, or until tender.
4. Turn into a large bowl. Refrigerate, covered, overnight.
5. Spoon peaches into 4 pint jars.
6. Remove spice bag. Bring syrup to boiling. Pour over peaches, filling jars to ½ inch from top.
7. Cover with lids and process in a boiling-water bath, following manufacturer's directions for peaches. *Makes 4 pints.*

McCall's Chocolate Spice Cake
(pictured)

3 **squares unsweetened chocolate**
2¼ **cups sifted cake flour**
2 **teaspoons baking soda**
½ **teaspoon salt**
½ **teaspoon ground cinnamon**
¼ **teaspoon ground cloves**
½ **cup (1 stick) butter or margarine, softened**
2½ **cups firmly packed light-brown sugar**
3 **eggs**
2 **teaspoons vanilla extract**
½ **cup sour milk (see Note) or buttermilk**
1 **cup boiling water**

   Seven-Minute Allegretti Frosting, recipe follows

1. Melt chocolate over hot, not boiling, water. Let cool.
2. Preheat oven to 350F. Grease well and flour two 9-by-1½-inch round layer-cake pans or three 8-by-1½-inch layer-cake pans.
3. Sift flour with baking soda, salt, cinnamon and cloves; set aside.
4. In large bowl of electric mixer, at high speed, beat

Bounty from the Land and Sea

butter, sugar, eggs and vanilla until light and fluffy—about 5 minutes—occasionally scraping side of bowl with rubber spatula.

5. At low speed, beat in chocolate.
6. Beat in flour mixture (in fourths), alternately with milk (in thirds), beginning and ending with flour mixture. Beat just until smooth—about 1 minute.
7. Beat in water just until mixture is smooth. Batter will be thin.
8. Pour batter into prepared pans; bake 30 to 35 minutes, or until surface springs back when gently pressed with fingertip.
9. Cool in pans 10 minutes. Remove from pans; cool thoroughly on wire racks. Fill and frost with Seven-Minute Allegretti Frosting, or as desired. *Makes 2 (9-inch) or 3 (8-inch) layers.*

Note: To sour milk: Place 1½ teaspoons lemon juice or vinegar in measuring cup. Add milk to measure ½ cup; stir. Let stand a few minutes before using.

Seven-Minute Allegretti Frosting

    3 egg whites
2¼ cups sugar
1½ tablespoons light corn syrup
    ½ cup water
1½ teaspoons vanilla extract
    1 square unsweetened chocolate
    1 teaspoon butter or margarine

1. In top of large double boiler, combine egg whites, sugar, corn syrup and ½ cup water. With portable electric mixer at medium speed, beat about 1 minute, to combine ingredients.
2. Cook over rapidly boiling water (water in bottom should not touch top of double boiler), beating constantly, about 7 minutes, or until stiff peaks form when beaters are slowly raised.
3. Remove from boiling water. Add vanilla; continue beating until frosting is thick enough to spread—about 2 minutes. Use to fill and frost cake layers.
4. Melt chocolate with butter over hot, not boiling, water; stir until smooth. Drizzle from tip of spoon around top edge of cake, letting it run irregularly down side. *Makes enough to fill and frost a 9-inch layer cake.*

Tomato-Soup Spice Cake With Cream-Cheese Frosting

(pictured)

    4 cups all-purpose flour
1½ teaspoons baking soda
    2 teaspoons ground cinnamon
    1 teaspoon ground cloves
    ½ teaspoon ground nutmeg
    1 cup (2 sticks) butter or margarine, softened
    1 box (1 lb) light-brown sugar
    2 eggs
    1 can (10½ oz) condensed tomato soup, undiluted
      Water
    2 cups chopped walnuts
    1 cup dark raisins

Frosting
    1 pkg (8 oz) cream cheese, softened
    1 tablespoon butter or margarine, softened
    1 box (1 lb) confectioners' sugar

1. Preheat oven to 350F. Grease a 13-by-9-by-2-inch baking pan.
2. Sift flour with soda, cinnamon, cloves and nutmeg. Set aside.
3. In large bowl, with electric mixer at high speed, cream 1 cup butter until light. Gradually beat in brown sugar until light and fluffy. Add eggs and beat to combine well.
4. Combine soup with enough water to measure 2 cups; mix well.
5. At low speed, add flour mixture (in fourths) to sugar mixture, alternately with soup mixture (in thirds), beginning and ending with flour mixture. Beat just until combined.
6. Fold in nuts and raisins. Turn into prepared pan.
7. Bake 55 to 60 minutes, or until cake tester inserted in center comes out clean.
8. Cool in pan on wire rack 30 minutes. Turn out of pan; let cool completely on rack.
9. Make Frosting: In medium bowl, with electric mixer at medium speed, beat cheese with butter until creamy. Add confectioners' sugar; beat until light and fluffy. Spread thickly over top of cake; make swirl design with knife. *Makes 15 to 18 servings.*

Bounty from the Land and Sea

Coconut-Custard Pie
(pictured)

    9-inch pie shell, purchased or homemade
  4 **eggs**
1½ **cups heavy cream**
1⅓ **cups milk**
  1 **can (4 oz) shredded coconut (see Note)**
½ **cup granulated sugar**
  1 **teaspoon vanilla extract**
¼ **teaspoon coconut flavoring (optional)**
¼ **teaspoon salt**
  2 **tablespoons confectioners' sugar**

1. Prepare and bake pie shell. Cool.
2. Preheat oven to 350F. Butter a 9-inch pie plate.
3. In medium bowl, with wire whisk or rotary beater, beat eggs slightly. Add 1 cup cream, the milk, 1 cup coconut, the granulated sugar, vanilla, coconut flavoring and salt; beat until well mixed.
4. Pour into prepared pie plate. Place in shallow pan; pour cold water to about ½ inch around pie plate.
5. Bake 40 to 45 minutes, or until silver knife inserted in center comes out clean.
6. Remove pan from water. Let custard cool completely on wire rack; then refrigerate until well chilled—several hours or overnight.
7. Loosen custard from pie plate by carefully running a small spatula around edge and shaking plate gently. Holding plate just above rim of baked shell, carefully slip custard into shell.
8. Whip remaining cream with confectioners' sugar. Use to decorate edge of pie. Sprinkle cream with remaining coconut. *Makes 6 to 8 servings.*

Note: If desired, toast coconut: Spread coconut on a baking sheet; place in 375F oven 5 to 7 minutes, stirring occasionally, until golden.

Fresh Berry Pie
(pictured)

  1 **pkg (11 oz) piecrust mix**
  2 **pint boxes fresh blackberries, raspberries or blueberries**
  1 **tablespoon lemon juice**
  1 **cup sugar**
¼ **cup all-purpose flour**
¼ **teaspoon ground cinnamon**
⅛ **teaspoon ground nutmeg**
    Dash ground cloves
  2 **tablespoons butter or margarine**
  1 **egg yolk**
  1 **tablespoon water**

1. Prepare piecrust mix as package label directs. Shape into a ball; divide in half. On lightly floured surface, roll out half of pastry into an 11-inch circle. Use to line a 9-inch pie plate. Refrigerate with rest of pastry until ready to use.
2. Preheat oven to 400F.
3. Gently wash berries; drain well. Place in large bowl; sprinkle with lemon juice.
4. Combine sugar, flour, cinnamon, nutmeg and cloves. Add to berries and toss lightly to combine. Turn into pastry-lined pie plate, mounding in center. Dot with butter.
5. Roll out remaining pastry into an 11-inch circle. Make several slits near center for steam vents. Adjust over filling; fold edge of top crust under bottom crust; press together, and crimp decoratively.
6. Beat egg yolk with 1 tablespoon water. Brush lightly over top crust.
7. Bake 45 to 50 minutes, or until juices start to bubble through steam vents and crust is golden-brown.
8. Cool on wire rack at least 1 hour. *Makes 8 servings.*

Old-Fashioned Potato Bread
(pictured)

  2 **cups warm water (105 to 115F)**
  2 **pkg active dry yeast**
½ **cup sugar**
  1 **tablespoon salt**
  1 **cup warm unseasoned mashed potato**
½ **cup (1 stick) butter or margarine, softened**
  2 **eggs**
7½ **cups all-purpose flour**
  3 **tablespoons butter or margarine**

1. If possible, check temperature of warm water with thermometer. Sprinkle yeast over water in large bowl of electric mixer; stir until dissolved. Add sugar and salt, stirring until dissolved.
2. Add mashed potato, softened butter, eggs and 3½ cups flour; with mixer at medium speed, beat until smooth—about 2 minutes.
3. Gradually add remaining flour, mixing with a wooden spoon or hands until dough is smooth and stiff enough to leave side of bowl.
4. Melt 1 tablespoon butter and brush over dough. Cover with double thickness of foil or plastic wrap.
5. Let rise in refrigerator until double in bulk—at least 2 hours. Punch down dough. Refrigerate, covered, overnight.
6. Next day, turn out dough onto lightly floured pastry cloth. Knead until dough is smooth and elastic and blisters appear on surface—about 10 minutes.
7. Divide dough in half. Shape each half into a smooth ball about 6 inches in diameter. Place each in 9-inch round layer-cake pan.

Bounty from the Land and Sea

8. Melt remaining 2 tablespoons butter. Brush over balls of dough.

9. Cover with towel. Let rise in warm place (85F), free from drafts, until double in bulk—1½ to 2 hours.

10. With sharp knife, make 3 lengthwise cuts in surface of each loaf; then make 3 crosswise cuts, to make crisscross pattern.

11. Preheat oven to 400F. Bake loaves 40 to 45 minutes, or until they are well browned and sound hollow when tapped with knuckles.

12. Remove from pans; cool on wire rack. If desired, dust tops lightly with flour before serving. *Makes 2 round loaves.*

Swedish Apple Meringue Cake
(pictured)
Adapted from a recipe by Sheila Sherman, Lakewood, Chautauqua County, New York.

Crust
- ½ cup (1 stick) butter or margarine
- ¼ cup sugar
- 3 large egg yolks
- 1¼ cups all-purpose flour
- ¾ cup natural almonds, roasted and finely chopped
- 1½ tablespoons lemon juice
- 1 tablespoon grated lemon peel
- 1 egg white

Filling
- 3 lb medium Granny Smith apples (about 6)
- 1½ tablespoons lemon juice
- ⅓ cup sugar
- 2 tablespoons all-purpose flour

Meringue
- 3 large egg whites, at room temperature
  Dash salt
- ¼ cup sugar

- ¼ cup seedless raspberry jam

1. Make Crust: Preheat oven to 350F. In small bowl, with electric mixer, cream butter and ¼ cup sugar; add egg yolks; beat until smooth. With wooden spoon, stir in 1¼ cups flour, the almonds, 1½ tablespoons lemon juice and the peel.

2. Press crust mixture onto bottom and side of 9-inch fluted cake pan with removable bottom. Brush bottom of crust with a little egg white. Bake 20 to 25 minutes, or till golden-brown. Cool on wire rack. Increase oven temperature to 400F.

3. Make Filling: Peel and core apples; cut each into 12 wedges. In large bowl, toss apple with lemon juice,

⅓ cup sugar and the flour until evenly coated. In large skillet, over medium-low heat, cook apple mixture, gently stirring, until apple is glazed—about 4 minutes. Cover; reduce heat to low; cook 3 minutes longer.

4. Make Meringue: In small bowl, with electric mixer at high speed, beat egg whites with salt until soft peaks form. Gradually add sugar, 2 tablespoons at a time; beat until stiff peaks form.

5. Spread jam on crust; place apple on top. Spread meringue over apple, carefully sealing at edge of crust and swirling top decoratively. Bake 5 minutes, or until meringue is lightly browned. Let cake cool in pan on wire rack 15 minutes before cutting. To serve: Remove side of pan, leaving cake on pan bottom. Place on serving plate. *Makes 8 servings.*

Apple Crumble Pie
(pictured)
Recipe from Eileen Rumsey, Friendship, New York.

Piecrust
- 1¼ cups all-purpose flour
- ½ teaspoon salt
- ⅓ cup shortening or lard
- 3 to 4 tablespoons cold water

Filling
- 2 lb Golden Delicious or other cooking apples, pared, cored and thinly sliced (about 6 cups)
- 3 tablespoons lemon juice
- ½ cup sugar
- 2 tablespoons all-purpose flour
- 1 teaspoon grated lemon peel

Crumb Topping
- ½ cup sugar
- ½ cup all-purpose flour
- ½ teaspoon ground cinnamon
- ¼ teaspoon ground ginger
- ⅛ teaspoon ground mace
- ¼ cup (½ stick) butter or margarine

  Vanilla ice cream or American-cheese slices (optional)

1. Make Piecrust: In medium bowl, combine 1¼ cups flour and the salt. With pastry blender or 2 knives, cut in shortening until pieces are the size of small peas. Sprinkle with water, 1 tablespoon at a time, and toss with fork until flour mixture is moistened. Form dough into a ball. On lightly floured board or pastry cloth, roll dough to fit a 9-inch pie plate; trim and crimp edge decoratively. Chill in refrigerator until ready to use.

Bounty from the Land and Sea

2. Make Filling: In medium bowl, toss apple slices with lemon juice. Add remaining filling ingredients; stir to mix; set aside. Preheat oven to 375F.
3. Make Crumb Topping: In small bowl, combine sugar, flour, cinnamon, ginger and mace; mix well. With pastry blender or fork, cut in butter until mixture is crumbly.
4. Place apple filling in piecrust; sprinkle crumb topping evenly over filling. Bake 55 to 60 minutes, or until filling is bubbling and topping is golden. Serve warm with vanilla ice cream or American-cheese slices, if desired. *Makes 8 servings.*

Apple Kuchen
(pictured)

1¼ **cups sifted all-purpose flour**
¼ **cup sugar**
1½ **teaspoons baking powder**
½ **teaspoon salt**
¼ **cup (½ stick) butter or margarine**
1 **egg, beaten**
¼ **cup milk**
1 **teaspoon vanilla extract**
5 **cups thinly sliced, pared tart apple (about 2 lb)**

Topping

¼ **cup sugar**
1 **teaspoon ground cinnamon**
¼ **cup (½ stick) butter or margarine, melted**

⅓ **cup apricot preserves**
1 **tablespoon hot water**
　Soft vanilla ice cream or whipped cream

1. Preheat oven to 400F. Lightly grease a 13-by-9-by-2-inch baking pan.
2. Into medium bowl, sift flour with ¼ cup sugar, the baking powder and salt. With pastry blender, cut in ¼ cup butter until mixture resembles coarse crumbs.
3. Add beaten egg, milk and vanilla, stirring with a fork until mixture is smooth—about 1 minute.
4. Spread batter evenly in bottom of prepared pan. Arrange apple slices, thin sides down and slightly overlapping, in parallel rows over the batter.
5. Make Topping: Combine sugar, cinnamon and melted butter. Sprinkle sugar mixture over the apple slices.

6. Bake 35 minutes, or until apple slices are tender. Remove to wire rack.
7. Mix apricot preserves with hot water. Brush over apple. Cut apple kuchen into rectangles and serve warm, with ice cream or whipped cream. *Makes 12 servings.*

Frosted Apple Pie
(pictured)

1 **pkg (11 oz) piecrust mix**
1 **cup granulated sugar**
2 **tablespoons flour**
1 **teaspoon ground cinnamon**
⅛ **teaspoon ground nutmeg**
¼ **teaspoon salt**
7 **cups thinly sliced, pared tart cooking apples (2½ lb)**
2 **tablespoons lemon juice**
2 **tablespoons butter or margarine**
1 **egg yolk, slightly beaten**
1 **tablespoon water**

Frosting

1 **cup confectioners' sugar**
1 **tablespoon light corn syrup**
1 **tablespoon water**
½ **teaspoon vanilla extract**
½ **cup chopped walnuts**

1. Make pastry as package label directs. Shape into a ball. Divide in half; form each half into a round; then flatten each with palm of hand. On lightly floured pastry cloth, roll out half of pastry into a 12-inch circle.
2. Fold rolled pastry in half; carefully transfer to a 9-inch pie plate, making sure fold is in center of pie plate. Unfold pastry; fit carefully into pie plate. Refrigerate.
3. Preheat oven to 425F. In small bowl, mix granulated sugar, flour, cinnamon, nutmeg and salt. In a large bowl, toss the apple with the lemon juice. Add sugar mixture to sliced apple; toss lightly to combine.
4. Roll out remaining pastry into 12-inch circle. Fold over in quarters; cut slits for steam vents.
5. Turn apple mixture into pastry-lined pie plate, mounding high in center. Dot apple with butter cut in small pieces. Using scissors, trim overhanging edge

Bounty from the Land and Sea

of pastry so it measures ½ inch from rim of pie plate.

6. Carefully place folded pastry so that point is at the center of filling, and unfold. Using scissors, trim overhanging edge of pastry (for top crust) so it measures 1 inch from edge all around.

7. Moisten edge of bottom pastry with a little water. Fold top pastry under edge of bottom pastry. With fingers, press edges together to seal, so juices won't run out. Press upright to form a standing rim. Crimp edge.

8. Brush with egg yolk mixed with 1 tablespoon water. Bake 45 to 50 minutes, or until apple is fork-tender and crust is golden. Remove to rack; cool 30 minutes.

9. Make Frosting: In small bowl, combine confectioners' sugar, corn syrup, 1 tablespoon water and the vanilla; mix until smooth. Spread over pie; sprinkle with nuts. *Makes 8 servings.*

Apple Butter

```
4   lb tart apples
2   cups cider
3   cups sugar
¼   teaspoon salt
1   teaspoon ground cinnamon
¼   teaspoon ground cloves
2   tablespoons grated lemon peel
2   tablespoons lemon juice

    Paraffin
```

1. Sterlize five (8-ounce) jelly glasses.

2. Wash apples; remove stem and blossom ends; cut up; do not pare or core.

3. In large saucepan, combine cut-up apple and cider. Bring to boiling; reduce heat and cook until soft—about 15 minutes. Press mixture through strainer or food mill. Measure pulp; there should be about 7 cups.

4. Preheat oven to 300F.

5. Combine apple pulp with rest of ingredients; mix well. Divide evenly into two 13-by-9-by-2-inch baking dishes. Bake, uncovered, 2 hours, stirring occasionally.

6. Pour immediately into sterilized glasses.

7. Cover at once with ⅛-inch hot melted paraffin (see Note). *Makes 2½ pints.*

Note: When melting paraffin, it is best to cut up wax and place in a container in a pan of boiling water to melt. Never melt it over direct heat as it may catch fire.

Pumpkin Punch Bowl
With Hot Mulled Cider
(pictured)

```
1   gallon cider
½   cup firmly packed light-brown sugar (optional)
4   to 5 (3-inch) cinnamon sticks, broken into pieces
10  to 15 whole allspice
20  to 25 whole cloves
1   medium pumpkin (about 12 inches in diameter)
```

1. In 6-quart kettle, bring cider, brown sugar, cinnamon, allspice and cloves to boiling; simmer, uncovered, 30 minutes.

2. Wash and dry pumpkin. Remove a 2-inch slice from top. Scoop out seeds. Discard pulp; save seeds for toasted pumpkin seeds, if desired.

3. Using a 2-cup glass measuring cup or a small saucepan, pour cider and spices into pumpkin punch bowl and serve.

4. When cider has been used, prepare pumpkin shell for use in another recipe. Its flavor will be enhanced by the spicy cider. *Makes 15 servings.*

Pumpkin Upside-Down Cake
(pictured)

Adapted from a recipe by Lorraine Venable.

Filling
```
3     large eggs
2     cans (1-lb size) pumpkin
1¼    cups sugar
1     can (12 or 13 oz) evaporated milk
2     teaspoons ground cinnamon
1     teaspoon ground nutmeg
½     teaspoon ground ginger
```

Topping
```
1     pkg (1 lb, 2½ oz) yellow-cake mix
¾     cup (1½ sticks) butter or margarine, melted
1     cup walnuts, chopped

      Whipped cream (optional)
```

Bounty from the Land and Sea

1. Preheat oven to 350F. Make Filling: In medium bowl, lightly beat eggs. Add remaining filling ingredients; stir until well combined. Pour into ungreased 13-by-9-by-2-inch baking dish or 3-quart shallow oval casserole.
2. For the topping, sprinkle the *dry* cake mix evenly over filling. Drizzle butter evenly over cake mix.
3. Bake 30 minutes. Remove from oven; sprinkle nuts on top; return to oven; bake 30 minutes longer, or until topping is golden-brown. Let cake cool completely on wire rack. Serve with whipped cream. *Makes 16 servings.*

Mexican Pumpkin Casserole
(pictured)

Adapted from a recipe by Mrs. L.D. Elder, Spartanburg, South Carolina.

  2 tablespoons butter or margarine
  1 medium onion, diced
  2 cloves garlic, minced
  2 cans (1-lb size) pumpkin
  1 jar (8 oz) taco sauce
  1 can (4 oz) chopped green chiles, drained
  ½ teaspoon salt
  ¼ teaspoon pepper
  4 large eggs, lightly beaten
1½ cups crushed tortilla chips
  1 pkg (8 oz) Monterey Jack or Cheddar cheese, shredded (2 cups)
 10 whole tortilla chips (optional)

1. In large skillet, over medium heat, melt butter. Add onion and garlic; sauté, stirring, until tender—about 5 minutes. Remove from heat; add pumpkin, taco sauce, chiles, salt and pepper; stir until well mixed. Add eggs; stir until blended. Preheat oven to 400F.
2. In 2- or 2½-quart clear glass soufflé dish or straight-sided casserole, place crushed tortilla chips to cover bottom. Spoon one-third of pumpkin mixture evenly over chips. Reserve 2 tablespoons shredded cheese for garnish. Sprinkle half of remaining cheese on pumpkin layer.
3. Continue layering a third of pumpkin mixture, the remaining cheese and the remaining third of pumpkin mixture. Bake 30 to 40 minutes, or until slightly puffed and heated through. Garnish with reserved shredded cheese and tortilla chips. *Makes 10 servings.*

Pumpkin-Oatmeal Bars
(pictured)

  1 cup quick-cooking or old-fashioned oats
  1 cup all-purpose flour
  1 cup lightly packed brown sugar
  1 teaspoon baking powder
  ¼ teaspoon salt
  1 cup canned pumpkin
  1 large egg, lightly beaten
  ½ cup (1 stick) butter or margarine, melted
  1 teaspoon vanilla extract
  ½ cup dark seedless raisins
  ½ cup unsalted dry-roasted peanuts, coarsely chopped

1. Grease 9-by-9-by-2-inch baking pan; set aside. Preheat oven to 350F.
2. In medium bowl, combine oats, flour, brown sugar, baking powder and salt; stir to mix. Make well in center; add pumpkin, egg, butter and vanilla; stir just until dry ingredients are moistened. Stir in raisins and peanuts. Spread mixture in prepared pan. Bake 35 to 40 minutes, or until firm and lightly browned. Let cool in pan on wire rack. Cut into bars. *Makes 12 bars.*

Glazed Pumpkin Cookies
(pictured)

  2 cups all-purpose flour
  2 teaspoons baking powder
  ½ teaspoon salt
  2 teaspoons ground cinnamon
  ½ teaspoon ground nutmeg
  ¼ teaspoon ground ginger
  ½ cup (1 stick) butter or margarine, softened
  1 cup granulated sugar
  2 eggs
  1 cup canned or fresh puréed pumpkin
  1 cup golden raisins
  1 cup chopped walnuts or pecans

Lemon Glaze

1¾ cups confectioners' sugar
  1 tablespoon grated lemon peel
  1 tablespoon lemon juice

1. Preheat oven to 350F. Lightly grease cookie sheets. Sift flour, baking powder, salt, cinnamon, nutmeg and ginger onto waxed paper.
2. In large bowl, with electric mixer at medium speed, beat butter, granulated sugar and eggs until fluffy.
3. At low speed, beat in pumpkin. Then beat in flour mixture just until combined.
4. Stir in raisins and walnuts.
5. Drop by tablespoons, 2 inches apart, onto prepared cookie sheets.

Bounty from the Land and Sea

6. Bake 12 to 15 minutes, or until golden. Remove to wire rack.
7. Make Lemon Glaze: In medium bowl, combine confectioners' sugar, lemon peel and lemon juice; stir until smooth.
8. While cookies are slightly warm, spread tops with glaze. *Makes about 3½ dozen.*

Peach-Pumpkin Upside-Down Cake
(pictured)

 1 **can (1 lb, 13 oz) peach halves in heavy syrup**
1⅔ **cups all-purpose flour**
 1 **teaspoon baking soda**
 ¼ **teaspoon baking powder**
 ½ **teaspoon salt**
 ½ **teaspoon ground cinnamon**
 ½ **teaspoon ground nutmeg**
 ½ **cup salad oil**
 1 **cup sugar**
 2 **eggs**
 1 **cup canned or fresh puréed pumpkin**
 ⅓ **cup pecan halves**
 ¼ **cup peach preserves**

1. Preheat oven to 350F. Grease and flour a 10-inch springform or layer-cake pan.
2. Drain peach halves, reserving ¼ cup of the syrup. Set peaches aside to drain well. On waxed paper, sift flour with baking soda, baking powder, salt and spices.
3. In large bowl of electric mixer, beat oil and sugar at medium speed until well combined. Beat in eggs, one at a time. Beat in pumpkin; then, at low speed, beat in flour mixture just until combined.
4. Pour cake batter into prepared pan. Arrange peach halves and pecans on top, as pictured. Bake 40 to 45 minutes, or until surface of cake springs back when gently pressed with fingertip.
5. Combine reserved syrup and preserves in a small saucepan. Bring to boiling, stirring until preserves melt. Remove cake from pan and place on serving plate. Brush with peach glaze. Serve warm or cool. *Makes 8 servings.*

Sliced-Pumpkin Tart
(pictured)

 1 **small sugar pumpkin, calabasa or winter squash (3 lb)**
 1 **cup water**
 ¼ **cup sugar**
 ½ **teaspoon ground cinnamon**
 1 **teaspoon cornstarch**
 ½ **cup apricot preserves**
   9-inch baked tart shell
 1 **tablespoon coarsely chopped walnuts**

1. Scrub pumpkin. Cut into quarters. Remove seeds and pulp. Place quarters, shell side down, in a 5-quart Dutch oven with 1 cup water. Sprinkle pumpkin with ¼ cup sugar. Simmer, covered, until tender—20 to 30 minutes.
2. Let pumpkin pieces cool slightly on wire rack over a pan. Measure drippings from pumpkin pieces. Add enough cooking liquid to make ½ cup.
3. In a small saucepan, stir together cinnamon and cornstarch. Gradually stir in reserved ½ cup liquid. Bring mixture to boiling, stirring until thickened. Remove from heat. Stir in apricot preserves.
4. Peel pumpkin pieces. Cut into 2-inch-wide strips. Slice crosswise into ⅛-inch-thick pieces. Spoon 2 cups pumpkin into tart shell, making a flat layer. Pour on half of sauce.
5. Arrange remaining pumpkin on top of sauce in concentric circles. Top with remaining sauce. Sprinkle with chopped walnuts. Refrigerate until chilled through—2 to 3 hours. *Makes 8 servings.*

Pumpkin-Rum Mousse
(pictured)

 6 **egg whites**
 2 **env unflavored gelatine**
 ¼ **cup cold water**
 ¼ **cup golden rum**
 6 **egg yolks**
 ½ **cup sugar**
1½ **cups canned or fresh puréed pumpkin**
 ½ **teaspoon ground cloves**
 ¼ **teaspoon ground cinnamon**
 ¼ **teaspoon ground ginger**
 ¼ **teaspoon ground nutmeg**
 2 **cups heavy cream (1 pint)**
   Pecan or walnut halves

1. Fold 26-inch-long piece of waxed paper in thirds; with string, tie collar around 1-quart soufflé dish, to form a rim 2 inches high. In large bowl of electric mixer, let egg whites warm to room temperature—1 hour.
2. In small saucepan, sprinkle gelatine over water and rum; let stand 5 minutes to soften. Place over low heat, stirring until gelatine is dissolved. Remove from heat.
3. In small bowl of electric mixer, beat egg yolks until thick—about 3 minutes. Gradually beat in ¼ cup sugar, 2 tablespoons at a time; beat until very thick. Add pumpkin and spices; stir in softened gelatine. Beat 1½ cups cream until stiff; refrigerate.
4. In large bowl, at high speed, beat whites (use clean beaters) until soft peaks form when beaters are slowly raised. Beat in remaining ¼ cup sugar, 2 tablespoons

Bounty from the Land and Sea

at a time, beating well after each addition. Beat until stiff peaks form when beaters are slowly raised.
5. With whisk, using an under-and-over motion, fold pumpkin mixture into egg whites just to combine. Fold in whipped cream. Turn into soufflé dish.
6. Refrigerate until firm—4 hours or overnight.
7. To serve: Remove collar. Whip remaining cream; put through pastry bag with number-5 tip. Pipe on rosettes, as pictured; garnish with pecan halves. *Makes 10 servings.*

Blueberry Cornbread

- **1 cup sifted all-purpose flour**
- **¼ cup sugar**
- **3 teaspoons baking powder**
- **½ teaspoon salt**
- **1 cup yellow cornmeal**
- **1 egg, beaten**
- **½ cup (1 stick) butter or margarine, melted**
- **1 cup milk**
- **¾ cup blueberries, washed and drained**

1. Preheat oven to 375F. Grease an 8-by-8-by-2-inch baking pan.
2. In a small bowl, sift flour with sugar, baking powder and salt. Add cornmeal, mixing well; set aside.
3. In medium bowl, combine egg, butter and milk, mixing well. Add flour mixture, stirring only until moistened.
4. Spoon batter into prepared pan; sprinkle blueberries on top. Bake 20 to 25 minutes, or until golden-brown. To serve, cut into squares. Serve hot, with butter. *Makes 9 servings.*

Frozen Maple Mousse

- **1¼ cups maple or maple-flavored syrup**
- **2 egg yolks**
- **⅛ teaspoon salt**
- **1 pint heavy cream (2 cups)**
- **Whipped cream (optional)**

1. In the top of a double boiler, over direct heat, heat the maple syrup just until it is bubbly around the edge of the pan.
2. In small bowl, with electric mixer or rotary beater,

beat egg yolks with salt until light-colored. Gradually beat in all the syrup. Return mixture to top of double boiler.
3. Cook over simmering water, stirring constantly, until mixture is slightly thickened and forms a coating on a metal spoon—10 to 15 minutes.
4. Set top of double boiler in ice water; beat mixture until thick and fluffy and well chilled—5 minutes.
5. In large, chilled bowl, beat 2 cups heavy cream just until stiff. Fold in syrup mixture. Pour into an 8-by-8-by-2-inch baking pan.
6. Freeze until firm about 1 inch from edge. Turn into large bowl; beat with wire whisk until smooth. Turn into 6-cup mold, preferably one with a tube.
7. Freeze, covered with plastic wrap, until firm—8 hours or overnight.
8. To serve: Unmold onto chilled serving plate. Garnish with whipped cream. *Makes 8 servings.*

Sheriff's Pecan Casserole
(pictured)

Adapted from a recipe by Shirley H. Phelps, Leesburg, Georgia.

- **1 pkg (14 or 16 oz) white or caraway-rye yeast-bread mix**
- **1 env (1⅛ oz) à-la-king-sauce mix**
- **1 cup milk**
- **1 pkg (1 lb) bulk pork sausage**
- **2 cups pecans, chopped**
- **1 can (1 lb) cut green beans, drained**
- **1 jar (4 oz) whole pimientos, drained and diced (optional)**
- **2 cups shredded sharp Cheddar cheese (8 oz)**

1. Prepare bread mix as package label directs. When dough forms a ball, on lightly floured surface, knead 5 minutes. Invert bowl over dough; let rise 20 minutes.
2. Meanwhile, in small saucepan, combine sauce mix with milk; stir until smooth. Over medium-high heat, cook, stirring, until sauce thickens and comes to boiling; remove from heat.
3. In large skillet, break up sausage with a wooden spoon; brown; drain excess fat. Add pecans, beans, pimientos and prepared sauce to sausage in skillet; stir to mix. Preheat oven to 350F.

Bounty from the Land and Sea

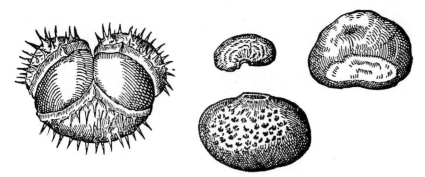

4. On lightly floured surface, with rolling pin, roll bread dough into a 19-by-14-inch rectangle. Fit dough crosswise into a 13-by-9-by-2-inch baking pan, leaving a 3- to 4-inch overhang on long sides of pan. Spoon sausage mixture onto bread dough in pan, spreading evenly over entire surface; sprinkle cheese over sausage mixture.

5. With scissors, cut bread-dough overhangs into 1-inch-wide strips, beginning at outer edges and ending at sausage-cheese filling. Alternately fold strips over filling, tucking ends under to seal. Bake 35 to 40 minutes, or until bread is golden. *Makes 10 servings.*

Butter-Pecan Cheesecake
(pictured)

Adapted from a recipe by Jolie Mercer, Albany, Georgia.

4 tablespoons (½ stick) butter or margarine
1 cup pecans, chopped
1 cup graham-cracker crumbs
1¾ cups sugar
4 pkg (8-oz size) cream cheese, softened
4 large eggs
1 container (1 lb) sour cream
1 teaspoon vanilla extract
Pecan halves (optional)

1. In medium skillet, over medium heat, melt 1 tablespoon butter. Add chopped pecans; cook, stirring, until lightly toasted. Transfer to small bowl; set aside.

2. In same skillet, melt remaining butter; remove from heat; stir in graham-cracker crumbs and 2 tablespoons sugar until well mixed. Pat crumb mixture on bottom of 9-inch springform pan; place in freezer to chill. Preheat oven to 475F.

3. In large bowl of electric mixer, beat cream cheese and 1½ cups sugar until smooth. Add eggs, one at a time, beating after each addition. Add 1 cup sour cream and the vanilla; beat until well mixed. Stir in toasted pecans.

4. Pour cream-cheese mixture into prepared pan. Bake 10 minutes; reduce oven to 300F; continue baking 45 to 50 minutes, or until center of cheesecake is almost firm.

5. Meanwhile, add remaining 2 tablespoons sugar to remaining sour cream in its container; stir to mix. When cheesecake is done, remove from oven. In-

crease oven temperature to 400F. Spread sour-cream mixture evenly on cheesecake; return to oven; bake 5 minutes, or until topping is set. Let cool in pan on wire rack; refrigerate until cold—3 hours or overnight.

6. To serve: Remove side of springform pan. Place cheesecake on serving plate; garnish top with pecan halves. *Makes 16 serivngs.*

Bucky Badger Ice-Cream Sundae
(pictured)

Cranberry Sauce
1 pkg (12 oz) fresh or frozen cranberries
1 cup sugar
1 cup water

Vanilla ice cream

1. To make Cranberry Sauce in a microwave oven: In medium-size glass bowl or microwave-safe dish, combine cranberries, sugar and water. Cover with plastic wrap; turn back one corner to vent. Microwave at HIGH 15 minutes, stirring every 5 minutes. Let stand, covered, 10 minutes. Refrigerate several hours or overnight. (Sauce will thicken as it cools.) Without a microwave oven, combine cranberries, sugar and water in medium saucepan; bring to boiling. Reduce heat; simmer, uncovered, 10 minutes. Refrigerate several hours or overnight.

2. To make sundaes: Scoop ice cream into dishes; top with Cranberry Sauce. *Makes 2½ cups sauce.*

Note: If desired, ½ cup golden raisins or chopped nuts may be stirred into Cranberry Sauce before refrigerating.

Hot Cranberry Grog
(pictured)

1 bottle (1 quart) cranberry-juice cocktail
2 tablespoons brown sugar
2 (3-inch-long) cinnamon sticks
½ teaspoon whole allspice
½ teaspoon whole cloves
Dash ground nutmeg
Dash salt
½ cup light rum
4 (6-inch-long) cinnamon sticks
Butter (optional)

Bounty from the Land and Sea

In medium saucepan, combine juice, brown sugar, small cinnamon sticks, spices and salt; bring to boiling. Simmer, covered, 20 minutes. Stir in rum; bring back to boiling. Place a long cinnamon stick and, if desired, a pat of butter in each mug. Strain cranberry grog into mugs. *Makes 4 (1-cup) servings.*

Cranberry-Cream-Cheese Torte
(pictured)

Adapted from the Eagle River, Wisconsin, *Cranberry Festival Cookbook.*

Cranberry Filling
 1 **pkg (12 oz) fresh or frozen cranberries**
 1 **cup sugar**
½ **cup water**
 1 **teaspoon grated lemon peel**

Cake
⅓ **cup cornstarch**
⅓ **cup all-purpose flour**
 5 **large eggs, separated**
½ **teaspoon salt**
⅓ **cup sugar**
 1 **teaspoon vanilla extract**

Cream-Cheese Filling
 1 **pkg (8 oz) cream cheese, softened**
 3 **tablespoons butter or margarine, softened**
⅓ **cup sugar**
 1 **tablespoon lemon juice**
 1 **teaspoon grated lemon peel**
½ **teaspoon vanilla extract**

 2 **tablespoons light rum**
    Candied lemon peel (optional; see Note)

1. Make Cranberry Filling: In medium saucepan, combine cranberries, 1 cup sugar, the water and 1 teaspoon lemon peel; bring to boiling. Reduce heat; simmer, uncovered, 10 minutes. Set aside to cool.
2. Make Cake: Grease bottom of 15½-by-10½-by-1-inch jelly-roll pan and line with waxed paper. In small bowl, stir cornstarch and flour to mix well. In large bowl, with electric mixer at high speed, beat egg whites and salt until soft peaks form. Gradually add ⅓ cup sugar, 2 tablespoons at a time; beat until stiff peaks form.
3. Preheat oven to 375F. In small bowl of electric mixer, with same beaters, beat egg yolks and 1 teaspoon vanilla until thick and lemon-colored. Spoon yolk mixture over whites; sprinkle with cornstarch mixture; with rubber spatula, fold gently, just until egg mixtures are combined. Spread batter evenly in prepared pan. Bake 10 to 12 minutes, or until top is

golden. Let cake cool in pan on wire rack 30 minutes. Remove from pan; discard waxed paper.
4. Meanwhile, make Cream-Cheese Filling: In small bowl, with electric mixer, beat all filling ingredients until smooth.
5. Cut cake crosswise into four 10-by-3¾-inch rectangles. Brush top of each cake layer with rum. Place a layer, rum side up, on serving platter; spread on half of Cream-Cheese Filling. Top with another cake layer; spread on half of Cranberry Filling. Repeat with remaining cake layers and fillings. Garnish with candied lemon peel. *Makes 12 servings.*

Note: To make candied lemon peel, with sharp paring knife or vegetable peeler, remove lemon peel from a lemon in a continuous spiral. Remove and discard white membrane. Cut into 2½-by-¼-inch pieces. In small saucepan, combine ¼ cup sugar, ¼ cup water and ¼ cup light corn syrup; bring to boiling; stir until sugar is dissolved. Add lemon peel; simmer until syrup thickens—about 10 minutes. Drain.

Potato-Rye Rolls
(pictured)

Adapted from recipe by Freddie McKoen, Merrill, Oregon.

 1 **large (10 oz) baking potato, pared and cubed (about 1½ cups)**
    Water
2½ **to 3 cups all-purpose flour**
 1 **cup rye flour**
 1 **pkg fast-rising yeast**
 2 **teaspoons caraway seeds**
1½ **teaspoons onion salt**
½ **cup milk**
¼ **cup molasses**
 1 **tablespoon butter or margarine**
 1 **cup shredded Monterey Jack cheese (4 oz)**
 1 **large egg white, mixed with 1 tablespoon water**

1. In small saucepan, bring potato cubes in water to cover to boiling. Over low heat, cook, covered, till tender—about 15 minutes. Drain, reserving ¼ cup potato water; set aside. Mash potato cubes.
2. In large bowl of electric mixer, combine 1 cup all-purpose flour, the rye flour, yeast, caraway seeds and onion salt; mix well. In medium saucepan, heat reserved potato water, milk, molasses and butter until very warm (120 to 130F).
3. With electric mixer at low speed, gradually beat milk mixture into flour mixture until ingredients are moistened. Beat at medium speed 2 minutes. Add mashed potato; beat at high speed 2 minutes.
4. With wooden spoon, gradually stir in cheese and

Bounty from the Land and Sea

enough remaining all-purpose flour to make dough stiff enough to leave side of bowl. Turn dough out onto a lightly floured pastry cloth or board. Knead until smooth and elastic, adding more flour, if necessary, to make a smooth, not sticky, dough—8 to 10 minutes.

5. Place in lightly greased medium bowl, turning dough over to bring up greased side. Cover with towel. Let rise in warm place (85F), free from drafts, until double in bulk—about 45 minutes.

6. Grease a 10-inch Bundt or tube pan. Punch dough down; divide into 15 pieces; shape into balls. Place 9 balls in bottom of prepared pan. Place 6 balls on top; cover; let rise in warm place until double in bulk—about 30 minutes.

7. Preheat oven to 375F. Bake 25 minutes. Remove pan from oven; brush rolls with egg-white mixture; bake 5 minutes longer, or until shiny brown. Cool in pan on wire rack 10 minutes. Remove from pan; cool completely. *Makes 15 rolls.*

Gold Coast Stew
(pictured)

2 tablespoons peanut or salad oil
2 medium onions, thinly sliced
1 large green pepper, halved, seeded and cut into ½-inch strips
1 large red pepper, halved, seeded and cut into ½-inch strips
3 cups canned or fresh chicken broth (see Note)
1 can (6 oz) tomato paste
¾ cup creamy or chunky peanut butter
1 teaspoon sugar
1 teaspoon chili powder
½ teaspoon salt
½ teaspoon ground nutmeg
4 cups cubed cooked chicken (see Note) or leftover turkey
Cooked rice
Chopped peanuts (optional)

1. In large saucepan, over medium-high heat, heat oil. Add onion and green- and red-pepper strips; cook, stirring occasionally, until tender—about 5 minutes. Add chicken broth, tomato paste, peanut butter, sugar, chili powder, salt and nutmeg; stir to mix well. Cook, stirring frequently, until mixture boils; add chicken; cook until heated through.

2. Serve stew with cooked rice; garnish with chopped peanuts. *Makes 8 servings.*

Note: For fresh broth and cooked chicken, cook a whole or cut-up 4-pound roasting chicken, partially covered, in 8 cups simmering water until tender—about 40 minutes.

Peanut-Butter-Fudge Cake
(pictured)

Cake
2 large eggs
1 cup (2 sticks) butter or margarine
1 cup water
½ cup buttermilk
¼ cup unsweetened cocoa
1 teaspoon vanilla extract
2 cups granulated sugar
2 cups all-purpose flour
1 teaspoon baking soda

Topping
1 jar (12 oz) creamy peanut butter, at room temperature
1 teaspoon peanut or salad oil

Frosting
¼ cup (½ stick) butter or margarine
3 tablespoons buttermilk
2 tablespoons unsweetened cocoa
1½ cups confectioners' sugar
½ teaspoon vanilla extract

1. Make Cake: Grease and flour 13-by-9-by-2-inch baking pan; set aside. Preheat oven to 350F.

2. In small saucepan, lightly beat eggs; add 1 cup butter, the water, ½ cup buttermilk, ¼ cup cocoa and the vanilla. Over medium heat, cook, stirring occasionally, just until mixture begins to boil. Meanwhile, in medium bowl, combine granulated sugar, the flour and baking soda. Pour hot mixture over sugar mixture; stir until well mixed. Pour into prepared pan, spreading evenly. Bake 25 minutes, or until a cake tester inserted in center of cake comes out clean. Cool in pan on wire rack 15 minutes.

3. Cake may be left in pan to cool completely or removed from pan: Cover a 13-by-9-inch piece of cardboard with foil. Run knife around edge of pan to loosen cake. Place foil-covered cardboard, smooth side down, on cake. Place large wire rack or cutting board, upside down, on cardboard. Grasping rack and pan firmly, invert so that cake drops onto cardboard and rack; remove pan. Let cake cool.

4. Make Topping: In small bowl, stir peanut butter with oil to make spreading consistency; spread evenly over top of cooled cake.

5. Make Frosting: In small saucepan, combine butter, buttermilk and cocoa. Over medium heat, bring to boiling; remove from heat. Stir in confectioners' sugar and vanilla until smooth. With teaspoon, drop frosting on peanut topping in three crosswise and five lengthwise rows. Working quickly before frosting sets, with metal spatula, draw edge through frosting crosswise, then lengthwise, to make decorative design. *Makes 15 servings.*

Fine Foods
From Restaurants And Country Inns

The Early American traditions of fine food and warm hospitality still live on in our historical country inns and restaurants. For your at-home dining pleasure, this section reveals the well-guarded secret recipes of some of the best establishments throughout the country. They have all been adapted for easy preparation in your own kitchen and just might win you a reputation as a five-star chef. Recipes start on page 60.

For lovers of good food, San Francisco's fine restaurants are a special drawing card. Here are some of their most popular dishes. Beginning at **top, center**: a creamy Almond Tart from Chez Panisse. **Continuing clockwise**: Artichaut Chatelaine from Maurice et Charles; Middle Eastern Chicken Tabaka; Oriental Onion Cakes; and a tart citrus dessert, Cold Soufflé Milanaise. *Recipes begin on page 60.*

55

The festive platter of Cornish hens comes from the Lake Superior region in Michigan. The hens are roasted with tarragon, white wine and garlic, then heaped around a mound of fragrant Turkish Pilaf. *See recipes on page 62.*

56

The Elms Inn in Ridgefield, Connecticut, is in a 1760 building, with furnishings of the period. Breast of Chicken Scala with sour cream, spicy Scampi and Coupe Elizabeth, made with Bing cherries and ice cream, are typical of the delectable fare that has been pleasing travelers since 1799. *Recipes begin on page 63.*

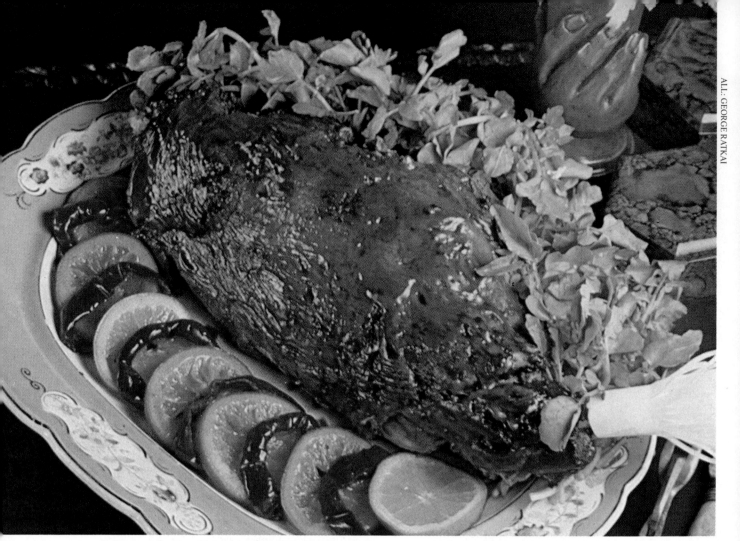

In Portsmouth, New Hampshire, The Blue Strawberry offers a touch of Americana and a delightful menu that includes this mouth-watering Roast Leg of Lamb served with a spiced Orange-And-Pepper Sauce. Glazed rings of orange and red pepper join with watercress in embracing this beauty. *See recipes on page 64.*

From Florida comes this very popular Grasshopper Pie with its filling of melted marshmallows, crème de menthe, crème de cacao and whipped cream frozen firm and fabulous in a chocolate crumb crust. *See recipe on pages 64, 65.*

The simple, sophisticated Vacherin Glacé au Kirsch—scoops of luscious ice cream nestled in meringue shells, splashed with kirsch, and crowned with whipped cream and strawberries—has become the trademark of L'Auberge Chez François, in Great Falls, Virginia. *See recipe on page 67.*

58

When in Tulsa, Oklahoma, don't miss the Garden Restaurant, the place to go for light, flaky Icebox Rolls. Hot from the oven and slathered with butter, they're a favorite with one and all. *See recipe on page 65.*

A specialty of the New York area is this succulent Rack of Lamb in red wine, flanked by baked Aubergine Provençale, an eggplant-and-to-mato dish with definitely French accents. *See recipes on page 66.*

An elegant meal awaits the discriminating diner in Mobile, Alabama. Delicate sherried Crabmeat au Gratin is served bubbly hot in scallop shells. *See recipe on page 67.*

This sausage-stuffed roast-pork platter, from Saint Paul, is Minnesota fare at its hearty best. The kielbasa, pork loin and vegetables simmer together to tender perfection in a caraway-accented garlic-wine broth. *See recipe on page 65.*

Fine Foods from Restaurants and Country Inns

continued from page 55

Chicken Tabaka
(pictured)
(San Francisco, California)

6 **whole breasts of chicken, with all bones except wishbone removed**
½ **cup chopped parsley**
½ **cup chopped cilantro (Chinese parsley)**
½ **cup (1 stick) butter, melted**
½ **tablespoon dried oregano leaves**
6 **to 8 cloves garlic, chopped**
½ **tablespoon salt**
½ **tablespoon pepper**
1 **tablespoon all-purpose flour**
½ **cup lemon juice**
1 **can (13 ¾ oz) chicken broth**
½ **cup catsup**
½ **cup pomegranate juice (see Editor's Note)**

Watercress (optional)

1. Flatten the chicken breasts slightly so they are of uniform thickness.
2. In a large bowl, combine all the remaining ingredients to make a sauce.
3. Pour half the sauce into a roasting pan just large enough to hold all the chicken breasts without overlapping them. Place the chicken breasts, skin side up, over the sauce and pour the remaining sauce over them. Marinate, refrigerated, overnight or, better, at least 24 hours.
4. When ready to cook, weight down the chicken with three or four heavy plates or a slightly smaller pan weighted down with some full cans of food. Set the pan of chicken over low heat until the sauce comes to a boil. Lower the heat to a simmer, and let it cook for 15 minutes.
5. Preheat oven to 350F.
6. Remove the plates and bake the chicken, uncovered, in the preheated oven for 15 minutes, basting chicken occasionally.
7. Arrange chicken breasts on a serving platter. Garnish with watercress, if desired. Serve sauce separately. *Serves 6.*

Editor's Note: Or use 2 tablespoons grenadine syrup.

Hunan Onion Cakes
(pictured)
(San Francisco, California)

12 **flour tortillas, 7 or 8 inches in diameter**
6 **tablespoons sesame oil**
2 **eggs, lightly beaten**
  Salt
1 **cup finely chopped scallions, including tender green portion**
4 **to 6 cups vegetable oil**

1. Set up an assembly line: a stack of tortillas, a bowl of sesame oil with a brush, a bowl of beaten eggs, a salt shaker and a bowl of scallions next to or surrounding a work area large enough to accommodate one of the 7- or 8-inch tortillas. Put the vegetable oil in a heavy frying pan slightly bigger than one of the tortillas. Heat the oil over moderate heat to about 350 to 365F. It should be hot enough for a tortilla to brown in about 1 minute.
2. Place a tortilla flat on the work area. Brush it with sesame oil, then egg. Sprinkle it lightly with salt and scatter 2 to 3 tablespoons of the scallions over it. Align a second tortilla over the first one and press them firmly together.
3. Slide the onion cake into the hot oil. When it is brown on one side, use a pair of tongs or chopsticks to turn it over to brown on the other side. Meanwhile, prepare the next onion cake.
4. When the cake is browned on both sides, hold it vertically over the oil to drain; then place it on a cutting board. With a chef's knife or a large cleaver, cut it into sixths. Slide in the next onion cake. Repeat until all onion cakes are cooked. *Makes 6.*

Note: This may seem like a lot of onion cakes, but most dedicated eaters can easily polish off one whole onion cake.

Cold Soufflé Milanaise
(pictured)
(San Francisco, California)

8 **eggs, separated**
1 **tablespoon sugar**
2 **tablespoons all-purpose flour**
2 **cups milk**
2 **env unflavored gelatine**
½ **cup cold water**
4 **limes**
2 **lemons**
2 **oranges**
¾ **cup sugar**
1 **cup heavy cream, whipped**

1. In a small mixing bowl, beat the egg yolks with the 1 tablespoon of sugar and the flour.
2. In a medium-size saucepan, bring the milk to a boil. Add about ½ cup of the hot milk to the egg yolks. Stir well; then beat the yolks into the hot milk in the saucepan. Heat this custard gently until it thickens—about 2 minutes. Remove from heat.
3. In a small bowl, sprinkle the gelatine over ½ cup cold water to soften. Place over a pan of hot water to melt the gelatine; then stir it into the custard.
4. Grate the zest (colored portion of the skin) of the citrus fruits into the custard. Squeeze the juices and

Fine Foods from Restaurants and Country Inns

add the strained juices to the custard (see Editor's Note 1).

5. In a large bowl, beat the egg whites until they form soft peaks. Add ½ cup of the sugar and continue beating until the meringue forms stiff peaks. Using a wire whisk or rubber spatula, with an over-and-under motion, fold the custard mixture into the meringue.

6. Mix the remaining ¼ cup sugar and the whipped cream. Fold it into the soufflé mixture. Butter and sugar a 2-quart soufflé mold. Tie a collar of buttered waxed paper around it (see Editor's Note 2).

7. Pour in the soufflé mixture right up to the top. Chill the soufflé at least 4 hours. (It is not necessary to make this in a soufflé mold. It can just as easily be chilled in a large bowl and served as a citrus mousse.) If you do use a soufflé mold, remove the collar before serving (see Editor's Note 3). *Serves 8 to 10.*

Editor's Notes:

1. Place the pan of custard in a bowl of ice water, stirring occasionally, until the consistency of unbeaten egg whites—15 to 20 minutes.

2. In our photograph we used a 1½-quart soufflé dish. Fold a 26-inch piece of waxed paper lengthwise in thirds. Grease with 1 tablespoon butter. Form a 2-inch collar around dish; tie.

3. If desired, decorate with whipped cream (as pictured) and orange, lime and lemon slices.

Almond Tart
(pictured)
(Chez Panisse, Berkeley, California)

Pastry
 1 **cup all-purpose flour**
 1 **tablespoon sugar**
 ¼ **lb (1 stick) butter**
 1 **tablespoon (or more) water**
    Few drops almond extract
 ½ **teaspoon vanilla extract**

Filling
 1 **cup sliced almonds**
 ¾ **cup sugar**
 ¾ **cup heavy cream**
 ¼ **teaspoon salt**
    Few drops almond extract
 1 **teaspoon Grand Marnier**

1. In a medium-sized bowl, mix the flour with 1 tablespoon sugar. Cut in the butter until the mixture resembles coarse meal. Work in the water, few drops almond extract and the vanilla to make a paste. Press the paste into a 9-inch tart pan (with a removable bottom) and chill for 1 hour.

2. Preheat oven to 400F.

3. Bake the tart for 10 minutes, or until it turns a golden-brown.

4. To make the Filling: Combine all the ingredients and let them stand until the sugar dissolves—about 20 minutes.

5. Pour the filling into the prebaked shell; return it to the oven and bake for 40 minutes or until the top is brown and the sugar has caramelized. Serve the tart at room temperature. *Makes 6 to 8 servings.*

Editor's Note: We suggest reducing oven temperature to 375F for baking filling 40 minutes.

Artichaut Chatelaine
Artichoke and Mushroom Salad
(pictured)
(Maurice et Charles, San Rafael, California)

Artichokes
 6 **small artichokes, partially peeled, if necessary (see Note)**
 2 **tablespoons butter**
 2 **teaspoons salt**
 ½ **teaspoon pepper**
 1 **lemon, sliced**
    Water

Salad
 6 **large mushrooms, approximately the same size as the artichoke hearts**

Dressing
 ½ **cup olive oil**
 2 **tablespoons vinegar or lemon juice**
 1 **tablespoon Dijon-style mustard**
 ½ **cup sour cream, lightly whipped**
 1 **tablespoon fresh dill, chopped (optional)**
    Salt
    Pepper

1. Put the artichokes in a saucepan with the butter, salt, pepper and lemon. Add water to cover artichokes; cover the pan with a lid and boil the artichokes 20 minutes or until they are cooked through. Test by piercing the stem end with a fork. Drain.

2. When artichokes are cool enough to handle, cut them in half lengthwise and scoop out the hairy choke with a teaspoon.

3. Cut the mushrooms in half lengthwise. Arrange artichoke halves and mushroom halves on a salad plate.

4. With a wire whisk, beat the olive oil with the vinegar or lemon juice and the mustard. When it forms a creamy sauce, mix in the sour cream, the dill and salt and pepper to taste. Serve the sauce with the salad. *Serves 6.*

Note: This can also be made with 1 package (10 oz) frozen artichoke hearts, cooked according to package directions, drained thoroughly.

Fine Foods from Restaurants and Country Inns

Baked Whole Garlic
(Chez Panisse, Berkeley, California)

1 **whole head of garlic**
Salt
Pepper
2 **tablespoons olive oil**

1. Carefully make an incision around the garlic about the middle, just piercing the skin. The object is to lift off the outer skin, exposing the tops of the cloves. Put it in a baking dish. Lightly salt and pepper the garlic. Pour the olive oil over the garlic.
2. Preheat the oven to 200F. Bake the garlic for 15 minutes, uncovered; then cover the baking dish and continue baking 1 hour or longer, until the garlic is tender. Baste occasionally with the oil.
3. Serve the garlic whole and warm (it can be reheated easily), with plenty of fresh, crusty bread. *Makes 1 serving.*

Menu

(Lake Superior Region, Michigan)
Shrimp Bisque
Roast Cornish Hens*
With Turkish Pilaf*
Blue Cloud Dessert*
Coffee

Roast Cornish Hens
(pictured)

6 **Cornish hens (see Note), about 1¼ lb each**
Salt
Pepper
7 **tablespoons dried tarragon leaves**
6 **cloves garlic, peeled**
Garlic salt
¾ **cup (1½ sticks) butter or margarine**
¾ **cup dry white wine**
2 **tablespoons all-purpose flour**
1 **cup water**
Turkish Pilaf, recipe follows

1. Wash hens under cold running water; drain. Pat dry, inside and out, with paper towels.
2. Sprinkle inside of each hen with ¼ teaspoon salt, ⅛

*Recipes given for starred dishes.

teaspoon pepper and 1 tablespoon tarragon. Place one clove of garlic inside each. Sprinkle outside of each liberally with garlic salt. Refrigerate.
3. Meanwhile, make basting sauce: Melt butter in saucepan; stir in wine and 1 tablespoon tarragon.
4. About 1 hour before serving, preheat oven to 450F. Place hens in a shallow roasting pan without a rack. Roast, basting often with sauce, 1 hour, or until hens are browned and tender.
5. Place hens on platter; keep warm.
6. To make gravy: Dissolve flour in 1 cup water; stir into drippings in pan. Bring to boiling, stirring until thickened.
7. To serve: Turn Turkish Pilaf into center of platter; arrange hens on top. *Makes 6 servings.*

Note: If frozen, let thaw overnight in refrigerator.

Turkish Pilaf
(pictured)

2 **cups cracked wheat**
2 **cans (13¾-oz size) chicken broth**
¼ **teaspoon pepper**
¼ **cup (½ stick) butter or margarine**
1 **can (3 oz) chow-mein noodles, crumbled**

1. In medium saucepan, combine cracked wheat and chicken broth. Cover; bring to boiling; reduce heat and simmer 20 minutes. Remove from heat; let stand 10 minutes longer, or until all liquid is absorbed.
2. Add pepper, butter and chow-mein noodles; toss gently to combine. *Makes 6 to 8 servings.*

Blue Cloud Dessert

1½ **cups graham-cracker crumbs**
3 **tablespoons sugar**
⅓ **cup (⅔ stick) butter or margarine, melted**

Topping
1 **lb marshmallows**
1 **cup milk**
½ **teaspoon salt**
1 **cup heavy cream, whipped**
1 **teaspoon vanilla extract**
1 **can (1 lb, 5 oz) blueberry-pie filling**
½ **cup graham-cracker crumbs**

Fine Foods from Restaurants and Country Inns

1. Preheat oven to 375F. In bowl, combine 1½ cups crumbs with the sugar and melted butter; mix well. Turn into a 13-by-9-by-2-inch baking dish. Press to bottom of dish to make an even layer. Bake 8 minutes; set aside to cool.
2. Make Topping: In top of double boiler, over hot water, melt marshmallows with milk and salt. Remove from hot water; let cool until very thick.
3. Fold in whipped cream and vanilla until well combined.
4. Spread half of marshmallow mixture over crust; then spread with blueberry-pie filling. Top with rest of mixture. Sprinkle with ½ cup crumbs. Chill well—2 hours. *Makes 12 servings.*

Menu

(The Elms Inn, Ridgefield, Connecticut)
Scampi*
Breast of Chicken Scala*
Buttered White Rice
Green Beans, French Style
Green Salad With Herb Dressing
Coupe Elizabeth*
Chilled White Wine   Coffee

Scampi
(pictured)

1½ **lb raw medium-size shrimp**
¼ **cup (½ stick) butter or margarine**
½ **cup olive oil**
8 **shallots, chopped very fine (about ¾ cup)**
4 **cloves garlic, chopped fine**
1 **cup canned stewed tomatoes**
½ **cup sliced mushrooms**
1 **teaspoon salt**
Dash pepper
⅓ **cup lemon juice**
¼ **cup chopped parsley**

1. Shell shrimp, leaving last tail segment of shell in place. To butterfly: Split each shrimp lengthwise, from head to tail, leaving intact at tail. Remove dark vein from center of shrimp.
2. In hot butter and oil in large skillet, sauté shallot and

garlic, stirring, 3 minutes. Add tomatoes and mushrooms; cook, stirring, 5 minutes longer.
3. Add salt, pepper, lemon juice, 2 tablespoons parsley and the shrimp; toss to mix well.
4. Divide shrimp mixture into six individual baking dishes.
5. Broil, 4 to 5 inches from heat, 10 minutes, or just until shrimp are tender. Sprinkle each with rest of parsley. *Makes 6 servings.*

Breast of Chicken Scala
(pictured)

3 **whole chicken breasts, boned, halved and skin removed (about 2¼ lb in all)**
2 **tablespoons all-purpose flour**
¼ **cup (½ stick) butter or margarine**
1 **can (10½ oz) condensed beef consommé, undiluted**
½ **cup sour cream**
1 **teaspoon salt**
¼ **teaspoon pepper**
1 **tablespoon grated Parmesan cheese**

1. Wipe chicken with damp paper towels. Sprinkle evenly with flour.
2. In hot butter in large skillet or Dutch oven, sauté chicken until golden-brown on each side—takes about 15 minutes in all. Add consommé; simmer, covered, about 45 minutes. Stir in sour cream, salt and pepper; simmer 10 minutes longer.
3. Remove chicken breasts to heatproof serving dish. Stir sauce in pan to mix well; strain over chicken. (If desired, refrigerate chicken overnight in sauce to improve flavor. Heat slightly just before serving.)
4. To serve: Sprinkle cheese over top. Run under broiler a few minutes, until golden-brown. Serve at once. *Makes 6 servings.*

Coupe Elizabeth
(pictured)

1 **can (1 lb, 1 oz) Bing cherries**
1 **tablespoon cornstarch**
½ **cup Cherry Heering**
1½ **quarts vanilla ice cream**
Whipped cream
Ground cinnamon

*Recipes given for starred dishes.

Fine Foods from Restaurants and Country Inns

1. Drain cherries; measure 1 cup juice. In small bowl, dissolve cornstarch in ½ cup juice. Combine with rest of juice in medium saucepan.
2. Bring to boiling, stirring; reduce heat and simmer until thickened and translucent—about 5 minutes. Let stand until cool.
3. Meanwhile, in small bowl, combine cherries and Cherry Heering; let stand about 1 hour.
4. Add cherries and liquid to thickened juice; mix well.
5. Make scoops of ice cream; pour cherry sauce over ice cream in serving dishes. Top with ruffle of whipped cream (put cream through a pastry bag with a number-6 decorating tip). Sprinkle cream lightly with cinnamon. Serve at once. *Makes 6 servings.*

Roast Leg of Lamb
With Orange-And-Pepper Sauce
(pictured)
(The Blue Strawberry, Portsmouth, New Hampshire)

5- to 6-lb leg of lamb
½ cup (1 stick) butter, melted
½ cup olive oil
¼ cup lemon juice
2 teaspoons prepared mustard
½ teaspoon pepper
1 teaspoon dried sage leaves
1 teaspoon salt
2 cups dry white wine
   Orange-And-Pepper Sauce, recipe follows
   Glazed Oranges and Peppers, recipe follows

1. Preheat oven to 550F.
2. Wipe lamb with damp paper towels. Trim excess fat. Place, fat side up, in large, shallow roasting pan, without rack.
3. Combine butter, olive oil, lemon juice, mustard, pepper, sage and salt; mix well. Brush lamb well all over with this mixture. Pour remaining mixture over lamb.
4. In very hot oven, roast lamb, uncovered, 45 minutes. Pour off excess grease.
5. Pour wine over lamb. Reduce oven temperature to 400F. Roast 45 minutes longer. Baste with the pan drippings several times during the last 20 minutes.
6. Meanwhile, make Orange-And-Pepper Sauce and Glazed Oranges and Peppers.
7. Remove lamb from oven. Drain juices; measure 1 cup. Pour into Orange-And-Pepper Sauce. Bring to boiling; simmer 3 minutes, stirring to blend well. Pour sauce over lamb; return to oven; roast 20 to 30 minutes longer, depending on desired doneness (see Note).
8. Arrange lamb on platter; garnish with Glazed Oranges and Peppers. *Makes 8 to 10 servings.*

Note: The internal temperature for rare lamb is 145-150F; for medium, 160F; and for well-done, 175F.

Orange-And-Pepper Sauce

¼ cup (½ stick) butter
3 shallots, chopped
1 leek, sliced
¼ cup chopped onion
1 strip orange peel
2 cloves garlic, crushed
1 tablespoon lemon juice
1 hot red pepper, cut into long thin strips
2 tablespoons flour
1 cup dry red wine
1 cup water
½ teaspoon salt

1. In hot butter in saucepan, sauté shallots, leek, onion, orange peel, garlic, lemon juice and red-pepper strips until tender but not browned.
2. Remove from heat; stir in flour; then stir in wine, water and the salt. Return to heat and simmer, covered, stirring occasionally, ½ hour.
3. Add any juices from roast lamb; strain. Serve with lamb.

Glazed Oranges and Peppers

½ cup granulated sugar
½ cup water
¼ cup light corn syrup
2 medium oranges, sliced ¼ inch thick
1 large sweet red pepper, cut into ½-inch rings

1. Combine sugar, water and the corn syrup in large saucepan. Bring to boiling; reduce heat and simmer 10 minutes.
2. Add orange slices and pepper rings; simmer, uncovered and stirring often, 20 minutes, or until orange rind becomes translucent.

Grasshopper Pie
(pictured)
(Islamorada, Florida Keys, Florida)

1½ cups very fine chocolate-wafer crumbs
¼ cup (½ stick) butter, melted

Filling
24 large marshmallows
½ cup milk
⅓ cup green crème de menthe
¼ cup crème de cacao
1 cup heavy cream, whipped

Fine Foods from Restaurants and Country Inns

1. In large bowl, combine 1¼ cups chocolate-wafer crumbs and ¼ cup melted butter; mix until crumbs hold together when pressed.
2. Turn into an 8-inch pie plate; press evenly to side and bottom. Refrigerate.
3. Make Filling: In top of double boiler, over hot water, melt marshmallows with milk. Stir to mix well; place in bowl of ice to cool quickly. To cooled mixture, add crème de menthe and crème de cacao; mix well. With rubber spatula, using an over-and-under motion, gently fold whipped cream into mixture to combine thoroughly.
4. Pour into pie shell. Sprinkle center of pie with remaining crumbs. Freeze several hours, or until firm. *Makes 8 servings.*

Roast Pork Stuffed With Sausage
(pictured)
(St. Paul, Minnesota)

1- **lb piece of kielbasa (Polish sausage)**
5- **lb loin of pork, center cut, all bones except ribs removed**
2 **tablespoons seasoned salt**
2 **teaspoons caraway seed**
2 **cloves garlic, crushed**
1 **cup dry white wine**
4 **medium onions, peeled**
6 **stalks celery, cut in half**
8 **small carrots, pared**
  Water
¼ **cup all-purpose flour**

1. Cut sausage in half; freeze until firm—2 hours.
2. Preheat oven to 325F. Wipe pork with damp paper towels. Trim fat from loin and reserve.
3. With a long sharp knife, make two deep slits, one on each end, straight through the length of roast, twisting knife around to make pocket for sausage.
4. Stuff each end with half of frozen sausage; use finger to push all the way in.
5. In large oval 8- or 10-quart Dutch oven, place pork, fat side down. Over medium heat, cook until lightly browned—about 15 minutes. Turn fat side up.
6. Sprinkle seasoned salt over pork. Add caraway seed, garlic and wine to roasting pan.
7. Cook, tightly covered, 1 hour. Place onions, celery and carrots around the roast pork. Cook, covered, 2 hours longer.
8. In medium skillet, sauté reserved pork fat until crisp and lightly browned; drain on paper towel. Reserve.
9. Remove roast to heated platter. Garnish with browned pork fat. Surround roast with onions, celery and carrots. Keep warm.
10. Make gravy: Strain pan drippings into a 1-quart measure. Remove excess fat. Add water to make 2½ cups. Return to roasting pan. In small bowl, mix flour with ½ cup water until smooth. Stir into pan drippings; bring to boiling, stirring constantly. Reduce heat and simmer 3 minutes. Adjust seasoning, if necessary. Serve with roast and vegetables. *Makes 8 servings.*

Icebox Rolls
(pictured)
(The Garden, Tulsa, Oklahoma)

1 **cup shortening**
¾ **cup sugar**
1½ **teaspoons salt**
1 **cup boiling water**
2 **pkg active dry yeast**
½ **cup warm water (105 to 115F)**
3 **eggs, slightly beaten**
7½ **cups sifted all-purpose flour**
1 **cup water**
  Melted butter

1. In small bowl, combine shortening, sugar and salt. With wooden spoon, beat until smooth and creamy.
2. Add boiling water; stir until smooth. Set aside to cool to lukewarm.
3. In large bowl, sprinkle yeast over ½ cup warm water (check temperature of water with thermometer, if possible); stir until dissolved.
4. Add shortening mixture and beaten eggs to yeast; mix well.
5. Add flour alternately with 1 cup water. Beat until smooth.
6. Grease top of dough; cover bowl tightly with foil. Refrigerate overnight.
7. To shape: Remove a fourth of the dough from the refrigerator. (Cover remaining dough tightly and keep refrigerated until ready to use.) On lightly floured pastry cloth or floured surface, roll into a rectangle 12 by 10 inches. Brush with 2 tablespoons melted butter.
8. Roll up jelly-roll fashion. With sharp knife, cut crosswise into 12 pieces.
9. Place, cut side down, in greased (2½-inch) muffin-pan cups.
10. Cover with towel; let rise in warm place (85F), free from drafts, until double in bulk—about 1 hour.
11. Meanwhile, preheat oven to 400F.
12. Bake 15 to 20 minutes, until golden-brown. Serve hot. *Entire recipe makes 4 dozen.*

Fine Foods from Restaurants and Country Inns

Menu

(Hillsdale, New York)
Country-Style Pâté
Rack of Lamb*
Aubergine Provençale*
Salad Dutch Hearth*
Bananas Flambé*
Red Bordeaux Wine   Coffee

Rack of Lamb
(pictured)

4 **small racks (see Note) of lamb (each about ¾ lb, 3 or 4 lamb chops each)**
   Salt
   Garlic salt
   Cracked black pepper
1 **teaspoon dried thyme leaves**
3 **tablespoons salad oil**
3 **tablespoons butter or margarine**
2 **carrots, pared and sliced**
2 **onions, sliced**
1½ **cups dry red wine**

1. Wipe lamb with damp paper towels; rub each rack with a little salt, garlic salt, pepper and the thyme leaves. In large skillet, heat oil and butter. In hot fat, brown lamb, turning on all sides until brown and crispy—about 15 minutes. Remove lamb to shallow roasting pan without wire rack (lamb will rest on bones). Preheat oven to 350F.
2. Sauté sliced carrot and onion in skillet until browned all over; add to roasting pan.
3. Roast lamb 25 minutes, basting several times with 1 cup red wine.
4. Remove lamb to heated serving platter. Pour off fat from roasting pan. Add remaining red wine to pan; stir to dissolve particles in pan. Bring to boiling; reduce heat and simmer several minutes. Strain, if necessary; pour over lamb.
5. Decorate racks of lamb with paper frills. *Makes 8 servings.*

   Note: Tips of bones should be "Frenched" by butcher (bone tips are clean and skin and fat removed).

*Recipes given for starred dishes.

Aubergine Provençale
Eggplant, Country Style
(pictured)

1 **lb eggplant**
2 **to 3 large tomatoes**
   Salt
   Pepper
¼ **cup olive oil**
2 **tablespoons packaged dry bread crumbs**
2 **cloves garlic, finely chopped**
2 **tablespoons chopped parsley**

1. Preheat oven to 375F. Wash eggplant; trim ends. Halve eggplant lengthwise. Remove peel in ½-inch-wide strips, leaving three strips on each half. Slice crosswise in ⅓-inch slices.
2. Wash tomatoes; remove stems; cut in half; slice thinly.
3. In shallow baking dish, alternate eggplant and tomato slices, standing on flat end, rounded side up. Sprinkle lightly with salt and pepper; then sprinkle with 3 tablespoons olive oil.
4. Bake 30 minutes, or until eggplant is tender. Combine bread crumbs, garlic and parsley; sprinkle over vegetables; sprinkle with remaining tablespoon of olive oil. Bake 5 minutes longer, or until crumbs are golden. Remove to serving platter with broad spatula. *Makes 8 servings.*

Salad Dutch Hearth

1 **bunch watercress**
½ **lb mushrooms**

Vinaigrette Dressing

1 **teaspoon salt**
¼ **cup white-wine vinegar**
½ **teaspoon cracked black pepper**
1 **tablespoon prepared Dijon mustard**
¼ **cup salad oil**

1. Wash watercress and mushrooms; drain. Slice raw mushrooms thinly into shallow dish. Refrigerate watercress.
2. Make Vinaigrette Dressing: In small bowl, stir salt and vinegar to dissolve salt. Stir in pepper and mustard.
3. Slowly add oil, whisking with a fork until dressing is smooth and slightly thickened. Pour over mushrooms; refrigerate 1 hour.

Fine Foods from Restaurants and Country Inns

4. To serve: Pour mushrooms and dressing over watercress; toss. *Makes 8 servings.*

★

Bananas Flambé

4 large bananas
½ cup (1 stick) unsalted butter
½ cup superfine sugar
⅓ cup dark rum
Vanilla ice cream (optional)

1. Peel bananas, removing any strings; cut bananas in half lengthwise, then cut crosswise on the diagonal, to make 1½-inch pieces.
2. In large skillet, melt butter; add sugar; heat, stirring, until golden.
3. Add bananas; sauté, turning occasionally, until tender—about 5 minutes.
4. Ignite rum; add, flaming, to bananas.
5. Serve at once, over vanilla ice cream, if desired. *Makes 6 servings.*

★

Crabmeat au Gratin
(pictured)
(Mobile, Alabama)

1 lb fresh crabmeat or 2 cans (6- or 7½-oz size) crabmeat
½ cup dry sherry
¼ cup (½ stick) butter or margarine
2 tablespoons finery chopped onion
¼ cup all-purpose flour
½ cup milk
1 cup light cream or half-and-half
1 teaspoon salt
Dash pepper
1 egg yolk, lightly beaten
1 can (3 oz) sliced mushrooms, drained
½ cup grated Cheddar cheese (2 oz)

1. Preheat oven to 350F. Lightly grease six to eight scallop shells or a 1-quart casserole.
2. Drain crabmeat, removing any cartilage. Sprinkle crabmeat with ¼ cup sherry; toss to mix well.
3. In hot butter in medium saucepan, sauté onion until tender—5 minutes.
4. Remove from heat. Stir in flour. Gradually stir in milk and cream; bring to boiling, stirring; reduce heat and simmer until quite thick—8 to 10 minutes.

5. Remove from heat; add salt, pepper and remaining sherry. Stir a little of sauce into egg yolk; return to rest of sauce in saucepan; mix well. Stir in crabmeat mixture and mushrooms.
6. Turn into shells or casserole.
7. Sprinkle grated cheese evenly over crabmeat.
8. Place shells on cookie sheet; bake 15 to 20 minutes, or until mixture is bubbly. (Bake casserole 25 minutes.) *Makes 6 to 8 servings.*

★

Vacherin Glacé au Kirsch
(pictured)
(L'Auberge Chez François, Great Falls, Virginia)

Meringue Shells

6 egg whites
1 teaspoon cream of tartar
2 cups sifted granulated sugar
1 teaspoon vanilla extract
1 teaspoon grated lemon peel

1 quart strawberry or vanilla ice cream
Kirsch
1 cup heavy cream, whipped
8 fresh strawberries, with hulls on

1. Make Meringue Shells: In large bowl of electric mixer, let egg whites warm to room temperature—about 1 hour.
2. At high speed, beat egg whites with cream of tartar just until soft peaks form when beaters are slowly raised.
3. Gradually beat in sugar, ¼ cup at a time, beating well after each addition. Beat in vanilla and lemon peel. Continue beating until very stiff—12 minutes longer.
4. Preheat oven to 250F. Lightly grease a large cookie sheet.
5. Spoon meringue into a pastry bag fitted with a number-6 star tube; form eight meringue rings on prepared cookie sheet. (Makes 16 shells; use rest another time.)
6. Bake 1 hour, or until very lightly colored. Store in an airtight container until ready to use.
7. To serve: Fill each ring with a scoop of ice cream; sprinkle with a generous teaspoonful of kirsch. Decorate with whipped cream put through a pastry tube or spooned over ice cream. Top each with a strawberry. *Makes 8 servings.*

Fine Foods from Restaurants and Country Inns

Chicken San Joaquin
(Golden Eagle, San Francisco, California)

- **3 chicken breasts, halved**
- **6 chicken legs**
- **6 chicken thighs**
- **Salt**
- **Pepper**
- **⅔ cup olive oil**
- **1½ cups dry white wine**
- **¾ lb fresh mushrooms, sliced**
- **⅓ cup finely chopped shallots**
- **1½ cups pitted ripe olives**
- **3 cups chopped fresh or canned tomatoes**

1. Preheat the oven to 375F. Have ready a casserole large enough to hold the chicken and the vegetables. Lightly salt and pepper the chicken.
2. In a large skillet, heat the olive oil and brown the chicken pieces. Do not crowd the pan; brown the chicken in shifts, if necessary.
3. When chicken is browned on all sides, put it in the casserole. Pour off the oil and reserve it. Deglaze the pan with the white wine (bring it to a boil and scrape up any browned bits that adhere to the bottom of the pan to dissolve them). Pour the wine into the casserole.
4. Return the reserved oil to the skillet. Add the mushrooms and shallots and cook until the mushrooms have browned. Add them to the casserole, along with the olives and tomatoes.
5. Cover the casserole and bake for 45 minutes. *Makes 6 to 8 servings.*

Mousseline of Bay Scallops
(Towson, Maryland)

Mousse
- **1 lb bay scallops, washed and well drained**
- **2 egg whites**
- **¾ cup heavy cream**
- **½ teaspoon white pepper**
- **¼ teaspoon salt**
- **2 dashes hot red-pepper sauce**
- **2 dashes Angostura bitters**
- **Boiling water**

Sauce
- **3 tablespoons butter or margarine**
- **3 tablespoons all-purpose flour**
- **½ teaspoon salt**
- **⅛ teaspoon pepper**
- **1 can (10 ¼ oz) baby clams**
- **½ cup dry white wine**
- **⅔ cup light cream or half-and-half**
- **10 small cooked shrimp (½ lb), optional**

1. Preheat oven to 350F. Butter a 1-quart mold or baking dish.
2. Make Mousse: Place scallops, egg whites, heavy cream, white pepper, ¼ teaspoon salt, the red-pepper sauce and bitters in food processor; blend 30 seconds, or only until smooth. Do not overblend.
3. Fill mold with mousse. Cover top of mold with a buttered square of waxed paper. Place mold in a 13-by-9-by-2-inch baking pan; then pour enough boiling water around mold to measure 1 inch.
4. Bake 25 to 30 minutes, or just until firm.
5. Meanwhile, make Sauce: In small saucepan, melt butter. Remove from heat. Stir in flour, salt and pepper until smooth. Drain clams; liquid should measure ½ cup. Gradually stir in clam juice, wine and light cream.
6. Over medium heat, bring to boiling, stirring constantly until mixture thickens. Add clams and shrimp; simmer gently, stirring, 2 minutes.
7. To serve: With spatula, loosen edge of mold. Invert over heated serving dish. Remove mold. Spoon some of sauce over mousse. Pass rest of sauce. *Makes 6 servings.*

Menu

(Swiss Hotel, Sonoma, California)
*Smoked Salmon Canapé**
*Chicken Sautéed in Wine**
*Snow Peas and Water Chestnuts**
Salad of California Greens
*Zabaglione**
Chilled White Wine   Coffee

Smoked Salmon Canapé

- **8 oz smoked salmon**
- **½ cup finely chopped chives**
- **1 pkg (8 oz) cream cheese, softened**
- **1 container (8 oz) plain yogurt**
- **½ to 1 teaspoon Worcestershire sauce**
- **Party rye bread or pumpernickel**

1. Cut salmon into ½-inch cubes. Combine with chives.
2. In medium bowl, combine cream cheese, yogurt and Worcestershire; beat with a whisk or portable electric mixer until smooth and creamy.

*Recipes given for starred dishes.

Fine Foods from Restaurants and Country Inns

3. Add salmon and chives to cheese mixture; mix well. Refrigerate in serving bowl at least 3 hours, or until well chilled. Serve on rye-bread rounds. *Makes about 25 canapés.*

Chicken Sautéed in Wine

2 broiler-fryers (about 1¾ lb each), cut up
1 teaspoon salt
¼ teaspoon pepper
¼ cup all-purpose flour
3 tablespoons salad oil
2 tablespoons all-purpose flour
1 clove garlic, crushed
1 tablespoon dried rosemary leaves
1 cup canned chicken broth
1 cup Chablis

1. Wipe chicken with damp paper towels. On sheet of waxed paper, combine salt, pepper and ¼ cup flour; mix well. Roll chicken pieces in flour mixture to coat evenly; shake off any excess.
2. Slowly heat oil in large skillet. Add chicken pieces, skin side down, a few at a time (just enough to cover bottom of pan). Sauté chicken until nicely browned on all sides, removing pieces with tongs as they are browned. Continue until all of chicken is browned.
3. Remove skillet from heat. Into drippings in pan, stir 2 tablespoons flour, the garlic and rosemary leaves. Cook, stirring, over low heat to brown flour—several minutes. Slowly add chicken broth and wine; mix well.
4. Return chicken to skillet; cook, covered, over low heat until tender—about 45 minutes. If sauce is too thick, add a little more wine. Serve with sauce spooned over chicken. *Makes 4 to 6 servings.*

Snow Peas and Water Chestnuts

2 tablespoons peanut oil
10 canned water chestnuts, sliced ¼ inch thick
1 small onion, sliced
1 lb fresh snow peas (see Note), washed
Monosodium glutamate (optional)
1 teaspoon salt
1 tablespoon water

1. In hot oil in a large skillet with tight-fitting cover or in a wok, sauté water chestnuts and onion, stirring, until onion is tender—about 5 minutes.
2. Add snow peas, a dash monosodium glutamate, salt and 1 tablespoon water; mix well. Simmer, covered,

5 minutes, or until peas are tender but still crisp. *Makes 4 to 6 servings.*

Note: Or use 3 packages (6-ounce size) frozen Chinese pea pods.

Zabaglione

4 egg yolks
⅓ cup sugar
Dash salt
½ cup blended Marsala (see Note)
Fresh strawberries or raspberries (optional)

1. In top of double boiler, combine egg yolks, sugar, salt and Marsala. Blend well.
2. Cook over hot (not boiling) water; water in bottom should not touch top of double boiler.
3. While cooking, beat with portable electric mixer until mixture stands in stiff peaks when beaters are raised—about 5 minutes. Serve warm in tall sherbet glasses, or serve cold with fruit. *Makes 4 servings.*

Note: Blend ¼ cup cream Marsala with 2 tablespoons sherry and 2 tablespoons almond Marsala (if not available, use cream Marsala); mix well.

Baked Fudge
(The Garden, Tulsa, Oklahoma)

4 eggs, well beaten
2 cups sugar
½ cup all-purpose flour
½ cup unsweetened cocoa
¼ teaspoon salt
1 cup (2 sticks) butter or margarine, melted
1 cup finely chopped pecans
2 teaspoons vanilla extract

Boiling water
½ cup heavy cream, whipped

1. Preheat oven to 325F.
2. In medium bowl, with wooden spoon, beat eggs, sugar, flour, cocoa and salt until well blended.
3. Mix in butter. Add remaining ingredients, mixing until well blended.
4. Pour mixture into a 9-by-9-by-2-inch baking pan. Set pan in a 13½-by-10½-by-2-inch roasting pan. Pour boiling water into roasting pan to measure 1 inch.
5. Bake 45 minutes, or until fudge is set like custard and crusty on top (or until a knife inserted ½ inch from edge comes out clean). Do not overbake.
6. Remove from hot water to wire rack. Let cool 20 minutes or longer. Refrigerate.
7. Cut into squares. Serve topped with whipped cream. *Makes 12 to 16 servings.*

CHAPTER

2

AMERICA'S INTERNATIONAL FLAVOR

People immigrating to our country came with their hopes and dreams for a better way of life. They also brought their own cultures, especially their unique and distinctive cuisines. Over the years, many of these international favorites have been incorporated into America's national cooking style, becoming standard fare all across the country. You can enjoy a Chinese, Mexican, French or an Italian meal in a specialty restaurant or prepare it easily at home. Neighborhood markets are stocked with exotic fresh produce, spices and imported ingredients—all for the creation of homemade, authentic ethnic foods. Within this chapter you'll find a collection of our favorite international recipes—each one contributed by the men and women who came from afar, each one a creative influence on us all.

The Spicy and Spectacular Taste Of Mexico

Mexican foods are really hot, and we don't just mean spicy. Popular for decades in the Southwest, this colorful and exciting cuisine has swept the nation in recent years to become a favorite in cities and towns from Maine to California. One bite of our special selection of Mexican dishes will convince you that the taste of olé is here to stay. Recipes begin on page 80.

Left: Our Roast Pork in Orange-Almond Sauce is decidedly Mexican: The roast is rubbed with spices before baking, then served with a fruity sauce of oranges, raisins, almonds and capers. *See recipe on page 80.*

73

Above: Pineapple Sopapillas are mouth-watering fritters that resemble plump little pastry pillows, fried golden-brown, then stuffed with pineapple chunks. *See recipe on page 80.*

At right: Ground beef, kidney beans, chili powder and a splash of tequila fill these Beef Enchiladas, smothered in tomato sauce and baked with cheese. *See recipe on page 81.*

74

Above: This dazzling Magic Mocha Cake has fudgy-rich layers stacked between mocha cream, all frosted with coffee-tinged chocolate and a web of white icing. *See recipe on page 81.*

At left: Beef Empanadas are marvelous sugar-dusted meat pies filled with spicy ground beef, raisins and green chiles. *See recipe on page 80.*

Below: Fried Bananas are a two-way treat. Sprinkled with salt, they're a versatile vegetable perfect with ham, pork and poultry; sprinkled with sugar and served hot with a rich Chantilly Sauce, they become a favorite delectable dessert. *See recipes on page 83.*

Above: Crushed corn chips supply the tasty crunch in this Mexican Salad Bowl of grated cheese, olives, onion and tomato wedges all awaiting a toss with creamy avocado dressing. *See recipe on page 82.*

At right: Chicken With Rice, Mexican style: Chicken browns in olive oil, then combines with saffron rice, green chili peppers, tomatoes, peas, pimientos and olives for a one-dish bake that's moist, tender and terrific. *See recipe on page 82.*

At left: Sliced fresh cauliflower florets marinate in oil-and-vinegar dressing, then mix with sliced ripe olives and red- and green-pepper cubes in this bowl of crisp salad lined with escarole leaves. *See recipe on page 82.*

The Spicy and Spectacular Taste of Mexico

continued from page 73

Roast Pork in Orange-Almond Sauce
(pictured)

        5 - lb loin of pork
    2 teaspoons ground cinnamon
    1 teaspoon salt
    ¼ teaspoon ground cloves
    ⅛ teaspoon ground pepper
    1 cup chopped onion
    1 clove garlic, crushed
 1 ½ cups orange juice
    ½ cup golden raisins
    1 tablespoon capers
    ¼ cup slivered blanched almonds
    2 navel oranges, peeled and sliced
       Cilantro

1. Preheat oven to 325F. Wipe pork with damp paper towels.
2. In small bowl, combine cinnamon, salt, cloves and pepper. Rub spice mixture on surface of meat.
3. Insert meat thermometer in center of roast, away from bone. Place roast, fat side up, in shallow roasting pan without rack. (Roast will rest on bones.) Scatter onion and garlic around roast.
4. Roast, uncovered, 1 hour. Remove from oven. Pour 1 cup orange juice over pork. Cover completely with foil.
5. Roast about 2 hours or until meat thermometer registers 170F.
6. Remove roast to heated platter. Make sauce: To drippings in roasting pan, add ½ cup orange juice, the raisins, capers and almonds. Bring to boiling, stirring occasionally; cook 10 minutes. Makes 1 ½ cups.
7. Garnish roast with orange slices and cilantro and serve with sauce. *Makes 8 servings.*

Pineapple Sopapillas
(pictured)

Pillows

    2 cups all-purpose flour
    3 teaspoons baking powder
    ½ teaspoon salt
    2 tablespoons shortening
    ¾ cup water

Filling

 2 ½ tablespoons granulated sugar
    2 tablespoons cornstarch
    1 can (1 lb, 4 oz) crushed pineapple, undrained

       Peanut or salad oil for frying
       Confectioners' sugar

1. Make Pillows: Into medium bowl, sift flour with baking powder and salt. With two knives, cut in short-

ening until mixture resembles coarse meal. Add water; mix well to form a soft dough.
2. On lightly floured pastry cloth, knead dough until smooth.
3. Cover with bowl; let stand 20 minutes.
4. Meanwhile, make Filling: In a medium saucepan, combine granulated sugar and cornstarch. With wooden spoon, stir in pineapple. Cook mixture over medium heat, stirring, until boiling; boil 1 minute, stirring constantly. Set aside to cool.
5. Divide dough into four parts. On lightly floured pastry cloth, roll each part into a rectangle 8 inches long, 4 inches wide and ¼ inch thick. Cut each rectangle into four pieces (4 inches by 2 inches); move to edge of pastry cloth.
6. In deep skillet, slowly heat peanut oil (at least 2 inches) to 375F on deep-frying thermometer. Gently drop dough pieces, three or four at a time, and fry until puffy — about 1 minute. Turn and brown other side. With slotted utensil, lift from oil; drain well on paper towels.
7. While pillows are still hot, with a sharp knife, make a slit along one long side and one short side of each. Gently lift up tops and fill each with a slightly rounded tablespoon of the filling.
8. Sprinkle tops with sifted confectioners' sugar. Serve warm. *Makes 16.*

Beef Empanadas
(pictured)

Filling

    2 tablespoons butter or margarine
    ½ cup chopped onion
    ¾ lb ground beef
    1 large tomato, peeled and chopped
    1 can (4 oz) chopped green chiles, undrained
    ¼ cup chopped seedless raisins
    1 teaspoon salt

Pastry

    2 cups all-purpose flour
    ½ teaspoon salt
    ½ cup shortening
    4 to 5 tablespoons ice water

       Salad oil or shortening for deep-frying
       Confectioners' sugar (optional)

1. Make Filling: In hot butter in large skillet, sauté onion until tender. Add beef; sauté until no longer red.
2. Add tomato, chiles, raisins and 1 teaspoon salt. Simmer, stirring occasionally, 20 to 25 minutes, or until most of liquid has evaporated. Remove from heat.
3. Meanwhile, make Pastry: In medium bowl, combine flour and salt. With pastry blender, cut in ½ cup shortening until well blended. Sprinkle with ice water;

The Spicy and Spectacular Taste of Mexico

stir with fork until mixture holds together. Shape into a ball.

4. Divide pastry into 12 pieces. On lightly floured surface, roll each piece into a 5-inch round. Place about ¼ cup filling on one-half of each round; fold over other half. Press edges together with finger to seal; press edges with tines of fork.

5. In deep, heavy saucepan or electric skillet, slowly heat oil (1½ to 2 inches) to 375F on deep-frying thermometer.

6. Gently drop beef pies, a few at a time, into hot oil. Cook, turning with slotted utensil, until golden-brown on both sides — 3 to 4 minutes.

7. Drain on paper towels. Serve hot. If desired, sprinkle lightly with confectioners' sugar. *Makes 12.*

Beef Enchiladas
(pictured)

Filling
1 lb ground beef chuck
1 clove garlic, finely chopped
1 teaspoon salt
1 tablespoon vinegar
1 tablespoon tequila, cognac or water
1 tablespoon chili powder
1 can (1 lb) kidney beans, undrained

Tomato Sauce
3 tablespoons salad oil
1 clove garlic, very finely chopped
¼ cup chopped onion
2 tablespoons all-purpose flour
2 cans (10 ½-oz size) tomato purée
1 tablespoon vinegar
1 beef-bouillon cube
1 cup boiling water
2 tablespoons finely chopped canned green chiles
   Dash ground cumin
½ teaspoon salt
   Dash ground pepper

Enchiladas
10 canned or frozen corn tortillas
1 cup grated sharp Cheddar cheese or 1 cup cubed
   Monterey Jack cheese (4 oz)

1. Prepare Filling: In medium skillet, over low heat, sauté beef with 1 clove chopped garlic, 1 teaspoon salt, 1 tablespoon vinegar, the tequila and chili powder until chuck is browned. Stir in kidney beans.

2. Make Tomato Sauce: In hot oil in skillet, sauté garlic and onion until golden.

3. Remove from heat. Stir in flour until smooth; stir in tomato purée, vinegar and bouillon cube dissolved in boiling water.

4. Bring mixture to boiling, stirring, over medium heat.

5. Add chiles, cumin, salt and pepper; simmer, uncovered and stirring occasionally, about 5 minutes.

6. Preheat oven to 350F.

7. To assemble Enchiladas: Place about ⅓ cup filling in center of each tortilla; roll up. Arrange, seam side down, in 13-by-9-by-2-inch baking dish. Pour tomato sauce over all; sprinkle with cheese.

8. Bake 25 minutes. *Makes 10 small or 5 large servings.*

Note: Meat Filling and Tomato Sauce may be made ahead of time and refrigerated. Reheat slightly when ready to use.

Magic Mocha Cake
(pictured)

1 pkg (1 lb, 2.25 oz) devil's-food-cake mix
1 teaspoon ground cinnamon

Mocha-Whipped-Cream Filling
1½ cups heavy cream
½ cup confectioners' sugar
1 tablespoon instant-coffee granules

Chocolate Frosting
3 sq (1-oz size) unsweetened chocolate, cut up
½ cup (1 stick) butter or margarine
1 egg yolk
2 cups confectioners' sugar
¼ cup strong coffee
½ teaspoon vanilla extract

White Icing
½ cup confectioners' sugar
1½ teaspoons water

1. Preheat oven to 350F. Grease and flour two 8-by-8-by-2-inch layer-cake pans. Prepare cake mix according to package directions, adding cinnamon to mix.

2. Bake according to package directions. Remove to cake rack; cool 10 minutes before removing from pans. Cool completely.

3. Meanwhile, in medium bowl, combine all Mocha-Whipped-Cream-Filling ingredients; refrigerate, covered, 30 minutes.

4. With portable electric mixer at high speed, beat filling until stiff. Refrigerate until ready to use.

5. Make Chocolate Frosting: In top of double boiler, combine chocolate and butter. Melt over hot, not boiling, water, stirring occasionally. Stir in egg yolk; mix well. Remove top of double boiler from hot water.

6. Add 2 cups confectioners' sugar, the coffee and vanilla; with wooden spoon, mix until smooth.

7. Place top of double boiler in pan of ice water, stirring occasionally, 8 to 10 minutes or until frosting is thick enough to spread.

The Spicy and Spectacular Taste of Mexico

8. To assemble cake: Slice layers in half horizontally to make four layers. Place a layer, cut side up, on cake plate. Spread with 1 cup filling. Repeat with remaining layers, with top layer cut side down.
9. Frost top and side of cake with Chocolate Frosting.
10. Make White Icing: In small bowl, combine confectioners' sugar and water; mix well. Turn into pastry bag with writing tip.
11. Starting in the center, pipe a spiral design 1 inch apart on top of cake. Starting in the center, with toothpick, draw lines toward edge 1 inch apart, all around the cake, as pictured. For easier cutting, refrigerate 1 hour. *Makes 12 servings.*

Arroz con Pollo
Chicken With Rice
(pictured)

   3 - lb broiler-fryer, cut into 8 pieces
½ **cup olive oil**
 2 **cups chopped onion**
 1 **clove garlic, crushed**
½ **teaspoon crushed red pepper**
2½ **teaspoons salt**
½ **teaspoon ground pepper**
 2 **cups converted white rice**
¼ **teaspoon saffron threads**
 1 **can (1 lb, 12 oz) tomatoes, undrained**
 1 **canned green chile pepper, chopped**
 1 **can (10¾ oz) condensed chicken broth, undiluted**
½ **cup water**
½ **package (10-oz size) frozen peas**
½ **cup pimiento-stuffed green olives, sliced**
 1 **can (4 oz) pimientos, drained and sliced**

1. Wipe chicken pieces with damp paper towels.
2. In heavy 6-quart Dutch oven, heat olive oil. Brown chicken, a few pieces at a time, until golden-brown all over. Remove chicken as it browns.
3. Preheat oven to 325F.
4. Add chopped onion, garlic and red pepper to Dutch oven; sauté, stirring, over medium heat until golden—about 3 minutes.
5. Add salt, pepper, rice and saffron to Dutch oven; cook, stirring, until rice is lightly browned—10 minutes.

6. Add tomatoes, chile pepper and chicken broth to rice mixture. Add chicken pieces. Bring just to boiling.
7. Bake, covered, 1 hour.
8. Add water. Sprinkle peas, olives and pimiento strips over top; do not stir. Bake, covered, 20 minutes longer or until chicken is tender and peas are cooked.
9. Serve hot. *Makes 6 servings.*

Mexican Salad Bowl
(pictured)
Dressing
 1 **small ripe avocado (8 oz)**
 2 **tablespoons lemon juice**
½ **cup sour cream**
⅓ **cup salad oil**
½ **teaspoon sugar**
 1 **teaspoon seasoned salt**
½ **teaspoon chili powder**

 2 **quarts bite-size crisp salad greens**
¼ **cup grated Cheddar cheese**
¼ **cup chopped green onion**
¼ **cup pitted ripe olives, sliced**
 2 **medium tomatoes, each cut into 8 wedges**
 1 **cup coarsely crushed corn chips**

1. Make Dressing: Halve avocado lengthwise; remove pit and peel. In medium bowl, crush avocado with lemon juice, using potato masher. Add remaining dressing ingredients; mix well. Refrigerate, covered with plastic wrap, several hours or until well chilled.
2. To serve: In salad bowl, combine salad greens, Cheddar cheese, green onion and olives. Garnish with tomato wedges. Sprinkle with corn chips. Add dressing; toss lightly and serve immediately. *Makes 6 to 8 servings.*

Cauliflower Salad Bowl
(pictured)

 1 **medium head cauliflower**
   Ice water
 1 **small head escarole**
½ **cup bottled oil-and-vinegar dressing**
 1 **can (6 oz) pitted ripe olives, drained and slivered**
 1 **green pepper, stemmed, seeded and cut into cubes**
 1 **red pepper, stemmed, seeded and cut into cubes**

The Spicy and Spectacular Taste of Mexico

1. In a large bowl, separate cauliflower into flowerets. Cover with ice water and let stand 1 hour.
2. Meanwhile, wash escarole; separate leaves and dry well on paper towels or spin in a salad dryer. Store in a plastic bag in refrigerator until serving time.
3. Drain cauliflower. Cut flowerets into ¼-inch slices; place in a shallow glass baking dish. Pour bottled dressing over cauliflower; cover and refrigerate 2 hours.
4. When ready to serve, line a chilled salad bowl with escarole leaves. Toss sliced olives and pepper cubes with marinated cauliflower. Pile into center of serving bowl. Pour any remaining dressing over salad. *Makes 4 servings.*

Fried Bananas (as a vegetable)

 2 firm green-tipped bananas
 2 tablespoons flour
 ¼ cup (½ stick) butter or margarine
   Salt

1. Peel bananas. Cut in half lengthwise and then in half crosswise.
2. Sprinkle flour on a sheet of waxed paper. Roll cut bananas in flour to coat well.
3. Heat 2 tablespoons of the butter in the blazer of a chafing dish or a large skillet over medium heat. Add bananas and cook until lightly browned; turn to brown other side, adding remaining 2 tablespoons of butter as needed. Cooked bananas should be heated through but not mushy.
4. Sprinkle bananas lightly with salt. Serve hot with ham, pork or poultry. *Makes 4 servings.*

Fried Bananas (as a dessert)
(pictured)

 Fried Bananas, recipe above
 1 tablespoon lemon juice
 3 tablespoons sifted confectioners' sugar
   Chantilly Sauce, recipe follows

1. Prepare Fried Bananas according to recipe above, omitting salt.

2. Sprinkle cooked bananas with 1 tablespoon lemon juice and 3 tablespoons sifted confectioners' sugar. Serve hot with Chantilly Sauce. *Makes 4 servings.*

Chantilly Sauce
(pictured)

 1½ cups confectioners' sugar
  2 tablespoons butter or margarine, melted
  1 egg
  1 tablespoon vanilla extract
  2 tablespoons brandy
  ½ pint whipping cream

1. In a medium bowl, with a portable electric mixer, beat together the sugar, butter, egg, vanilla and brandy until smooth and creamy. Cover and refrigerate at least 1 hour.
2. At serving time, whip cream until stiff and fold it into chilled sauce. Serve over hot bananas. *Makes about 2 cups sauce.*

Pork-And-Hominy Soup

 2 lb pork ribs
 1 large onion, peeled and quartered
 1 clove garlic, peeled
 1 can (10¾ oz) condensed chicken broth
 5 cups cold water
 ½ teaspoon salt
 ¼ teaspoon ground pepper
 2 cans (1-lb size) white hominy
 1 teaspoon chili powder
 1 cup shredded lettuce
 ½ cup chopped green onion
 6 radishes, washed and sliced

1. In 5-quart Dutch oven, combine pork ribs, onion, garlic, chicken broth, cold water, salt and pepper. Bring to boiling; reduce heat; simmer, covered, 1 hour.
2. Drain hominy; rinse under cold running water; add to pork mixture. Continue cooking one hour.
3. Remove pork ribs from broth; cool; remove meat from bones; discard bones. Skim fat from broth; discard.

The Spicy and Spectacular Taste of Mexico

4. Before serving, add chili powder; simmer, covered, 10 minutes. Serve, sprinkled with shredded lettuce, green onion and radishes. Nice with French bread. *Makes 8 servings (8 cups).*

Vegetable-Beef Soup

    3 - lb shin of beef
    1 onion, quartered
1½ teaspoons salt
    2 quarts water
    3 carrots, peeled, sliced on the diagonal
    1 cup celery, cut into 1-inch pieces
    2 pared potatoes, cubed (2 cups)
    2 ears corn, sliced ½ inch thick
    2 zucchini, sliced ¼ inch thick
      Chopped onion
      Cilantro sprigs

1. In a deep, 8-quart kettle, place beef, quartered onion, salt and 2 quarts water. Cover and bring to boiling; skim surface. Reduce heat; simmer, covered, 2 to 2½ hours or until tender. Remove from heat.
2. Lift out beef and bone; discard bone; skim off fat. Let meat cool. Cut into cubes; return to broth.
3. Add carrot, celery and potato. Bring to boiling; simmer, covered, 15 minutes.
4. Add corn and zucchini; simmer, covered, 10 minutes or until vegetables are tender.
5. Serve soup at once, garnished with chopped onion and cilantro. *Makes 10 servings (3½ quarts).*

Avocado Soup

    2 ripe avocados (about 1 lb each), peeled and cut
      into small chunks
½ teaspoon salt
      Dash ground white pepper
    1 cup heavy cream
    1 can (13¾ oz) chicken broth
⅓ cup dry sherry
    1 small avocado, peeled and thinly sliced
      Chopped pimiento

1. In food processor or blender, combine avocado chunks, salt, pepper and half of the cream; blend until completely smooth. Add the remaining ½ cup of cream; blend just to mix.
2. In large saucepan, bring chicken broth to boiling; stir in avocado mixture and sherry; remove from heat.
3. Serve soup, hot or cold, with sliced avocado and chopped pimiento on top. (If soup seems too thick, add a little broth.) *Makes 8 servings.*

Pork in Sherry

    6 pork-loin chops, ¾ inch thick (2½ lb)
    1 tablespoon oil
    2 cloves garlic, pressed
½ cup chopped blanched almonds
    1 cup chopped onion
    2 tortillas, cut into eighths
    1 tablespoon white-wine vinegar
    1 can (10¾ oz) condensed chicken broth
    1 can (8 oz) tomato sauce
¼ teaspoon ground coriander
    2 tablespoons chili powder
½ cup dry sherry
    1 tablespoon sesame seed, toasted

1. Wipe chops with damp paper towels. Heat oil in a large, heavy skillet. Sauté chops until golden on both sides—about 10 minutes. Remove from pan.
2. Add garlic, almonds, onion and tortillas to the skillet. Sauté until golden. Turn into blender or processor, along with vinegar and ¼ cup broth. Blend to make a smooth paste; add more broth, if needed.
3. Add tomato sauce, coriander, chili powder, sherry and remaining broth to skillet. Stir in almond-onion mixture. Return to boiling, stirring constantly.
4. Return pork chops to skillet. Cover tightly and cook over low heat until pork is tender—60 or 70 minutes. Stir occasionally to make sure sauce does not stick to pan.
5. Arrange chops on platter. Pour sauce over them; sprinkle with sesame seed. *Makes 6 servings.*

Green Peas, Northern Mexico Style

    2 medium carrots
    1 medium potato
    2 medium onions
    1 head Bibb lettuce
¼ cup (½ stick) butter or margarine
    2 tablespoons chopped parsley
¼ teaspoon crushed dried bay leaf
¼ teaspoon dried thyme
½ teaspoon salt
      Dash ground pepper
    2 pkg (10-oz size) frozen green peas, thawed
    1 tablespoon all-purpose flour
    1 cup heavy cream

1. Peel carrots; slice lengthwise. Peel potato; cut into small cubes. Peel and finely chop onions. Wash lettuce; trim stem end.
2. Melt butter in a large, heavy skillet or Dutch oven. Add carrot, potato, onion, lettuce, parsley, bay leaf, thyme, salt and pepper. Cover and cook over low

The Spicy and Spectacular Taste of Mexico

heat, stirring occasionally, until just tender—20 minutes. Add peas; cook 5 minutes longer.
3. Place flour in a small bowl; gradually add cream, beating until smooth. Add to vegetables. Cook, stirring, until thick. *Makes 8 servings.*

Mexican Caramel Flan

¾ cup sugar
2 tablespoons water

Custard

1 cup milk
1 cup light cream or half-and-half
3 eggs
¼ cup sugar
¼ teaspoon salt
1 teaspoon vanilla extract
2 tablespoons brandy

Boiling water
½ cup heavy cream, whipped stiff

1. Place ¾ cup sugar in medium-size, heavy skillet. Cook over low heat, stirring constantly, just until sugar melts and forms a syrup. Gradually stir in water.
2. Immediately pour syrup into six 6-ounce custard cups. Set aside.
3. Preheat oven to 325F.
4. Make Custard: In medium saucepan, heat milk and cream just until bubbles form around edge of pan.
5. In medium bowl, with rotary beater, beat eggs slightly. Add sugar, salt and vanilla. Gradually stir in hot milk mixture and the brandy. Pour ½ cup custard into each prepared custard cup.
6. Set cups in shallow pan; pour boiling water to ½-inch level around cups.
7. Bake 30 to 35 minutes or until silver knife inserted in center comes out clean. Remove cups from water. Cool; then refrigerate 3 hours or overnight.
8. To serve: Run small spatula around edge of cups, to loosen. Invert on serving dish; shake gently to release.
9. Turn whipped cream into a pastry bag with small star tip; pipe around edges. *Makes 6 servings.*

Mexican Butter Cookies

¾ cup (1½ sticks) butter or margarine, softened
⅔ cup granulated sugar
¼ teaspoon salt
2 egg yolks
1 tablespoon light cream or half-and-half
1 teaspoon vanilla extract
2 cups all-purpose flour
1 cup chopped walnuts, pistachios, pecans or almonds
Confectioners' sugar (optional)

1. In large bowl, with electric mixer at medium speed, beat butter, granulated sugar and salt until light. Add egg yolks, cream and vanilla; beat until fluffy.
2. Gradually add flour, stirring with wooden spoon until dough is smooth. Shape into a ball; flatten; cut in half. Wrap each half in waxed paper or foil. Refrigerate until firm—about 1 hour.
3. Preheat oven to 350F.
4. On lightly floured surface, with floured rolling pin, roll out half of dough to about ¼-inch thickness. Cut with 2-inch plain or scalloped round cookie cutter. Place, 1 inch apart, on ungreased cookie sheets. Sprinkle with ¾ cup chopped nuts.
5. Bake 12 to 15 minutes or just until edges of cookies are golden. Remove to wire rack; let cool.
6. Roll remaining dough into a long strip 2½ inches wide and ¼ inch thick. Trim edges evenly. Sprinkle with ¼ cup chopped nuts. Then, with sharp knife, cut crosswise into ¾-inch-wide strips. Bake as above.
7. When cookies are cool, sprinkle with confectioners' sugar, if desired. *Makes about 6½ dozen.*

Cheese Enchiladas

Filling

1 can (4 oz) chopped green chiles
2 cups grated sharp Cheddar cheese (8 oz)
1 carton (16 oz) cream-style cottage cheese
1 clove garlic, crushed
½ teaspoon ground coriander
¼ teaspoon salt

Enchiladas

Salad oil
1 pkg (11 oz) refrigerated corn tortillas (1 dozen)
1 can (8 oz) tomato sauce
½ cup sour cream
2 tablespoons chopped green chiles
½ cup grated sharp Cheddar cheese (2 oz)

1. Preheat oven to 350F.
2. In medium bowl, combine Filling ingredients; mix well. Makes 3½ cups.
3. Prepare Enchiladas: In half inch hot oil, over medium heat, fry tortillas a few seconds on each side (just until limp). Drain on paper towels.
4. Spoon 2 rounded tablespoons filling on each tortilla. Roll up; place, seam side down, in 13-by-9-by-2-inch baking dish.
5. Combine tomato sauce, sour cream and green chiles; spoon over enchiladas. Sprinkle ½ cup Cheddar cheese in a row over center of enchiladas. Bake, uncovered, 25 to 30 minutes or until sauce bubbles and cheese melts. *Makes 6 servings.* ∎

Buongusto!
Italian Specialties

Who doesn't love Italian food? We certainly do, and here are some of the best of those light, subtly blended dishes and *molto elegante* desserts, all in the grand tradition, that have been Italian family secrets for generations. Now they can belong to your own family. Recipes begin on page 92.

Milanese Pork Stew With Polenta is a plentiful platter of braised pork and sausage, cabbage wedges and vegetables, with slices of polenta (cornmeal pasta). Sicilian Meatball Soup—homemade meatballs and noodles served with a sprinkle of Parmesan cheese and parsley—cooks up simple and satisfying in less than 30 minutes. Roast Chicken With Vegetables gets its Italian flair from olive oil, garlic and oregano.

Above: Chicken, anchovies, capers and olives in a parsley-wine sauce fill a crispy bread loaf to become Spicy Chicken Breasts Pagnotta. Cold Pasta With Tomato Sauce is a refreshingly light meal for a warm afternoon. The rigatoni is al dente, and the sauce is flavored with basil and garlic. Irmana's Spinach, Sausage, Mozzarella and Ham is enveloped in fresh bread dough, then baked till golden brown. Each hot slice reveals the marvelous, moist filling. *Recipes begin on page 93.*

At right: Fruit Spumone, a frozen mountain of lavishly creamy fruit, is a tempting twist on the popular Italian ice cream. Almond Cake is a traditional cookie-like torta, abundant with almonds, accented with lemon and laced with brandy. Crème de menthe provides the refreshing, spirited tingle in luscious Mint Bavarian Cream, layered with crunchy almond pralines. *Recipes begin on page 94.*

Mushrooms in Lemon Sauce is a creamy, delicately flavored appetizer or accompaniment that is sophisticated, yet amazingly uncomplicated to prepare. *See recipe on page 95.*

Chicken Rolls With Anchovy Sauce: Prosciutto is at the center of boneless chicken breasts, rolled up and threaded with bread squares and bay leaves, then splashed with anchovy butter. *See recipe on page 97.*

Above: Spaghetti With Zucchini is a fabulous spur-of-the-moment toss of golden fried zucchini, Parmesan cheese, fresh chopped parsley and basil. *See recipe on page 96.*

At left: Rice Salad is a cool, make-ahead mix of rice, ham, Gruyère cheese and chopped pickle dressed in a light Dijon sauce. Add olives, red-pepper strips and a lettuce-lined bowl for an elegant presentation. *See recipe on page 97.*

Buongusto!

continued from page 87

Milanese Pork Stew With Polenta
(pictured)

   2 **tablespoons butter or margarine**
 ¼ **lb salt pork, cubed**
   1 **cup sliced onion**
   1 **lb carrots, pared and cut on diagonal in 1½-inch pieces**
   1 **stalk celery, cut into 1½-inch pieces**
1½ **lb lean pork, cut in 1½-inch pieces**
   3 **Italian sweet sausages, cut in half**
   1 **teaspoon salt**
 ⅛ **teaspoon ground pepper**
   1 **bay leaf, crumbled**
   2 **tablespoons all-purpose flour**
   1 **cup dry white wine**
 ½ **cup water**

Polenta

   4 **cups water**
   1 **tablespoon salt**
   2 **cups yellow cornmeal**

   1 **head cabbage (2 lb)**
   1 **teaspoon salt**

1. In hot butter in 6-quart Dutch oven or heavy kettle, sauté salt pork, onion, carrot and celery, stirring, about 5 minutes. Remove vegetables and reserve, leaving salt pork in pan.
2. In remaining fat, brown pork and sausage on all sides about 25 minutes.
3. Add 1 teaspoon salt, the pepper, bay leaf and flour; mix well. Add wine and ½ cup water. Simmer, covered, about 1½ hours, or until pork is tender. Add reserved vegetables last half hour of cooking.
4. Prepare Polenta: Grease well a 9-by-5-by-3-inch loaf pan. In heavy 6-quart kettle, bring 4 cups water and 1 tablespoon salt to a full, rolling boil. Slowly add cornmeal, stirring constantly with wire whisk. Mixture will be thick. Turn heat low; cook, uncovered and without stirring, until very thick—about 15 minutes. Spoon into prepared pan, spreading evenly. Keep warm.
5. Meanwhile, cook cabbage: Discard outer leaves from cabbage; wash head; cut into 8 wedges.
6. Pour 1 cup water in large skillet; bring to boiling. Add salt, then cabbage. Cook, covered, over medium heat, 10 minutes. Remove from heat.
7. Arrange cabbage wedges, spoke fashion, in center of round platter. Spoon meat and vegetables into center. Turn polenta out of pan. Cut into ½-inch slices; arrange around edge. Spoon pan liquid over cabbage and meat. *Makes 6 to 8 servings.*

Sicilian Meatball Soup
(pictured)

Meatballs

   1 **egg**
   1 **lb ground chuck**
 ½ **cup soft white-bread crumbs (1 slice)**
   2 **tablespoons chopped parsley**
   2 **tablespoons grated Parmesan cheese**
 ½ **clove garlic, crushed**
 ½ **teaspoon salt**
 ⅛ **teaspoon ground pepper**

   3 **cans (10½-oz size) condensed beef broth, undiluted**
      Water
   1 **pkg (8 oz) ribbon or other noodles**
      Grated Parmesan cheese
      Chopped parsley

1. Make Meatballs: In medium bowl, using a fork, beat egg slightly. Add rest of meatball ingredients; mix until well blended.
2. Shape into 36 balls (one rounded teaspoon per ball).
3. In large kettle or 6-quart Dutch oven, bring to boiling beef broth plus water to make 9 cups liquid.
4. Add meatballs; simmer 5 minutes. Using slotted utensil, remove meatballs.
5. Bring back to boiling; add noodles. Cook, uncovered and stirring occasionally with long fork, about 10 minutes.
6. Return meatballs to soup. Simmer 5 minutes or until meatballs are heated through and noodles are tender.
7. Serve in bowls. Sprinkle with Parmesan cheese and parsley. *Makes 8 servings (9 cups).*

Roast Chicken With Vegetables
(pictured)

   2 **(2- to 2½-lb size) broiler-fryers, quartered**
   1 **large green pepper, seeded and cut in 1-inch strips**
   4 **medium potatoes, pared and quartered**
   1 **clove garlic, crushed**
 ⅓ **cup salad or olive oil**
   1 **teaspoon dried oregano leaves**
1½ **teaspoons salt**
 ¼ **teaspoon ground pepper**
 ¼ **teaspoon paprika**

   Cooked spaghetti (optional)

1. Wash chicken; pat dry with paper towels. In large, shallow baking pan, arrange chicken pieces, green-pepper strips and potatoes in a single layer.
2. Preheat oven to 350F.
3. Combine garlic, oil and oregano; mix well. Drizzle

Buongusto!

over chicken and vegetables. Sprinkle all over with salt, pepper and paprika.

4. Bake, uncovered and basting frequently with pan juices, 1 hour or until chicken and potatoes are tender.
5. Increase oven temperature to 400F. Bake 15 minutes to brown.
6. Arrange chicken with vegetables on warm serving platter, discarding garlic. If desired, serve with spaghetti with tomato sauce or cheese. *Makes 6 to 8 servings.*

Pagnotta Scaldavivande
Spicy Chicken Breasts Served in
a Loaf of Bread
(pictured)

4 tablespoons (½ stick) unsalted butter
3 cloves garlic, crushed
3 tablespoons extra-virgin olive oil
½ teaspoon hot red-pepper flakes, or more to taste
2 lb boneless chicken breasts, cut into 1½-inch square chunks
3 salt-packed anchovies, washed, filleted and dried with paper towels or 6 oil-packed anchovy fillets, drained on paper towels
3½ tablespoons chopped Italian parsley
½ cup capers, rinsed and dried
1 cup pitted black olives, Gaeta, if possible, or packed in oil
¾ cup dry white wine
Coarse salt
Freshly ground black pepper
1 round loaf (2 lb) of homemade-style bread (pagnotta)

1. Melt 2 tablespoons of the butter in a small saucepan, along with one clove of garlic. Set aside for 30 minutes before using.
2. Heat 2 tablespoons of the butter and the oil in a 12-inch skillet. Add the remaining 2 cloves of garlic; brown and discard. Remove the skillet from the heat and add the hot red-pepper flakes. Turn the heat to medium; add the chicken and cook for 5 minutes, stirring. Turn the heat to low and add the anchovies, putting them in the center of the skillet. Mash to a paste with the back of a wooden spoon. Add the parsley, capers, olives and wine and simmer for 15 minutes in all. Add salt and pepper to taste. The pan juices should be abundant.
3. Preheat the oven to 400F.
4. While the chicken mixture is simmering, prepare the pagnotta by cutting a lid from the loaf with a serrated knife. Remove the soft part of the bread from inside the lid. Cut around the inside edge of the bottom part

of the loaf and remove the soft part, leaving about a 1-inch layer all around.

5. When ready to serve, remove the garlic from the melted butter and dribble the butter over the inside of the loaf and the lid. Put the loaf in the oven 10 minutes before the chicken is to be done and bake for 10 minutes.
6. Pour the chicken mixture into the bread shell, cover with the lid and serve on a wooden platter or large serving dish. To serve, spoon out the filling and slice the bread with a serrated knife. *Makes 6 to 8 servings.*

Note: This dish may be prepared in advance, then assembled and heated at the last minute. It will take about 10 minutes to heat the chicken, the time you will need to heat the pagnotta.

Pasta Alla Checca
Cold Pasta With Tomato Sauce
(pictured)

2 lb ripe Italian plum tomatoes, if available (if using other tomatoes, they must be firm but very ripe)
¼ cup salt-packed capers, rinsed and dried
1 cup pitted black olives, Gaeta, if possible, cut in half
40 fresh basil leaves, washed, dried and torn into pieces (see Notes)
½ cup extra-virgin olive oil
Coarse salt
Freshly ground black pepper
1 clove garlic, crushed or chopped
Water
1 lb ribbed rigatoni, mezzi ditali or conchiglie

1. Dip the tomatoes in boiling water for a minute; then peel and dice, discarding the seeds.
2. Place the diced tomatoes in a bowl large enough to contain the pasta. Add the capers, olives, basil leaves, ¼ cup of the olive oil, and salt and pepper to taste. Add the garlic, crushed or chopped. (If crushed, remove before serving.) Place in the sun for 2 to 3 hours, if possible. Otherwise, leave at room temperature for 3 or 4 hours.
3. Bring 4 quarts of water and 1½ tablespoons salt to a boil in a large pasta pot, and cook the pasta until *very* al dente, just barely cooked. Pour 2 cups of cold water into the pot to stop the cooking process; then drain.
4. Add the remaining ¼ cup olive oil to the pasta and mix. Add the pasta to the sauce and mix again. *Makes 6 servings.*

Notes: If serving cold, let the pasta cool at room temperature; add to the sauce at the last minute.

Use 2 teaspoons dried basil leaves if fresh basil is not available.

Buongusto!

Spinaci al Pane d'Irmana
Irmana's Spinach, Sausage, Mozzarella and Ham
Cooked in Dough
(pictured)

Dough

3 cups all-purpose flour
1 egg yolk, at room temperature
2 tablespoons unsalted butter, melted
  Coarse salt
1 oz (2 cakes) compressed yeast or 2 pkg active dry yeast
½ cup lukewarm water, plus 1 to 2 tablespoons additional water if necessary

  Corn oil, for oiling pan

Filling

2 lb fresh spinach or 2 pkg (10-oz size) frozen spinach
3 tablespoons unsalted butter
  Coarse salt
  Freshly ground black pepper
7 oz boiled ham, thinly sliced (see Note)
8 oz mozzarella cheese, coarsely grated
2 hot Italian sausages, skinned, crumbled and cooked in 2 tablespoons water

1 egg, lightly beaten, for painting crust

1. Make Dough: Combine the flour, egg yolk, butter and a pinch of salt in a bowl. Dissolve the yeast in the ½ cup warm water and add to the other dough ingredients. Stir with a wooden spoon until well mixed, adding 1 to 2 tablespoons water, if necessary, to obtain a fairly soft dough.

2. Turn out on a marble or wooden surface and knead for a few minutes, until the dough is smooth and elastic. Place in a floured bowl, cover with towel and put in a warm, draft-free place until the dough has doubled in size, between 1 and 2 hours.

3. When the dough has doubled, remove from the bowl and knead for a minute or two. Replace in bowl and let rise a second time until doubled in bulk, 1 to 1½ hours.

4. Meanwhile, preheat oven to 375F.

5. Make Filling: Wash the spinach and boil with the water clinging to its leaves until tender, about 4 minutes. Drain and squeeze free of excess moisture. Melt the butter in a skillet and add the spinach. Cook over medium heat for 3 minutes; then season with salt and pepper to taste and set aside off the heat.

6. Oil the bottom of a 13-by-9-by-2-inch baking pan. Place the dough directly into the pan, flattening it with your hands as for pizza, until the dough covers the pan, leaving a ½-inch border all around edge of the dough.

7. Place the filling on the rectangle of dough as follows: Arrange half the ham slices evenly over the dough. On top of the ham slices, arrange half the grated mozzarella; then place half the spinach on top. Add all of the sausage meat next and over this the balance of the mozzarella, the balance of the spinach and, last, the remaining slices of ham.

8. Fold the longer side of the dough toward you over the filling; fold the other side over this and the filling like an envelope and press down to close with your hands. Make sure that your hands are not oily, because this will prevent the dough from sealing. Press with a fork all around the edges to seal thoroughly.

9. Bake for 40 to 50 minutes, or until lightly colored. After 20 minutes, remove from the oven and paint the top of the bread with beaten egg. Replace in the oven and finish baking. Serve hot. *Makes 6 to 8 servings.*

Note: Mortadella can take the place of the ham, and chicory or dandelion greens the place of the spinach.

Editor's Note: We used 2 packages active dry yeast dissolved in ½ cup warm water (105 to 115F). To make a fairly soft dough, we added about ½ cup additional water.

Torta Fregolotta
Almond Cake
(pictured)

2⅔ cups all-purpose flour
1¼ cups finely chopped almonds
  Pinch of coarse salt
1 cup (2 sticks) plus 1 tablespoon unsalted butter, at room temperature, cut into small pieces
1 cup sugar
2 tablespoons grappa (Italian brandy)
  Grated zest of 1 lemon
2 tablespoons fresh lemon juice

Buongusto!

1. Preheat the oven to 350F. Butter a round 12-inch pie tin with low sides; then flour lightly, shaking out excess flour.
2. *If using an electric mixer:* Put all the ingredients in the large mixer bowl. Using either the paddle or the dough hook, mix until the dough masses. Wrap a towel around and over the top of mixer and bowl to keep the flour from scattering. The mixture should be crumbly, not smooth. *If mixing by hand:* Use a large spoon and mix all ingredients to the crumbly stage.
3. Empty the mixture into the prepared tin, smoothing the top with a spatula or with hands. Bake for about 1 hour (see Editor's Note). Check the *torta* after 50 minutes. It should be lightly browned, darker around the edges.
4. Place on a rack to cool for 10 minutes; remove from the tin. Place cake on the rack to cool completely. *Makes 10 to 12 servings.*

Note: This is a traditional hard, flat cake, like a large cookie, served with ice cream in Italy. It is also served with sweet wine, such as Vin Santo, at the end of a meal. It is never cut with a knife, but broken into pieces by hand. It is best served the day after baking. The shortbread also keeps crisp and fresh for a long time in an airtight tin box or wrapped in aluminum foil.

Editor's Note: Before baking, sprinkle ½ cup chopped blanched almonds around cake one inch from edge. We baked it for 40 to 50 minutes.

Funghi Brodettati
Mushrooms in Lemon Sauce
(pictured)

5 **tablespoons (½ stick plus 1 tablespoon) unsalted butter**
2 **lb mushrooms, washed and sliced**
  Coarse salt
  Freshly ground black pepper
1 **tablespoon all-purpose flour**
½ **cup dry white wine**
2 **egg yolks**
2 **tablespoons lemon juice**
1 **tablespoon chopped parsley**

1. Melt 4 tablespoons of the butter in a skillet large enough to contain the mushrooms; then add the mushrooms and sauté over high heat. Add salt and pepper to taste and cook until all the liquid from the mushrooms has been absorbed. Remove skillet from heat and sprinkle the flour over the mushrooms. Stir to blend well and add the white wine. Return skillet to heat and cook for 5 to 7 minutes, or until the sauce has thickened.
2. Mix the egg yolks and lemon juice together and add to the skillet off the heat. Mix thoroughly with a wooden spoon. Add the chopped parsley and mix well. Add the remaining 1 tablespoon butter and briefly replace the skillet on low heat, stirring constantly for 1 or 2 minutes, until the mixture becomes creamy. Serve immediately. *Makes 6 servings.*

Note: If desired, mushrooms can also be served as a main course with hot triangles of bread fried in butter.

Editor's Note: If whole medium-size mushrooms are used (as pictured): Wash mushrooms; trim ends of stems.

Spuma di Frutta
Fruit Spumone
(pictured)

1 **cup plus 2 tablespoons sugar**
¾ **cup water**
8 **medium egg yolks**
1¼ **lb strawberries, peaches, apricots, raspberries or any good fresh ripe fruits in season (see Notes)**
¼ **cup strained fresh lemon juice**
3 **cups heavy cream (1½ pt)**
  Corn oil

1. Put the 1 cup sugar and the water in a small saucepan and bring to a boil. Turn down heat and simmer for 5 minutes.
2. Beat the egg yolks for 2 minutes in an electric mixer. With mixer running at medium speed, add the boiling syrup *a drop at a time* to begin with, then slowly until all the syrup has been absorbed.
3. Put the mixture in the top of a double boiler and cook over barely simmering water for about 15 minutes, stirring constantly until the yolks thicken. (The water must simmer, not boil, and the top of the double boiler should not touch the water, or eggs will scramble.)

Buongusto!

4. After removing from the heat, set the saucepan in cold water and beat the yolks with a whisk until cool.

5. Measure the fruit; add the lemon juice and purée in a blender.

6. Beat the cream until fairly stiff, slowly adding the 2 tablespoons sugar. Fold the fruit into yolks; then fold in cream.

7. Oil a 10-cup mold lightly and line with plastic wrap, leaving enough wrap to hang over the sides of the mold. Pour the fruit mixture into the mold and cover tightly with two layers of aluminum foil. Freeze overnight.

8. To unmold, place a serving platter over the mold and turn upside down. Leave for a few minutes. Gently unmold by holding the plastic wrap to the platter and pulling at it. *Makes 12 servings.*

Notes: If using berries, press them through a sieve to remove seeds; weigh peaches or apricots *after* pitting and peeling.

This dessert can be made in one mold or in individual molds or glasses, covered with plastic wrap and placed in the freezer for at least 1 hour. It will be cold but not frozen.

Editor's Note: If desired, mold can be garnished with whipped cream, using pastry bag with number-5 tip, and fresh strawberries, as pictured.

Spaghetti con le Zucchini
Spaghetti With Zucchini
(pictured)

 2 **lb small firm zucchini**
 2 **cups peanut oil**
    Water
    Coarse salt
 ½ **cup (1 stick) unsalted butter**
 ⅓ **cup chopped fresh parsley**
 1 **cup fresh basil leaves**
 1 **lb, 4 oz spaghetti**
 4 **oz Parmesan cheese, freshly grated, plus additional cheese for serving**

1. Wash and dry the zucchini and cut in ¼-inch slices.

2. Heat the peanut oil in a heavy skillet over medium-high heat and fry the zucchini, in two batches, until golden. Drain on paper towels.

3. Bring 6 quarts water and 2 tablespoons coarse salt to a boil in a large pasta pot.

4. Cut the butter into pieces and place in the bowl in which the pasta is to be served. (When the pasta water boils, place the bowl over the pot so that the butter melts and the bowl is heated.) Put the chopped parsley into the bowl with the butter. Tear the basil into small pieces and add to the butter, reserving a sprig for garnish. Set aside in a warm place.

5. Cook the pasta until al dente and stop the cooking process by adding a cup of cold water to the pot. Drain, reserving 2 tablespoons of the pasta water.

6. Pour the spaghetti into the heated bowl and mix thoroughly. Add the Parmesan and mix to coat the pasta. Add the zucchini, reserving a cup for garnish. If too dry, add the reserved pasta water. Arrange the reserved zucchini on top and place the sprig of basil in the center. Serve the pasta at once with a pepper mill and extra Parmesan. *Makes 6 servings.*

Bavarese Alla Menta
Mint Bavarian Cream
(pictured)

Praline
    Corn oil
 1 **lemon or 1 orange**
 ⅓ **cup plus 1 tablespoon sugar**
    Generous ½ cup blanched whole almonds, lightly toasted

Bavarian Cream
 1¼ **cups milk**
  3 **egg yolks**
  ½ **cup plus 2 tablespoons sugar**
  2 **env unflavored gelatine**
  ½ **cup cold water**
  2 **scant cups heavy cream (about 1 pt)**
  5 **tablespoons crème de menthe**

    Fresh mint for garnish

1. Make the Praline: Oil a marble surface or cookie sheet with corn oil. Have the lemon or orange at room temperature.

2. Melt the sugar in a small heavy saucepan (*not* non-stick) over medium heat, stirring to prevent burning. When the sugar is caramel colored, add the almonds, stirring to coat them evenly.

3. Empty the pan onto the oiled surface and quickly flatten the mixture with the lemon or orange, pressing down hard. (The oil in the fruit keeps the praline from sticking and makes it easy to smooth out.) Leave praline to harden at least 1 hour. (If prepared in advance, cool completely, wrap in foil and place in tightly covered container.)

4. To make Bavarian Cream: Scald the milk in a small saucepan.

5. Beat the egg yolks in the large bowl of an electric mixer. Add the sugar gradually and beat until thick and lemon colored. On lowest speed, slowly add the hot milk to the yolks; then return the mixture to the saucepan and heat almost to the boiling point, stirring constantly. (Do *not* boil.) When thickened, the mixture will coat a metal spoon thickly.

Buongusto!

6. Soften the gelatine in the cold water and add to the hot mixture, stirring to dissolve. Cool the cream over a basin of ice water, stirring occasionally. Add the crème de menthe.

7. Using a food processor fitted with the metal blade, chop the praline fine.

8. Beat the cream until stiff but not dry and fold into the cooled gelatine mixture.

9. Lightly oil a 7- or 8-cup mold, preferably nonstick, with corn oil. Spoon some of the Bavarian Cream into the bottom of the mold and sprinkle with praline. Add more Bavarian Cream, sprinkle generously with praline (reserving some for garnish) and end with the remaining Bavarian Cream. Cover tightly with plastic wrap and refrigerate for several hours.

10. Unmold onto a round serving dish. Should there be difficulty unmolding, wrap a hot towel around the mold for 7 or 8 seconds. It also helps to run a small, sharp paring knife around the edges in a continuous motion (do not saw), but generally the cream turns out easily. Sprinkle the reserved praline over the top and around the sides. Decorate with fresh mint. *Makes 8 servings.*

Editor's Note: If desired, spoon into sherbet glasses, as pictured.

❧

Insalata di Riso
Rice Salad
(pictured)

2 lb raw long-grain rice
1 cup pitted green olives
1 cup pitted ripe black olives, preferably Gaeta
7 oz Gruyère cheese, diced
7 oz cooked ham, sliced thickly and then diced
7 oz roasted red peppers, cut in thin strips
7 oz firm, ripe tomatoes, skinned and diced in small
    pieces (to be prepared at the last minute)
    Chopped gherkins to taste

Dressing

1 cup extra-virgin olive oil
½ cup fresh lemon juice
½ cup Dijon mustard
    Coarse salt and freshly ground black pepper to taste

    Black olives
3 roasted red peppers

1. Cook the rice al dente according to package directions. (It is important not to overcook, or it will become mushy in the salad.) Drain the rice and spread on clean towels to dry.

2. Prepare the other salad ingredients; turn into a large chilled bowl and add the cold rice. Mix gently. If serving at once, the tomatoes can be included. If

prepared in advance, add the tomatoes at the last moment.

3. Make Dressing: Put the oil, lemon juice and mustard in a small bowl and mix together, beating with a fork. Add salt and pepper to taste and pour over the rice mixture.

4. Garnish with black olives and peppers. *Makes 12 servings.*

Note: The salad can be prepared the day before, with the dressing. If prepared in advance, leave out the tomatoes until just before serving.

Editor's Note: If desired, serve on a bed of romaine, as pictured.

❧

Involtini con Salsa d'Alici
Chicken Rolls With Anchovy Sauce
(pictured)

4 whole boneless chicken breasts, split (about 1½ lb)
7 oz prosciutto crudo, thickly sliced
2 thick slices Italian bread, or more as needed
    Freshly ground black pepper
    Bay leaves, fresh, if possible
1 cup (2 sticks) unsalted butter, melted
12 anchovy fillets, salt-packed, if possible, washed and
    filleted (6 whole anchovies)

1. Preheat oven to 400F.

2. Place the chicken breasts on a cutting board and, pressing them flat with one hand, slice in half parallel to the board. Pound each piece between two sheets of waxed paper until very thin.

3. Cut the prosciutto into squares a little smaller than the chicken pieces and the bread into squares somewhat larger (1 inch).

4. Have the pepper ready in a saucer. Place a piece of prosciutto at the center of each breast slice, then dip your fingers into the pepper and rub over the meat. Roll up the breasts.

5. Thread the chicken rolls on skewers, alternating with the bread and bay leaves, as follows: bread/bay leaf/ chicken roll/prosciutto (use what is left)/bay leaf/ bread. Place the skewers in a roasting pan; then pour ¼ cup of the melted butter over the skewers. Place in the hot oven for about 20 minutes.

6. Dissolve the anchovies in the remaining ¾ cup butter by mashing them with a wooden spoon. Heat the anchovy butter and pour over the hot skewers before serving. *Makes 6 to 8 servings.*

Editor's Note: If fresh bay leaves are not available, pour boiling water over dried bay leaves; let stand for 20 minutes; drain. We used a 1-pound round loaf of Italian bread, crusts trimmed and cut into 1-inch cubes. Rolls in picture were threaded with 2 chicken rolls and 2 bread cubes. ∎

Favorites From Afar:
China, Greece and The Tropics

Every country and culture has its own rich heritage of foods, distinctively flavored with native ingredients and prepared as tradition dictates. We've collected the favorite delicacies from three exotic countries and brought them home to you to enjoy. Recipes begin on page 104.

From China comes this luscious fare: **clockwise from top,** Deviled Short Ribs, Szechwan Chicken, Clams With Black-Bean-And-Garlic Sauce, Duck With Peaches, Red-Cooked Fish Fillets and Lion's Head Casserole (Chinese meatballs).

Recipes from Lilah Kan's *Chinese Casserole Cookery.*

99

The Greek Islands boast an abundance of fresh fish and vegetables and a treasure trove of delicious, authentic Greek dishes. These *dolmathes* (stuffed grape leaves) are a classic combination of ground meat, rice, pine nuts, onion, tomato and lots of dill, enveloped in fresh or prepared grape leaves. Other specialties include mussels from Andros, stuffed zucchini from Skorpios and nutty, spiced baklavas. *Recipes begin on page 107.*

GEORGE RATKAI

The islands of the South Pacific are blessed with an unspoiled beauty, a warm tropical climate and delightful creations such as this array that makes use of the always abundant pineapples and bananas. **Clockwise from top right:** ham-filled banana fritters, a spectacular shrimp-and-pineapple salad in quartered pineapple shells, banana crêpes in apricot sauce, molded pineapple-rice cream, glazed banana tart, marinated chicken broiled with bananas and a rum-inspired fresh-pineapple flambé. *Recipes begin on page 110.*

Favorites from Afar

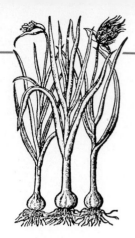

continued from page 99

Szechwan Chicken and Peanuts in Brown Sauce
(pictured)

6 dried black oriental mushrooms

Braising Liquid
 2 tablespoons light soy sauce
 2 tablespoons sherry
¼ teaspoon sugar
 3 tablespoons hoisin sauce
 1 tablespoon ground-brown-bean sauce
 1 tablespoon vinegar (rice, cider or white)
 2 cloves garlic, peeled and flattened
   ⅛-inch slice fresh ginger root, flattened
 2 dried chili peppers, broken in half (use both seeds and pods)
¼ cup of the mushroom-soaking liquid

   Vegetable oil for browning the chicken and onion
 1 (3- to 3½-lb) frying chicken, cut into small pieces
 1 large onion, cut in half from top to bottom, peeled and sliced along the grain into ¼-inch segments
¼ cup bamboo shoots, sliced about ⅛ inch thick into ½-inch-by-2-inch pieces
⅓ cup roasted, unsalted peanuts, walnuts or cashews
 2 teaspoons cornstarch
 2 teaspoons water
½ teaspoon sesame oil
 1 scallion, cut into ¼-inch rounds (both white and green parts), or fresh coriander leaves

1. Soak the mushrooms in warm water to cover for at least an hour; then cut off and discard stems and cut mushroom caps into quarters. Set aside the mushrooms and soaking water.
2. Prepare the Braising Liquid: In a flameproof casserole large enough to hold all the chicken (3½- to 4-quart size), mix together soy sauce, sherry, sugar, hoisin sauce, brown-bean sauce, vinegar, garlic, ginger root, chili peppers and ¼ cup of the mushroom-soaking liquid.
3. Heat a heavy cast-iron skillet or a wok over high heat until the pan is hot. Pour enough oil into the pan to coat the cooking surface, plus about a tablespoon extra. When the oil is hot, add half the chicken pieces and brown them, turning as necessary, for 8 to 10 minutes. When the pieces are browned, transfer them with a slotted spoon to the casserole, leaving behind any excess oil. Add more oil, if needed, to the pan.

Brown the remaining pieces of chicken, the onion and the mushrooms. When the chicken is browned, transfer it, with the vegetables, to the casserole. Mix well.
4. Bring liquid in casserole to a boil; lower the heat, cover and simmer the chicken for 15 minutes. Add bamboo shoots and peanuts; mix and simmer another 20 minutes.
5. Blend the cornstarch and water, stir it into the sauce and cook a few moments to thicken. Add the sesame oil and give a final stir. Sprinkle the garnish of scallion or coriander over the chicken. Serve hot. *Makes 4 servings.*

Lion's Head Casserole
(pictured)

 1 small head Chinese cabbage (about 1½ lb), cut crosswise into ¼-inch slices
1½ lb boned pork loin, minced to hamburger consistency with two cleavers or a food processor
 6 water chestnuts, diced into ⅛-inch cubes
 2 tablespoons smoked ham, minced fine
 1 egg, lightly beaten
 4 teaspoons light soy sauce
 4 teaspoons dry sherry
 1 teaspoon sugar
½ teaspoon sesame oil
⅛ teaspoon grated fresh ginger root
¼ teaspoon ground white pepper
 2 tablespoons cornstarch mixed with
   2 teaspoons cold water
   Vegetable oil for browning the meatballs

 1 cup chicken broth
 4 tablespoons oyster sauce
 1 tablespoon cornstarch
 1 tablespoon cold water
½ teaspoon sesame oil

1. Line a 10½-inch flameproof casserole (or a heavy frying pan with a tight-fitting cover) with half the shredded Chinese cabbage. Set aside the rest of the cabbage.
2. Mix the pork, water chestnuts, ham, egg, soy sauce, sherry, sugar, ½ teaspoon sesame oil, ginger, pepper and cornstarch-water mixture until well blended.

Favorites from Afar

3. From this mixture, shape meatballs 1¾ inches in diameter—you'll have about 16—laying the finished ones on a large plate. Because this is a rather wet mixture, the meatballs will tend to flatten out.

4. Heat a heavy black skillet or wok over medium-high heat and add a tablespoon or so of oil to the pan. Tilt the pan to coat it completely with oil. When the pan is hot, place the meatballs in it and brown them on all sides—about 8 minutes. Depending upon the size of your pan, you may have to brown the meatballs in two or more batches.

5. Carefully transfer the browned meatballs, using a pair of tongs or a slotted spoon, to the cabbage-lined casserole. Sprinkle the remaining cabbage on top of the meatballs.

6. Mix the chicken broth and oyster sauce and pour the mixture over the cabbage and meatballs.

7. Set the casserole over high heat and bring the sauce to a boil. Immediately turn the heat to low or medium-low, cover the casserole and simmer the Lions' Heads for 45 minutes.

8. Stir the cornstarch and water together and mix it into the sauce. Cover the casserole and simmer another few minutes, until the sauce has thickened. Stir in the ½ teaspoon sesame oil.

9. Serve hot, accompanied with hot white rice or fried rice and a salad. *Makes 4 to 6 servings.*

Red-Cooked Fish Fillets
(pictured)

Enough lettuce leaves to line a 10½-inch casserole
1 **lb fresh or frozen fish fillets, defrosted and patted dry**

Braising Liquid
2 **tablespoons light soy sauce**
2 **tablespoons sherry**
¼ **teaspoon sugar**
1 **clove garlic, peeled and flattened**
  ⅛-inch slice fresh ginger root
2 **tablespoons oyster sauce**
½ **cup water**

1 **to 2 teaspoons cornstarch**
1 **to 2 teaspoons cold water**
¼ **teaspoon sesame oil**

1. Line a 10½-inch casserole with lettuce leaves and arrange the fish on them.

2. Prepare the Braising Liquid: Mix soy sauce, sherry, sugar, garlic, ginger root, oyster sauce and water and pour over the fish. If it doesn't cover the fillets (this will depend upon the size and type of the fillets), mix enough more sauce, in the same proportions, to cover the fish.

3. Bring the liquid barely to a boil over high heat; lower heat, cover the casserole and simmer the fish fillets 20 minutes.

4. Mix the cornstarch and water and stir enough into the sauce to thicken it lightly. Be careful not to break the fish. Drizzle the sesame oil over the fish. *Makes 2 to 4 servings.*

Duck With Peaches
(pictured)

4- to 5-lb duckling
1 **teaspoon coarse or regular salt for browning the duck**

Braising Liquid
¼ **cup dark soy sauce**
¼ **cup sherry**
1 **cup canned peach nectar (or peach syrup, if canned peaches are being used)**
1 **whole star anise**
1 **dried chili pepper, broken in half (use both seeds and pod)**
2 **cloves garlic, peeled and flattened**
  ⅛-inch slice fresh ginger root, flattened

1½ **teaspoons cornstarch**
1½ **teaspoons cold water**
½ **teaspoon sesame oil**

2 **medium-size peaches, peeled, sliced and covered with water containing juice of half a lemon; or 1 small can peach halves, if fresh peaches are unavailable**
  Syrup from peaches, if canned peaches are used

1. Remove excess fat from the duck cavity. Remove the wing tips (save them, the neck and the gizzard to make duck broth—bag them and freeze them until

Favorites from Afar

you accumulate enough; duck livers can be frozen separately until you have enough to make a duck-liver pâté). Rinse the duck under cold running water, drain and pat dry inside and out with paper towels.

2. Put a large black iron skillet or a wok over high heat. Sprinkle the salt into the pan. When the pan is hot, place the duck, breast down, in the pan. Turn heat to medium-high. The subcutaneous fat will be drawn into the pan, and the duck will start to brown in its own fat. Turn the duck from time to time so the entire surface is browned; use tongs to hold the duck at an angle to brown out-of-the-way parts of the duck. This process will take 8 to 10 minutes.

3. Prepare the Braising Liquid: In a 4-quart flameproof casserole, mix soy sauce, sherry, peach nectar, star anise, chili pepper, garlic and ginger root. Transfer the duck to the casserole, breast down.

4. Bring the liquid to a boil, lower heat, cover the casserole and simmer 1½ to 2 hours, turning the duck with tongs every so often.

5. When duck is done, transfer it to a platter. (To tell if the duck is done, pierce the thigh with the point of a knife. If the juices are slightly pink, the duck is medium-rare; if the juices are clear, it is well done.)

6. Strain the braising liquid into a smaller pot and skim off the fat. Put the pot over medium-high heat and reduce the liquid by half. Blend the cornstarch and water and stir into the liquid; cook a few moments to thicken. Add the sesame oil and give a final stir.

7. Serve the sauce on the side or pour it over the duck. Garnish the duck with the drained peach slices. Carve the duck at the table. *Makes 2 main-dish servings or 4 servings if duck is served with other Chinese food.*

Clams With
Black-Bean-And-Garlic Sauce
(pictured)

1 dozen cherrystone clams (in the shell), well scrubbed under running water
1 teaspoon light soy sauce
⅛ teaspoon finely grated fresh ginger root
¼ cup water
Vegetable oil for frying the black-bean-and-garlic mixture
1½ tablespoons salted black beans, rinsed, drained and mashed
1 tablespoon minced garlic
2 teaspoons cornstarch
2 teaspoons cold water
½ teaspoon sesame oil
2 scallions, cut into ¼-inch rounds (both white and green parts)

1. Put clams in a 4-quart flameproof casserole.

2. Mix together the soy sauce, ginger and water; set aside.

3. Put a wok or a frying pan over high heat and add about a teaspoon of vegetable oil, enough to coat the bottom of the pan (you may need more oil, depending upon the size of the pan). When the oil is hot, add the black beans and garlic. Fry for a few minutes, stirring; then reduce heat and add the soy-sauce mixture.

4. Pour the black-bean sauce over the clams; bring it to a boil over high heat; lower heat, cover the casserole and simmer the clams 15 to 20 minutes, or until they have opened. (After the first 7 or 8 minutes, stir the clams, making sure the bottom clams go to the top and the top clams go to the bottom.)

5. When all the clams have opened, transfer them to a large serving bowl (a pair of tongs is helpful here). Bring the sauce to a boil. Blend the cornstarch and water together and mix into the sauce; cook for a minute or two, until thickened.

6. Stir in sesame oil. Pour sauce over clams and sprinkle scallion rounds on top. Serve hot. *Makes 4 first-course servings.*

Deviled Short Ribs
(pictured)

Salt for browning the short ribs
4 lb meaty beef short ribs, trimmed of surplus fat, separated and cut into 2-inch pieces

Braising Liquid

1 cup dark soy sauce
1 cup sherry
1 teaspoon sugar
4 cloves garlic, peeled and flattened
¼-inch piece fresh ginger root
2 whole star anise
2 dried chili peppers, broken in half (use both seeds and pods)
½ cup water

1 large onion, cut in half from top to bottom, peeled and cut into ¼-inch segments
6 carrots, peeled and cut into 1-inch diagonal chunks
3 celery stalks, cut into 1-inch diagonal pieces
1 tablespoon cornstarch
1 tablespoon water
½ teaspoon sesame oil
2 tablespoons Dijon mustard

1. Set a large frying pan or a wok over high heat and sprinkle about a teaspoonful of salt into it. When the pan is hot, add half the short ribs and brown them on all sides—about 8 minutes.

Favorites from Afar

2. Meanwhile, prepare Braising Liquid: In a 4-quart flameproof casserole, combine soy sauce, sherry, sugar, garlic, ginger root, star anise, chili peppers and water. Stir to mix well.
3. Transfer the browned short ribs to the casserole with a slotted spoon, draining them of excess fat. Brown the remaining short ribs in the same fat and transfer them to the casserole. Turn the short ribs in the sauce to coat them well.
4. Bring the sauce to a boil over high heat. Lower the heat, cover the casserole and simmer the short ribs for about 2½ hours, turning them from time to time.
5. Add the onion, carrot and celery and mix in well. Simmer the meat and vegetables for another hour.
6. Blend the cornstarch and water and mix into the sauce. Remove about 1 cup of sauce from the casserole and stir the sesame oil and the mustard into it. Pour the mixture back into the pot and mix everything well. Cook, stirring, for a few minutes, until the sauce has thickened slightly.
7. Serve hot, with boiled potatoes and a green vegetable. *Makes 4 to 6 servings.*

Dolmathes
Stuffed Grape Leaves
(pictured)

⅓ **cup olive oil**
1 **onion, finely chopped**
1 **lb ground lean meat**
½ **cup rice**
⅓ **cup pignolias (pine nuts)**
2 **tablespoons tomato paste**
½ **cup fresh dill, chopped (or 2 tablespoons dry dillweed)**
¾ **cup water**
Salt and pepper to taste
1 **jar grape leaves**
Additional water as needed

1. Heat olive oil in skillet; add onion and cook until transparent. Add ground meat and cook until it crumbles. Add rice, pignolias, tomato paste, dill and ¾ cup water. If using fresh grape leaves, add salt and pepper to taste; if using prepared grape leaves, omit salt. Simmer rice mixture for 10 minutes or until water is absorbed (rice will be half-cooked). Cool mixture before stuffing grape leaves.
2. Put 1 tablespoon mixture in center of leaf, fold in edges like an envelope and roll. Layer bottom of saucepan with single leaves. Cover this layer with closely fitted layers of stuffed grape leaves. Repeat layering until all stuffing and leaves are used up. Put small

plate, upside down, on top, and push down gently to prevent leaves from unrolling.
3. Add water to cover all but top layer of leaves. Bring to boil, reduce heat and simmer until water is absorbed—approximately ½ hour. Cool slightly before serving. *Makes about 40.*

Editor's Note: We like to serve this cold as an appetizer or with cocktails. We used a 1-pound jar of grape leaves, drained. Use imperfect leaves for bottom of pan.

Plaki Salonika
Baked Bass, Salonika Style

3 - **lb bass, haddock or cod, about ¾ inch thick**
¼ **cup olive or salad oil**
2 **medium tomatoes, sliced**
½ **cup chopped parsley**
2 **cloves garlic, crushed**
1 **teaspoon salt**
½ **teaspoon ground pepper**

1. Preheat oven to 425F.
2. Wipe fish with damp paper towels; cut crosswise into 6 to 8 slices.
3. Arrange fish slices in half of olive oil in a shallow, 3-quart baking dish.
4. Cover each fish slice with a tomato slice. Sprinkle with parsley, garlic, salt, pepper and remaining olive oil. Bake, uncovered, 25 to 30 minutes or until fish flakes easily with fork. *Makes 6 to 8 servings.*

Youvetsi

3 - **lb leg of lamb or 2 lb lean lamb meat, cubed**
2 **to 4 tablespoons olive oil**
1 **medium onion, chopped**
6 **large fresh tomatoes**
1 **clove garlic, slit in half**
¼ **cup fresh savory, chopped, or 1½ teaspoons dried savory**
Salt and pepper to taste
2 **cups kritheraki or orzo**

1. Preheat oven to 350F.
2. Bone leg; cut meat into walnut-size pieces.
3. Heat olive oil over burner in ovenproof pan. Add meat and brown on all sides. Add onion; stir. Add tomatoes, garlic and savory. Add salt and pepper to taste. Cover tightly and simmer about 25 minutes, or until meat is almost cooked.
4. When lamb is almost cooked, parboil kritheraki or orzo. Drain and add to lamb mixture.

Favorites from Afar

5. Cook in 350F oven for 20 minutes, or until liquid is absorbed. If orzo absorbs all the moisture of the meat mixture before fully cooked, add water; stir. *Serves 6.*

   Editor's Note: When we tried this in our kitchens, we used 1 cup uncooked orzo (a pasta). Also, you may substitute 1 can (2 pounds, 3 ounces) tomatoes, undrained, for fresh tomatoes.

Baklavas

Syrup
   2 cups sugar
1¼ cups water
      Juice of ½ lemon
      Peel of 1 orange
      Peel of 1 lemon
   2 cinnamon sticks

   1 lb clarified unsalted butter

Nut-Spice Mixture
1¼ lb crushed walnuts
   ⅔ cup sugar
   1 teaspoon ground nutmeg
   4 teaspoons ground cinnamon

   1 lb phyllo (see Editor's Note)
      Rosewater (optional)

1. Make Syrup: In a saucepan, combine sugar and water. Add lemon juice, peels and cinnamon sticks. Bring to boil, reduce heat and simmer for 15 minutes. Let cool.
2. To clarify butter: Melt butter over low heat. Remove from heat and set aside until separated into 3 layers. Skim off top layer and discard. Pour middle layer into bowl for use. Discard lower, milky layer.
3. Make Nut-Spice Mixture: Combine thoroughly crushed walnuts, the sugar, nutmeg and cinnamon. Set aside.
4. Preheat oven to 325F.
5. To assemble Baklavas: Cut phyllo with sharp knife to fit an 11-by-9-inch baking pan (see Note). Set aside four sheets of phyllo for finishing layer. Keep phyllo covered with dish towel when not in use. Butter baking pan thoroughly, using clarified butter. Place

one sheet of phyllo on bottom and butter phyllo generously. Place a second, third and fourth sheet of phyllo on top, buttering each sheet.
6. Distribute approximately ½ cup nut-spice mixture evenly over phyllo. Make another phyllo layer, using 2 sheets (whole or scraps), always buttering between each sheet. Alternate ½ cup nut-spice mixture with 2-sheet phyllo layers until mixture is used up. Finish with four whole sheets of phyllo previously set aside, buttering each.
7. With very sharp knife, cut through top layer of phyllo, making diamond-shape pattern.
8. Bake at 325F for 45 minutes, or until golden-brown. Remove from oven. When cool, pour syrup evenly over top. Following pattern, cut through Baklavas and let stand until syrup is absorbed. If you wish, sprinkle top with rosewater before serving. *Makes about 30 pieces.*

   Editor's Note: We used the more standard 13-by-9-inch baking pan. Phyllo leaves are packaged, very thin pastry leaves. They are available fresh or, more commonly, frozen.

Andros Island Mussels

24 mussels
   1 bottle (8 oz) clam juice
   1 pkg (2½ oz) pignolias (pine nuts)
   3 tablespoons olive oil
   ½ cup chopped onion
   ¼ cup dried currants
   ½ cup long-grain white rice
   ½ cup white wine
   1 teaspoon salt
   ¼ teaspoon ground pepper
   2 tablespoons chopped parsley

1. Scrub mussels well and scrape with a knife until shells are clean and free of beards. Rinse well in cold water.
2. In medium saucepan, bring half the clam juice to boiling; add mussels and cook just until shells open— 3 to 5 minutes. Drain, reserving liquid; strain liquid.

Arrange mussels in a single layer in shallow baking dish. Discard any mussels that do not open.

3. Preheat oven to 400F. Place pignolias in a single layer in shallow baking pan; toast in oven 5 minutes.
4. In hot oil in medium saucepan, sauté onion until golden. Add remaining clam juice and reserved liquid, currants, rice, wine, salt and pepper; bring to boiling. Reduce heat and simmer, covered, 20 minutes, or until all liquid is absorbed. Remove from heat.
5. Add toasted pignolias and parsley; mix well. Place a tablespoonful of mixture in each mussel shell. (If desired, mussels may be prepared several hours ahead. Refrigerate until just before serving.)
6. Bake, uncovered, at 400F 10 minutes, or until hot. *Makes 8 appetizer servings.*

Kolokythakia Yemista, Skorpios
Stuffed Zucchini With Egg-And-Lemon Sauce

8 to 10 medium zucchini (3½ to 4 lb in all)

Stuffing
- **1 lb ground beef or lamb**
- **1 medium onion, coarsely chopped**
- **½ teaspoon dried oregano leaves**
- **2 tablespoons chopped parsley**
- **1 teaspoon salt**
- **¼ teaspoon ground pepper**
- **1 cup cooked rice**

- **1 tablespoon olive oil**

Sauce
- **3 eggs**
- **¼ cup lemon juice**
- **½ cup canned condensed beef consommé, undiluted**

1. Wash and scrub zucchini. Trim stem ends. If zucchini are long, halve crosswise.
2. With apple corer, carefully scoop out center of zucchini; discard.
3. Make Stuffing: Combine beef with onion, oregano, parsley, salt, pepper and rice; toss with fork to mix well.

4. Preheat oven to 375F. Grease a 13-by-9-by-2-inch baking dish with olive oil.
5. Using a small spoon, stuff zucchini with meat mixture. Arrange in single layer in baking dish. Bake, uncovered, 45 minutes, or until zucchini are fork-tender.
6. Meanwhile, make Sauce: In medium saucepan, with rotary beater, beat eggs with lemon juice; gradually beat in consommé.
7. Heat gently, stirring, until slightly thickened; do not boil. Serve over zucchini. *Makes 8 servings.*

Arni Me Kolokythakia
Lamb With Little Zucchini

- **¾ cup olive oil**
- **2 lb boned lamb, cut in walnut-size pieces**
- **1 onion, diced**
- **6 medium tomatoes, peeled and diced**
- **½ cup chopped fresh dill (or 2 tablespoons dried dillweed)**
- **Salt and pepper to taste**
- **3 lb small zucchini, ends cut off and split lengthwise (2 to 3 inches long)**

1. Preheat oven to 350F.
2. Heat ¼ cup olive oil in large saucepan. Add lamb and brown on all sides. Add onion. When onion is transparent, add tomato, dill, salt and pepper. Cover, reduce heat and simmer until lamb is cooked but not falling apart (about 25 minutes).
3. Heat remaining olive oil (½ cup) in large skillet. Add zucchini and sear on both sides until golden. Drain zucchini on paper towel.
4. Line an 11-by-9-inch baking pan with zucchini, close to each other, to cover the bottom. Distribute cooked-meat mixture evenly on top of zucchini. Bake at 350F for 20 minutes, or until zucchini are cooked. *Serves 4 to 6.*

Editor's Note: When we tried this dish we used 1 teaspoon salt and ¼ teaspoon pepper and 2 cans (1-pound size) tomatoes, undrained, for fresh.

Favorites from Afar

Ravanie

Sauce

   2 **cups water**
1¼ **cups sugar**
   ⅓ **cup rum**
   2 **(¼-inch) orange slices with skin**

Cake

2½ **cups finely crushed walnuts**
 10 **finely crushed zwiebacks**
   8 **eggs**
   1 **teaspoon cream of tartar**
  ⅔ **cup sugar**
     Grated rind of 1 orange
  ¼ **lb (1 stick) unsalted butter, melted**

1. Make Sauce: Combine water, sugar and rum in saucepan. Add orange slices. Bring to boil, reduce heat and simmer 10 minutes. Set aside to cool.
2. Make Cake: In a small bowl, combine walnuts and zwieback. Lightly butter an 11-by-9-inch baking pan (see Note).
3. Separate eggs; in large bowl of electric mixer, let egg whites warm to room temperature—about 1 hour. Put yolks in small mixer bowl.
4. Add cream of tartar to egg whites and beat until whites are stiff—about 5 minutes. Using same beaters, beat sugar with yolks until thick and pale yellow—about 5 to 7 minutes.
5. Preheat oven to 350F.
6. Fold egg yolks into whites using an under-and-over motion. Fold in walnut-zwieback mixture and orange rind. Add melted butter and fold in.
7. Pour batter into prepared pan. Bake 45 minutes or until golden-brown and sides pull away from pan.
8. Pour cooled sauce evenly over cake; cut in diamond shapes. *Makes about 30 pieces.*

   Editor's Note: We used the more standard 13-by-9-inch baking pan.

Tzatziki, Mykonos
Yogurt Salad

 1 **medium cucumber**
 1 **cup yogurt**
 1 **teaspoon white vinegar**
 1 **teaspoon olive oil**
 1 **small clove garlic, chopped**
 ½ **teaspoon salt**
    Chopped parsley

1. Pare cucumber; halve lengthwise. Scoop out seeds by running tip of spoon down center of each half; discard seeds. Grate cucumber coarsely.

2. In medium bowl, combine grated cucumber, the yogurt, vinegar, oil, garlic and salt; stir with wooden spoon until thoroughly combined.
3. Taste and add more salt if necessary. Sprinkle with chopped parsley. Serve at once. *Makes 4 servings.*

Sofrito
Beef Stew, Corfu Style

2½ **lb beef chuck or round**
 ⅓ **cup all-purpose flour**
 1 **teaspoon salt**
 ½ **teaspoon ground pepper**
 ¼ **teaspoon paprika**
 ¼ **teaspoon dried thyme leaves**
 ¼ **cup olive or salad oil**
 2 **cloves garlic, crushed**
 ¼ **cup red-wine vinegar**
 1 **can (10½ oz) condensed beef broth, undiluted**
 ½ **cup chopped parsley**
 1 **cup packaged toasted croutons**

1. Cut beef into ½-inch-thick slices. In medium bowl, combine flour, salt, pepper, paprika and thyme; mix well. Add beef slices, a few at a time; toss to coat beef with flour mixture.
2. In large heavy skillet, slowly heat half of oil. Over high heat, brown meat slices, a few at a time, turning to brown on both sides. Remove beef as it browns. Add more oil as needed; continue until all of beef is browned.
3. Return beef to skillet, along with garlic, vinegar, beef broth and parsley. Bring to boiling; reduce heat; simmer, covered, 1 hour, or until meat is tender and sauce is thickened.
4. Serve with croutons. Sprinkle with more chopped parsley, if desired. *Makes 4 to 6 servings.*

Banana-And-Ham Fritters
(pictured)

 6 **medium-size, medium-ripe whole bananas (about 2 lb), peeled**
1½ **teaspoons salt**
 ⅛ **teaspoon ground pepper**

Filling

 2 **cups ground cooked ham or 1 can (12 oz) luncheon meat, ground**
 ¼ **cup milk**

 ¾ **cup packaged dry bread crumbs**
 2 **eggs, beaten**
    Salad oil for frying
 8 **lemon quarters**

Favorites from Afar

1. In medium skillet, bring 1 inch water to boiling. Add bananas, salt and pepper. Cook, covered, over medium heat just until bananas are soft.
2. Drain bananas well. Return to skillet; heat slightly to dry out. Mash. Let cool. Makes 2 cups.
3. Meanwhile, make Filling: In medium bowl, combine ham and milk; mix well. Divide mixture into eight parts.
4. On sheet of waxed paper, flatten ¼ cup mashed banana into a 3½-inch round. Place ground ham in center; fold banana over ham, covering completely. Roll in bread crumbs; dip in egg. Reroll in crumbs. Shape into an oval croquette, 4 inches long. Repeat with rest of mixture. Set aside while heating oil.
5. In deep, heavy saucepan, heat salad oil (2 inches deep) to 375F on deep-frying thermometer.
6. Deep-fry a few at a time, turning once, until golden— 2 to 3 minutes on each side. Drain on paper towels. Serve with lemon quarters. *Makes 8 servings.*

Shrimp-And-Pineapple Salad
(pictured)

1 **medium-size fresh pineapple**
1 **medium cucumber**
1 **stalk celery, diagonally sliced**
¼ **lb seedless green grapes**
 Boiled Shrimp, recipe follows
½ **cup mayonnaise or cooked salad dressing**
1 **tablespoon sugar**
½ **teaspoon salt**
1 **tablespoon lemon juice**
¼ **teaspoon curry powder**
 Parsley or watercress

1. Wash pineapple. With sharp knife, cut pineapple into quarters lengthwise, right through frond, leaving frond in place.
2. Using a sharp knife or grapefruit knife, cut pineapple meat from each quarter; do not cut shell. Remove and discard cores. Cut pineapple meat into ¼-inch-thick slices; turn into large bowl. (Drain pineapple shells very well; refrigerate.)
3. Pare cucumber; cut into ¼-inch-thick slices; cut slices in half.
4. Add cucumber and celery to pineapple; toss to combine.
5. Peel grapes, if desired, or cut in half. Add to pineapple mixture along with shrimp. Refrigerate, covered, to chill well—several hours.
6. In small bowl, combine mayonnaise, sugar, salt, lemon juice and curry powder; mix well. Refrigerate, covered, until ready to use—several hours.

7. To serve: Add dressing to shrimp-and-fruit mixture; toss gently. Spoon into pineapple shells, mounding high. Garnish with parsley or watercress. *Makes 4 servings.*

Boiled Shrimp

½ **lb unshelled raw shrimp**
½ **small onion, peeled and thinly sliced**
1 **sprig parsley**
½ **tablespoon salt**
½ **bay leaf**
⅛ **teaspoon dried thyme leaves**
¼ **teaspoon curry powder**

1. Rinse shrimp; remove shells and devein: Using a small, sharp knife, slit each shrimp down back; lift out sand vein.
2. In large skillet, combine 2 cups water, the onion, parsley, salt, bay leaf, thyme and curry powder. Bring to boiling, covered, over medium heat; simmer 10 minutes.
3. Add shrimp; return to boiling. Reduce heat and simmer, covered, 3 to 5 minutes, or just until tender.
4. Drain; let cool. Refrigerate, covered, until ready to use.

Molded Pineapple-Rice Cream
(pictured)

⅓ **cup regular white rice**
2½ **cups milk**
⅓ **cup sugar**
½ **teaspoon salt**
2 **env unflavored gelatine**
1 **can (1 lb, 4 oz) crushed pineapple, undrained**
⅓ **cup flaked coconut**
1 **teaspoon vanilla extract**
½ **teaspoon almond extract**
1 **cup heavy cream, whipped**
4 **canned pineapple slices, halved**
¼ **cup apricot preserves**
 Whipped cream for garnish (optional)

1. In top of double boiler, combine rice, milk, sugar and salt. Cook over boiling water, covered and stirring occasionally, until rice is tender—about 1 hour and 15 minutes.
2. In small bowl, sprinkle gelatine over crushed pineapple; let stand 5 minutes to soften. Turn into hot rice mixture, stirring to dissolve gelatine completely. Stir in coconut and vanilla and almond extracts. Refrigerate until cool—about 1 hour (or place in freezer to cool more quickly) until mixture is firm enough to mound.

Favorites from Afar

3. With rubber spatula, fold whipped cream into cooled gelatine mixture, mixing thoroughly.
4. Turn into a fancy 1½-quart mold. Refrigerate until firm enough to unmold—at least 3 hours or overnight.
5. To unmold, run a sharp knife around edge of mold to loosen. Invert on serving platter; shake to unmold. (If necessary, place a hot, damp cloth on bottom of mold to loosen.)
6. Around base of mold, arrange halves of pineapple slices (see picture). Over low heat, melt preserves; use to brush surface of mold completely. If desired, decorate with rosettes of whipped cream, as pictured. Refrigerate until serving. *Makes 8 servings.*

Glazed Banana Tart
(pictured)

1 pkg (10 oz) frozen patty shells
1 egg yolk
1 tablespoon water

Pastry Cream

¼ cup sugar
  Dash salt
1 tablespoon cornstarch
1 cup milk
2 egg yolks, slightly beaten
½ teaspoon vanilla extract

¼ cup orange marmalade
3 small bananas, very thinly sliced, about ⅛ inch thick (1 lb)
  Confectioners' sugar

1. Remove patty shells from package; let stand at room temperature 30 minutes to soften. Cover a small cookie sheet with brown paper.
2. On lightly floured pastry cloth, overlap pastry shells in two rows of three shells each. With rolling pin, roll into a rectangle 12 inches long and 8 inches wide. From long end, fold over in thirds; press edges to seal. Refrigerate, wrapped in waxed paper, ½ hour.
3. With fold at right, again roll into a rectangle 12 inches long and 8 inches wide. Fold into thirds; press edges to seal. Repeat, rolling 14 inches long, 8 inches wide. Trim edges to make even.
4. Make tart shell: From each end and side, cut a 1-inch strip of pastry. Beat egg yolk with 1 tablespoon water.

Use to brush a 1-inch strip all around pastry rectangle. Place long strips on each side. Cut short strips to make 4 inches long; place at each end. Prick inside all over with fork.
5. Place on prepared cookie sheet; refrigerate ½ hour.
6. Make Pastry Cream: In small saucepan, combine sugar, salt and cornstarch; mix well. Stir in milk. Cook, stirring constantly, over medium heat until mixture thickens and begins to boil; boil 1 minute. Remove from heat.
7. Stir a little hot mixture into egg yolks; mix well; stir back into saucepan. Cook, stirring, until thickened and bubbly. Stir in vanilla. Let cool; then refrigerate, covered.
8. Meanwhile, preheat oven to 450F. Bake tart shell 10 minutes. Reduce heat to 350F; bake 25 to 30 minutes, or until puffed and golden. Remove to wire rack to cool.
9. To assemble tart: Heat orange marmalade gently just to melt. Spread pastry cream in bottom of tart shell. Arrange sliced banana in seven crosswise rows over pastry cream (see picture). Brush lightly with melted marmalade. Sprinkle edge all around with confectioners' sugar. Refrigerate about 30 minutes. To serve, slice crosswise, cutting between rows of banana. *Makes 8 servings.*

Banana Crêpes With Apricot Sauce
(pictured)

1 jar (12 oz) apricot preserves
¼ cup water
8 medium-size ripe bananas
¼ cup lemon juice
4 tablespoons (½ stick) butter or margarine
8 Crêpes, recipe follows
2 tablespoons light-brown sugar
⅓ to ½ cup golden rum

1. Melt preserves with ¼ cup water in small saucepan, stirring occasionally, over medium heat—10 minutes.
2. Peel bananas; remove tips at stem end. Brush with lemon juice. In 2 tablespoons hot butter in medium skillet, gently sauté bananas, turning gently, until tender—about 5 minutes. Do not break bananas.
3. Spread one side of each crêpe with 1 tablespoon

sauce; top with a banana; fold crêpe around banana.

4. In chafing dish or skillet, heat 2 tablespoons butter with the brown sugar until melted. Add crêpes; cook gently about 5 minutes; add remaining apricot sauce and golden rum; cook 5 minutes longer. Serve warm with some of sauce spooned over crêpes. *Makes 8 servings.*

Crêpes

½ **cup all-purpose flour**
2 **tablespoons butter or margarine, melted and cooled, or 2 tablespoons salad oil**
1 **whole egg**
1 **egg yolk**
¾ **cup milk**
Butter for brushing skillet

1. In small bowl, combine flour, melted butter, egg, egg yolk and ¼ cup milk. Beat with rotary beater until smooth. Beat in the remaining milk until the mixture is well blended. Refrigerate, covered, at least 30 minutes.
2. Slowly heat a 7-inch skillet until a drop of water sizzles and rolls off. For each crêpe, brush skillet lightly with butter. Pour in about 3 tablespoons batter, rotating pan quickly to spread batter completely over bottom.
3. Cook until lightly browned; then turn and brown other side. Turn out onto wire rack. (Stack crêpes with a piece of waxed paper between each two if not using for several hours.) *Makes 8 crêpes.*

Broiled Chicken With Bananas
(pictured)

2 **(2½-lb size) broiler-fryers, quartered**

Marinade
⅓ **cup lemon juice**
⅓ **cup salad oil**
1 **clove garlic, crushed**
⅛ **teaspoon ground nutmeg**
1½ **teaspoons salt**
⅛ **teaspoon ground pepper**
1½ **teaspoons dried thyme leaves**

8 **medium-size bananas**
2 **tablespoons dark corn syrup**
Lemon quarters for garnish

1. Wash chicken; pat dry with paper towels. Arrange in single layer in large, shallow baking pan.
2. Make Marinade: Combine lemon juice, oil, garlic, nutmeg, salt, pepper and thyme; mix well; pour over chicken. Refrigerate, covered, several hours or overnight, turning several times.
3. To cook, pour off marinade and reserve. Broil chicken, skin side down, in same pan, about 8 inches from heat, 25 minutes, basting several times with reserved marinade. Turn chicken with tongs; broil 20 minutes longer.
4. Peel bananas; arrange in pan with chicken. Brush with corn syrup. Broil bananas and chicken about 10 minutes, or until bananas are golden. Serve with lemon quarters. *Makes 8 servings.*

Fresh-Pineapple Flambé
(pictured)

1 **large pineapple (about 4 lb)**
2 **tablespoons butter or margarine**
½ **cup firmly packed light-brown sugar**
½ **cup dark rum**
1 **sugar cube**
Lemon extract

1. Preheat oven to 350F.
2. Slice top from pineapple about 1½ inches below frond. Set top aside.
3. With grapefruit knife or other sharp knife, remove meat from pineapple shell, leaving shell intact. Discard core of pineapple; cut meat into ½-inch chunks.
4. Place pineapple shell in shallow pan; heat in oven about 10 minutes.
5. In medium skillet, melt butter; add brown sugar and rum; stir to combine. Add pineapple chunks; over low heat, stir until heated through—about 10 minutes.
6. To serve: Place warm pineapple shell on serving platter. Spoon in pineapple chunks and sauce, mounding high. Place top of pineapple on serving dish next to pineapple.
7. Soak sugar cube in lemon extract; place on top of pineapple chunks. Ignite with match. Serve flaming. (This dessert is nice served over ice cream, too.) *Makes 6 to 8 servings.*

The Fabulous French Influence

From the Continental provinces to Canada to New Orleans, French cuisine has long been inspired and has captivated the rest of the world with its subtle elegance and superb taste. Such culinary savoir faire is exemplified in these next few pages. Recipes begin on page 120.

Provence

At left: The land of the Riviera has a cuisine more Mediterranean than French. Here, olive and citrus groves abound, and the cooking favors oil and herbs. **At top** is roast-pepper salad in vinaigrette; **below,** orange-scented Beef Stew Provençal. Between are Fresh Orange Sherbet with Cointreau and Almond Tile Cookies.

French Canada

At right: The French who settled in Canada created a very special cuisine—French in style but enriched by their new country's native foods. **Clockwise, from top:** Quebec's hearty Yellow Pea Soup; Tourtière, a ground-pork pie with cloves and allspice; Veal Loaf; and that staple of French country cooking, herbed Chicken in Wine. *Recipes begin on page 124.*

Normandy

Below: Normandy is dairy country, famous for cheese and poultry and the fruit of its orchards. Rich cream goes into Sole Normande, **at top,** and into the Madeira sauce for Poulet Vallée d'Auge, **below.** With them are pears in pastry and Calvados, the regions renowned apple brandy. *Recipes begin on page 122.*

BOTH: GEORGE RATKAI

New Orleans

This city is world famous for the birth of jazz, Mardi Gras and its cooking—a unique blend of classic French, a bit of British, some spicy Spanish, plus a dash of Chickasaw Indian. **Clockwise, from keyboard center:** Pecan Pralines; saucy Chicken Creole; deep-fried Creole Doughnuts, sprinkled with sugar; Creole Jambalaya, a classic mix of shrimp, ham, rice, tomatoes and spices; and delicate Strawberry Cookie-Shell Sundaes, with fresh strawberries and pecans. *Recipes begin on page 125.*

The Fabulous French Influence

continued from page 115

Menu from Provence

Vermouth Cassis or Pastis
Green-Pepper Salad Platter*
Beef Stew Provençal*
Risotto With Artichoke Hearts
and Tomatoes*
Banon and Chèvre Cheeses
French Bread
Fresh Orange Sherbet*
Almond Tile Cookies*
Coffee   Rosé Wine

Green-Pepper Salad Platter
(pictured)

Vinaigrette Dressing
- 1 **cup olive or salad oil**
- ⅓ **cup red-wine vinegar**
- 1 **clove garlic, crushed**
- 1 **teaspoon salt**
- 1 **teaspoon dried tarragon leaves**
- ¼ **teaspoon ground pepper**
- 2 **tablespoons chopped parsley**
- 2 **tablespoons chopped chives**

- 8 **medium-size green peppers (2½ lb)**
- 2 **small onions, peeled, thinly sliced and well chilled**
- 4 **large ripe tomatoes, thinly sliced and well chilled (2 lb)**
- 2 **cans (2-oz size) anchovy fillets, drained and well chilled**
- 10 **ripe olives**
- 1 **canned pimiento, cut in ¼-inch strips**
  Freshly grated black pepper

1. Make Vinaigrette Dressing: Combine oil, vinegar, garlic, salt, tarragon, pepper, parsley and chives in jar with tight-fitting lid. Shake vigorously. Refrigerate until ready to use. Shake again before using. *Makes 1½ cups.*
2. Wash peppers; drain well.
3. Place peppers on cookie sheet; broil about 6 inches from heat, turning frequently, until the skin of the peppers becomes blistered and charred—about 15 minutes.
4. Place peppers in a large kettle; cover; let stand 15 minutes.
5. Do not peel off charred skin. Cut each pepper into fourths. Remove the ribs and seeds; cut into julienne strips ½ inch wide. Toss with 1 cup vinaigrette dressing in shallow glass bowl; refrigerate several hours.

6. To serve as pictured: In center of round serving platter, mound green-pepper strips. Arrange onion slices around peppers, overlapping; next, tomato slices, overlapping. Garnish tomatoes with anchovies and olives. Garnish peppers with pimiento strips. Spoon rest of dressing over tomatoes. Grate fresh black pepper over all. Nice as a first course or salad. *Makes 10 to 12 servings.*

Beef Stew Provençal
(pictured)

- 3 **lb lean beef chuck, cut into 1½-inch cubes**
- ⅓ **cup all-purpose flour**
- 2 **teaspoons salt**
- ¼ **teaspoon ground pepper**
- ¼ **cup (½ stick) butter or margarine**
- 4 **tablespoons olive or salad oil**
- 8 **small onions, peeled (1 lb)**
- 1 **clove garlic, crushed**
- 1 **cup chopped leek or shallot**
- 1½ **teaspoons dried thyme leaves**
- 2 **bay leaves**
- 1 **can (1 lb, 12 oz) tomatoes, undrained**
- 2 **beef-bouillon cubes**
- 1½ **cups dry red wine**
- 1 **strip orange peel, 1 inch wide and 3 inches long**
- 8 **small new potatoes, scrubbed**
- 4 **zucchini, cut into ½-inch-thick slices (1½ lb)**
- 12 **pitted green olives**
- 12 **ripe olives**
- 1 **can (15 oz) coeur de celeri, drained (see Note)**

- ¼ **cup water**
  Chopped parsley

1. Wipe meat with damp paper towels. On waxed paper, combine flour with salt and pepper. Roll beef cubes in flour mixture to coat. Reserve remaining flour mixture for later use.
2. In hot butter and 2 tablespoons oil in 6-quart Dutch oven, sauté beef, half at a time, until well browned on all sides—about 30 minutes in all. Remove as browned.
3. Sauté whole onions until golden-brown—about 5 minutes; remove and set aside.
4. Add remaining oil to drippings in pan; sauté garlic, leek, thyme and bay leaves until leek is golden—5 minutes. Add tomatoes, bouillon cubes, wine, browned beef and orange peel.
5. Bring to boiling; simmer, covered (place waxed paper on top, under lid), for 2 hours or until meat is tender. The last hour of cooking, add potatoes and sautéed onions; cook 40 minutes; add zucchini and green and ripe olives; cook until meat and vegetables are tender. Add drained coeur de celeri.

*Recipes given for starred dishes.

The Fabulous French Influence

6. In small bowl, combine reserved flour mixture with ¼ cup water; mix until smooth. Stir into stew; simmer, stirring, until mixture thickens—about 5 minutes. Sprinkle with chopped parsley. Serve with French bread. *Makes 8 servings.*

Note: If canned coeur de celeri is not available, use 2 fresh celery hearts; cut each into quarters, vertically. Add to stew with potatoes and onions, as directed in Step 5.

Risotto With Artichoke Hearts and Tomatoes

Butter or margarine
1 medium onion, chopped
2 cups long-grain white rice
3 cans (10½-oz size) condensed beef broth, undiluted
   Water
1 teaspoon salt
¼ teaspoon ground pepper
1 pkg (9 oz) frozen artichoke hearts
3 medium tomatoes
½ cup grated Parmesan cheese
½ cup sliced pimiento-stuffed olives

1. Preheat oven to 350F. In 3 tablespoons hot butter in 4½-quart Dutch oven, sauté onion, stirring, about 5 minutes, or until golden and tender. Stir in rice; cook, stirring, several minutes or until rice is golden.
2. Pour broth into a 1-quart measure; add water to make 4 cups. Stir broth into rice mixture; bring to boiling. Cover Dutch oven; bake rice 20 minutes, or until tender and all liquid is absorbed. Add salt and pepper.
3. Meanwhile, prepare vegetables: In a medium skillet, cook artichokes as package label directs; drain. In same skillet, sauté artichokes in 2 tablespoons hot butter until golden. Meanwhile, peel tomatoes; remove seeds; chop pulp finely. In 2 tablespoons butter in medium skillet, cook tomato 5 minutes.
4. Fluff up rice with fork; lightly mix in tomato, artichokes and half of grated cheese. Pile into warm serving dish. Sprinkle with remaining cheese and the olives. *Makes 8 servings.*

Fresh Orange Sherbet in Orange Shells
(pictured)

2 tablespoons grated orange peel
7 large oranges
½ cup honey or light corn syrup
⅔ cup sweet orange marmalade
2 cups light cream or half-and-half
¼ cup Cointreau
   Fresh mint sprigs

1. Grate peel from one orange. Cut tops from 6 oranges, cutting about one-third of the way down. Squeeze juice from tops and bottoms of 7 oranges. Juice should measure 2 cups. With a teaspoon, scrape white membrane from the tops and bottoms of 6 oranges. Set aside.
2. In blender container, combine grated orange peel and juice, honey, marmalade, cream and Cointreau. Blend ½ minute at high speed. Pour into 13-by-9-by-2-inch baking pan; freeze until firm 1 inch from edge all around—about 3 hours.
3. Blend again in blender ½ minute—until soft but not melted. Turn back into baking pan, or mound in reserved orange-shell bottoms. Freeze until firm— several hours or overnight. (Flavor improves overnight.)
4. Serve in orange shells, filling bottoms and putting tops in place. Decorate each with a mint sprig inserted through hole in top. *Makes 6 servings.*

Almond Tile Cookies
(pictured)

2 egg whites at room temperature
½ cup sugar
¼ teaspoon vanilla extract
3 tablespoons butter or margarine, melted
3 tablespoons all-purpose flour
½ cup sliced blanched almonds

1. Preheat oven to 400F. Grease a large cookie sheet with salad oil and dust with flour.
2. In medium bowl, combine egg whites, sugar and vanilla; beat with wire whisk 2 minutes, or until sugar is dissolved and mixture is syrupy.
3. Add butter and flour; beat until smooth. Stir in almonds.
4. Drop by teaspoonfuls, 4 inches apart, onto prepared cookie sheet. With small spatula, spread each to a 3-inch circle. Make no more than 8 at a time.
5. Bake 4 to 5 minutes, or until cookies are golden-brown around edges and lightly browned in centers.
6. With small spatula, immediately remove cookies carefully and place over rolling pin to curve them. (If cookies get too cool, return to oven just until hot and soft again.)
7. Repeat with remaining batter, oiling and flouring cookie sheet each time. *Makes about 3 dozen.*

The Fabulous French Influence

Menu from Normandy

Moules Marinière
Poulet Vallée d'Auge* or
Sole Normande*
Buttered Green Beans or Salsify
Green Salad Bowl
Camembert or Pont-l'Éveque Cheese
French Bread
Douillons (Pear Dumplings)*
Cider   Chilled White Wine
Coffee   Calvados or Benedictine

Poulet Vallée d'Auge
Chicken in Madeira Cream Sauce
(pictured)

  5- lb ready-to-cook roasting chicken
  Salt
  Ground pepper
¾ cup (1½ sticks) butter or margarine
  Water
1 lb very small white onions
1 lb fresh mushrooms, washed and cut in half
  lengthwise
3 tablespoons all-purpose flour
½ cup Madeira wine or dry sherry
1½ cups light cream or half-and-half
1 egg yolk
  Chopped parsley

1. Rinse chicken well; dry with paper towels. Sprinkle inside with 1½ teaspoons salt and ⅛ teaspoon pepper. Tuck wings under body; tie legs together. If necessary, fasten skin at neck with a skewer.
2. In ¼ cup hot butter in 6-quart Dutch oven, brown chicken well all over—takes about 30 minutes. Turn chicken carefully with two wooden spoons so as not to break skin.
3. Add two tablespoons water; cover tightly and simmer gently until chicken is tender—about 1 hour and 20 minutes. Remove the chicken to a serving platter; keep warm. If desired, the chicken may be cut into serving pieces.

4. In a large skillet, cook onions in 1 inch boiling water until tender—15 to 20 minutes; drain well. Toss with ¼ cup butter; sauté, stirring, about 5 minutes.
5. In another large skillet, heat ¼ cup butter. Sauté mushrooms, stirring, about 5 minutes. Add ½ teaspoon salt and dash pepper; mix well.
6. Combine flour and Madeira; stir until smooth. Stir into drippings left in Dutch oven. Add ½ teaspoon salt. Mix cream with egg yolk; slowly stir into flour mixture. Cook, stirring until the sauce is thick—about 5 minutes.
7. To serve: Pour some of the sauce over the chicken; serve rest of sauce in gravy boat; surround chicken with mushrooms and onions, as pictured. Sprinkle parsley on vegetables. *Makes 8 servings.*

Sole Normande
(pictured)

6 fillets of sole (2½ lb)
3 tablespoons lemon juice
1 teaspoon salt
⅛ teaspoon ground white pepper
2 tablespoons butter or margarine
½ cup dry white wine
1 small onion, sliced
1 bay leaf
½ teaspoon dried tarragon leaves
½ pint oysters or mussels in liquid (optional)
  Sauce Normande, recipe follows
½ lb cooked shrimp, shelled and deveined, recipe
  follows (optional)

1. Preheat oven to 350F.
2. Rinse fillets under cold water; dry well on paper towels; fold over in thirds. Arrange in a single layer in a lightly buttered 13-by-9-by-2-inch baking dish. Sprinkle with lemon juice, salt and pepper; dot with butter.
3. Pour wine over all. Top with onion, bay leaf and tarragon.
4. Bake, uncovered, 20 minutes, or until fish flakes easily when tested with fork.
5. Meanwhile, in small saucepan, cook oysters in their liquid just until edges begin to curl. Drain; set aside.

*Recipes given for starred dishes.

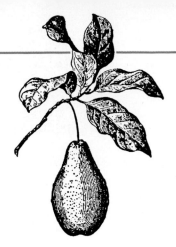

The Fabulous French Influence

6. With slotted spatula, lift fillets to a large, shallow serving dish; keep fillets warm. Reserve cooking stock.
7. Meanwhile, make Sauce Normande. Add oysters and shrimp to sauce; drain off any liquid from fillets in dish; pour sauce over all and serve at once. *Makes 6 servings.*

Sauce Normande

 3 tablespoons butter or margarine
 ½ lb fresh mushrooms, washed and sliced
 3 tablespoons all-purpose flour
 1 cup reserved fish stock
 ½ cup dry white wine or cider
 2 egg yolks, slightly beaten
 ½ cup heavy cream

1. Melt butter in saucepan. Add mushrooms; sauté, stirring occasionally, about 5 minutes. Remove from heat; stir in flour until smooth. Add reserved fish stock and the wine. Cook over medium heat, stirring constantly, until mixture comes to boiling. Reduce heat; simmer 3 minutes.
2. In medium bowl, combine egg yolks and cream; mix well. Stir in a little of hot mushroom mixture. Pour back into saucepan. Cook, stirring, several minutes, or until slightly thickened.

Cooked Shrimp

 ½ lb unshelled raw shrimp
 ½ small onion, peeled and thinly sliced
 ¼ lemon, thinly sliced
 1 sprig parsley
 ½ tablespoon salt
 3 black peppercorns
 ½ bay leaf
 ⅛ teaspoon dried thyme leaves

1. Rinse shrimp; shell and devein.
2. In large skillet, combine 2 cups water, the onion, lemon, parsley, salt, peppercorns, bay leaf and thyme. Bring to boiling, covered, over medium heat; simmer 10 minutes.

3. Add shrimp; return to boiling. Reduce heat and simmer, covered, 2 to 3 minutes, or just until tender.
4. Drain. Add to Sauce Normande.

Pear Dumplings
(pictured)

1½ pkg (11-oz size) piecrust mix
 6 ripe (but not soft) pears (about 2½ lb)
 ¼ cup sugar
 1 teaspoon ground cinnamon
 ¼ cup lemon juice
 1 egg yolk
 1 teaspoon water

Custard Sauce
 2 cups milk
 4 egg yolks
 ⅓ cup sugar
 Dash salt
 1 teaspoon vanilla extract

1. Preheat oven to 400F. Prepare pastry as package label directs. On lightly floured surface, divide pastry into seven parts. With a stockinette-covered rolling pin, roll six pieces of pastry into 7-inch squares.
2. Pare pears, leaving stems on. Combine ¼ cup sugar and the cinnamon. Sprinkle each pear with lemon juice, then with cinnamon-sugar.
3. Slip center of a square of pastry over stem of each pear; mold pastry around pears, covering completely. Place in lightly greased, shallow 15½-by-10½-inch baking pan.
4. Roll remaining piece of pastry into a 9-inch circle. Using a 3-inch cookie cutter, cut out 3 rounds. Cut centers from each with a one-inch cutter. Reroll trimmings for three more rounds.
5. Slip a circle of pastry over each stem. Blend 1 egg yolk with 1 teaspoon water. Brush pastry with egg-yolk mixture. Bake 45 to 50 minutes.
6. Meanwhile, make Custard Sauce: Heat milk in top of double boiler over direct heat until bubbles form around the edge.
7. In small bowl, slightly beat egg yolks with sugar and salt. Gradually add hot milk, stirring constantly. Return to double-boiler top.

The Fabulous French Influence

8. Cook, stirring constantly, over simmering water (double-boiler top should not touch water) until mixture coats a metal spoon. Stir in vanilla. Refrigerate, covered, until chilled.
9. Serve warm dumplings with chilled custard sauce. *Makes 6 servings.*

Veal Loaf
(pictured)

   2 tablespoons butter or margarine
 ½ cup finely chopped onion
   2 lb ground veal
 ½ lb ground salt pork
   1 teaspoon salt
 ½ teaspoon ground pepper
   2 tablespoons chopped parsley
   1 tablespoon lemon juice
1¾ cups fresh white-bread crumbs (5 slices)
   2 tablespoons catsup or tomato sauce
 ¼ cup milk
   1 egg
   4 slices bacon

1. Preheat oven to 350F.
2. In hot butter in medium skillet, sauté onion, stirring, until tender—about 5 minutes. In large bowl, combine remaining ingredients except bacon with sautéed onion. Mix with wooden spoon until well combined.
3. Line a 9-by-5-by-3-inch loaf pan with foil, leaving some overhanging edge. Turn mixture into pan; smooth; place bacon on top. Bake about 1 hour.
4. Let stand several minutes before lifting from pan by grasping foil. May be served hot or cold. *Makes 8 servings.*

Sugar Pie
Recipe from Jehane Benoit, Canada.

 ½ teaspoon baking soda
 ¼ teaspoon vanilla extract
1½ cups maple or maple-flavored syrup
      9-inch unbaked pie shell
   1 cup all-purpose flour
   1 cup firmly packed dark-brown sugar
      Dash ground nutmeg
 ⅓ cup (⅔ stick) butter

1. Preheat oven to 350F. Stir baking soda and vanilla into maple syrup; pour into pie shell.
2. Blend remaining ingredients with fingertips until mixture is crumbly; then spread over surface.

3. Bake 30 minutes (with foil underneath in case pie bubbles over).
4. Let cool on rack; serve cold. *Makes 8 servings.*

   Editor's Note: Pie may not be thick at first; it will thicken on refrigeration.

Yellow Pea Soup
(pictured)

   1 lb dried yellow split peas
      Water
 ½ lb lean salt pork, finely chopped, or a ham bone
   5 medium onions, finely chopped
   2 tablespoons butter or margarine
   1 leek, chopped (1 cup)
 ½ teaspoon dried savory leaves
   1 teaspoon snipped chives or minced scallion
   1 teaspoon salt
 ½ teaspoon ground pepper

1. Night before, soak peas in cold water to cover. Store, covered, in refrigerator.
2. Next day, drain and wash peas. In a 6-quart kettle, cover peas with 1 quart water.
3. Add salt pork and half of chopped onion to kettle. Bring to boiling; reduce heat and boil gently, covered, 1½ hours. Add more water (about 2 cups) as needed during cooking.
4. In hot butter, cook remaining chopped onion and the leek until just tender—several minutes. Add to kettle with savory, chives, salt, pepper and 2 cups water.
5. Bring back to boiling; reduce heat and boil gently, covered, about 30 minutes, or until peas are tender. *Makes 2½ to 3 quarts.*

Marie Lamarre's Tourtière
(pictured)

1½ lb ground pork
 ½ cup finely chopped onion
 ½ cup water
   2 large potatoes (1 lb)
 ½ teaspoon salt
 ¼ teaspoon ground allspice
 ¼ teaspoon ground cloves
 ⅛ teaspoon ground pepper
      Pastry for a 2-crust, 9-inch pie
   1 egg yolk
   2 tablespoons water

The Fabulous French Influence

1. In a medium saucepan, combine pork, onion and ½ cup water; mix well. Cook, covered, over very low heat 2 hours.
2. Meanwhile, peel potatoes; quarter. Cook in small amount of boiling salted water until tender; drain.
3. Add potato to meat mixture, along with salt, allspice, cloves and pepper; mash with a potato masher.
4. Preheat oven to 450F. Roll half of pastry to make an 11-inch circle; fit into bottom of a 9-inch pie plate. Turn meat mixture into shell.
5. Roll other half of pastry to make an 11-inch circle. Adjust pastry over top; crimp edges; make several slits in top for steam vents. Mix egg yolk with 2 tablespoons water; use to brush over pastry. Bake 20 minutes, or until pastry is golden-brown. Serve warm or cold. *Makes 6 servings.*

Chicken in Wine
(pictured)

```
3   (2 lb-size) whole broiler-fryers
2   tablespoons salad oil
2   tablespoons butter or margarine
1   medium onion, thinly sliced
¼   cup chopped celery leaves
3   small bay leaves
¼   teaspoon dried thyme leaves
¼   teaspoon dried marjoram leaves
1   whole clove
1   can (1 lb) tomatoes, drained
2   teaspoons salt
¼   teaspoon ground pepper
1¼  cups sherry
3   tablespoons all-purpose flour
```

1. Wash chickens under cold running water; dry well on paper towels. Wash giblets; set aside.
2. To hot oil and butter in a 7-quart Dutch oven, add onion, celery leaves, bay leaves, thyme, marjoram and clove; mix well. Sauté until lightly browned—about 5 minutes. Add chickens; brown well, turning to brown all over. (Brown one or two at a time, if necessary—each chicken will take about 15 minutes to brown.)
3. Add drained tomatoes, 1 teaspoon salt and the pepper with chicken giblets (except livers). Simmer gently, covered, 1 hour. Add livers and 1 cup sherry; cook 15 minutes longer.
4. Lift chickens to serving platter; keep warm. Strain broth. Cup up livers and reserve; save remaining giblets for another use. Dissolve flour in ¼ cup sherry; stir into broth. Bring to boiling, stirring until thickened. Stir in cut-up chicken livers and 1 teaspoon salt. Serve with chickens. *Makes 6 servings.*

Pecan Pralines
(pictured)

```
1    cup granulated sugar
1    cup firmly packed light-brown sugar
½    cup light cream or half-and-half
1½   cups pecan halves
2    tablespoons butter or margarine
```

1. In heavy 2-quart saucepan, combine sugars and cream. Over medium heat, bring to boiling, stirring occasionally with wooden spoon. Continue cooking, stirring occasionally, to 228F on candy thermometer, or until syrup spins a 2-inch thread when dropped from spoon.
2. Add pecans and butter. Cook over medium heat, stirring frequently, to 236F on candy thermometer, or until a little in cold water forms a soft ball.
3. Remove from heat to wire rack. Let cool 10 minutes to 200F; stir till slightly thick but still glossy.
4. Drop by rounded tablespoonfuls, 2 inches apart, onto buttered cookie sheet or double thickness of waxed paper. Pralines will spread into large patties. If mixture becomes too stiff, stir in a small amount of cold water. *Makes 1 dozen.*

Chicken Creole
(pictured)

```
2    tablespoons butter or margarine
     3- to 3½-lb ready-to-cook broiler-fryer, cut in
     serving pieces
1    cup sliced onion
2    cloves garlic, crushed
2    tablespoons all-purpose flour
1    can (1 lb) tomatoes, undrained
1    teaspoon dried thyme leaves
2    teaspoons chopped parsley
2    bay leaves
1½   teaspoons salt
¼    teaspoon hot red-pepper sauce
3    cups chopped green pepper
```

1. In hot butter in large skillet, sauté chicken until golden-brown; remove pieces as they brown.
2. Add onion and garlic to drippings and sauté until soft—about 5 minutes. Remove from heat. Blend in flour until smooth.
3. Stir in tomatoes, thyme, parsley, bay leaves, salt and red-pepper sauce. Add browned chicken pieces.
4. Cook, covered, over low heat, 15 minutes; stir occasionally.
5. Add green pepper. Cook, covered, over low heat 30 minutes longer, or until chicken is tender. *Makes 4 servings.*

The Fabulous French Influence

Creole Jambalaya
(pictured)

2 tablespoons butter or margarine
½ cup chopped onion
1 clove garlic, crushed
¼ lb cooked ham, diced (¾ cup)
1 can (1 lb) tomatoes, undrained
¾ cup canned condensed chicken broth, undiluted
1½ lb raw shrimp, shelled and deveined
1 tablespoon chopped parsley
1 bay leaf
1 teaspoon salt
¼ teaspoon dried thyme leaves
½ teaspoon hot red-pepper sauce
⅛ teaspoon ground pepper
1 cup long-grain white rice

1. Preheat oven to 350F.
2. In hot butter in Dutch oven, sauté onion until soft—about 5 minutes. Add garlic and ham; sauté 5 minutes longer.
3. Stir in tomatoes, chicken broth, shrimp, parsley, bay leaf, salt, thyme, red-pepper sauce and pepper. Bring to boiling, covered.
4. Pour into a 2-quart casserole. Sprinkle rice over top of mixture; gently press into liquid just until rice is covered—do not stir. Cover.
5. Bake 40 minutes, or until rice is tender and liquid is absorbed. Toss gently before serving. *Makes 6 servings.*

Creole Doughnuts
(pictured)

½ cup boiling water
¼ cup granulated sugar
2 tablespoons shortening
½ teaspoon salt
½ cup evaporated milk, undiluted
1 teaspoon active dry yeast (about ½ pkg)
¼ cup warm water (105 to 115F)
1 egg, beaten
3½ cups sifted all-purpose flour

Salad oil or shortening for deep-frying
Confectioners' sugar

1. Pour boiling water over granulated sugar, shortening and salt in large bowl; stir until sugar is dissolved. Add milk. Let cool to lukewarm.
2. Sprinkle yeast over warm water in small bowl; stir to dissolve. Stir into milk mixture with egg.
3. Add 2 cups flour; beat with a wooden spoon until smooth. Add remaining flour, beating dough about 2 minutes or until smooth—dough will be soft.
4. Place dough in lightly greased bowl; turn to bring up greased side. Cover with waxed paper and towel. Refrigerate until well chilled—about 4 hours.
5. In electric skillet or heavy saucepan, slowly heat salad oil (from 1½ to 2 inches deep) to 360F on deep-frying thermometer.
6. Meanwhile, remove dough from refrigerator; divide in half; return half to refrigerator until ready to use. On lightly floured surface, roll out other half of dough into 9-by-8-inch rectangle; cut into 20 pieces.
7. Gently drop pieces, 4 at a time, into hot oil. As they rise to surface, turn with slotted utensil. Fry until golden-brown on both sides—about 3 minutes in all. Repeat with other half of dough.
8. Drain on paper towels. Sprinkle with confectioners' sugar. Serve warm. *Makes 40.*

Strawberry Cookie-Shell Sundaes
(pictured)

1 pint fresh strawberries (see Note)
½ cup granulated sugar

Cookie Shells

1 egg
⅓ cup sifted confectioners' sugar
2 tablespoons brown sugar
¼ teaspoon vanilla extract
¼ cup sifted all-purpose flour
   Dash salt
2 tablespoons melted butter or margarine
2 tablespoons chopped pecans

1 quart vanilla ice cream
½ cup chopped pecans

The Fabulous French Influence

1. Wash strawberries; slice. Add granulated sugar. Refrigerate.
2. Preheat oven to 300F. Grease and flour 2 cookie sheets.
3. Make Cookie Shells: In medium bowl, with electric mixer, beat egg until soft peaks form when beaters are raised. With a wire whisk or rubber spatula, gradually stir in confectioners' sugar and brown sugar, folding until sugars dissolve. Add vanilla.
4. Stir in flour and salt, mixing well. Gradually blend in butter and 2 tablespoons pecans.
5. Spoon about 2 tablespoons batter onto prepared cookie sheet. Spread thin, to make 5-inch round. Make 2 more rounds on cookie sheet and 3 rounds on other cookie sheet.
6. Bake, one sheet at a time, 12 minutes. Remove hot cookies from sheet with broad spatula. Mold each cookie, bottom side down, over outside of 6-ounce custard cup to form shell. Cool.
7. To serve: Fill shells with ice cream. Spoon strawberries over ice cream. Top with chopped nuts. *Makes 6 servings.*

Note: Or use 1 package (10 ounces) frozen sliced strawberries, thawed. Omit sugar.

Bananas Foster

¼ cup (½ stick) butter or margarine
½ cup firmly packed light-brown sugar
4 ripe bananas, peeled and split lengthwise
⅛ teaspoon ground cinnamon
½ cup white rum
¼ cup banana liqueur (crème de banana)
   Vanilla ice cream or sweetened whipped cream

1. Melt butter and brown sugar in flat chafing dish or attractive skillet. Add bananas in a single layer and sauté, turning once, until tender—about 5 minutes.
2. Sprinkle with cinnamon; pour in rum and banana liqueur. Ignite with match; remove from heat and baste bananas until the flame burns out.
3. Serve at once, with vanilla ice cream or sweetened whipped cream. *Makes 4 servings.*

Mrs. Simmons' Pecan Pie

¼ cup (½ stick) butter or margarine
½ cup sugar
3 eggs
½ cup light corn syrup
½ cup dark cane syrup (see Note)
1 teaspoon vanilla extract
   Dash salt
1 cup chopped pecans
2 teaspoons grated orange peel (optional)
   9-inch unbaked pie shell
½ cup pecan halves
   Whipped cream

1. Preheat oven to 350F.
2. In large bowl, let butter soften to room temperature. Add sugar and beat until light, using electric mixer or wooden spoon.
3. Add eggs, one at a time, beating until light and fluffy, not foamy.
4. Add both syrups, vanilla, salt, chopped pecans and orange peel; mix until well blended.
5. Turn into pie shell. Sprinkle with pecan halves. Bake 45 minutes, or until firm when gently shaken.
6. Let cool on wire rack. Serve with whipped cream. *Makes 6 to 8 servings.*

Note: Dark cane syrup is available in specialty markets.

Mrs. Simmons' Chocolate Whip

1 env unflavored gelatine
¼ cup cold water
1 pkg (6 oz) semisweet chocolate pieces
½ cup milk
¼ cup sugar
⅛ teaspoon salt
1 teaspoon vanilla extract
4 eggs, separated

½ cup heavy cream, whipped

1. Sprinkle gelatine over ¼ cup cold water in measuring cup to soften.
2. Combine chocolate pieces, milk, sugar and salt in top of double boiler. Heat over hot, not boiling, water,

The Fabulous French Influence

stirring occasionally, until chocolate is melted. Stir in softened gelatine; heat until melted. Add vanilla.

3. Beat egg yolks in medium bowl until thick and lemon-colored. Stir into chocolate-gelatine mixture until well blended. Heat 2 minutes.
4. Remove from heat; cool at room temperature 30 to 45 minutes, or until consistency of unbeaten egg white.
5. Beat egg whites until stiff peaks form when beaters are raised. Fold into cooled chocolate-gelatine mixture.
6. Gently turn into a 1-quart mold, spreading evenly.
7. Refrigerate several hours, or until firmly set.
8. To unmold: Loosen around edge with small spatula. Invert over serving platter; shake gently to release. If necessary, place a hot, damp dishcloth over mold; shake again to release. Decorate with whipped cream. Refrigerate until serving time. *Makes 6 servings.*

Miss Ruth's Praline Cookies

1 cup firmly packed light-brown sugar
1 tablespoon all-purpose flour
¼ teaspoon salt
1 egg white
1 teaspoon vanilla extract
2 cups pecan halves

1. Sift brown sugar, flour and salt onto a sheet of waxed paper.
2. With rotary beater, beat egg white in a small bowl just until stiff but not dry. With rubber spatula, fold in sugar mixture and vanilla.
3. Preheat oven to 275F. Grease several cookie sheets well.
4. Add egg-white mixture to pecans in a large bowl. Gently fold together, to coat pecans completely with mixture.
5. Drop by tablespoonfuls on prepared cookie sheet, to make 24 cookies. Bake 25 to 30 minutes, or until lightly browned.
6. With spatula, remove cookies at once to wire rack to cool. *Makes 24 cookies.*

Papin's Club Sauce for Steak

6 tablespoons Dijon mustard
6 tablespoons Worcestershire sauce
10 tablespoons (1 stick plus 2 tablespoons) butter

1. In small saucepan, combine mustard, Worcestershire and butter.

2. Place over low heat, stirring constantly, until butter is melted and sauce is hot. Do not boil. *Makes 1⅓ cups.*

Coquilles St. Jacques

1 lb bay or sea scallops
½ lb mushrooms, washed and sliced
¾ cup dry white wine
½ bay leaf
2 parsley sprigs
½ small onion, chopped
¼ teaspoon salt
⅛ teaspoon ground pepper

Sauce

3 tablespoons butter or margarine
¼ cup all-purpose flour
½ teaspoon salt
¼ teaspoon ground pepper
¾ cup milk
¼ cup heavy cream
2 egg yolks, slightly beaten
1 tablespoon lemon juice

½ cup packaged dry bread crumbs
2 tablespoons butter or margarine, melted
6 tablespoons grated Parmesan cheese

1. Wash and dry scallops; if using sea scallops, cut into quarters.
2. In large skillet, combine scallops, mushrooms, wine, bay leaf, parsley, onion, ¼ teaspoon salt and ⅛ teaspoon pepper; simmer gently 5 minutes.
3. Strain; reserve stock; reserve scallops and mushrooms.
4. Make Sauce: In large heavy saucepan, melt 3 tablespoons butter; remove from heat. Stir in flour, salt and pepper; heat gently until mixture bubbles.
5. Remove from heat; stir in 1 cup reserved stock and the milk. Bring to boiling; cook, stirring, until slightly thickened.
6. Add cream to egg yolks; mix well. Stir in a little of hot sauce; mix well; pour back into rest of sauce, stirring.
7. Cook, stirring, 1 to 2 minutes.
8. Remove from heat; stir in scallops, mushrooms and lemon juice; mix well.
9. Turn into six scallop shells or six (4-inch) round baking dishes.
10. Toss crumbs with melted butter; sprinkle over top, along with Parmesan cheese.
11. Place baking dishes on cookie sheet; place under broiler several minutes to brown top and heat through. *Makes 6 servings.*

The Fabulous French Influence

Menu

*Tarte à Pâté**
(Pâté Tart)
*Poule au Pot**
(Poached Chicken With Vegetables)
*Artichauts à la Mayonnaise**
(Leaf Artichokes With Mayonnaise)
*Gâteau au Chocolat**
(Chocolate Cake)
Café   Beaujolais

Pâté Tart

9-inch unbaked pie shell
3 cans (4¾-oz size) liver pâté
¼ cup minced onion
2 cloves garlic, crushed
Ground nutmeg
2 eggs
1 cup heavy cream
½ teaspoon salt
Dash ground red pepper
1 cup finely grated natural Swiss cheese (¼ lb)
⅓ cup grated Parmesan cheese

1. Prepare pie shell; refrigerate until ready to use.
2. Preheat oven to 375F.
3. In medium bowl, combine pâté, onion, garlic and ¼ teaspoon nutmeg; mix well. Spread evenly over bottom of pie shell.
4. In medium bowl, with rotary beater, beat eggs with cream, salt, dash nutmeg and red pepper until well combined but not frothy. Stir in cheeses.
5. Pour into pie shell; bake 40 to 45 minutes or until top is golden and firm when pressed with fingertip.
6. Let cool in pan on wire rack about 1 hour. Serve warm, cut into wedges. *Makes 6 to 8 servings.*

Poached Chicken With Vegetables

4- to 5-lb ready-to-cook roasting chicken, with giblets
Salt
⅛ teaspoon ground pepper
¼ cup (½ stick) butter or margarine
8 leeks
1½ to 2 lb small carrots, pared
1½ lb small new potatoes, pared
¼ cup (½ stick) butter or margarine, melted
4 teaspoons all-purpose flour
½ cup dry white wine
½ cup canned chicken broth
2 bunches chives
Chopped parsley

1. Remove giblets from chicken; rinse and set aside on paper towels. Rinse chicken well; dry with paper towels. Sprinkle inside with 1½ teaspoons salt and the pepper. Tuck wings under body; tie legs together. If necessary, fasten skin at neck with a skewer.
2. In ¼ cup hot butter in Dutch oven, brown chicken well all over—takes about 30 minutes. Turn chicken carefully with two wooden spoons—do not break skin.
3. Meanwhile, coarsely chop giblets. Wash leeks well; cut off roots and discard. Remove some of top leaves and add to giblets. Then halve leeks crosswise and set aside.
4. Place giblet-leek mixture under browned chicken. Cover tightly and simmer over low heat 30 minutes.
5. Arrange carrots (halved, if necessary) around the chicken; simmer, covered, 40 minutes longer or until chicken and carrots are tender. Remove from heat.
6. Meanwhile, cook potatoes in 1 inch boiling water in medium saucepan, covered, 20 to 25 minutes or until tender. Drain; then drizzle with 2 tablespoons melted butter.
7. Cook halved leeks in 1 inch boiling water in medium saucepan, covered, 10 minutes or until tender. Drain and drizzle with 2 tablespoons melted butter.
8. Carefully remove chicken and carrots to heated platter; keep warm.
9. Strain drippings; return to Dutch oven. Stir in flour until smooth. Gradually stir in wine and chicken broth; bring to boiling. Reduce heat and simmer 3 minutes. Taste and add salt, if needed.
10. To serve: Arrange potatoes, leeks and bunches of chives around chicken and carrots. Sprinkle potatoes with parsley. Pass gravy. *Makes 4 to 6 servings.*

Leaf Artichokes With Mayonnaise

¼ cup salad or olive oil
2 tablespoons lemon juice
1 clove garlic, split
1 teaspoon salt
Dash ground pepper
4 large artichokes (about 3 lb)

Tarragon Sauce

1 cup mayonnaise or cooked salad dressing
2 tablespoons lemon juice
½ teaspoon dried tarragon leaves
4 mushroom caps, dipped in lemon juice (optional)

*Recipes given for starred dishes.

The Fabulous French Influence

1. In large kettle, combine 6 quarts water with the oil, 2 tablespoons lemon juice, the garlic, salt and pepper; bring to boiling.
2. Meanwhile, trim stalk from base of artichokes; cut a 1-inch slice from top of each. Remove discolored leaves; snip off spike ends of leaves.
3. Wash artichokes in cold water; drain. Tie twine around each to hold leaves in place.
4. Add to boiling water mixture. Reduce heat and simmer, covered, 30 minutes or until bases of artichokes feel soft. Drain well and remove twine. Cool; then refrigerate until serving time.
5. Meanwhile, make Tarragon Sauce: In small bowl, combine mayonnaise with 2 tablespoons lemon juice and the tarragon; mix well. Refrigerate, covered.
6. To serve: Top each chilled artichoke with a mushroom cap. Arrange on large platter or individual serving dishes. Serve the sauce in individual dishes. *Makes 4 servings.*

Chocolate Cake

4 eggs
4 bars (4-oz size) sweet cooking chocolate
½ cup (1 stick) unsalted butter, softened
4 teaspoons sugar
4 teaspoons all-purpose flour
Chocolate curls (optional)

1. Lightly grease a 9-by-5-by-3-inch loaf pan; line with waxed paper. Separate eggs, placing whites and yolks in large bowls. Let whites warm to room temperature—about 1 hour.
2. Preheat oven to 425F.
3. In top of double boiler, melt chocolate over hot, not boiling, water, stirring occasionally. Remove from water; beat in butter with spoon.
4. Meanwhile, with portable electric mixer, beat egg whites until stiff peaks form when beaters are slowly raised. Set aside.
5. With same beaters, beat yolks until thick and lemon-colored. Slowly add sugar, beating constantly. Add flour; beat just until blended.
6. Stir into chocolate mixture. Then, with rubber spatula or a wire whisk, gently fold chocolate mixture into beaten egg white.

7. Turn into prepared pan. Reduce oven temperature to 350F. Bake 25 minutes.
8. Let cool completely in pan on wire rack. Cake will settle like a cheesecake. Refrigerate until well chilled—about 4 hours.
9. To serve: Loosen cake; remove from pan by inverting on serving plate. If desired, decorate with chocolate curls. Cut cake into ¾-inch slices. *Makes 16 servings.*

Note: This is a heavy, rich, moist cake, almost like a pudding, that keeps well under refrigeration.

Crêpes Soufflés
(The Pontchartrain Hotel, New Orleans, Louisiana)

Crêpes

2 eggs
1 cup sifted all-purpose flour
1 cup milk
1 tablespoon vanilla extract
1 teaspoon butter or margarine, melted

Sauce

3 egg yolks
½ cup granulated sugar
½ cup milk
¼ light cream or half-and-half
¼ teaspoon ground mace
¼ cup golden rum

Soufflé Filling

3 egg whites
1 cup confectioners' sugar
½ teaspoon grated orange peel
¼ teaspoon vanilla extract
⅛ teaspoon almond extract
⅛ teaspoon yellow food color (optional)

1. Make Crêpes: In medium bowl, beat 2 eggs well. Add flour, 1 cup milk, 1 tablespoon vanilla and the butter. Stir until smooth.
2. For each crêpe, lightly grease hot 7-inch skillet. Pour in about 2 tablespoons batter, rotating pan quickly to spread batter completely over bottom of pan.
3. Cook over medium heat until lightly brown on each side—about 2 minutes per side. Place crêpes on a plate as they are removed from skillet. (Stack crêpes, if desired, with pieces of waxed paper between them.)

The Fabulous French Influence

4. Make Sauce: Place egg yolks in top of double boiler; gradually stir in granulated sugar, milk, cream and mace. Cook over simmering water, stirring constantly, until thickened—about 10 minutes. Remove from water; stir in rum. Keep warm.
5. Make Soufflé Filling: In small bowl, with electric mixer at low speed, beat egg whites for 3 minutes. Gradually beat in confectioners' sugar; continue beating about 10 minutes, until stiff peaks form when beaters are slowly raised.
6. Add orange peel, extracts and yellow food color; beat until well blended.
7. Preheat oven to 450F.
8. Spoon about 2 rounded tablespoons filling on center of each crêpe; fold in half, keeping filling inside. Place in shallow pan.
9. Bake, uncovered, 5 minutes or until very hot and puffed. Spoon a little sauce over crêpes. Pass remaining sauce. *Makes 6 servings (12 crêpes).*

Cherries Jubilee

1 can (1 lb, 14 oz) pitted dark sweet cherries in extra-heavy syrup
1 cup brandy
¼ cup sugar
¼ cup currant jelly
1 quart vanilla ice cream

1. Drain cherries, reserving ½ cup syrup. Turn cherries into a small bowl.
2. In small saucepan, combine reserved syrup, ½ cup brandy and the sugar. Bring to boiling; reduce heat and simmer, uncovered, until mixture thickens slightly and is reduced to ½ cup. Pour over cherries. Let stand several hours.
3. Just before serving, in small saucepan, heat cherries in syrup until hot. Add currant jelly; stir until melted. Stir in 6 tablespoons brandy. Pour mixture into a small silver bowl.
4. Pour remaining 2 tablespoons brandy into ladle; heat over low heat just until vapor rises. Ignite with a match and lower ladle of flaming brandy into cherries. When flame fades, ladle cherry mixture over individual servings of ice cream. *Makes 8 servings.*

Pain Perdu

2 eggs
½ cup granulated sugar
1 cup milk
1 teaspoon vanilla extract
½ teaspoon grated lemon peel
8 slices day-old French bread (1 inch thick)
2 tablespoons butter or margarine

Confectioners' sugar
Ground nutmeg

1. In small bowl, with rotary beater, beat eggs with granulated sugar. Stir in milk, vanilla and lemon peel.
2. Arrange bread in single layer in shallow dish. Pour egg mixture over slices. Let stand 30 minutes.
3. In hot butter in large skillet, sauté bread until golden-brown—about 6 minutes per side.
4. Arrange on serving platter. Sprinkle with confectioners' sugar and nutmeg . Nice with preserves or syrup. *Makes 4 servings.*

Marc's Omelet
Recipe from Doris Hamel, Québec, Canada.

2 tablespoons butter or margarine
¼ cup green scallions, snipped with scissors
10 fresh mushrooms, washed and coarsely chopped
1 medium tomato, washed and thickly sliced
6 eggs
¼ cup milk
½ teaspoon salt
¼ teaspoon ground pepper
¼ lb sliced brick cheese

1. Preheat oven to 350F. In an omelet pan or 9-inch skillet (see Note), heat butter. Add scallions, mushrooms and tomato slices; cook slowly.
2. Beat eggs with milk, salt and pepper just to combine. Pour over vegetables; cook until almost set.
3. Place cheese slices on top to cover completely. Place in oven until cheese melts. Serve at once, in wedges. *Makes 6 servings.*

Note: Skillet should have a heat-resistant handle. ■

CHAPTER

3

THE BEST OF PARTIES

✸

Think back to the last great party you attended or gave and what made it so memorable. Was it simply being with old friends and family? Was it the special occasion that drew you all together? Was it the gorgeous weather and setting? Or the witty conversation and fabulous food? The answer is probably a combination of all the above, because the secret of a successful party is a friendly group of people gathered anywhere to share good times and good food. We want your next party to be your most memorable, and so we selected for this chapter only the very best of our entertaining themes, recipes, menus and tips. Please accept our invitation to make the most of them.

Picnic Salad

Pots de Crème

Cold
Veal-And-H

Rose-Wine Spritzer

Fresh-Fruit
Melon-Go-Round

GEORGE RATKAI/PAUL DOME

Entertaining In the Great Outdoors

There's something about open-air dining that makes every morsel of food taste wonderful. Whether you choose to step out onto your own patio or journey to a favorite park or secluded beach, you're sure to have a delightful day with the help of our entertaining menus, which begin on page 140.

Picnic in the Park

Left: Europeans long ago learned that *le pique-nique* can be as artful and elegant as the most formal dining-room luncheon. Spread a colorful cloth on any grassy stretch of garden or woodland and serve this memorable meal of Veal-And-Ham Pie, salad, fresh fruits, luscious Pots de Crème and the Continental go-alongs: crusty bread, cheese and wine.

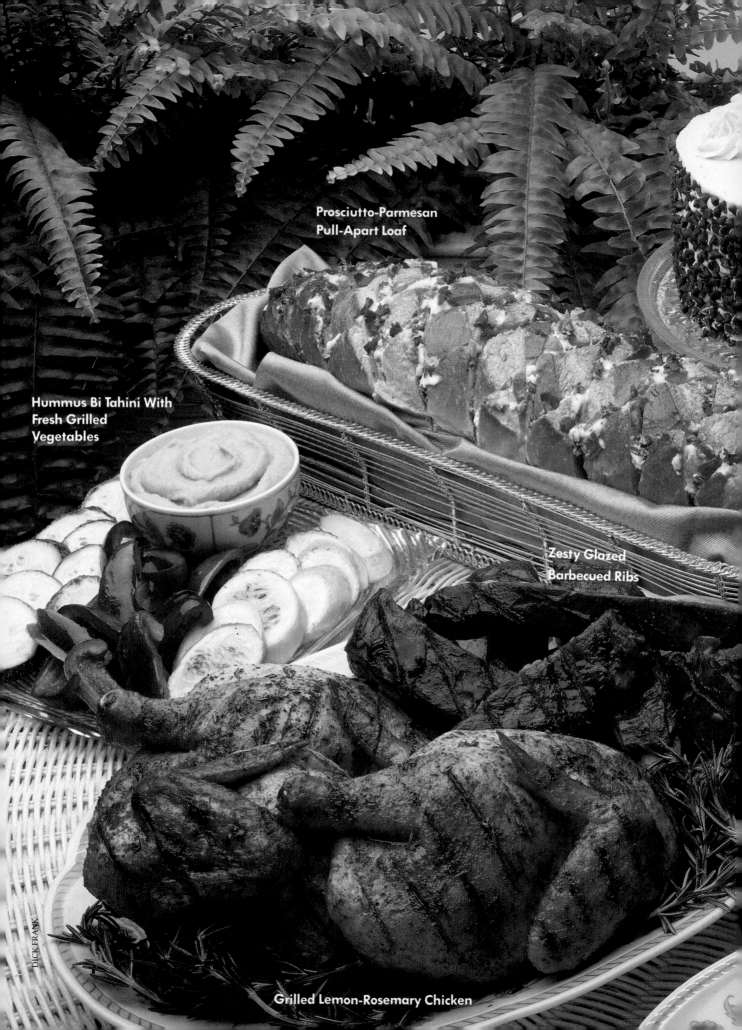

Prosciutto-Parmesan
Pull-Apart Loaf

Hummus Bi Tahini With
Fresh Grilled
Vegetables

Zesty Glazed
Barbecued Ribs

DICK FRANK

Grilled Lemon-Rosemary Chicken

Backyard Barbecue

Fire up the grill and let the tantalizing aroma of Southwest-style ribs and crisp Lemon-Rosemary Chicken halves beckon your guests to this fun-filled feast. *Recipes begin on page 142.*

White-Grape Spritzer

Orange-Chocolate-Chip Chiffon Cake

Sesame-Noodle-Stuffed Tomatoes

Shrimp-Crowned Avocado Mold

Chili-Cheese Cornsticks

All-American Blueberry Tartlets

Celery Slaw

Chicken Twists With Tarragon-Avocado Dipping Sauce

Marinated Seafood Wraps

Seaside Spread

Above: This easy-to-prepare fare is perfect to pack and tote to the beach, where you'll relish everything in the picnic hamper from savory Chicken Twists to Chili-Cheese Cornsticks and mini blueberry pies. *Recipes begin on page 146.*

Patio Party

At Right: Alfresco dining with a light touch: a swirl of delicious and refreshing flavors, from smoky to sweet, all guaranteed to please as an afternoon or evening repast. *Recipes being on page 148.*

Pineapple-Glazed Baba

Fresh-Fruit Gazpacho

Smoked-Turkey Salad

Almond-Butter Brie

Crunchy Marinated
Vegetables

Entertaining in the Great Outdoors

continued from page 135

A Picnic in the Park

(Planned for 8)
Cold Veal-And-Ham Pie*
Picnic Salad*
French Bread   Wedge of Blue Cheese
Pots de Crème*
Fresh-Fruit Melon-Go-Round*
Rosé-Wine Spritzer*   *Iced Tea*

Cold Veal-And-Ham Pie
(pictured)

1½ **lb veal cutlets, ¼ inch thick**
    1- lb fully cooked ham slice, ½ inch thick
  2 **tablespoons finely chopped onion**
  2 **tablespoons finely chopped parsley**
 ½ **teaspoon salt**
 ¼ **teaspoon dried marjoram leaves**
 ¼ **teaspoon dried thyme leaves**
    Dash ground pepper
1½ **pkg (9.5-oz size) piecrust mix**
  1 **can (4½ oz) deviled ham**
  4 **hard-cooked eggs, shelled**
  1 **egg, slightly beaten**
  1 **env unflavored gelatine**
  1 **cup chicken broth**

1. Wipe veal with damp paper towels. Cut into 12 pieces as even in size as possible; pound each with mallet. Trim excess fat from ham. Cut ham into strips 2 inches by ¾ inch.
2. In small bowl, combine onion, parsley, salt, marjoram, thyme and pepper; blend well.
3. Preheat oven to 350F.
4. Prepare piecrust mix as package label directs. Shape into a ball; remove one-third pastry and set aside.
5. On lightly floured surface, roll out larger portion of pastry into a 12-inch circle. Set aside trimmings. Use to line a 9-inch, deep, fluted pie plate, letting pastry stand up around edge.

6. Roll out remaining pastry into an 11-inch circle. Set aside trimmings. Then roll out all trimmings and cut into diamond-shaped pieces, about 1 inch wide and 1¼ inches long, to decorate top of pie.
7. Spread deviled ham over pastry in pie plate. Arrange half of veal in pie plate; sprinkle with half of herb mixture; then add half of ham strips. Arrange whole hardcooked eggs in center, spoke fashion. Repeat layering, mounding in center over eggs and using rest of veal, herb mixture and ham.
8. Adjust 11-inch pastry circle over filling. Fold edge of bottom crust over top crust; press the edges together to seal well; crimp decoratively. With tip of sharp paring knife, cut a 1½-inch round hole in center for steam vent.
9. Arrange diamond-shaped pastry pieces on top, as pictured. Brush with beaten egg.
10. Bake 1½ hours.
11. Meanwhile, sprinkle gelatine over chicken broth in small saucepan; let stand to soften. Heat, stirring, until gelatine is dissolved. Let stand at room temperature.
12. Let pie cool on wire rack 30 minutes. Then slowly pour broth mixture through a small funnel into center of pie. Let cool 2 hours longer; then refrigerate, loosely covered, overnight. *Makes 8 to 10 servings.*

Note: If traveling to picnic, remove pie from refrigerator just before leaving and carry in cooler or insulated bag. Remember to take a pie server.

Picnic Salad
(pictured)

  1 **large head romaine**
  3 **Belgian endives**
  2 **pint boxes cherry tomatoes**
 ½ **teaspoon dried tarragon leaves**
  1 **bottle (8 oz) Italian-style salad dressing or herb-and-garlic French dressing**

1. Day before serving: Wash romaine and endives; separate into leaves. Halve lengthwise large outer leaves of romaine. Spin-dry greens or pat dry with paper

Recipes given for starred dishes.

Entertaining in the Great Outdoors

towels. Refrigerate separately in plastic bags in crisper. Wash and dry tomatoes and refrigerate in plastic bag.

2. Add tarragon to salad dressing; shake well. Refrigerate.

3. To serve: Mound tomatoes in center of salad bowl; line side of bowl first with romaine leaves, then with endive leaves. Pour dressing into 8 to 10 paper soufflé cups (one per person) for dipping greens. *Makes 8 to 10 servings.*

Note: If traveling to picnic, pack greens, tomatoes and dressing in cooler just before leaving. Arrange bowl of salad at picnic spot.

Pots de Crème

(pictured)

3 cups (1½ pts) heavy cream
½ cup sugar
1 tablespoon vanilla extract
5 egg yolks
2 squares (1-oz size) semisweet chocolate
Sweetened whipped cream (optional)

1. Preheat oven to 325F.
2. In medium saucepan, combine cream and sugar; cook over medium heat, stirring occasionally, until sugar is dissolved and mixture is hot. Remove from heat; stir in vanilla.
3. In medium bowl, with wire whisk or rotary beater, beat egg yolks until blended but not frothy. Gradually add hot cream mixture, beating constantly.
4. Strain into 8 (5-oz) or 10 (3-oz) ungreased soufflé dishes or custard cups. Place in shallow pan; pour hot water to ½-inch level around dishes.
5. Bake 30 minutes or until mixture just begins to set around edges. Remove from water. Let cool 30 minutes on wire racks; then refrigerate, each covered with plastic wrap or foil, until well chilled—4 hours or overnight.
6. To serve: Garnish each with chocolate curls made from semisweet chocolate squares. If desired, pass sweetened whipped cream. *Makes 8 to 10 servings.*

Note: If traveling to picnic spot, remove pots de crème from refrigerator just before leaving, and carry in cooler.

Fresh-Fruit Melon-Go-Round

(pictured)

1 large Spanish or honeydew melon
8 unpeeled nectarines or peaches
1½ lb grapes
Fresh mint sprigs

1. Using sharp knife, cut ¼-inch slice from bottom of melon. Halve melon lengthwise; cut each half into 5 even wedges. Remove seeds.
2. Use a round serving platter, 9 inches in diameter and about ½ inch deep. Stand wedges, cut end down, to resemble a whole melon, holding wedges together at top, while placing a nectarine at base of alternate slices, to hold melon in place. Gently pull out the slices not held by nectarines (see picture). Secure top of wedges with wooden picks.
3. Garnish with remaining nectarines, small bunches of grapes and mint sprigs. *Makes 8 servings.*

Note: If traveling to picnic, assemble fruit plate at home; cover with plastic wrap and refrigerate until leaving. Carry the fruit plate in a basket.

Rosé-Wine Spritzer

(pictured)

1 bottle (25.6 fl oz) rosé wine, chilled
1 bottle (12 oz) club soda, chilled
1 large lemon
1 lemon wedge

1. Pour rosé wine and club soda into large pitcher; stir just to combine.
2. Using a sharp knife, remove skin from lemon in one spiral. Spear one end of spiral with metal skewer. Wind peel around skewer and spear other end. Top with lemon wedge. Stand in pitcher.
3. Serve in wineglasses or tall, ice-filled glasses. *Makes about 6 (6-oz) servings.*

Note: If traveling to picnic, carry wine and soda in cooler. Prepare at picnic spot.

Entertaining in the Great Outdoors

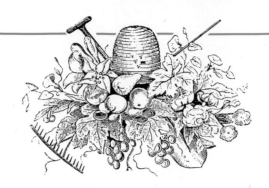

Backyard Barbecue

(Planned for 8)

Shrimp-Crowned Avocado Mold*
Hummus Bi Tahini
With Fresh Grilled Vegetables*
White-Grape Spritzer*
Zesty Glazed Barbecued Ribs*
Grilled Lemon-Rosemary Chicken*
Prosciutto-Parmesan Pull-Apart Loaf*
Tossed Green Salad
Sesame-Noodle-Stuffed Tomatoes*
Orange-Chocolate-Chip Chiffon Cake*

Shrimp-Crowned Avocado Mold
(pictured)

2 env unflavored gelatine
⅓ cup water
3 tablespoons lemon juice
4 large ripe avocados
1 small onion, quartered (see Note)
2 medium cloves garlic, halved (see Note)
1 teaspoon salt
⅛ teaspoon hot red-pepper sauce
1 container (8 oz) sour cream
¾ lb large shrimp
2 shallots, minced
1 medium clove garlic, minced
2 tablespoons olive or salad oil
¼ cup cry white wine
½ teaspoon salt

1. Lightly oil a 10-inch tart pan with removable bottom. In small saucepan, sprinkle gelatine over water and lemon juice; let soften 5 minutes. Meanwhile, peel avocados; remove and discard pits; place in processor or mash with fork. Add onion, halved garlic, 1 teaspoon salt and the red-pepper sauce; purée 3 minutes or until smooth and well blended, stopping processor several times to scrape side of bowl and push ingredients down into blade.

2. Over low heat, melt softened gelatine, stirring constantly. Turn processor on and slowly add gelatine through feed tube; purée 1 minute to blend thoroughly. Add sour cream and purée 15 seconds.

3. Pour avocado mixture into prepared pan; cover with plastic wrap, pressing wrap onto surface to prevent darkening. Refrigerate 3 to 5 hours. (Do not prepare day ahead.)

4. Wash shrimp thoroughly; remove and discard shells, leaving last section of tail intact; devein shrimp. In large skillet, sauté minced shallots and garlic in hot oil 1 minute. Add shrimp, white wine and salt to skillet; cook 2 to 3 minutes longer or until shrimp are pink and firm; cool 10 minutes at room temperature. Place shrimp in a bowl and cover with plastic wrap; chill until serving time.

5. Just before serving, with tip of sharp knife, loosen mold from side of pan; remove side of pan. Place large serving plate upside down over mold; invert mold onto plate; gently remove tart-pan bottom from mold. Arrange 2 shrimp upright in center of mold; arrange remaining shrimp around outer edge. *Makes 10 servings.*

Note: If mashing avocado mixture with a fork, dice the onion and mash or mince the garlic so mixture will be as smooth as possible.

Hummus Bi Tahini
With Fresh Grilled Vegetables
(pictured)

1 can (15 to 19 oz) chick-peas (garbanzos)
1 large clove garlic
3 tablespoons tahini (sesame paste)
2 tablespoons lemon juice
½ teaspoon salt
   Paprika
   Grilled Vegetables, recipe follows

1. Drain chick-peas, reserving liquid; set aside. In blender or processor, finely chop garlic and tahini.

*Recipes given for starred dishes.

Entertaining in the Great Outdoors

Add 3 tablespoons chick-pea liquid, the lemon juice and salt. Purée until smooth.

2. Add chick-peas and blend or process until smooth; add more liquid if necessary to blend smoothly. Turn into serving bowl; dust with paprika. Use as a dip for Grilled Vegetables. *Makes about 2 cups.*

Grilled Vegetables

1 medium zucchini
1 medium yellow squash
1 small eggplant
1 green pepper
1 red pepper
　Salad oil

1. Cut zucchini, yellow squash and eggplant into ½-inch-thick slices. (If the eggplant is over 2 inches in diameter, halve or quarter the slices.)
2. Cut each pepper into 1-inch-wide lengthwise strips. Brush vegetables on one side with oil.
3. To broil vegetables: Preheat broiler. Place vegetables on foil-covered jelly-roll pan. Broil, at least 4 inches from heat, 3 to 5 minutes. (Do not overcook, or vegetables will be too limp to use as dippers.) To grill vegetables: Place vegetables, oiled side down, in a metal barbecue basket in single layer; grill just until starting to brown. Serve with Hummus Bi Tahini. *Makes 8 servings.*

White-Grape Spritzer
(pictured)

5 cups ice cubes (see Note)
1 can (6 oz) frozen apple-juice concentrate, thawed
　Lemon and lime slices
1 bottle (50.7 fl oz) sparkling white-grape juice, chilled
1 bottle (33.8 fl oz) club soda, chilled

1. In 4-quart pitcher, combine 1 cup ice cubes, the apple juice and lemon and lime slices; add sparkling grape juice and club soda; stir quickly to blend juices.
2. Place remaining ice cubes in eight (12-ounce) glasses, dividing evenly; pour spritzer over ice in glasses. *Makes 8 servings.*

Note: If using a punch bowl, freeze a 6- to 8-cup ring mold of water one day before serving. At serving time, blend juices and club soda in punch bowl; unmold ice ring and float in punch bowl with lemon and lime slices. Serve in punch cups. *Makes 24 (4-ounce) servings.*

Zesty Glazed Barbecued Ribs
(pictured)

6 lb pork spareribs
2 teaspoons salt
¼ teaspoon ground pepper
　Water
1½ cups red-wine vinegar
1½ cups catsup
1 medium onion, finely chopped
3 large cloves garlic, crushed
2 tablespoons Worcestershire sauce
1 tablespoon dry mustard
2 teaspoons chili powder
¼ cup firmly packed brown sugar

1. In large kettle or saucepot, place ribs, salt and pepper; add water to cover. Over high heat, bring to boiling. Reduce heat; simmer, covered, 45 minutes. Drain, discarding liquid.
2. In each of two 13-by-9-by-2-inch baking dishes, place half the ribs. In bowl, combine 2 cups water, the vinegar, 1 cup catsup, the onion, garlic, Worcestershire, mustard and chili powder; mix well. Pour over ribs, dividing evenly; cover with plastic wrap; refrigerate 2 hours or overnight, turning occasionally.
3. Remove 1 cup marinade; combine with remaining catsup and the brown sugar; mix well.
4. Prepare outdoor grill for barbecuing or preheat indoor grill or broiler. Grill ribs, using the **indirect method** (see Barbecue Basics, this page), 6 inches from source of heat, 40 minutes, brushing every 10 minutes with the sweetened marinade. Or broil, 5 inches from heat, turning and brushing occasionally with marinade, until ribs are fork-tender—about 15 minutes. Cut ribs into one or two sections; transfer to serving platter. *Makes 8 servings.*

✳ Barbecue Basics ✳

Here's all you need to know about grilling with grandeur—and the how-to's for cooking with wood chips.

Foods can be cooked by either the **direct method**—great for searing meats such as chops, steaks and burgers—or the **indirect method,** which is best for ribs, roasts, vegetables and fish.

To barbecue using the **direct method,** simply place food over the hottest part of the fire. To barbecue using the **indirect method,** cover the grill—or wrap foods in foil—then place your food on the grill, away from the heat source. (If you're using a charcoal-type barbecue, simply arrange briquettes on one side and cook on the other.)

For really smoky, outdoor flavor, you can barbecue with wood chips, using either of the above methods; just be sure to soak the chips in water for at least 30 minutes first. With a charcoal-type grill, wait until coals are red-hot and covered with white ash; then spread chips evenly

Entertaining in the Great Outdoors

over the coals. If yours is a gas grill, preheat it at least 10 minutes on HIGH; then sprinkle on the wet chips. Start to cook food when the chips begin to smoke.

For maximum mouth-watering flavor, cover the grill to allow smoke to penetrate food fully. For even more flavor—you guessed it!—use more chips. We tested oak, ash, alder, hickory and mesquite chips and loved every single one. Alder has a delicate flavor that enhances fish and chicken dishes. Other varieties, like mesquite, impart a robust taste. The most versatile choice? Oak. It complements most kinds of food.

Note: The recipes were tested under the broiler, on a countertop grill and with both charcoal and gas grills.

Grilled Lemon-Rosemary Chicken
(pictured)

Marinade
 1 tablespoon grated lemon peel
½ cup lemon juice
½ cup white-wine vinegar
¼ cup chopped shallots
 2 tablespoons chopped fresh rosemary
 2 tablespoons Dijon-style mustard
 2 medium cloves garlic, minced
 1 teaspoon salt
½ teaspoon freshly ground black pepper
1½ cups salad oil

 4 (2½-lb size) broiler-fryer chickens, halved
    Rosemary sprigs (optional)
    Bottled dipping sauce (optional)

1. Make Marinade: In medium bowl, combine all marinade ingredients except oil; stir until mixed. Slowly pour oil into mixture, whisking until well blended.
2. Wash chickens with cold water; pat dry with paper towels.
3. In large stainless-steel or glass bowl, combine chickens with marinade; turn to coat well. Refrigerate several hours or overnight, turning chickens occasionally.
4. Prepare outdoor grill for barbecuing, or preheat indoor grill or broiler. Grill chickens, using **indirect method** (see Barbecue Basics, page 143), 6 inches from heat, brushing with marinade every 10 minutes, 20 to 30 minutes on each side. Or broil, 6 inches

from heat, 30 minutes, brushing with marinade frequently and turning once, until chickens are browned and juices run clear when leg is pierced with fork.
5. Transfer to serving plate lined with rosemary sprigs. Serve with dipping sauce. *Makes 8 servings.*

Prosciutto-Parmesan Pull-Apart Loaf
(pictured)

¾ cup (1½ sticks) butter or margarine, softened
⅓ cup grated Parmesan cheese
½ cup coarsely chopped prosciutto (2 oz)
¼ cup chopped fresh basil or ¼ cup chopped fresh parsley and 1 tablespoon dried basil leaves
 1 teaspoon freshly ground pepper
 1 loaf (1 lb) Italian bread

1. In a small bowl, combine all the ingredients except Italian bread and blend well.
2. With serrated knife, slice bread diagonally almost all the way through 12 times, at 1½-inch intervals; spread 1 rounded tablespoon prosciutto butter between sections, using half of butter mixture. Turn loaf around so that ends are reversed; slice loaf diagonally almost all the way through 12 times, making diamond patterns of 1½-inch sections of bread; spread with remaining prosciutto butter.
3. Preheat oven to 450F. Tear off a sheet of heavy-duty aluminum foil 5 inches longer than bread; center bread on foil. Fold over long sides of foil to come halfway up sides of loaf, and fold or crimp short ends of foil to secure. Heat 10 minutes or until crust is crisp and loaf is heated through.
4. To heat on grill: Bring long sides of foil together over top of bread; fold together 1 inch of foil and crease; continue folding foil until it fits loosely over bread. Repeat folding technique at short ends of foil. Place loaf, right side up, 5 to 6 inches from heat; heat 8 minutes or until loaf is heated through. *Makes 12 servings.*

Sesame-Noodle-Stuffed Tomatoes
(pictured)

 4 oz Chinese-style thin noodles or vermicelli
 1 teaspoon salad oil

Entertaining in the Great Outdoors

Sesame Dressing
- 1 tablespoon cider vinegar
- 1 tablespoon soy sauce
- 1 tablespoon sesame seeds
- 1 small clove garlic, minced
  Dash ground red pepper
- 2 tablespoons dark sesame oil
- 1 tablespoon salad oil

- 4 green onions, cut into narrow 2-inch-long strips
- 1 medium carrot, coarsely shredded
- 8 medium tomatoes
  Sesame seeds for garnish (optional)

1. Break noodles into 5-inch lengths; cook as package label directs. Drain; rinse with cold water. Toss with 1 teaspoon oil; set aside.
2. Make Sesame Dressing: In medium bowl, combine cider vinegar, soy sauce, sesame seeds, garlic and pepper; stir to mix. Slowly add sesame and salad oils, whisking until blended. Add noodles, green onion and carrot; toss to coat thoroughly with dressing. Refrigerate until ready to serve.
3. To serve: From stem end of each tomato, cut a ½-inch-thick slice. Cut thin strips from each slice around core; add strips to sesame noodles. With spoon, scoop pulp and juice from each tomato (save pulp for another use, if desired). Place tomatoes on serving plate. Fill with sesame noodles. Garnish with additional sesame seeds, if desired. *Makes 8 servings.*

Orange-Chocolate-Chip Chiffon Cake
(pictured)

- ½ cup semisweet chocolate mini pieces
- 2 cups cake flour
- 1 cup granulated sugar
- 1 tablespoon baking powder
- ½ teaspoon salt
- ½ cup salad oil
- 4 large egg yolks
- ½ cup milk
- 1 tablespoon grated orange peel
- ¼ cup orange juice
- 6 large egg whites, at room temperature
- ½ teaspoon cream of tartar

Frosting
- ¼ cup (½ stick) butter or butter-flavored shortening
- 2 large egg yolks
- 1 tablespoon grated orange peel
- 2 pkg (1-lb size) confectioners' sugar
- ¼ cup orange juice

- ½ cup orange marmalade
- 1 cup semisweet chocolate mini pieces
  Orange sections

1. Preheat oven to 350F. Cut two 9-inch circles of waxed paper. Grease two round 9-by-1½-inch layer-cake pans. Place one waxed-paper circle in bottom of each pan; grease paper.
2. In blender or food processor, chop ½ cup chocolate pieces; set aside. In large bowl, combine cake flour, granulated sugar, baking powder and salt; mix well. Make well in center; add oil, 4 egg yolks, the milk, 1 tablespoon orange peel and ¼ cup orange juice. With spoon, beat until smooth; stir in chopped chocolate pieces.
3. In large bowl, with electric mixer at high speed, beat 6 egg whites and the cream of tartar until stiff peaks form. Fold egg whites gently into batter just until blended. Pour into prepared pans; bake 30 to 35 minutes or until cake tester comes out clean. Cool in pans on wire racks 5 minutes. Remove from pans; peel off waxed paper. Cool completely.
4. Meanwhile, make Frosting: In large bowl, combine butter, 2 egg yolks, the orange peel, confectioners' sugar and orange juice. With electric mixer at medium speed, beat until mixture is smooth and spreadable. (If too thick, gradually add more orange juice.) Set aside ½ cup frosting for decorating.
5. Spread half the marmalade over bottom of each cake layer. Place one cake layer, top side down, on serving plate. Spread with ½ cup frosting. Top with second cake layer, top side up. Frost side and top with remaining frosting. With palm of hand, pat chocolate pieces onto side of cake. Spoon reserved frosting into pastry bag fitted with ½-inch star tip. Pipe swirls on top of cake; garnish with orange sections. *Makes 10 servings.*

Entertaining in the Great Outdoors

Seaside Spread

(Planned for 10)

Marinated Seafood Wraps*
Ice-Cold Beer
Chicken Twists With
Tarragon-Avocado Dipping Sauce*
Celery Slaw*
Chili-Cheese Cornsticks*
All-American Blueberry Tartlets*
Iced Coffee and Tea

Marinated Seafood Wraps
(pictured)

- 1 **lb small shrimp, in shell**
- 1 **lb medium sea scallops, halved crosswise**
- ½ **lb squid, cleaned, cut into ¼-inch slices**
- ⅔ **cup olive or salad oil**
- ⅓ **cup freshly squeezed lime or lemon juice**
- 1 **medium clove garlic, crushed**
- ½ **teaspoon salt**
- ¼ **teaspoon ground white pepper**
- ½ **lb imitation crab**
- 1 **large red pepper**
- 2 **green onions**
- 1 **large head Boston lettuce, crisped**

1. In 3-quart saucepan, bring 1½ quarts water to boiling. Add shrimp; reduce heat; cover; simmer 2 minutes. With slotted spoon, remove shrimp to strainer. Rinse with cold water; drain. Bring water in saucepan back to boiling; add scallops. Reduce heat; cover; simmer 2 minutes or until just opaque; remove scallops to strainer. Bring water in saucepan back to boiling; add squid. Reduce heat; simmer 1 minute; drain. Rinse squid with cold water; drain.
2. In large bowl, combine oil, lime juice, garlic, salt and pepper; mix well; set aside. Remove shells from shrimp and devein; cut crab into bite-size pieces. Remove and discard stem, ribs and seeds from red pepper; cut pepper into 2-by-¼-inch strips; thinly

Recipes given for starred dishes.

slice green onions. Toss shrimp, scallops, squid, crab, red pepper and onions in lime marinade; cover; refrigerate overnight. Serve in lettuce cups. *Makes 10 servings.*

Chicken Twists With
Tarragon-Avocado Dipping Sauce
(pictured)

- 1 **lb boneless chicken breasts, skinned**
- 1 **lb boneless chicken thighs, skinned**
- 1 **cup all-purpose flour**
- 2 **large eggs, beaten with 2 tablespoons water**
- 2 **to 2½ cups packaged unseasoned bread crumbs**
  Salad oil for deep frying
  Tarragon-Avocado Dipping Sauce, recipe follows

1. With flat side of meat mallet or rolling pin, pound chicken lightly until ¼ inch thick. Cut diagonally into strips, about 4 by 1 inches. Dip each piece in flour, shaking off excess; set aside on tray while flouring remaining pieces. Then dip chicken in beaten egg; coat with crumbs.
2. Twist each strip gently several times. Chill chicken pieces 30 minutes. In Dutch oven, heat oil to 365F on a deep-fat thermometer. Fry chicken, five pieces at a time, ½ minute, or until cooked through and golden-brown. With tongs, remove to paper towels; drain well.
3. Allow oil to return to 365F; fry remaining chicken. Refrigerate until thoroughly chilled. Serve with Tarragon-Avocado Dipping Sauce. *Makes 10 servings.*

Tarragon-Avocado Dipping Sauce

- 1 **ripe avocado**
- 1 **cup sour cream**
- ¼ **cup lime juice**
- 3 **tablespoons fresh or 1 tablespoon dried tarragon leaves**
- 1 **tablespoon honey**
- 1 **teaspoon salt**
- ⅛ **teaspoon ground pepper**
  Avocado slices (optional)

Entertaining in the Great Outdoors

Peel and remove pit from avocado; cut into 1-inch cubes. Purée in blender or food processor with remaining ingredients, scraping down bowl once. (Or you may mash avocado with a fork and mix in remaining ingredients.) Place in serving bowl; cover with plastic wrap, pressing wrap to surface. Chill until serving time. Garnish with avocado slices, if desired. *Makes 2 cups.*

Celery Slaw
(pictured)

- **1 head celery (about 2 lb), trimmed**
- **1 small onion**
- **⅔ cup salad oil**
- **½ cup sour cream**
- **¼ cup white-wine vinegar**
- **1 teaspoon sugar**
- **¼ teaspoon paprika**
- **Parsley sprigs (optional)**
- **Cherry tomatoes, trimmed and halved**

1. Slice celery in thin diagonal pieces; slice onion into thin rings; place in large bowl.
2. In small bowl, combine remaining ingredients except parsley and tomatoes; pour over vegetables; stir to combine. Cover and chill 1 hour.
3. Just before serving, stir well; arrange in serving bowl; garnish with parsley sprigs and tomatoes. *Makes 10 servings.*

Chili-Cheese Cornsticks
(pictured)

- **1¼ cups yellow cornmeal**
- **½ cup all-purpose flour**
- **2 tablespoons sugar**
- **1 tablespoon baking powder**
- **½ teaspoon salt**
- **1 large egg**
- **1 cup milk**
- **¼ cup salad oil**
- **½ cup shredded Cheddar cheese (2 oz)**
- **2 tablespoons chopped mild green chiles**

1. Preheat oven to 425F. Grease well two cornstick pans.
2. In medium bowl, combine cornmeal, flour, sugar, baking powder and salt; mix well. Add egg, milk and oil. With wire whisk, beat just until smooth—1 minute. Stir in cheese and chiles.
3. Spoon into prepared pans. Bake 12 to 15 minutes or until golden. Loosen with tip of knife; turn out of pans. *Makes 10 large or 14 smaller cornsticks.*

All-American Blueberry Tartlets
(pictured)

Tart Shells
- **1 cup slivered almonds, finely ground**
- **½ cup (1 stick) butter, softened**
- **½ cup sugar**
- **½ teaspoon salt**
- **1 large egg white**
- **½ teaspoon almond extract**
- **1¼ cups all-purpose flour**

Blueberry Filling
- **1 container (1 pint) fresh blueberries**
- **¾ cup sugar**
- **2 tablespoons cornstarch**
- **1 teaspoon ground cinnamon**
- **3 tablespoons lemon juice**
- **¼ cup water**
- **2 tablespoons butter**
- **1 teaspoon grated lemon peel**

- **1 pkg (8 oz) cream cheese, softened**
- **1 tablespoon milk**

1. Early in day or day before, make Tart Shells: In medium bowl, with fork, combine almonds, ½ cup butter, ½ cup sugar, the salt, egg white and almond extract. Beat with a wooden spoon until smooth and well blended. Gradually stir in flour, mixing till smooth.
2. With pastry brush, oil 12 (4- to 5-inch) fluted tart pans. Divide dough into 12 equal portions; press into prepared pans, being careful to press dough up to top edges of pans. Prick bottoms of tart shells with fork; place on baking sheet; freeze 30 minutes.

Entertaining in the Great Outdoors

3. Meanwhile, make Blueberry Filling: Wash berries; drain. Reserve 1 cup berries; place remaining berries in saucepan.
4. In small bowl, combine ¾ cup sugar, the cornstarch and cinnamon; add to saucepan and toss with berries. Using bottom of a drinking glass, crush berries in saucepan to make juice; add lemon juice and water; allow to stand 10 minutes.
5. Bring crushed berry mixture to boiling over medium-high heat, stirring often; boil 3 minutes, stirring constantly. Remove from heat; stir in 2 tablespoons butter and the lemon peel; allow to cool to room temperature. Stir in reserved berries; transfer to bowl; cover with plastic wrap; refrigerate.
6. Preheat oven to 350F. Bake tart shells 15 to 18 minutes or until golden-brown. Place shells on wire rack; cool 10 minutes in pan. With tip of sharp knife, loosen shells from edge of pan; gently remove shells; allow to cool completely. Wrap in foil, or store in airtight containers, until ready to fill.
7. Three to six hours before serving: In small bowl, combine softened cream cheese with milk. Place half of cream cheese in a pastry bag fitted with a ¼-inch star tip; cover tip with plastic wrap; refrigerate. Divide remaining cream cheese among tart shells, spreading over bottoms. Pour about ¼ cup blueberry filling into each tart shell. With cream-cheese-filled pastry bag, pipe 6 strips of cream cheese in a lattice pattern on top of each tart. Carefully arrange tarts in a covered box or container, allowing 1 inch of space above top of tarts to prevent smearing. Refrigerate tarts until ready to serve. *Makes 12 tarts.*

Patio Party

(Planned for 8)

Almond-Butter Brie
With Fruit and Crackers*
Fresh-Fruit Gazpacho*
Smoked-Turkey Salad*
Crunchy Marinated Vegetables*
Pineapple-Glazed Baba*
California White Wine

*Recipes given for starred dishes.

Almond-Butter Brie
With Fruit and Crackers
(pictured)

½ cup (1 stick) butter or margarine, softened
¼ cup finely chopped toasted almonds (see Note)
 3 tablespoons light rum
¼ teaspoon lemon juice
⅛ teaspoon garlic salt
⅛ teaspoon paprika
  6-inch wheel brie cheese (about 1 lb)
  Whole toasted almonds
  Fresh fruits
  Assorted crackers

1. In small bowl, beat butter with chopped almonds, rum, lemon juice, garlic salt and paprika.
2. Cut white crust from top of brie; spread brie with butter mixture; garnish edge with whole almonds. Cover with plastic wrap; refrigerate until 1 hour before serving. Serve with fruits and crackers. *Makes 16 servings.*

Note: To toast almonds, place in small skillet; heat, shaking the pan frequently, just until nuts turn golden-brown.

Fresh-Fruit Gazpacho
(pictured)

1 cup diced cantaloupe
1 cup diced honeydew melon
1 cup whole strawberries, hulled
1 large green apple, pared and diced
2 teaspoons sugar
1 teaspoon grated orange peel
¼ teaspoon grated lemon peel
1 cup orange juice
½ cup fresh blueberries

  Lemon and lime slices (optional)
  Blueberries (optional)

1. In processor or blender, combine melons, strawberries, apple, sugar and peels with orange juice; process till smooth. (If using blender, blend half at a time.)
2. Pour into serving bowl; stir in blueberries. Cover and chill at least 1 hour or up to 6 hours.
3. Serve in chilled bowls. Garnish with lemon and lime slices and additional blueberries, if desired. *Makes 8 servings.*

Entertaining in the Great Outdoors

Smoked-Turkey Salad
(pictured)

- 2 lb smoked turkey or chicken
- ½ lb Jarlsberg cheese
- 2 cups seedless green grapes, halved
- 2 cups seedless red grapes, halved
- 1 cup thinly sliced celery
- 1 cup salted cashews
- 1½ cups mayonnaise
- ¼ cup medium-dry sherry
- 2 tablespoons Dijon-style mustard
  Green-leaf lettuce, crisped

1. Cut turkey in 1-inch cubes; cut cheese in 1½-by-¼-inch strips. In bowl, mix turkey, cheese, grapes, celery and cashews.
2. In small bowl, blend mayonnaise, sherry and mustard until smooth. Pour over salad and toss to blend. Cover and chill until ready to serve.
3. To serve: Arrange greens in serving bowl; spoon salad into center. *Makes 12 servings.*

Crunchy Marinated Vegetables
(pictured)

- 1 can (14 oz) whole artichoke hearts
- 1 pkg (9 oz) frozen whole green beans
- ½ lb slender carrots
- ¼ lb whole pearl onions
- 1 jar (4 oz) whole pimientos
- 1 cup pitted large ripe olives

Marinade

- 1 cup olive or salad oil
- ⅓ cup wine vinegar
- ½ teaspoon salt
- 3 small cloves garlic, crushed
- 1 teaspoon dried basil leaves
- ¾ teaspoon crushed red pepper
- 6 black peppercorns

1. Drain and halve artichoke hearts; thaw beans. Pare carrots; cut into 1½-inch pieces; peel onions. Cook carrot and onions in boiling water until tender-crisp; drain. Cut pimientos into 1-inch-wide strips.
2. Arrange all vegetables and olives in a 5-cup container with a tight-fitting lid. In small saucepan, heat marinade ingredients to boiling; pour over vegetables. Allow to cool; cover and chill. *Makes 8 servings.*

Pineapple-Glazed Baba
(pictured)

- 1 pkg fast-rising or regular dry yeast
- 3 tablespoons warm water (110 to 115F)
- 1 tablespoon sugar
- 1 teaspoon salt
- 1½ cups all-purpose flour
- 3 large eggs, beaten
- ½ cup (1 stick) butter or margarine, softened
- ½ cup currants

Glaze

- 1 cup sugar
- 2 cups unsweetened pineapple juice

  Fresh dark sweet cherries (optional)

1. In small bowl of electric mixer, dissolve yeast in warm water with 1 tablespoon sugar. Let stand 10 minutes or until bubbly.
2. Add salt, flour and eggs to yeast mixture. Stir to blend. With mixer at medium speed, beat 5 minutes or until dough is smooth, scraping side of bowl with rubber spatula.
3. Cover bowl with plastic wrap; let stand in warm place (85F) 45 to 60 minutes or until dough doubles in bulk. Meanwhile, generously grease an 8-cup mold or Bundt pan. When dough has risen, stir; then beat butter into dough; add currants. Place dough in prepared mold; cover with plastic wrap; let rise in warm place 45 minutes or until double in bulk.
4. Preheat oven to 350F. Bake baba 30 minutes or until evenly browned. Remove baba from mold and place on wire rack.
5. Meanwhile, make Glaze: In medium saucepan, combine sugar and pineapple juice; bring to boiling. Lower heat; cover and simmer gently until slightly thickened—about 10 minutes.
6. With long, thin metal or wood skewer, prick baba all over, penetrating about 2 inches. Place a rimmed plate or pan under the wire rack. Brush baba with pineapple glaze, concentrating on the top. (This will allow juice to filter down through the cake.) Reapply glaze that has dripped off baba. Serve with fresh cherries. *Makes 8 servings.*

Note: Baba can be made a day in advance.

Entertaining In the Great Indoors

Come on in and help yourself to our fabulous menus that will help make your next house party an event to remember. No matter the weather, time of day or number of invited guests (the buffet pictured at left can feed up to 25 people!), you'll have the inside track on easy, elegant entertaining. Our great indoor menus begin on page 155.

Buffet for a Crowd

Left: Cooking for large numbers of people needn't be a monumental task if the menu is easy to prepare and serve, is economical and is one that everyone will like. This Baked Manicotti casserole dinner for 25 fills the bill perfectly. The saucy meat-stuffed pasta dish is a real crowd-pleaser, as are its accompaniments of salad, bread and Custard-Filled Cream Puffs.

151

Friendly Fare

At right: For a night of casual entertaining, consider this delectable Sole With Shrimp Sauce, a dilled medley of fish fillets and shrimp, topped with fluffy mashed potatoes. Serve with a Jellied Madrilène, vegetables, French bread and Cold Strawberry Soufflé...then relax and enjoy the company of good friends. *Recipes begin on page 161.*

Dining Room Favorites

Below: We'd like to share one of our favorite menus that have lavishly graced the table in McCall's own dining room. It serves 12, and you may enjoy sharing it with a dozen of your favorite people. The first course (not shown) is a delicate Mousse of Sole With Lobster Sauce, served with glasses of chilled Pouilly-Fumé. Following, **at center,** is our robust and spicy Rack of Lamb Provençal with a Dijon mustard-crumb topping, surrounded by Savory Stuffed Mushrooms and Baked Tomato Halves. Our big, beautiful Brioche, **at left,** plus a green salad (not shown) and a good Bordeaux complete the main course. For dessert, we like to offer a choice. Pictured here, **from center left:** Apricot-Rum Cake with apricots, figs and whipped cream; fresh strawberries with Sabayon Sauce; Pear Tart Tatin garnished with marrons, whipped cream and candied violets; and, **at top,** a refreshing Crème-De-Menthe-Sherbet ring with strawberries. *Recipes begin on page 157.*

153

An Elegant Tea

Bring out your best silver for an elegant afternoon tea. For those with a sweet tooth, serve a tempting array of Petits Fours **(at top)** and a selection of Strawberry Cream Puffs, Almond Cookies and Madelons **(bottom)**. For savory delights, the platter **(right)** offers Tomato-Curry Rounds, Rolled Watercress Sandwiches and Cream-Cheese-And-Olive Ribbon Sandwiches. And, with everything, pots of steaming brewed tea. *Recipes begin on page 162.*

Entertaining in the Great Indoors

continued from page 151

Buffet for a Crowd

(Planned for 25)
Manicotti* or Lasagne*
Tossed-Green-Salad Bowl*
Bread Sticks   Italian Bread
Pickled Garden Relish
Custard-Filled Cream Puffs*
Red or White Jug Wine
Tea   Coffee

Baked Manicotti
(pictured)

Tomato Sauce
- ½ **cup olive or salad oil**
- 2 **cups finely chopped onion**
- 2 **cloves garlic, crushed**
- 2 **cans (1-lb size) tomato purée**
- 2 **cans (2-lb, 3-oz size) Italian plum tomatoes, undrained**
- ¼ **cup chopped parsley**
- 2 **tablespoons sugar**
- 1 **tablespoon salt**
- 3 **teaspoons dried oregano leaves**
- 2 **teaspoons dried basil leaves**
- ½ **teaspoon ground pepper**
- 1 **teaspoon fennel seed**
- 2 **cups water**

Filling
- ⅓ **cup olive or salad oil**
- 2 **cups chopped onion**
- 2 **cloves garlic, crushed**
- 2½ **lb ground chuck**
- 2 **eggs, slightly beaten**
- 1 **tablespoon salt**
- 2 **teaspoons dried oregano leaves**
- 1 **teaspoon dried basil leaves**
- ½ **teaspoon ground pepper**
- 3 **pkg (10-oz size) frozen chopped spinach, thawed, drained and finely chopped**
- 1 **pkg (8 oz) mozzarella cheese**

- 2 **pkg (8-oz size, 16 shells each) manicotti**
- 2 **cups grated Parmesan cheese**
- 2 **pkg (8-oz size) mozzarella cheese**

- **Parmesan cheese (optional)**
- **Chopped parsley (optional)**

1. Make Tomato Sauce: In ½ cup hot oil in 5-quart Dutch oven or kettle, sauté 2 cups onion and 2 cloves garlic until tender—5 minutes.
2. Add remaining sauce ingredients (mash tomatoes with a fork) and 2 cups water; bring to boil. Lower heat; simmer, covered and stirring occasionally, 1 hour.
3. Meanwhile, make Filling: In ⅓ cup hot oil in large skillet, sauté onion and garlic until tender—about 5 minutes. Turn into large bowl.
4. In same skillet, brown chuck, stirring (break up beef with wooden spoon), until well browned—about 20 minutes. Remove with slotted spoon to onion mixture; add eggs, salt, herbs, pepper, chopped spinach and 3 cups sauce; mix well.
5. Coarsely grate 1 package mozzarella; stir into meat mixture.
6. Preheat oven to 375F. In about 6 quarts rapidly boiling salted water, carefully place manicotti, a few at a time; stir gently. Boil 2 minutes just to soften; drain. With small spoon, fill manicotti with meat mixture; set aside.
7. Spoon a third of sauce into bottom of round cake pan, 16½ inches in diameter, 2 inches deep; arrange, spoke fashion, half of the filled shells on top of the sauce (see Note). Cover with a third of sauce; sprinkle with half of Parmesan cheese. Place remaining manicotti on top, spoke fashion. Top with rest of sauce. Arrange slices of mozzarella on top of each manicotto; sprinkle with remaining Parmesan cheese.
8. Cover tightly with foil; bake 60 minutes; remove foil; bake, uncovered, 15 minutes or until bubbly. If desired, sprinkle with Parmesan and chopped parsley before serving. *Serves 25.*

Note: Two 13-by-9-by-2-inch baking pans may be used; divide sauce and filled manicotti shells between the two pans. Bake, covered, 40 minutes; uncovered, 10 minutes. Sauce and filling can be made day ahead and refrigerated. Assemble before baking.

Lasagne

Meatballs
- 2 **eggs**
- ½ **cup milk**
- 3 **slices white bread, crumbled**
- 2 **lb ground chuck**
- ½ **cup finely chopped onion**
- 2 **tablespoons chopped parsley**
- 1 **clove garlic, crushed**
- 1 **teaspoon salt**
- ½ **teaspoon ground pepper**

*Recipes given for starred dishes.

Entertaining in the Great Indoors

Sauce

½   **cup olive or salad oil**
2   **lb Italian sweet sausages**
½   **cup finely chopped onion**
2   **cloves garlic, crushed**
¼   **cup chopped parsley**
2   **cans (2-lb, 3-oz size) Italian plum tomatoes, undrained**
4   **cans (6-oz size) tomato paste**
4   **teaspoons dried oregano leaves**
2   **teaspoons dried basil leaves**
2   **tablespoons sugar**
1   **tablespoon salt**
½   **teaspoon ground pepper**
¼   **teaspoon ground red pepper**
1   **cup water**

1½ **pkg (1-lb size) lasagne**
1½ **lb mozzarella cheese, diced**
2   **lb ricotta cheese**
2   **cups grated Parmesan cheese**

1. Preheat oven to 450F. Make Meatballs: In medium bowl, beat eggs slightly. Add milk and bread; mix well. Let stand 5 minutes.
2. Add chuck, ½ cup onion, 2 tablespoons parsley, 1 clove garlic, 1 teaspoon salt and ½ teaspoon pepper; mix until well blended. Shape into 60 meatballs—1 tablespoon per meatball. Place in well-greased shallow baking pan.
3. Bake, uncovered, 30 minutes.
4. Meanwhile, make Sauce: In 1 tablespoon hot oil in large skillet, brown sausages on all sides, pricking with fork to release fat. Remove from skillet; set aside. In remaining hot oil in a 5-quart Dutch oven or heavy kettle, over medium heat, sauté onion and garlic until golden. Add rest of sauce ingredients, ending with red pepper and 1 cup water, mashing tomatoes with wooden spoon. Add sausages. Bring to boiling; reduce heat and simmer, covered, 1½ hours, stirring occasionally.
5. Add meatballs and drippings from baking pan; simmer, covered, 20 minutes, stirring occasionally.
6. Preheat oven to 350F.
7. Lightly grease a large 17-by-11½-by-2¼-inch baking pan (see Note). Cook lasagne as package label directs. Drain; rinse in hot water. Drain again.
8. Remove sausages from sauce; slice in ¼-inch pieces.

In baking pan, layer half the ingredients in this order: lasagne, mozzarella, ricotta, tomato sauce with meatballs, sausage and Parmesan cheese; then repeat. If desired, additional mozzarella cubes or strips can be arranged on top before baking.

9. Bake 50 to 60 minutes or until hot and bubbly and cheese is melted and lasagne is heated through. Let stand 20 minutes before cutting. *Makes 25 servings.*

To do ahead: Complete through Step 8; cover pan with foil; refrigerate overnight. Next day, preheat oven to 350F. Bake 1½ hours or until hot and bubbly.

Note: You can use two 13-by-9-by-2-inch baking pans. Bake 35 to 40 minutes.

Tossed Green Salad
(pictured)

2   **medium heads iceberg lettuce**
1   **head (8 oz) escarole**
2   **heads (1½-lb size) romaine**
1   **bunch radishes**

Oil-And-Vinegar Dressing

½   **cup red-wine vinegar**
1½ **cups salad or olive oil**
½   **teaspoon ground pepper**
1   **teaspoon dried basil leaves**
3   **cloves garlic, split**
2   **teaspoons salt**
1   **teaspoon sugar**

1. Prepare salad greens: Wash lettuce, escarole and romaine; separate into leaves, discarding discolored or bruised leaves. Drain well, placing on paper towels to remove excess moisture, or spin them in a salad dryer. Wash and slice radishes.
2. Place cleaned greens in large plastic bag. Refrigerate until crisp and cold—several hours or overnight.
3. Make Oil-And-Vinegar Dressing: Combine all ingredients in jar with tight-fitting lid; shake vigorously.
4. Refrigerate, covered, several hours or overnight. Remove garlic before using. *Makes 2 cups.*
5. At serving time, tear greens into bite-size pieces into bowl; keep small leaves whole. Add radishes. *Makes 25 servings (12 quarts).*

Entertaining in the Great Indoors

Custard-Filled Cream Puffs

Custard Filling

- **2** pkg (3¼-oz size) vanilla-pudding-and-pie-filling mix
- **3** cups milk
- **1** cup heavy cream
- **¼** cup confectioners' sugar
- **1** teaspoon vanilla extract

Cream Puffs

- **1** cup water
- **½** cup (1 stick) butter or margarine
- **¼** teaspoon salt
- **1** cup all-purpose flour
- **4** large eggs
-   Confectioners' sugar

1. Make Custard Filling: Prepare pudding as package label directs, using the 2 packages and 3 cups milk.
2. Pour into medium bowl; place waxed paper directly on surface. Refrigerate until chilled—at least 2 hours.
3. In small bowl, combine heavy cream, ¼ cup confectioners' sugar and the vanilla; with portable electric beater, beat at medium speed just until stiff. Fold whipped-cream mixture into pudding until combined. Refrigerate to chill well—several hours or overnight. Makes enough filling for 24 cream puffs.
4. Make Cream Puffs: Preheat oven to 400F. In medium-size, heavy saucepan, combine 1 cup water with the butter and salt. Over medium heat, bring to boiling; remove from heat.
5. With wooden spoon, beat in flour all at once. Over low heat, beat until mixture leaves side of pan and forms a ball—1 to 2 minutes. Remove from heat.
6. With portable electric mixer, beat in eggs, one at a time, beating hard after each addition until mixture is smooth.
7. Continue beating until dough is shiny and satiny—about 1 minute.
8. Drop by generous tablespoonfuls, 2 inches apart, onto ungreased cookie sheet.
9. Bake 40 to 45 minutes or until puffed and golden-brown. Puffs should sound hollow when lightly tapped with fingertip.
10. Remove puffs from cookie sheet to wire rack. Cool completely, away from drafts.
11. To serve: With sharp knife, cut off tops of cream puffs. With fork, gently remove any soft dough from inside.
12. Fill each puff with 2 tablespoons custard; replace tops. Sprinkle with confectioners' sugar. Serve as soon as possible after filling. *Makes 12 puffs.*

Note: Make 2 batches of cream-puff dough for 24.

Dining Room Favorites

(Planned for 10 to 12)
Mousse of Sole With Lobster Sauce*
Rack of Lamb Provençal *
Savory Stuffed Mushrooms*
Baked Tomato Halves*
Green Salad   Hot Brioche*
Dessert Cart:
Pear Tart Tatin*   Apricot-Rum Cake*
Strawberries Sabayon*
Crème-De-Menthe Sherbet*
Coffee
Pouilly-Fumé de Ladoucette
Chateau Belgrave

Mousse of Sole With Lobster Sauce

- **1½** lb sole fillets

Lobster Filling

- **3** tablespoons butter or margarine
- **¼** cup all-purpose flour
- **¾** teaspoon salt
- **1¼** cups light cream or half-and-half
- **⅓** cup dry sherry
- **1** can (3 oz) whole mushrooms, drained
- **1** tablespoon catsup
- **2** egg yolks
- **2** cups cubed cooked lobster

- **¼** cup all-purpose flour
- **1½** teaspoons salt
- **⅛** teaspoon ground white pepper
- **2** egg whites
- **1¾** cups light cream or half-and-half
-   Boiling water
-   Watercress (optional)
-   Lemon slices (optional)

1. Rinse sole; pat dry with paper towels. Cut each fillet into four to six strips. Put through meat grinder, using finest blade, four times or purée in a food processor fitted with the steel blade. Place in large bowl of electric mixer; refrigerate, covered, 30 minutes. Generously grease a 2-quart metal charlotte mold, 7 inches in diameter; refrigerate.
2. Make Lobster Filling: Melt butter in a saucepan. Remove from heat.
3. Stir in ¼ cup flour and ¾ teaspoon salt until well blended. Gradually stir in 1 cup cream. Bring to boiling, stirring constantly; reduce heat and simmer 1 minute. Stir in sherry, mushrooms and catsup; cook over medium heat until hot.

*Recipes given for starred dishes.

Entertaining in the Great Indoors

4. Beat egg yolks with ¼ cup cream. Stir into sauce mixture, along with lobster; cook, stirring, 1 minute. Remove from heat.

5. Add flour, salt and pepper to ground sole; stir until well blended. With electric mixer at medium speed, beat in egg whites. Gradually beat in cream, 2 tablespoons at a time, until smooth and stiff—about 10 minutes.

6. Preheat oven to 325F.

7. Set aside 1 cup sole mixture. Use remaining mixture to line bottom and side of prepared mold to within 1 inch of top. Reserve 1 cup Lobster Filling; refrigerate. Use remaining filling to fill lined mold. Cover with reserved sole mixture, spreading to edge of mold.

8. Cover mold loosely with oiled waxed paper. Place in roasting pan; pour boiling water to 2-inch level.

9. Bake 45 to 50 minutes or until firm at edge when pressed with finger.

10. About 10 minutes before mousse is done, heat reserved lobster filling over hot water.

11. To serve: Loosen mousse around side with small spatula. Invert onto heated serving platter; lift off mold. Spoon heated filling over top. Garnish with watercress and lemon, if desired. Cut into wedges and serve with sauce. *Makes 10 to 12 first-course servings.*

✴

Rack of Lamb Provençal
(pictured)

3   (3½- to 4-lb size) racks of lamb (24 chops)
2   cups fresh bread crumbs
½   cup chopped parsley
2   cloves garlic, crushed
2   teaspoons salt
½   teaspoon ground pepper
4   tablespoons Dijon mustard
½   cup (1 stick) butter or margarine, melted
    Watercress or parsley (optional)

1. Preheat oven to 375F. Wipe lamb with damp paper towels; trim off all fat. Place lamb, using ribs as rack, in shallow, open roasting pan.

2. Roast, uncovered, 15 minutes for each pound.

3. Remove roast from oven; let cool about 15 minutes.

4. Combine bread crumbs, parsley, garlic, salt and pepper.

5. Spread mustard over top of lamb. Firmly pat crumb mixture into mustard. Drizzle with butter. Insert meat thermometer in center of middle chop.

6. Roast 20 minutes or until thermometer registers 150F

for rare; if you prefer medium, roast to 160F; if well done, 175F. Garnish with watercress or parsley, if desired. *Makes 12 servings.*

Savory Stuffed Mushrooms
(pictured)

24   fresh medium-size mushrooms
1   cup (2 sticks) butter or margarine
6   tablespoons finely chopped green pepper
6   tablespoons finely chopped onion
3   cups fresh-bread cubes (¼-inch)
1   teaspoon salt
¼   teaspoon ground black pepper
    Dash ground red pepper

1. Preheat oven to 350F. Wipe mushrooms with damp cloth. Remove stems. Chop stems fine; set aside.

2. Heat 3 tablespoons butter in large skillet. Sauté mushroom caps, on bottom side only, 2 to 3 minutes; remove. Arrange, rounded side down, in shallow baking pan.

3. Heat rest of butter in same skillet. Sauté chopped stems, green pepper and onion until tender–about 5 minutes.

4. Remove from heat. Stir in bread cubes and seasonings. Use to fill mushroom caps, mounding high in center.

5. Bake 15 minutes. *Makes 12 servings.*

✴

Baked Tomato Halves
(pictured)

12   small tomatoes (3 lb)
8   tablespoons (1 stick) butter or margarine
½   cup finely chopped onion
2   teaspoons prepared mustard
1   teaspoon Worcestershire sauce
4   slices white bread, torn into coarse crumbs
4   teaspoons chopped parsley

1. Preheat oven to 350F. Wash tomatoes and remove stems. Cut off tops crosswise. Place, cut side up, in shallow baking pan.

2. In 4 tablespoons hot butter in small skillet, sauté onion until tender. Stir in mustard and Worcestershire. Spread on tomatoes.

3. Melt remaining butter in same skillet. Stir in bread crumbs and parsley. Sprinkle over tomatoes.

4. Bake, uncovered, 20 minutes or until tomatoes are heated through and crumbs are golden-brown. *Makes 12 servings.*

Entertaining in the Great Indoors

Brioche
(pictured)

⅓ cup warm water (105 to 115F)
1 pkg active dry yeast
3 tablespoons sugar
1¼ teaspoons salt
⅔ cup (1⅓ sticks) butter, softened
4 large eggs, at room temperature
3 cups sifted all-purpose flour
1 egg yolk
2 teaspoons water

1. Day ahead: If possible, check temperature of water with thermometer, or test by dropping a little water on inside of wrist; it should feel warm, not hot. Sprinkle yeast over water in large electric-mixer bowl; stir to dissolve. Add sugar and salt.
2. Stir to dissolve; add the butter, eggs and 2 cups flour. Beat at medium speed 4 minutes, occasionally scraping bowl and beaters with rubber spatula. Add remaining cup of flour. Beat at low speed 1 minute or until smooth (dough will be soft).
3. Let rise in warm place (85F), covered with towel, free from drafts, until double in bulk–2 to 2½ hours. With rubber spatula, beat down dough. Cover with a sheet of waxed paper and damp towel; refrigerate overnight. Next day, grease 1½-quart brioche pan.
4. Cut off one-sixth of dough for cap. On lightly floured surface, form into ball, coating with flour. Turn out rest of dough onto lightly floured surface. Knead dough until smooth–about 1 minute; shape into 5-inch round. Fit evenly into prepared pan.
5. Make 1½-inch-wide indentation in center. Insert ball of dough. Let rise in warm place (85F), covered with towel, free from drafts, until dough rises to top of pan–takes about 2½ hours. Preheat oven to 375F. Beat the egg yolk with 2 teaspoons water.
6. Gently brush surface of dough (do not let egg run between brioche and cap). Bake 20 minutes. Cover loosely with foil; bake 40 minutes or until cake tester comes out clean. Cool 15 minutes. With small spatula, loosen from pan; remove. Serve warm. *Makes 10 to 12 servings.*

Pear Tart Tatin
(pictured)

2 cans (1-lb, 14-oz size) pear halves, drained
1 cup sugar
1 tablespoon butter or margarine
½ pkg (11-oz size) piecrust mix
1 jar (9½ oz) marrons (chestnuts) in syrup, drained (optional)
1 cup heavy cream, whipped and sweetened
Candied violets (optional)

1. Preheat oven to 450F.
2. Cut pears in half lengthwise; drain on paper towels.
3. To caramelize sugar: In large skillet, cook sugar over medium heat, stirring occasionally, until sugar melts and becomes a light-brown syrup.
4. Immediately pour into bottom of an 8½-inch round baking dish. Arrange pears, rounded side down, spoke fashion, in syrup. Top with a second layer of pears, rounded side up, fitting to fill open spaces.
5. Dot with butter. Bake, uncovered, 25 minutes or just until caramelized sugar is melted.
6. Let stand in baking dish on wire rack until cooled to room temperature—about 1½ hours.
7. Meanwhile, prepare pastry, following package directions. On lightly floured surface, roll out to a 9-inch circle. Place on ungreased cookie sheet; prick with fork. Refrigerate ½ hour.
8. Bake pastry at 450F for 10 minutes or until golden-brown. Let stand on cookie sheet on wire rack.
9. To serve: Place pastry circle over pears in baking dish. Top with serving plate; invert; remove baking dish. Mound marrons in center. Decorate with mounds of whipped cream. Garnish with candied violets. Serve with whipped cream. *Serves 6 to 8.*

Apricot-Rum Cake
(pictured)

Chiffon Cake

1 cup egg whites
2 cups sifted all-purpose flour
1½ cups sugar
3 teaspoons baking powder
1 teaspoon salt
½ cup salad oil
5 egg yolks
¾ cup water
3 tablespoons grated orange peel
1 teaspoon vanilla extract
½ teaspoon cream of tartar

Rum Syrup

1½ cups sugar
1½ cups water
1 unpeeled medium orange, sliced
½ unpeeled lemon, sliced
1 cup light or amber rum

Apricot Glaze

½ cup apricot preserves
½ tablespoon lemon or orange juice

1 can (1 lb, 14 oz) whole peeled apricots, drained and pitted
1 can (1 lb, 1 oz) whole Kadota figs, drained
¼ cup pecans or walnuts
1 cup heavy cream, whipped

Entertaining in the Great Indoors

1. Make Chiffon Cake: Let egg whites warm to room temperature in large bowl of electric mixer–about 1 hour.
2. Preheat oven to 325F. Sift flour with 1½ cups sugar, the baking powder and salt into another large bowl. Make well in center.
3. Add, in order, oil, egg yolks, ¾ cup water, the orange peel and vanilla; beat with spoon until smooth.
4. In large bowl of electric mixer, at high speed, beat egg whites with cream of tartar until stiff peaks form when beaters are slowly raised.
5. Pour egg-yolk mixture gradually over egg whites; with rubber spatula or wire whisk, using an under-and-over motion, gently fold into egg whites just until blended.
6. Turn into ungreased 10-inch tube pan; bake 55 minutes.
7. Increase temperature to 350F; bake 10 minutes longer or until cake tester inserted in center comes out clean.
8. Invert pan over neck of bottle; let cake cool completely–1½ hours.
9. Meanwhile, make Rum Syrup: In medium saucepan, combine sugar with 1½ cups water; bring to boiling, stirring until sugar is dissolved. Add orange and lemon slices. Boil, uncovered, 10 minutes or until syrup measures 1 cup. Remove from heat. Add rum.
10. With cake tester, make holes, 1 inch apart, in top of cake in pan. Pour warm syrup over cake, ¼ cup at a time. Let stand at room temperature 1 hour or until all syrup is absorbed.
11. Make Apricot Glaze: In small saucepan, melt preserves over low heat. Stir in lemon juice; strain.
12. Carefully loosen cake from pan; invert onto wire rack; then turn, top side up, onto serving plate. Brush glaze over top and side of cake. Refrigerate.
13. To serve: Garnish cake with apricots, figs, nuts and, if desired, green leaves. Cut cake into wedges. Pass whipped cream to spoon over cake. *Makes 12 servings.*

✳

Strawberries Sabayon
(pictured)

Sabayon Sauce
- **4 egg yolks**
- **2 tablespoons sugar**
- **¼ cup Grand Marnier**
- **⅓ cup heavy cream, whipped**
- **2 pint boxes fresh strawberries, washed and hulled**

1. Make Sabayon Sauce: In top of double boiler, with portable electric mixer at medium speed, beat egg yolks until thick. Gradually beat in sugar; beat until mixture is light and soft peaks form when beaters are slowly raised.
2. Place double-boiler top over simmering water (water in bottom should not touch base of top). Slowly beat in Grand Marnier; continue beating until mixture is fluffy and mounds—takes about 5 minutes.
3. Remove double-boiler top from hot water; set in ice water. Beat the custard mixture until cool. Gently fold in whipped cream.
4. Refrigerate sauce, covered.
5. Place berries in serving bowl or dessert dishes. Stir sauce; pour over fruit. *Serves 6.*

✳

Crème-De-Menthe-Sherbet Ring
(pictured)

- **3 pints lemon sherbet**
- **⅓ cup green crème de menthe**
- **1 quart fresh strawberries**
  Confectioners' sugar

1. Let sherbet stand in refrigerator for 30 minutes to soften slightly.
2. Turn sherbet into large bowl; beat, with portable electric mixer, just until smooth but not melted.
3. Quickly stir in crème de menthe until well combined.
4. Turn mixture into a 5½-cup ring mold; freeze until firm—several hours.
5. Meanwhile, wash strawberries; drain. Do not hull. Refrigerate.
6. To serve: Invert ring mold over round, chilled serving platter. Place hot, damp cloth over mold; shake to release sherbet.
7. Fill center of ring with strawberries. Dust berries lightly with confectioners' sugar. *Makes 8 servings.*

Friendly Fare

(Planned for 8)

Jellied Madrilène
Sole With Shrimp Sauce*
Mashed Potato*
Petit Pois
Marinated Sliced Cucumbers
French Bread
Cold Strawberry Soufflé*
Chilled White Wine   Coffee

*Recipes given for starred dishes.

Entertaining in the Great Indoors

Sole With Shrimp Sauce
(pictured)

10 medium-size sole fillets
¾ teaspoon salt
¼ teaspoon ground white pepper
¼ cup lemon juice
¼ cup snipped fresh dill
¾ cup dry white wine
    Butter or margarine
½ lb mushrooms, sliced

Sauce

¼ cup all-purpose flour
    Reserved fish broth
1 cup light cream or half-and-half
1 can (3 oz) baby shrimp, drained

    Mashed Potato, recipe follows
    Fresh dill sprigs for garnish

1. Preheat oven to 350F.
2. Rinse fillets under cold running water; pat dry with paper towels.
3. Arrange fillets on a large ovenproof (2-inch-deep) platter.
4. Sprinkle with salt, pepper, lemon juice and snipped dill. Add wine. Cut 2 tablespoons butter in small pieces and place on top of fish.
5. Cover dish with foil. Bake 25 minutes.
6. Meanwhile, in 3 tablespoons hot butter in medium skillet, over low heat, sauté mushrooms until tender—about 10 minutes; remove from heat.
7. Remove fish from oven. Carefully drain off fish liquid. Drain fish very well. Liquid should measure 1½ cups.
8. Make Sauce: Add flour to mushrooms. Stir until smooth. Stir in reserved fish broth and cream. Cook over medium heat, stirring constantly, until mixture comes to a boil; reduce heat and simmer 5 minutes, stirring. Add shrimp.
9. Pour sauce over fish. Prepare Mashed Potato.
10. With mashed potato in a pastry bag with a number-6 tip, make lattice pattern over the fish and around edge. Refrigerate if not serving soon.
11. When ready to serve, preheat oven to 350F.
12. Place in oven until bubbly and hot and potato is lightly browned—about 40 minutes. Garnish with dill. *Makes 8 servings.*

Mashed Potato

3 lb white potatoes
⅓ cup (⅔ stick) butter or margarine
⅓ cup milk
1 teaspoon salt
⅛ teaspoon ground white pepper
1 egg yolk

1. Pare potatoes; cut in quarters. Cook in 1 inch salted boiling water, covered, until tender—20 minutes. Drain very well; return to saucepan; heat slightly over low heat to dry out potato.
2. Beat, with electric mixer (or mash with potato masher), until smooth.
3. In saucepan, heat butter and milk until butter melts—don't let milk boil.
4. Gradually beat in hot milk mixture until potato is smooth. Beat in salt, pepper and egg yolk until light and fluffy.

Cold Strawberry Soufflé
(pictured)

4 egg whites
2 pkg (10-oz size) frozen strawberries, thawed
1 env unflavored gelatine
4 egg yolks
3 tablespoons water
1 tablespoon lemon juice
⅛ teaspoon salt
½ teaspoon vanilla extract
⅓ cup sugar
1 cup heavy cream

1. Make a collar for a 1-quart, straight-sided soufflé dish: Cut a strip of foil 6 inches wide and long enough to go around edge of soufflé dish. Fold foil twice lengthwise. Place band of foil tightly around dish, so it extends above dish to form a 1½-inch-deep collar. Fasten securely with string.
2. In large bowl of electric mixer, let egg whites stand at room temperature about 1 hour.

Entertaining in the Great Indoors

3. Meanwhile, drain strawberries, reserving ½ cup syrup. Set aside a few large strawberries for garnish.
4. Sprinkle gelatine over reserved strawberry syrup in top of double boiler. Let mixture stand 5 minutes to soften gelatine.
5. In small bowl, beat egg yolks with 3 tablespoons water. Stir into gelatine mixture.
6. Cook, stirring, over boiling water until gelatine is dissolved and mixture is slightly thickened.
7. Remove from hot water. Stir in lemon juice, salt and vanilla to mix well. Refrigerate until mixture is cooled—about 20 minutes.
8. Press strawberries (except those reserved for garnish) through sieve to make a purée; this should measure about 1⅓ cups. Stir into gelatine mixture.
9. Beat egg whites at high speed just until soft peaks form when beaters are slowly raised. Gradually beat in sugar; beat until stiff peaks form.
10. With rotary beater, beat cream until stiff.
11. Using a rubber spatula or wire whisk, with an under-and-over motion, fold gelatine mixture and whipped cream into egg whites until well combined.
12. Turn evenly into prepared soufflé dish. Refrigerate until firm—about 4 hours.
13. To serve: Gently remove collar from soufflé. Garnish edge with reserved strawberries and more whipped cream, if desired. *Makes 8 servings.*

An Elegant Tea

(Planned for 25)

Rolled Watercress Sandwiches*
Tomato-Curry Rounds*
Cream-Cheese-And-Olive Ribbon Sandwiches*
Petits Fours*
Strawberry Cream Puffs*
Almond Cookies*
Jewel Cookies*   *Madelons**
Hot Tea   *Lemon With Fresh Mint*

*Recipes given for starred dishes.

Rolled Watercress Sandwiches
(pictured)

1 large bunch watercress
¾ cup (1½ sticks) butter or margarine, softened
¼ teaspoon salt
1 tablespoon lemon juice
1½ loaves (1-lb size) thinly sliced white bread

1. Wash and drain watercress. Reserve small center sprigs for garnish—about 50.
2. Remove stems from remaining watercress. Finely chop enough watercress to measure ½ cup.
3. Beat butter and salt with portable electric mixer until smooth. Gradually beat in lemon juice. Then beat in chopped watercress.
4. With sharp knife, trim crusts from bread. Roll each slice lightly with rolling pin.
5. Spread bread slices evenly with watercress butter, using about 1½ teaspoons for each. Roll up, jelly-roll fashion. Trim ends. Insert a reserved watercress sprig in each end.
6. Refrigerate, between damp paper towels, until serving. (Sandwiches may be made several hours ahead and stored this way.) *Makes about 25.*

Tomato-Curry Rounds
(pictured)

2 loaves (1-lb size) unsliced white bread
3 tablespoons butter or margarine, softened
½ teaspoon lemon juice
¼ teaspoon curry powder
   Dash salt
3 large tomatoes, washed and very thinly sliced

1. With sharp knife, trim crusts from bread. Slice lengthwise into ¼-inch-thick slices. Using a 2-inch scalloped cookie cutter, cut into 48 rounds.
2. With truffle cutter or sharp knife, remove and discard a small scalloped round, about ¾ inch in diameter,

Entertaining in the Great Indoors

from center of 24 bread rounds. Cover all rounds with damp paper towels.
3. In small bowl, combine butter, lemon juice, curry powder and salt; mix well. Spread over the 24 uncut bread rounds.
4. Using same 2-inch scalloped cutter, cut 24 tomato rounds. Place tomato rounds on bread. Top with cutout bread rounds; press together lightly.
5. To store: Arrange in shallow pan. Cover with damp paper towels, then with plastic wrap. Refrigerate until serving. *Makes 24.*

Cream-Cheese-And-Olive Ribbon Sandwiches
(pictured)

1 pkg (8 oz) cream cheese at room temperature
2 tablespoons mayonnaise
⅓ cup chopped pimiento-stuffed olives
½ cup (1 stick) butter or margarine, softened
12 thin slices white bread
12 thin slices whole-wheat bread

1. In medium bowl, combine cream cheese, mayonnaise and chopped olives. Blend well with wooden spoon.
2. Lightly butter 8 slices of white bread and 4 slices of whole-wheat bread. Spread 4 of the buttered white-bread slices and the buttered whole-wheat-bread slices with cream-cheese mixture, using about 2 teaspoons for each slice.
3. To make ribbon sandwiches: Place whole-wheat slices, cheese side up, on white slices, cheese side up. Top with 4 buttered white slices, buttered side down. With sharp knife, trim crusts from each stack. Cut each stack into 6 strips, or ribbons. Keep sandwiches covered with damp paper towels to prevent drying out.
4. Repeat with rest of bread, butter and olive mixture.

Place whole-wheat slices on top and bottom this time.
5. To store: Arrange close together in shallow pan. Cover with damp paper towels, then with plastic wrap. Refrigerate until serving. *Makes 48.*

Petits Fours
(pictured)

2 pkg (1-lb, 1-oz size) pound-cake mix
4 eggs
Peach Glaze, recipe follows
Fondant Frosting, recipe follows
Pink and green cake-decorating tubes

1. Preheat oven to 350F. Lightly grease and flour a 15½-by-10½-by-1-inch jelly-roll pan.
2. Prepare both packages of pound-cake mix as package label directs, using 4 eggs and liquid called for.
3. Turn into prepared pan. Bake 30 to 35 minutes or until top springs back when pressed with fingertip.
4. Cool 10 minutes in pan. Turn out on wire rack; let cool completely.
5. Meanwhile, make Peach Glaze and Fondant Frosting.
6. Using 2-inch cookie cutters, cut out diamond, heart and round shapes from cooled cake—32 or 33.
7. To glaze cakes: Place on fork, one at a time. Hold over bowl of glaze and spoon glaze over cake, completely covering top and sides.
8. Place cakes, uncoated side down and 2 inches apart, on wire racks placed on cookie sheets. Let stand until glaze is set—at least 1 hour.
9. To frost: Place glazed cakes on fork, one at a time. Spoon frosting over cake to run over top and down sides evenly. Frost half white and half pink.
10. Let cakes dry completely on wire racks—about 1 hour. Repeat frosting, if necessary. Let dry.
11. To decorate: Make little posies and leaves with decorating tubes, or drizzle any remaining frosting over tops. Refrigerate several hours. Let stand at room temperature 1 hour. *Makes 32 or 33.*

Entertaining in the Great Indoors

Peach Glaze

1½ cups peach preserves
½ cup sugar
½ cup water

1. In medium saucepan, combine preserves, sugar and water; bring to boiling over medium heat. Boil, stirring, 5 minutes.
2. Remove from heat. Press through sieve into a bowl. *Makes 1½ cups.*

Fondant Frosting

2¼ cups granulated sugar
     Dash salt
¼ teaspoon cream of tartar
1½ cups water
     About 2¼ cups sifted confectioners' sugar
½ teaspoon almond extract
     Food color (optional)

1. In medium saucepan, combine granulated sugar, salt and cream of tartar with water. Over low heat, cook, stirring, until sugar is dissolved.
2. Over medium heat, cook, without stirring, to 226F on candy thermometer.
3. Transfer to the top of double boiler; let cool to luke-warm (110F on candy thermometer).
4. With wooden spoon, gradually beat in just enough confectioners' sugar to make frosting thick enough to coat spoon but thin enough to pour. Add almond extract. Remove half of frosting (about 1½ cups) to small bowl. Add a few drops food color to tint a delicate color.
5. Keep white frosting over hot, not boiling, water, to keep thin enough to pour. If frosting is too thin, add a little more confectioners' sugar; if too thick, thin with a little warm water. After using white frosting, heat tinted frosting and use in same way. *Makes 3 cups.*

Strawberry Cream Puffs
(pictured)

Cream-Puff Dough
½ cup water
¼ cup (½ stick) butter or margarine
⅛ teaspoon salt
½ cup sifted all-purpose flour
 2 large eggs

Filling
½ cup heavy cream
 2 tablespoons confectioners' sugar
¼ teaspoon vanilla extract

36 medium strawberries, washed and hulled
     Confectioners' sugar

1. Preheat oven to 400F. Make Cream-Puff Dough: In small saucepan, slowly bring ½ cup water with the butter and salt to boiling.
2. Remove from heat. With wooden spoon, beat in flour all at once.
3. Return to low heat; continue beating until mixture forms ball and leaves side of pan.
4. Remove from heat. Beat in eggs, one at a time, beating hard after each addition until smooth.
5. Continue beating until dough is shiny and breaks into strands.
6. For cream puffs, drop dough by slightly rounded teaspoonfuls, 2 inches apart, onto ungreased cookie sheet.
7. Bake until puffed and golden-brown—20 to 25 minutes.
8. Let cool completely on wire rack, away from drafts.
9. Meanwhile, make Filling: Beat cream with 2 table-spoons confectioners' sugar until stiff. Stir in va-nilla. Refrigerate, covered.
10. With sharp knife, cut a slice from top of each puff. Fill each with a scant teaspoonful of whipped cream; press a strawberry into each; replace tops. Refrig-erate if not serving at once.
11. To serve, sprinkle with confectioners' sugar. *Makes 36 cream puffs.*

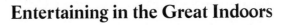

Entertaining in the Great Indoors

Almond Cookies
(pictured)

⅓ **cup egg whites**
½ **cup sugar**
¼ **teaspoon vanilla extract**
⅛ **teaspoon almond extract**
3 **tablespoons butter or margarine, melted**
3 **tablespoons all-purpose flour**
½ **cup sliced blanched almonds**

1. Preheat oven to 375F. Grease a large cookie sheet with salad oil; then dust with flour (omit if using a pan with nonstick coating).
2. In medium bowl, combine egg whites, sugar and vanilla and almond extracts; beat with wire whisk about 2 minutes or until sugar is dissolved and mixture is syrupy.
3. Add melted butter and flour; beat until smooth. Stir in almonds.
4. Drop by ½ teaspoonfuls, about 4 inches apart, onto prepared cookie sheet. With small spatula, spread each to a 1½-inch round. Make no more than 8 at a time.
5. Bake 5 minutes or until cookies are golden-brown around edge and very lightly browned in center.
6. With small spatula, carefully remove cookies at once and place over rolling pin to curve them. (If cookies get too cool, return to oven.)
7. Repeat with remaining batter, oiling and flouring cookie sheet each time. *Makes about 5 dozen.*

Jewel Cookies

½ **cup (1 stick) butter or margarine, softened**
¼ **cup firmly packed light-brown sugar**
1 **egg yolk**
1 **teaspoon vanilla extract**
1 **cup sifted all-purpose flour**
1 **egg white, slightly beaten**
½ **cup finely chopped walnuts or pecans**

4 **tablespoons confectioners' sugar**
2 **teaspoons milk**
3 **tablespoons peach preserves**

1. In medium bowl, with wooden spoon, beat butter, brown sugar, egg yolk and vanilla until smooth.
2. Stir in flour just until combined. Refrigerate 30 minutes.
3. Meanwhile, preheat oven to 375F. Using hands, roll dough into balls ½ inch in diameter. Dip in egg white; then roll in chopped nuts.
4. Place, 1 inch apart, on ungreased cookie sheets. With thimble or thumb, press center of each cookie.
5. Bake 8 minutes or just until a delicate golden-brown. Remove to wire rack; cool.
6. Meanwhile, in small bowl, combine confectioners' sugar and milk, mixing well.
7. Place ⅛ teaspoon icing in center of each cookie; top with a little of the peach preserves. *Makes 4 dozen.*

Madelons
(pictured)

Cream-Puff Dough, page 164
½ **cup heavy cream**
2 **tablespoons confectioners' sugar**
½ **teaspoon vanilla extract**
¾ **cup cherry preserves**
Confectioners' sugar

1. Preheat oven to 400F. Make Cream-Puff Dough.
2. Place dough in pastry bag with number-6 star tip. Pipe onto ungreased cookie sheet to make 12 S shapes 3 inches long, 2 inches apart.
3. Bake 25 to 30 minutes or until they are puffed and deep golden-brown. Remove to wire rack; cool completely.
4. Meanwhile, beat cream with 2 tablespoons confectioners' sugar and the vanilla until stiff. Refrigerate, covered.
5. To assemble Madelons: With sharp knife, cut puffs in half crosswise. Scoop out any filaments of soft dough.

Entertaining in the Great Indoors

6. Spoon 1 tablespoon cherry preserves into each bottom half, then a rounded tablespoon of whipped cream. Replace top. Sprinkle with confectioners' sugar. Refrigerate if not serving at once. *Makes 12.*

   Note: Make recipe two separate times for 24.

Luncheon Menu

(Planned for 24)

Hot Cheese-Ball Appetizer or
Warm Quiche Lorraine*
Breast of Chicken in White Wine*
Marinated-Asparagus Salad*
Assorted Hot Buttered Rolls
Raspberry-Sherbet Mold*
Champagne   Coffee*

Hot Cheese-Ball Appetizer

1 lb grated Parmesan cheese
2 pkg (8-oz size) cream cheese, softened
4 eggs
1 teaspoon salt
 Dash ground red pepper
2 cups fresh white-bread crumbs
 Peanut or salad oil for deep frying

1. In large bowl, combine both kinds of cheese, the eggs, salt and pepper. Beat with wooden spoon until smooth. Refrigerate, covered, 1 hour.
2. Form into 1-inch balls. Roll each ball lightly in bread crumbs on waxed paper. Refrigerate.
3. In a deep skillet or deep-fat fryer, slowly heat oil (about 2 inches) to 350F on deep-frying thermometer. Fry cheese balls, turning once, 1 minute or until golden-brown. Drain on paper towels. Serve hot. *Makes 60.*

   Note: If desired, make day ahead and refrigerate, covered. Fry as in Step 3.

*Recipes given for starred dishes.

Warm Quiche Lorraine

1½ pkg (11-oz size) piecrust mix
 1 lb sliced bacon
 2 cups finely chopped onion
 3 cups grated natural Swiss cheese (¾ lb)
 6 eggs
 4 cups light cream or half-and-half
1½ teaspoons salt
 1 teaspoon sugar
 ¼ teaspoon ground nutmeg
 ¼ teaspoon ground black pepper
 Dash ground red pepper

1. Prepare piecrust mix as package label directs.
2. On lightly floured surface, roll out pastry to an 18-by-15-inch rectangle. Use to line a 15½-by-10½-by-1-inch jelly-roll pan; flute edge. Refrigerate until needed.
3. Preheat oven to 375F.
4. Fry bacon until crisp. Drain on paper towels; crumble. Sauté onion in 2 tablespoons bacon drippings until golden.
5. Sprinkle cheese over bottom of pastry shell; sprinkle bacon and onion over cheese.
6. In large bowl, with rotary beater, beat eggs with cream, salt, sugar, nutmeg, black pepper and red pepper until well combined. Pour into prepared shell.
7. Bake 35 to 40 minutes or until golden and center is firm when gently pressed with fingertip.
8. Let cool on wire rack 10 minutes. To serve, cut quiche into squares—about 1½ inches. *Makes about 25 appetizer servings or 60 to 70 cocktail servings.*

Breast of Chicken in White Wine

12 chicken breasts (about 5 lb in all), halved, skinned and boned
 1 cup (2 sticks) butter or margarine
 ½ cup salad oil
 3 cups sliced onion
 2 lb small fresh mushrooms, washed and stems removed
1½ teaspoons salt
 1 teaspoon ground pepper
 1 tablespoon dried thyme leaves
 2 bay leaves, crushed
 2 cups dry white wine
 2 cans (13¾-oz size) chicken broth

Entertaining in the Great Indoors

Sauce

- ¼ cup dry white wine
- 2 tablespoons all-purpose flour

  Whole mushrooms for garnish
  Watercress for garnish

1. Wipe chicken breasts well with damp paper towels.
2. In a large skillet, heat ¼ cup butter and ¼ cup oil. Add chicken breasts, several pieces at a time; sauté until golden—about 10 minutes in all. Remove to large roasting pan. Continue to brown rest of chicken, adding more butter and oil as needed.
3. Overlap browned chicken breasts in bottom of 17-by-12½-by-2¼-inch roasting pan. Preheat oven to 350F.
4. Heat remaining butter and oil in skillet. Add onion and mushrooms; sauté, stirring, until onion is golden—about 5 minutes. Spread onion-mushroom mixture over chicken breasts.
5. Combine drippings left in skillet with salt, pepper, thyme and bay leaves. Add wine and chicken broth; bring to boiling, stirring. Pour over chicken. Cover pan tightly with foil.
6. Bake, basting twice, 1 hour or just until chicken breasts are tender.
7. Remove cooked chicken breasts and mushrooms; keep warm. Strain mixture remaining in roasting pan into large saucepan. Bring to boiling; boil, uncovered, to reduce to 2 cups—for sauce.
8. Make Sauce: Combine wine with flour; add to mixture in skillet. Bring to boiling; reduce heat and simmer 2 minutes.
9. Just before serving, spoon sauce over chicken breasts; garnish with whole mushrooms and watercress. *Makes 24 servings.*

   Note: If desired, bake in two 13-by-9-by-2-inch roasting pans. Chicken breasts may be cooked ahead: Bake 1 hour as in Step 6; cool completely; refrigerate, covered. Before serving, heat chicken breasts until hot; proceed with Step 7.

Marinated-Asparagus Salad

- 4 cans (15-oz size) green asparagus spears
- 3 cans (15-oz size) white asparagus spears

Lemon Vinaigrette

- 1 bottle (8 oz) herb-and-garlic salad dressing
- ½ cup lemon juice
- 2 tablespoons snipped chives
- ¼ teaspoon ground white pepper

- 2 heads Boston lettuce
- 1 bunch watercress

1. Drain asparagus spears.
2. Make Lemon Vinaigrette: In small bowl, combine vinaigrette ingredients.
3. In large, shallow, glass baking dish, arrange asparagus spears. Pour dressing over asparagus.
4. Refrigerate, covered, several hours to chill well.
5. Cut cores from lettuce; discard. Wash leaves; dry on paper towels or spin in a salad dryer. Refrigerate in crisper several hours or overnight. Wash watercress; drain. Refrigerate in crisper.
6. To serve: Arrange lettuce leaves on chilled large serving platter. Remove asparagus from vinaigrette; arrange around the outside of platter in groups, alternating green and white asparagus. Place watercress in center. Spoon vinaigrette over top. *Makes 20 to 24 servings.*

Raspberry-Sherbet Mold

- 6 pints raspberry sherbet
- ½ pint (1 cup) heavy cream, whipped stiff
  Crème de cassis

1. Day ahead: Line 3-quart heart-shaped mold with plastic wrap.
2. Remove sherbet from freezer; let stand at room temperature to soften—about 20 minutes. Pack into mold. Smooth surface with spatula.
3. Place in freezer until firm—overnight.
4. To unmold: Grasp plastic wrap and pull out sherbet mold; invert on chilled serving tray. Discard wrap.
5. Decorate outside edge and around bottom with whipped-cream ruching, using a pastry bag and number-6 rosette tip. Return to freezer until serving. (If stored more than one day, freezer-wrap in foil.)
6. Pass crème de cassis to serve over each portion of sherbet—about 1 tablespoon per serving. *Makes 24 servings.*

Sensational Celebrations

Life's special occasions deserve nothing less than festive dishes and glorious menus that help to express our heartfelt sentiment and best wishes. Our fabulous celebration recipes, beginning with the engagement brunch, at left, start on page 181.

Engagement Brunch

Left: The big question was popped, and the answer was a resounding "Yes!" Now celebrate the decision with this luscious, romantic brunch of His and Hers Eggs Benedict in two delicious variations — beef tenderloin and avocado-smoked salmon — and a custard-filled Cassatta.

169

Bridal Shower Buffet

With the "big day" fast approaching, honor the glowing bride-to-be with this lovely menu. **Clockwise, from center:** creamy Salmon-And-Asparagus Terrine in Watercress-Dill Sauce; hearts-of-palm salad; Breasts of Chicken in Wine With Julienne Vegetables; White-Chocolate-Dipped Kiwi; Meringue Kisses with chocolate-pistachio filling; Strawberries With Lemon Cream; and a Two-Tiered Shower Cake adorned with delicate Sugar Bells and a ribbon-handled umbrella. *Recipes begin on page 183.*

IRWIN HOROWITZ

A Wedding Reception at Home

Toast the happy couple and their new life together with this light, elegant fare that serves 50. Everything can be prepared a day in advance, and, with the help of a few friends, plus our preparation tips, the host or hostess can enjoy the celebration, too. **At bottom right** is a tray of assorted canapés filled with cucumber, egg salad, ham, cheese, pâté and pineapple. **In the center,** cream-cheese-and-watercress rolls stand in a toasted bread basket. **At left,** a chafing dish warms seafood-chicken Newburg, which is served in toast cups. White-wine-cassis punch provides the refreshment, and the traditional wedding cake bears cascades of fragrant, fresh blossoms. *Recipes begin on page 187.*

Happy Anniversary Dinner

This splendid menu is a fantastic and fitting tribute to the many years of life and love spent together. **At bottom,** artichokes are filled with Margarita Mayonnaise and pinwheeled with cooked shrimp. **To the left** is a magnificent Herbed Rack of Lamb, nestled in a bed of Saffron Rice and sautéed sugar snap peas; **above** is an elegant Red-Pepper-Endive Salad with tomato dressing. And the Deluxe Raspberry-Almond Cake salutes the couple with best wishes for many more happy anniversaries to come. *Recipes begin on page 192.*

IRWIN HOROWITZ

175

Celebration Cake-In-Bloom

All eyes will be on this spectacular dessert that turns any special occasion into a gala event. This rich, almond-flavored pound cake is glazed with apricots, then lavishly decorated with a profusion of pastel sugar flowers—roses, daisies, pansies and sweet peas. Our delectable recipes and easy, illustrated directions let you re-create this flower-topped beauty for your next exciting celebration. *See recipe on page 194.*

176

Chocolate Birthday Spectacular

Birthdays come but once a year (thankfully, some might say!). Whether the party is for someone in his or her young teens or swinging seventies, the celebration will be sensational with this dark, rich, creamy chocolate cake. The batter is homemade, as is the Mocha-Butter Filling and the Chocolate-Sour-Cream Frosting. And you can delight the children at the party with a special mini cake of their own. The finishing touches for both cakes: tiny candied lilacs and a special inscription hand-lettered in creamy icing. *See recipe on page 197.*

Creative Birthday Cakes for Children

The most exciting moment of any children's birthday party is the arrival of the cake, and the wilder and more colorful the cake is, the better. We've dreamed up some delightful cakes that anyone can make without using special pans. The secret lies in cutting a cake into different shapes and putting them together with icing. We used time-saving cake mixes and packaged frosting, but you can use your own favorite recipes. Raggedy Ann's hair is licorice, her eyes are gumdrops and she is dressed with enough candy and frosting to satisfy any sweet tooth. The passengers in the animal express are cookies, as are the wheels. The owl is feathered with frosting, and the firetruck uses a licorice hose. *Recipes begin on page 198.*

IRWIN HOROWITZ

Christening Brunch

On this special christening day, mark the occasion with a heavenly meal of Bacon Roses and Chived Eggs in Puff Pastry, lemon-buttered asparagus, Melon-Grape Mélange and a refreshing beverage, Grapefruit-Grenadine Sunrise. *Recipes begin on page 201.*

180

continued from page 169

Engagement Brunch

(Planned for 2)
Pink Champagne
Beef-Tenderloin Benedict*
Avocado-Smoked-Salmon Benedict*
Cassatta*
Cognac Cappucino*

His and Hers Eggs Benedict
(pictured)

Processor Hollandaise Sauce, recipe follows
Salt
2 eggs

Beef-Tenderloin Benedict (see Note)
1 slice filet of beef, 1 inch thick (about 6 oz)
  Salt
  Dash ground pepper
1 teaspoon butter or margarine
1 teaspoon salad oil
1 slice tomato, ½ inch thick

2 rounds (4-inch) of bread, toasted
2 slices ripe avocado
  Watercress

Avocado-Smoked-Salmon Benedict (see Note)
½ ripe medium avocado
4 thin slices smoked salmon

1. Prepare Processor Hollandaise Sauce. Keep warm over hot water.
2. Poach eggs: In medium skillet, bring 1 inch water to boiling; add ½ teaspoon salt; reduce heat to simmer.
3. Break one egg at a time into custard cups; quickly slip eggs into water, one by one. Cook, covered, 3 to 5 minutes. Lift out of water with slotted pancake turner or spoon. Drain well on paper towels. Keep warm.
4. Meanwhile, make Beef-Tenderloin Benedict: Gently flatten filet; sprinkle each side with salt and pepper. In hot butter and oil, in small heavy skillet, over medium heat, cook filet, turning every 3 minutes, about 9 minutes for rare.
5. Quickly sauté tomato slice, turning once, until warmed through. Place on toast; top with filet and a poached egg. Spoon hollandaise over egg. Garnish with 2 avocado slices and watercress. Serve at once.
6. To make Avocado-Smoked-Salmon Benedict, peel avocado; cut in slices. Arrange 2 slices salmon and

the avocado on toast on warm serving plate. Place egg on top; spoon hollandaise over egg. Garnish with remaining salmon slices, rolled, and watercress. Serve immediately. *Makes 2 servings.*

Note: Prepare one serving of each, as pictured, or double one recipe and prepare two alike.

Processor Hollandaise Sauce

3 egg yolks
3 tablespoons lemon juice
¼ teaspoon salt
  Dash ground red pepper
½ cup (1 stick) hot, melted butter or margarine

1. In processor with chopping blade or plastic mixing blade, or in blender container, combine yolks, lemon juice, salt and pepper. Cover and process 10 seconds.
2. Remove pusher from feed tube of processor or lid from blender. With motor running, gradually add melted butter in a steady stream.
3. Serve immediately or keep warm by placing bowl in 2 inches hot (not boiling) water. *Makes 1 cup.*

Cassatta
(pictured)

Sponge Cake
6 eggs
1½ cups cake flour
1 teaspoon baking powder
¼ teaspoon salt
¼ teaspoon cream of tartar
1½ cups granulated sugar
⅓ cup water
1 teaspoon vanilla extract
1 tablespoon lemon juice

  Filling, recipe follows
1½ cups heavy cream
¼ cup confectioners' sugar
  Few drops red food color (optional)
2 tablespoons light rum

1. Make Sponge Cake: Separate eggs, putting whites in large bowl and yolks in small bowl of an electric mixer. Let the egg whites warm to room temperature—1 hour.
2. Preheat oven to 350F.
3. Sift flour, baking powder and salt together on a sheet of waxed paper.
4. Add cream of tartar to egg whites. With electric mixer at medium speed, beat whites until foamy.

Sensational Celebrations

Gradually beat in ¾ cup granulated sugar, a tablespoon at a time. Continue beating until stiff, glossy peaks form when beaters are slowly raised.

5. With same beaters, beat egg yolks until thick and lemon-colored. Gradually beat in remaining granulated sugar, a tablespoonful at a time. Beat until thick and light—2 minutes.
6. In measuring cup, combine water, vanilla and lemon juice.
7. At low speed, blend flour mixture, one-third at a time, into egg-yolk mixture alternately with water mixture. Beat 1 minute.
8. With wire whisk or rubber spatula, using an over-and-under motion, fold into egg-white mixture.
9. Pour batter into three ungreased 8-inch heart-shaped or layer-cake pans.
10. Bake 25 to 30 minutes or just until surface springs back when lightly pressed with fingertip.
11. Invert pans, setting rims on two other pans. Cool 1½ hours.
12. Loosen around edge. Tap inverted pans on counter top; remove from pans.
13. Meanwhile, make Filling; refrigerate. In medium bowl, combine heavy cream, confectioners' sugar and red food color. With portable mixer, beat until stiff; refrigerate.
14. To assemble cake: Place one heart-shaped layer on plate, top side down. Brush with 1 tablespoon rum; spread with half of filling. Place second layer on top, top side down. Brush with 1 tablespoon rum; spread with remaining filling. Top with remaining layer, top side up.
15. With spatula, frost top and side with 1½ cups whipped cream. Turn remaining cream into pastry bag with number-5 star tip. Pipe a ruching around top edge and base of cake and a heart shape in center of cake. Refrigerate until ready to serve. *Makes 12 servings.*

Filling

1 **pkg (3⅛ oz) vanilla-pudding-and-pie-filling mix**
1½ **cups milk**
2 **tablespoons light rum**
½ **cup miniature semisweet chocolate pieces**
½ **cup (4 oz) chopped, mixed candied fruit**

1. In medium saucepan, combine pudding mix and milk; mix well. Cook, stirring, over medium heat, until mixture comes to a full, rolling boil. Turn into medium bowl; place waxed paper directly on surface.
2. Place in large bowl of ice to cool quickly. Add rum, chocolate and candied fruit. Refrigerate until needed.

Cognac Cappucino

1 **cup milk**
2 **teaspoons instant espresso coffee**
½ **cup cognac**
Dash ground cinnamon

1. Combine milk and instant coffee in a small saucepan. Bring just to boiling over low heat, stirring constantly.
2. Stir in cognac; sprinkle with cinnamon. Serve immediately. *Makes 2 servings.*

Bridal Shower Buffet

(Planned for 24)

Salmon-And-Asparagus
Terrine*
Breasts of Chicken in Wine
With Julienne Vegetables*
Hearts-of-Palm Salade Variée
White Wine
Two-Tiered Shower Cake*
Meringue Kisses*
White-Chocolate-Dipped
Kiwi*
Strawberries With
Lemon Cream*
Champagne or
Sparkling Wine

*Recipes given for starred dishes.

Salmon-And-Asparagus Terrine
(pictured)

12 fresh asparagus stalks (½ inch thick)
1½ lb fresh salmon steaks
1 small onion, peeled and quartered
2 tablespoons lemon juice
2 large egg whites
1½ cups heavy cream
½ teaspoon salt
  Dash ground red pepper
  Boiling water

Watercress-Dill Sauce
1 container (8 oz) sour cream
½ cup mayonnaise
½ cup watercress leaves
¼ cup freshly snipped dill or 1 tablespoon dried
  dillweed
1 tablespoon lemon juice
¼ teaspoon salt

1. Cut and discard woody ends from asparagus to make 6-inch stalks (see Note). Wash asparagus well with cold water. With vegetable parer, starting about 2 to 3 inches from tender tip, pare down each stalk to remove scales and tough skin from lower part of stalk. In large skillet, over medium-high heat, bring ½ inch water to boiling. Add asparagus; cook, covered, 5 minutes or until tender-crisp. Drain; rinse under cold water; drain well.
2. Preheat oven to 350F. Lightly oil a 12-by-4-by-3-inch (6 cup) loaf pan (see Note). With parchment or waxed paper, line bottom of pan. Remove and discard skin and most bones from the salmon (you should have 1 pound salmon remaining).
3. In food processor or electric blender, process or blend onion and lemon juice until onion is finely chopped. Add salmon, egg whites and heavy cream; process until very smooth. Stir in salt and ground red pepper.
4. Spoon 1⅓ cups salmon mixture into prepared pan. At one end of pan, lay 3 stalks asparagus, evenly spaced and with tips toward center, across salmon. Repeat at other end so there are three rows of two tip-to-tip stalks each.
5. Cover asparagus with 1⅓ cups salmon mixture; add remaining asparagus, arranged as in Step 4. Cover with remaining salmon mixture. Cover pan tightly

with foil; place in large roasting pan. Place in oven, and pour boiling water to within 1 inch of the top of loaf pan. Bake 1 hour. Carefully remove loaf pan from water bath; cool to room temperature; then refrigerate at least 3 hours or overnight.

6. Make Watercress-Dill Sauce: In food processor or electric blender, process or blend all sauce ingredients 3 minutes or until smooth. To serve: Unmold salmon terrine onto platter; spoon some sauce around terrine. Pass remaining sauce. *Makes 12 servings (24 [½-inch-thick] slices).*

Note: Salmon can be molded in a 9-by-5-by-3-inch loaf pan. Asparagus stalks should then measure 4½ inches when trimmed.

Breasts of Chicken in Wine With Julienne Vegetables
(pictured)

2 lb carrots, pared
2 bunches leeks
½ cup salad oil
12 chicken-breast halves with ribs (about 6 lb)
1 teaspoon dried tarragon leaves
½ teaspoon salt
¼ teaspoon ground pepper
½ cup (1 stick) butter or margarine
2 tablespoons lemon juice
1 can (10¾ oz) condensed chicken broth
½ cup white wine
3 tablespoons all-purpose flour

1. Preheat oven to 375F. Thinly slice half the carrots; place in large roasting pan. Cut remaining carrots into 2½-by-¼-inch strips; set aside. Cut and discard root end from leeks. Cut leeks in half lengthwise; wash thoroughly. Cut dark green tops off and coarsely chop; place in roasting pan with carrot. Cut remainder of leeks into 2½-by-¼-inch strips; set aside.
2. In large skillet, over medium heat, heat ¼ cup oil. Add 6 chicken-breast halves, skin side down. Cook 10 to 12 minutes or until golden-brown. As breasts brown, place on top of carrot and leeks in roasting pan. Repeat with remaining breasts and oil. Sprinkle breasts with tarragon, salt and pepper. Bake 15 minutes.

Sensational Celebrations

3. Meanwhile, with paper towel, wipe skillet clean. In same skillet, over medium heat, melt butter. Add carrot and leek strips and lemon juice. Cook, stirring constantly, 4 to 5 minutes or until carrot is tender-crisp. Place vegetables on large serving platter; cover; keep warm.

4. Place chicken breasts on top of carrot and leek strips; cover. Add chicken broth to roasting pan. Place roasting pan over two burners; over medium-high heat, bring to boiling; stir to dissolve browned bits. In small bowl, stir white wine into flour until smooth; gradually add to broth. Cook, stirring, until mixture thickens slightly. Strain; discard vegetables. Spoon some sauce over breasts; pass remaining sauce separately. *Makes 12 servings.*

Two-Tiered Shower Cake
(pictured)

Sugar Bells, recipe follows
Icing Shower Umbrellas, recipe follows

Orange Cake
(You will need to make this cake recipe *two* times in order to get 4 layers. Be sure to have sufficient ingredients on hand.)
2½ cups cake flour
  2 teaspoons baking powder
½ teaspoon salt
½ cup (1 stick) butter, softened
1½ cups granulated sugar
  2 teaspoons grated orange peel
  5 large eggs
  1 cup milk

Vanilla Buttercream
(You will need to make this recipe *three* times. Be sure to have sufficient ingredients on hand.)
½ cup (1 stick) butter, softened
  1 box (1 lb) confectioners' sugar
  4 tablespoons milk
1½ teaspoons vanilla extract
    Rose paste food color or red liquid food color

½ cup Grand Marnier or other orange-flavor liqueur
¼ cup orange juice
  1 (9-inch) cardboard circle
  2 (5-inch) cardboard circles

1. Two to three days ahead: Make Sugar Bells and Icing Shower Umbrellas.

2. Day ahead, make Orange Cake: Preheat oven to 350F. Grease and flour one 10-by-2-inch and one 6-by-2-inch round cake pan. In small bowl, with fork, combine flour, baking powder and salt; stir well. In large

bowl, with electric mixer at medium speed, cream butter, sugar and orange peel until well blended. Add eggs, one at a time, beating well after each addition until mixture is very light and fluffy.

3. At low speed, beat in flour mixture, in thirds, alternately with 1 cup milk, in halves, beginning and ending with flour mixture; beat just until combined.

4. Pour 1½ cups batter into the prepared 6-inch pan and the remaining batter into the prepared 10-inch pan. Bake 6-inch layer 25 minutes and 10-inch layer 30 minutes or until cake tester inserted in centers comes out clean. Cool in pans on wire racks 5 minutes. Remove cake layers from pans. Wash pans and prepare as directed above. Prepare another recipe of Orange Cake to make another 6-inch and 10-inch cake layer. When all layers are completely cooled, wrap separately in foil and refrigerate. (If desired, cake layers may be made several days ahead and frozen.)

5. Make Vanilla Buttercream: In large bowl, with electric mixer at low speed, beat butter, confectioners' sugar, 2 tablespoons milk and the vanilla. Beating at high speed, gradually add remaining milk; continue beating until buttercream is light and fluffy (makes about 2½ cups). Prepare a second buttercream recipe. Then prepare a third recipe, but use only 2 tablespoons milk (this recipe will be used for decorating and should be stiffer). Buttercream may be made several days ahead and refrigerated; let come to room temperature before filling and frosting cake.

6. In small bowl, place ½ cup of the stiffer buttercream; tint pink with small amount of food color. Place plastic wrap directly on surface and refrigerate. In another small bowl, place 2 cups of the stiffer buttercream; cover as above and refrigerate for decorating.

7. To assemble cake: If cake tops are too rounded, trim to make flat. In 1-cup measuring cup, combine Grand Marnier and orange juice. Brush each cake-layer top with orange-juice mixture. Place a 9-inch cardboard circle on serving plate; cover outer edge with pieces of waxed paper. Place one 10-inch cake layer, top side up, on cardboard; spread with 1 cup buttercream. Top with second 10-inch cake layer, bottom side up. In center of layer, spread ¼ cup buttercream in a 6-inch circle. Place one 5-inch cardboard circle directly on buttercream. Place 1 teaspoon buttercream on center of cardboard; top with second 5-inch cardboard circle. Place 6-inch cake layer, top side up, on cardboard circle; spread with ½ cup buttercream. Top with remaining 6-inch cake layer, bottom side up. Spread a thin layer of buttercream over top and sides of cake to seal. Refrigerate cake until frosting is slightly set—about 30 minutes.

Sensational Celebrations

8. With a long, flat icing spatula, spread remaining soft buttercream over entire cake–sides first, then tops. (To get a smooth finish, dip spatula frequently in warm water.) Pull waxed paper out from under 9-inch cardboard. Spoon the 2 cups reserved stiff buttercream into a pastry bag fitted with a ½-inch star tip. Pipe a "rope" border around the bottom and top edges of the 10-inch tier and around the bottom and top edges of the 6-inch tier. (To make rope border, pipe a downward arc. Then pipe an S shape, starting from the inside of the center of the arc. Continue making S shapes, starting each S from the center of the arc before it to make a continuous rope.)

9. With toothpick, mark the side of the 6-inch tier vertically in four equal parts. Mark the 10-inch tier in the same four equal parts. On the 10-inch tier only, mark each part in the middle–there will be eight equal parts. Spread small amount of buttercream onto the back of 8 sugar bells. Place a bell on each mark on the 6-inch tier. Place bells on the 10-inch tier, spacing them between bells on top tier. Spoon pink buttercream into a pastry bag fitted with a coupler and ¹⁄₁₆-inch writing tip. On the 6-inch tier, with even pressure, pipe one swag (double string) between the bells. On the 10-inch tier, pipe two swags between the bells, using the markings as a guide. With a toothpick, on top of the cake, outline five connecting half-circles to make a flower pattern. Pipe pink buttercream in small dots on top of pattern. Change tip of the pastry bag with pink buttercream to a ¼-inch star tip. At the beginning and end of each swag, pipe a star. (Cover star tip with foil or plastic wrap and store remaining pink buttercream in pastry bag to complete Icing Shower Umbrellas.) Place an Icing Shower Umbrella in the center of flower pattern on top of cake. *Makes 56 servings.*

Sugar Bells

1 **cup sugar**
2 **teaspoons water**
Rose paste food color or red liquid food color
Cornstarch
Small bell-candy mold
Cardboard

1. In medium-size plastic bag, combine sugar and water. With fingers, knead through bag to mix evenly. Transfer ⅓ cup sugar mixture to another plastic bag. With toothpick, add small amount of food color to bag; knead with fingers through bag until evenly distributed. Keep adding color, a little at a time, to reach desired intensity.

2. Sprinkle cornstarch over bell-candy mold. With small spatula, carefully pack pink sugar into the bow of the mold; pack white sugar into the bell. With spatula, scrape off excess. Mixture should be packed as firmly as possible into mold, with top perfectly flat and level with edge in order to unmold it smoothly.

3. Place a piece of cardboard over mold; invert; lift mold off. Dry at room temperature at least 5 hours or overnight, until hard. (Or place in 200F oven for 5 minutes.) Repeat with remaining pink and white sugar mixtures. Occasionally dust mold and spatula with cornstarch to prevent sticking. Save 8 sugar bells for cake; remainder may be used for favors. *Makes about 2½ dozen bells.*

Icing Shower Umbrellas

1 **large egg white**
1½ **cups confectioners' sugar**
⅛ **teaspoon cream of tartar**
Small plastic novelty umbrellas (about 3 inches in diameter) with separate plastic handles
Plastic wrap
Nonstick cooking spray

Leftover pink buttercream

1. Day ahead: In small bowl, with electric mixer at high speed, beat egg white, sugar and cream of tartar until icing is stiff enough to hold its shape.

2. Reserve 1 tablespoon icing; cover with plastic wrap; set aside. Spoon remaining icing into pastry bag fitted with a ⅛-inch writing tip. Cover one umbrella top with plastic wrap; gather excess below and use to hold umbrella while decorating. Spray top with nonstick cooking spray. Using small connecting dots, pipe icing onto plastic wrap to form the outline of umbrella, including ribs. Carefully rest umbrella on tray. Repeat with remaining icing in pastry bag and umbrellas. Let dry at room temperature, uncovered, overnight.

3. Next day, unmold icing umbrellas: With one hand cupped under, carefully turn umbrella upside down. With other hand, gently squeeze excess plastic wrap away from the umbrella—umbrella will drop into your hand. Using reserved icing, attach plastic handles to umbrellas. If necessary, prop up handles till dried.

4. After cake is decorated, use leftover pink buttercream in pastry bag with ¼-inch star tip; pipe small stars onto umbrella top. Tie a ribbon onto handle, if desired. Place an umbrella on top of cake. Extra umbrellas may be used as table decorations or favors. *Makes about 20 umbrellas.*

Sensational Celebrations

Meringue Kisses
(pictured)

2 large egg whites, at room temperature
¼ cup sugar
4 tablespoons finely chopped pistachios
¼ cup semisweet chocolate pieces

1. Preheat oven to 300F. Lightly grease 2 cookie sheets or line them with parchment paper.
2. In medium bowl, with electric mixer at high speed, beat egg whites until foamy. Gradually add sugar, 1 tablespoon at a time, beating just until soft peaks form. Fold in 2 tablespoons pistachios.
3. Spoon mixture into pastry bag fitted with ½-inch plain tip. Pipe into kisses on prepared cookie sheets or drop by teaspoonfuls. Bake 20 minutes or until meringues are crisp and lightly golden. With metal spatula, remove to wire rack.
4. Place chocolate in custard cup; set cup in small saucepan with ½ inch water. Place cup in pan; heat until chocolate melts.
5. Remove cup from pan. Dip bottom of a meringue in chocolate. Place base of another meringue against chocolate-dipped meringue and press gently to make thin rim of chocolate. Roll chocolate rim in remaining pistachios. Repeat with remaining meringues. Dry kisses on wire rack. Store in airtight container. *Makes about 4½ dozen.*

White-Chocolate-Dipped Kiwi
(pictured)

4 medium kiwi fruit (about ¾ lb)
¼ lb white chocolate

1. Pare kiwi; cut each crosswise into six ¼-inch slices. Place on paper-towel-lined tray. Chop white chocolate; place in small custard cup or bowl. Set custard cup in small saucepan with ½ inch water. Over medium heat, bring water just to boiling. Heat chocolate, stirring occasionally, just until melted.
2. Remove cup from water; let stand 5 minutes. Pat kiwi slices with paper towel. Dip each slice, one at a time, into chocolate, covering halfway; let excess drip off. Place on waxed-paper-lined tray. Refrigerate until set—about 1 hour. Place each slice in a paper petit-four cup. Keep refrigerated till ready to serve. *Makes 2½ dozen.*

Strawberries With Lemon Cream
(pictured)

1 pkg (8 oz) cream cheese, softened
⅓ cup confectioners' sugar
1 teaspoon grated lemon peel
1 tablespoon lemon juice
2 containers (1-pint size) strawberries (about 42)

1. In bowl, with portable electric mixer, beat cream cheese, sugar, lemon peel and juice till smooth. Cover; refrigerate. (Filling can be made ahead and kept refrigerated.)
2. Remove hulls from berries; place on paper-towel-lined tray, hulled end down. With sharp knife, cut an X through top of each berry (*don't* cut all the way through). Pull sections apart slightly.
3. Spoon filling into a pastry bag fitted with ½-inch star tip. Pipe a heaping teaspoon in center of each berry. (Berries may be filled 2 hours before serving.) To serve: Place in paper petit-four cups. *Makes about 3½ dozen.*

Notes on Preparation of
❋ **An Afternoon Wedding Reception** ❋

For 50 people, we have planned seven kinds of canapés, approximately 50 of each kind. In addition, there are about 60 Cream-Cheese-And-Watercress Sandwiches and 100 small servings of hot Seafood-And-Chicken Newburg.

Everything is finger food except for the cake. You may need to rent champagne glasses, plates and forks for the cake, a punch bowl and punch cups.

All of our canapés, the Cream-Cheese-And-Watercress Sandwiches and the Bread Basket can be made a day ahead and stored as directed. Several hours before serving, the canapés may be sliced and arranged on

Sensational Celebrations

serving trays, as pictured. These can then be refrigerated, covered with a damp towel, until serving. Arrange Cream-Cheese-And-Watercress Sandwiches in Bread Basket just before serving.

The Seafood-And-Chicken Newburg and Toast Cups may be made a day ahead and stored as directed. Reheat seafood mixture just before turning into heated chafing dish for serving. (If mixture seems too thick, add a little more sherry.)

The cake may be made and frosted the day before and stored in the refrigerator. Decorate with fresh flowers an hour or so before serving.

The champagne must be chilled in ice several hours ahead.

The Ice Ring may be made and frozen the day before. When it's frozen, it may also be unmolded and stored in freezer. The white wine and cassis for the punch bowl should be well chilled. Just before serving, combine wine and cassis in chilled punch bowl (to chill bowl, fill with ice until chilled, then empty out); float Ice Ring on top.

An Afternoon Wedding Reception

(Planned for 50)
Champagne
Assorted Canapés*
Cream-Cheese-And-
Watercress Sandwiches en Croûte*
Seafood-And-Chicken Newburg*
Devil's-Food Wedding Cake*
White-Wine-Cassis Punch Bowl*
Salted Almonds   Pastel Mints

Swiss-Cheese-And-Olive Rolls
(pictured)

 1 lb loaf unsliced white bread
 1 cup (2 sticks) butter or margarine, softened
24 to 32 large stuffed olives
 8 slices Swiss cheese (about 8 oz)
 2 tablespoons strong mustard
 2 cups chopped parsley

*Recipes given for starred dishes.

1. With long serrated knife, trim all crusts from bread. Slice into eight lengthwise slices. Using a rolling pin, gently roll bread to make thin.
2. Spread each slice with butter, using about ½ cup in all.
3. Place 3 or 4 olives at one end of each slice of bread.
4. Arrange cheese slices over rest of bread; spread lightly with mustard.
5. Roll up each slice of bread, starting from olive end.
6. Spread outside of rolls with remaining butter. Sprinkle ¼ cup parsley onto waxed paper and roll a sandwich roll in it to cover completely. Repeat with remaining rolls.
7. To store, wrap in damp paper towels and refrigerate. To serve, slice each roll crosswise into seven spirals. *Makes 56.*

Egg-Salad Ribbons
(pictured)

 1 lb loaf thin-sliced white bread
 1 lb loaf thin-sliced whole-wheat bread
 6 hard-cooked eggs, finely chopped
⅓ cup mayonnaise or cooked salad dressing
 2 tablespoons sour cream
¼ teaspoon salt
 1 tablespoon finely chopped onion
 1 tablespoon chopped fresh dill or ½ teaspoon dried dillweed
    Dash ground pepper
    Fresh dill sprigs (optional)

1. With sharp knife, trim crusts from bread.
2. Combine eggs, mayonnaise, sour cream, salt, onion, dill and pepper; mix well.
3. Make three-decker sandwiches, with 1 rounded tablespoon egg salad on two slices: five sandwiches with white, whole-wheat, then white bread; and five sandwiches with whole-wheat, white, then whole-wheat bread. Press each down with a plate for 30 minutes.
4. To store: Wrap in damp paper towels. Refrigerate. To serve, slice each into six ribbons; cut each ribbon crosswise in half; then cut in half again. Decorate each with sprig of dill. *Makes 120 ribbons of each design.*

Sensational Celebrations

Cucumber Spirals
(pictured)

1-lb loaf unsliced white bread
⅔ cup (1⅓ sticks) butter or margarine, softened
3 tablespoons chopped parsley
½ teaspoon grated lemon peel
2 teaspoons lemon juice
1 long cucumber, washed
½ cup (1 stick) butter or margarine, softened
2 cups chopped parsley

1. With long serrated knife, trim all crusts from bread. Slice into eight lengthwise slices. Using rolling pin, gently roll slices to make them thin.
2. Combine ⅔ cup butter, 3 tablespoons parsley, the lemon peel and lemon juice; mix well.
3. Spread bread with butter mixture.
4. Slice unpared cucumber into 8 lengthwise strips. Trim ends from each. Place 1 strip on each of 4 bread slices. (Refrigerate leftover cucumber to use another time.) Roll up from long side. Place each cucumber roll on a remaining slice of buttered bread, cut edge down; roll up again.
5. Spread outside of each roll with butter. Sprinkle 2 cups chopped parsley on waxed paper and roll sandwich rolls in it to cover them completely with parsley.
6. To store, wrap each in damp paper towels. To serve, slice each roll crosswise into 15 spirals. *Makes 60.*

Pineapple-Cream-Cheese-And-Walnut Rolls
(pictured)

1-lb loaf unsliced white bread
2 cans (8-oz size) crushed pineapple
2 pkg (8-oz size) cream cheese, softened
4 slices bacon, cooked and crumbled
2 tablespoons chopped walnuts
2 tablespoons chopped raisins
1 cup finely chopped walnuts

1. With long serrated knife, trim all crusts from bread. Slice into eight lengthwise slices. Using a rolling pin, gently roll bread to make thin.
2. Drain pineapple, reserving liquid. Mix 1 package cream cheese with the bacon, 2 tablespoons chopped walnuts, the raisins, pineapple and 1 tablespoon reserved pineapple juice.
3. Spread 3 tablespoons cream-cheese mixture on each bread slice; roll up from short end. Mix remaining package of cream cheese with 2 tablespoons reserved pineapple juice. Use to spread on outside of each

sandwich roll. Then roll each in finely chopped nuts placed on sheet of waxed paper.
4. To store: Wrap in damp paper towels; refrigerate. To serve, slice each roll crosswise into seven spirals. *Makes 56.*

Ham-And-Swiss-Cheese Rolls
(pictured)

1½ cups whipped cream cheese
2 teaspoons chopped parsley
2 pkg (8-oz size) sliced ham (12 slices in all)
6 slices Swiss cheese (about 8 oz)
2 tablespoons strong mustard

1. Combine cream cheese and parsley; mix well. Spread 1 slice ham with 2 tablespoons cream-cheese mixture; top with 1 slice Swiss cheese. Spread with 1 teaspoon mustard.
2. Top with 1 slice ham; spread with 2 tablespoons cream-cheese mixture. Repeat, to make six in all.
3. Roll up each from short side. To store: Arrange on tray; cover with damp towel. Refrigerate.
4. To serve: Slice each roll into eight crosswise slices. *Makes 48.*

Pâté Spirals
(pictured)

16 slices thin-sliced white bread
8 slices thin-sliced whole-wheat bread
1 can (4¾ oz) liver pâté
2 tablespoons mayonnaise or cooked salad dressing
2 tablespoons finely chopped scallion
1 tablespoon chopped parsley

1. Trim crusts from bread. Roll gently with rolling pin.
2. Combine pâté, mayonnaise, scallion and parsley; mix well.
3. Spread one slice white bread with 1 rounded teaspoon filling; top with whole-wheat slice; spread with 1 rounded teaspoon filling; then top with white slice and spread with 1 rounded teaspoon filling. Continue with rest of bread and filling, to make eight stacks of three slices each.
4. Roll up each from long side. To store: Refrigerate, wrapped with damp paper towels. To serve, cut crosswise into six spirals. *Makes 48 spirals.*

Ham Rolls
(pictured)

2 pkg (8-oz size) sliced ham (12 slices in all)
1½ cups whipped cream cheese
1 jar (8 oz) midget gherkins, drained

1. Spread 1 slice ham with 1 tablespoon cream cheese. Top with slice of ham; spread with 2 tablespoons cream cheese.
2. Arrange several gherkins in a row along short edge. Roll up from gherkin side. There will be six rolls.
3. To store: Arrange on tray; cover with damp towel. Refrigerate.
4. To serve: Slice each roll into eight crosswise slices. *Makes 48.*

Cream-Cheese-And-Watercress Sandwiches en Croûte
(pictured)

2 large bunches watercress
1½ cups (3 sticks) butter or margarine, softened
½ teaspoon salt
4 pkg (3-oz size) cream cheese with chives, softened
2 tablespoons lemon juice
4 loaves (1-lb size) thinly sliced white bread
Bread Basket, recipe follows

1. Wash and drain the watercress. Reserve small center sprigs for garnish—about 64.
2. Remove stems from remaining watercress. Finely chop enough watercress to measure ½ cup.
3. Beat the butter and the salt with electric mixer until smooth. Beat in the cream cheese. Gradually beat in lemon juice. Then beat in the chopped watercress.
4. With sharp knife, trim crusts from each slice of bread to make 3-inch squares. Roll each slice with rolling pin.
5. Spread bread slices evenly with watercress butter, using about 2½ teaspoons for each. Roll up, jelly-roll fashion. Insert a reserved watercress sprig in one end.
6. To store: Arrange rolls in single layer, seam side down, on tray; cover with damp paper towels. Refrigerate. To serve, arrange in Bread Basket. *Makes 64.*

Bread Basket
(pictured)

1 loaf (2 lb, 3 oz) unsliced sandwich bread (about 16 inches long)
¼ cup (½ stick) butter or margarine, melted

1. With a long serrated knife, slice off the top from bread lengthwise. Carefully cut all around the inside edge of the loaf to make a shell about ¼ inch thick.
2. Carefully remove bread from shell. (Save bread for bread crumbs.)
3. Cut scallops along sides of bread, as pictured. Cut four arcs on each long side and one on each end.
4. Preheat oven to 350F. Brush outside of basket with melted butter. Place on cookie sheet. Toast in oven just until light golden—about 8 to 10 minutes. Let cool.
5. Store at room temperature until ready to use. *Makes 1 basket.*

Seafood-And-Chicken Newburg
(pictured)

Toast Cups, recipe follows
Poached Chicken Breasts, recipe follows

2 cans (5-oz size) crabmeat
½ cup (1 stick) butter or margarine
6 tablespoons all-purpose flour
1 teaspoon salt
Dash ground white pepper
Dash ground red pepper
Reserved chicken broth from Poached Chicken Breasts
1 cup heavy cream (½ pt)
3 tablespoons dry sherry
2 hard-cooked eggs, finely chopped
2 tablespoons finely chopped onion
1 cup coarsely chopped fresh mushrooms
2 tablespoons finely chopped parsley
2 tablespoons finely chopped chives
3 jars (4.4-oz size) baby shrimp, drained
Chopped parsley

1. Day ahead: Prepare Toast Cups and Poached Chicken Breasts.
2. Drain crabmeat and remove any cartilage.

Sensational Celebrations

3. Melt 3 tablespoons butter in medium saucepan. Remove from heat; stir in flour, salt, white pepper and red pepper until smooth. Gradually stir in the reserved chicken broth and cream.
4. Bring mixture to boiling, stirring; sauce will be thickened and smooth.
5. Stir in sherry, chopped egg, crabmeat and chopped chicken.
6. Heat rest of butter in small skillet; sauté onion, mushrooms, parsley and chives until mushrooms are tender—about 5 minutes. Stir into crab-chicken mixture. Turn into chafing dish to keep warm. Decorate edge with shrimp, as pictured. Sprinkle with parsley.
7. To serve, fill Toast Cups with Newburg mixture (about 1 rounded teaspoon for each); decorate each with shrimp and parsley. *Makes about 100 servings.*

Toast Cups

50 **slices thin-sliced white bread
     (3½ [1-lb size] loaves)**
⅔ **cup (1⅓ sticks) butter or margarine, melted**

1. Preheat oven to 350F.
2. With 2-inch round cookie cutter, cut out 100 rounds of white bread. Brush both sides with melted butter. Press into 1¾-inch muffin-pan cups.
3. Bake 10 to 15 minutes or until golden around edge. Gently lift out of pans; cool on wire racks.
4. Store, lightly covered, at room temperature. To serve, fill each cup with 1 rounded teaspoon filling. *Makes 100 toast cups.*

Poached Chicken Breasts

1 **small onion, sliced**
1 **celery stalk, sliced**
1 **small carrot, sliced**
1 **parsley sprig**
½ **teaspoon salt**
¼ **teaspoon dried thyme leaves**
1 **can (13¾ oz) chicken broth**
½ **cup water**
2 **whole chicken breasts (2 lb), split**

1. In 3-quart kettle, combine onion, celery, carrot, parsley, salt, thyme, chicken broth, water and split chicken breasts; bring mixture to boiling.
2. Reduce heat and simmer, covered, 30 minutes or just until chicken breasts are fork-tender.
3. Remove kettle from heat. Let chicken breasts cool in broth.
4. Remove chicken breasts from broth; reserve broth. Remove skin and bone from chicken breasts. Chop meat into small cubes; store, covered, in refrigerator until next day.
5. Strain broth into a 2-cup measure; add water if necessary to make 1¾ cups broth. Store, covered, overnight in refrigerator.

Devil's-Food Wedding Cake
(pictured)

Cake
4 **pkg (1-lb, 2.5-oz size) devil's-food-cake mix**
8 **eggs**

White Frosting, recipe follows
1 **(8-inch) cardboard circle**
1 **(5-inch) cardboard circle**

Decoration
1½ **dozen fresh pink or white roses in various sizes
      Other small pink or white flowers, as pictured**

1. Day before serving, make Cake: Preheat oven to 350F. Grease well and flour a 12-by-2-inch tier-cake pan, a 9-by-2-inch tier-cake pan and a 6-by-2-inch tier-cake pan.
2. Prepare 2 packages cake mix together, as package label directs, using 4 eggs. Pour 6⅓ cups batter into prepared 12-inch pan. Pour 3 cups batter into prepared 9-inch pan. Pour 1½ cups batter into prepared 6-inch pan.
3. Bake large layer 40 to 45 minutes, medium-size layer 35 to 40 minutes and small layer 30 to 35 minutes or until surfaces spring back when gently pressed with fingertip.
4. Cool in pans on wire rack 15 minutes. Remove from pans; cool thoroughly on wire racks.
5. Prepare remaining 2 packages of cake mix together,

using 4 eggs. Bake in 12-, 9- and 6-inch tier-cake pans, as directed above.

6. When the six layers are completely cool, make White Frosting. Cut an 8-inch and a 5-inch circle from thin cardboard. Cover each with foil or plastic wrap.

7. To assemble and frost cake: If necessary, trim off rounded tops of layers so they will stack evenly. Spread a teaspoonful of frosting in the middle of a large round tray—at least 14 inches in diameter. Place one 12-inch layer, top side down, in center of tray; spread 1½ cups frosting on layer. Top with second 12-inch layer, bottom side down; spread with 1 cup frosting.

8. Place prepared 8-inch cardboard circle in center, then one 9-inch cake layer, top side down; spread with ¾ cup frosting. Add second 9-inch layer, bottom side down, and spread with ¾ cup frosting.

9. Top with prepared 5-inch cardboard circle, then one 6-inch cake layer, top side down; spread with ½ cup frosting. Then top with remaining 6-inch layer, bottom side down.

10. Reserve 3 cups frosting. Spread remaining frosting on cake: First, frost side of each layer; then, starting at top layer, frost remaining surfaces, making all frosting smooth with a spatula dipped in warm water.

11. Using reserved frosting in pastry bag with number-30 star tip, make a border on rim of each layer and around base of cake. To make border: Make slight curve on slant from left to right. Start second curve alongside first. Continue as shown in photograph on page 173.

12. Cover with a tent of foil and store in a cool place or, if possible, refrigerate overnight.

13. Early next day, decorate cake: Trim stems of roses; remove leaves and set aside.

14. Arrange roses on cake, as pictured. Arrange rose leaves around base of cake.

15. Keep cake in cool place or, if possible, refrigerate until shortly before serving.

16. To serve cake: Cut top layer into eight wedges; remove cardboard. Cut next layer into 16 wedges; remove cardboard. Cut a circle in 12-inch layer, 2½ inches from edge, to make a ring. Cut the ring into 20 pieces; cut remaining cake into eight wedges. *Makes 52 servings.*

White Frosting

¾ **cup shortening**
¼ **cup (½ stick) butter or margarine, softened**
2 **pkg (1-lb size) confectioners' sugar**
½ **cup water**
2 **teaspoons vanilla extract**
½ **teaspoon almond extract**

1. In large bowl of electric mixer, at low speed, beat shortening and butter until light and fluffy.
2. Beat in sugar, 1 cup at a time, alternately with water, beating until smooth after each addition.
3. Add vanilla and almond extracts; continue beating until smooth and of spreading consistency.
4. Keep frosting covered with damp cloth to prevent drying out. Beat again just before using.

Note: You will need to make this recipe twice. Make it in separate batches.

White-Wine-Cassis Punch Bowl
(pictured)

Ice Ring, recipe follows
3 **gallons dry white wine**
6 **cups crème de cassis**
1 **pint box strawberries, washed and hulled**

1. Day ahead: Prepare Ice Ring.
2. Several hours ahead, chill white wine and cassis. Fill punch bowl with ice to chill well.
3. Just before serving, empty punch bowl of ice. Combine 1 gallon white wine and 2 cups cassis in punch bowl; mix well. (The punch bowl may not be large enough to serve any more than this at one time. As more punch is needed, mix 1 gallon white wine with 2 cups cassis.) Float Ice Ring on top. Add strawberries. *Makes 108 (4 oz) servings.*

Ice Ring

2 **large navel oranges, washed**
Distilled water

1. Slice unpeeled oranges crosswise into slices about ⅛ inch thick. Arrange in single layer in bottom of a 5-cup ring mold, overlapping on sides.

Sensational Celebrations

2. Without disturbing orange slices, gradually pour in enough distilled water to measure 1 inch deep.
3. Freeze until firm. Then fill the rest of the mold with distilled water. Freeze until ice ring is firm—overnight.
4. When ice ring is firm, place in warm water a few seconds to loosen ice. Turn out on waxed paper. Return to freezer at once until ready to use.

Happy Anniversary Dinner

(Planned for 6)

Artichokes With
Margarita Mayonnaise*
Herbed Rack of Lamb*
Saffron Rice*
Sautéed Sugar Snap Peas
Red Wine
Red-Pepper-Endive Salade
Composée*
Deluxe Raspberry-Almond
Cake*
White Wine

Artichokes With Margarita Mayonnaise
(pictured)

6   medium (6- to 8-oz size) artichokes
1   tablespoon cider vinegar

Margarita Mayonnaise

2   limes
3   large egg yolks
1   tablespoon tequila
1   tablespoon Triple Sec or other orange-flavor liqueur
½   teaspoon salt
½   teaspoon dry mustard
1¼   cups salad oil

30   small shrimp (about ½ lb), cooked and shelled (leave last tail segment attached)

1. Trim stalk from base of each artichoke and cut a ½-inch slice from the top; remove all discolored leaves. With scissors, snip off spike ends; wash and drain artichokes.
2. In 8-quart kettle, bring 3 inches water and the vinegar to boiling; add artichokes; simmer, covered, over low heat 30 to 40 minutes or until artichoke bases can be pierced with a fork; drain. Cool; then refrigerate to chill completely.

Recipes given for starred dishes.

3. Make Margarita Mayonnaise: Grate peel from limes; wrap and refrigerate peel. Squeeze limes to make 2 tablespoons juice. In blender or food processor, combine egg yolks, lime juice, tequila, Triple Sec, salt and mustard. Blend or process 30 seconds. With motor running, gradually add oil in a thin stream, blending until mayonnaise is thick and smooth. Cover and refrigerate.
4. Assemble artichokes just before serving: Spread artichokes to reveal centers. With small spoon, scoop out and discard prickly choke. Place artichokes on individual plates. Spoon Margarita Mayonnaise into center of each artichoke, dividing evenly. Arrange 5 shrimp, tails outward, in a ring on top of each artichoke. Sprinkle some grated lime peel in center of shrimp ring. *Makes 6 servings.*

Herbed Rack of Lamb
(pictured)

2   racks of lamb, 2 to 3 lb each (6 to 8 chops each)
1   tablespoon chopped parsley
1½   teaspoons chopped fresh rosemary
¼   teaspoon salt
¼   teaspoon ground pepper
    Saffron Rice, recipe follows
    Sugar snap peas (optional)
    Fluted mushrooms (optional)
    Parsley sprigs (optional)

1. Remove the fell, or paperlike covering, from the fat on each rack. Trim excess fat from lamb, neatly tapering off at ends of meat. With small sharp knife, remove fat and meat 1½ inches from the top of bones, leaving bone ends bare. Cover bone ends with strips of foil to prevent scorching.
2. Preheat oven to 400F. With sharp knife, score fat surface of lamb racks, making an even pattern of ½-inch-wide diamonds. In cup, mix herbs, salt and pepper; use to coat scored surface. Place meat, fat side up, on wire rack in shallow pan. Insert meat thermometer into muscle of lamb rack (point should not rest on fat or bone). Roast 25 to 35 minutes or till meat thermometer registers 140F for rare or 160F for medium.
3. Place lamb on heated platter with Saffron Rice. Garnish with sugar snap peas, fluted mushrooms and parsley, if desired. Carve racks into chops, allowing at least two chops per person. *Makes 6 servings.*

Saffron Rice
(pictured)

1 **can (13¾ or 14½ oz) chicken broth**
¼ **teaspoon saffron threads**
2 **tablespoons salad oil**
½ **cup chopped onion**
1 **cup long-grain white rice**

1. In small saucepan, bring chicken broth to boiling; remove from heat. Crumble saffron with fingers; add to broth. Let stand, covered, 10 minutes.
2. Meanwhile, in medium saucepan, heat oil over medium heat. Add onion and rice; sauté, stirring occasionally, 3 minutes. Add saffron-chicken broth to saucepan; bring to boiling.
3. Reduce heat to low; simmer, covered, 15 to 20 minutes or until rice is tender and all liquid is absorbed. *Makes 6 servings.*

Red-Pepper-Endive Salade Composée
(pictured)

4 **medium-size red peppers (about 1½ lb)**

Sun-Dried-Tomato Dressing
12 **sun-dried tomatoes**
1¼ **cups olive oil**
¼ **cup lemon juice**
½ **teaspoon salt**
½ **teaspoon freshly ground black pepper**

4 **Belgian endives**
1 **bunch arugula or watercress**

1. Roast red peppers: Preheat broiler. Wash and drain peppers. Place on a foil-lined cookie sheet. Broil peppers 6 inches from heat, turning them every 5 minutes with tongs, about 15 minutes or until the peppers are completely charred. With tongs, transfer the peppers to a paper bag. Close the bag and let peppers stand 15 minutes.
2. With sharp knife, peel off charred skin. Cut each pepper lengthwise into fourths; remove ribs and seeds. Cut each quarter lengthwise into 1-inch-wide strips. Place peppers in a bowl and set aside.
3. Make Sun-Dried-Tomato Dressing: In food processor or electric blender, combine sun-dried tomatoes, olive oil, lemon juice, the salt and pepper. Process or blend until tomatoes are puréed. Pour tomato dressing over peppers and toss gently to mix. Cover with plastic wrap. Refrigerate several hours or overnight to develop flavor.
4. Wash endives and arugula under cold water; drain and pat dry with paper towels. Separate endives into

individual leaves. Arrange arugula, spoke fashion, on serving plate. Place endive leaves, round side up, between arugula leaves. With spoon, remove roasted red peppers from tomato dressing; reserve dressing. Roll pepper strips into curls and place in center of plate. Pass reserved dressing with salad. *Makes 6 servings.*

Deluxe Raspberry-Almond Cake
(pictured)

1½ **cups sliced blanched almonds**
½ **cup packaged dry bread crumbs**
2 **tablespoons all-purpose flour**
6 **large eggs**
¾ **cup granulated sugar**
¼ **teaspoon cream of tartar**
½ **cup raspberry preserves (see Note)**
2 **cups heavy cream (1 pint)**
3 **tablespoons confectioners' sugar**
½ **teaspoon almond extract**

11 **fresh or frozen whole raspberries (optional)**
Mint sprigs (optional)

1. Preheat oven to 350F. Place almonds in 15½-by-10½-by-1-inch jelly-roll pan. Toast, stirring occasionally, 10 to 15 minutes or until almonds are lightly browned. Remove from oven; place in small bowl, then in freezer 10 minutes to quick-chill. Meanwhile, cut three 9-inch circles of waxed paper. Grease three 9-by-1½-inch layer-cake pans. Place one waxed-paper circle in bottom of each pan; grease paper.
2. In small bowl, combine bread crumbs and flour; stir to mix. When almonds are cool, set aside 10 almond slices for garnish. In blender or food processor, coarsely chop ¾ cup almonds; set aside for garnish. Finely grind remaining ¾ cup almonds.
3. Separate eggs, placing whites in medium bowl and yolks in large bowl. With electric mixer at medium-high speed, beat yolks with ½ cup granulated sugar until thick and light; stir in finely ground almonds; set aside. With clean beaters, on high speed, beat egg whites with cream of tartar until soft peaks form; gradually add ¼ cup granulated sugar, beating until stiff. Alternately fold beaten whites and bread-crumb mixture into yolk mixture, beginning and ending with whites. Divide among prepared pans, spreading evenly.
4. Bake 15 to 20 minutes or until cakes spring back when gently touched with fingertip. Cool cakes in pans on wire racks 10 minutes; remove cakes from pans; remove paper and let cool completely.

Sensational Celebrations

5. In small saucepan, heat raspberry preserves. Press through strainer set over small bowl with back of spoon; discard seeds. In small bowl, with electric mixer at low speed, combine cream, confectioners' sugar and almond extract. At medium speed, whip cream mixture until stiff.

6. To assemble cake: Place one cake layer, bottom side down, on serving plate; with metal spatula, spread layer with a fourth of whipped cream. Place another layer on top; spread with a fourth of whipped cream. Place remaining layer, bottom side up, on top; spread raspberry preserves evenly to cover top. Spread a fourth of whipped cream to cover side of cake; pat the coarsely chopped almonds on side to cover.

7. Place remaining whipped cream in pastry bag fitted with coupler and ½-inch star tip. Pipe a decorative shell pattern around bottom of cake. Pipe shell pattern around top edge of cake, alternating with sliced almonds and 10 raspberries, as pictured. Insert small writing tip into coupler; write "Happy Anniversary" on raspberry-glazed top, if desired. Garnish with remaining raspberry and mint sprigs. *Makes 10 servings.*

Note: You may use seedless raspberry preserves and eliminate straining the preserves in Step 5.

Cakes for Special Occasions

Cake-In-Bloom

(pictured)

Frosting Flowers and Leaves, recipe follows
Pound-Cake Ring, recipe follows
½ **cup apricot preserves**
2 **teaspoons water**
Buttercream Frosting, recipe follows
Green, red and blue food colors

1. Day ahead: Make Frosting Flowers and Leaves: 9 large roses, 9 large and 6 small wild roses, 3 pansies, 3 daisies, 12 sweet peas and 16 leaves. Place in single layers on trays; cover with waxed paper. Let stand at room temperature until ready to use.

2. Make Pound-Cake Ring. Let cool; wrap in foil or plastic wrap until ready to use.

3. Next day: In small saucepan, combine apricot preserves with water. Heat, stirring, just until preserves are melted. Remove from heat; press through a coarse sieve to purée. Spread on top and around

side of cake. (Place cake on platter or stand.) Let cake stand 30 minutes to cool and set glaze.

4. Meanwhile, make Buttercream Frosting. Place ½ cup frosting in each of three small bowls. Tint one pale green, one pink and one blue. Leave rest of frosting white. Place plastic wrap directly on surface of frosting to prevent drying.

5. Place 1¼ cups white frosting in pastry bag fitted with coupler. Insert a ¹⁄₁₆-inch writing tip into coupler. Holding bag at an angle, press out frosting to make diagonal lines, 2 inches long and 1½ inches apart, all around lower side of cake. Make diagonal lines in opposite direction around base, joining top of one line to bottom of every other line, to make a diamond pattern, as pictured.

6. Insert a ¼-inch star tip into coupler of pastry bag with white frosting. Press out frosting at base of cake to make a shell; relax pressure on bag, drawing shell to a point. Continue making shells all around base of cake.

7. Insert ⅛-inch small star tip into coupler of pastry bag. Fill with green frosting. Holding bag upright, press out to form stars around inside center of cake. Repeat with pink frosting.

8. Insert a ¹⁄₁₆-inch small plain decorating tip into coupler of pastry bag. Fill bag with blue frosting. Press out frosting to decorate inside center of cake with forget-me-nots.

9. Place large roses on cake, in groups of three. Attach with a dab of pink Buttercream Frosting. Place leaves on cake around large roses. Place some of the flowers on cake, attaching each flower with a dab of pink Buttercream Frosting.

10. Insert a ¼-inch small star tip into coupler of pastry bag. Fill with remaining pink frosting. Press out frosting, forming larger stars, to fill in spaces on cake. Continue to attach rest of flowers to cake with pink stars. Press out blue forget-me-nots around other flowers. *Makes 12 servings.*

Frosting Flowers and Leaves

⅔ **cup egg whites, at room temperature (about 5 large)**
2 **pkg (1-lb size) confectioners' sugar**
1 **teaspoon cream of tartar**
½ **teaspoon almond extract**
Red, yellow and green food colors
Small paintbrush

1. In large bowl of electric mixer, combine all ingredients except food colors. Beat at low speed just until blended. At high speed, beat about 10 minutes or until smooth and stiff.

2. Cover directly with plastic wrap until ready to use. (If frosting becomes too soft on standing, beat in additional confectioners' sugar.)

3. Place about 1 cup frosting in each of several small bowls and add food colors appropriate for each kind of flower. Make each flower on a 2-inch square of waxed paper attached to pastry nail with a dab of frosting.

4. To make large roses: For each rose, press white frosting through a ¼-inch star tip onto center of waxed-paper square (Large Rose: illustration 1). Repeat to make nine in all (stars should be ¾ inch high). Let dry. Use a ½-by-¹⁄₁₆-inch rose tip (illustration 2). With wide part of tip resting on pastry nail, press out pink frosting around each star, spiral fashion, to form bud-like center of rose. Holding tip in same fashion, with pastry bag at a 45-degree angle, press out frosting to form four overlapping petals against center of rose (illustration 3). Holding pastry bag in same position, press out five to seven more petals against first row, to make another row of petals. Repeat to make nine large roses in all.

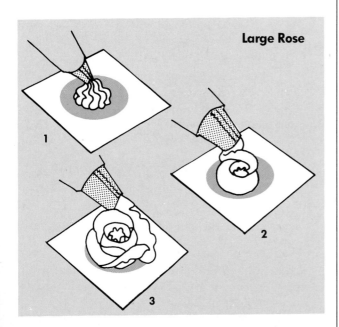

Large Rose

5. To make wild roses: Hold pastry bag with a ½-by-¹⁄₁₆-inch rose tip at a 45-degree angle in center of waxed paper at wide part of nail and press out yellow frosting toward edge of nail (Wild Rose: illustration 1); turn nail and press out frosting back toward center of the nail to make one large, round petal. Continue to make four more petals to form a round flower 1½ inches in diameter (illustration 2). (Smaller flowers are 1 inch in diameter.) Using a ¹⁄₁₆-inch round small plain tip and green frosting, press out five dots in center (illustration 3). Make five large yellow wild roses, four large pink wild roses and six small wild roses of various colors.

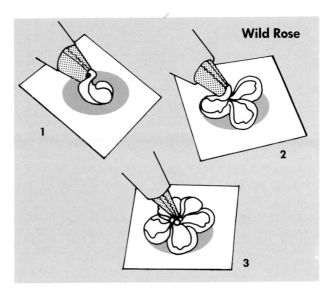

Wild Rose

6. To make pansies: Using a ½-by-¹⁄₁₆-inch rose tip, with wide part of tip resting on nail, press out yellow frosting, with a back-and-forth motion, to make two small petals with ruffled edges (Pansy: illustration 1). Insert same tip into pastry bag with white frosting (illustration 2). Press out frosting, with a slight back-and-forth motion, to make one large petal with a ruffled edge. Make two more pansies. Tint remaining yellow frosting a light orange; place in pastry bag fitted with a ⅛-inch small star tip. Press out small dabs of light orange frosting in center of each pansy (illustration 3, above). Using red food color diluted with water and a clean, small paintbrush, paint outer edge of large white petal of each pansy a pale pink.

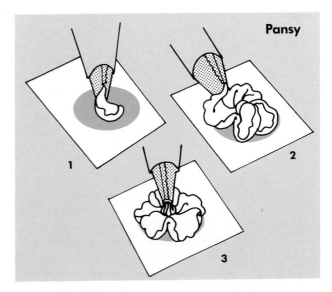

Pansy

Sensational Celebrations

7. To make daisies: Hold pastry bag with a ½-by-¹⁄₁₆-inch rose tip at a 45-degree angle and press out white frosting, moving pastry bag in and out, to form small, continuous daisy petals (Daisy: illustration 1). Make about 12 small petals, as close together as possible, to form round flower (illustration 2). Make two more round flowers. Tint rest of frosting a light orange; use to fill pastry bag with ⅛-inch small star tip. Press out frosting to make ruffled center of each flower (illustration 3).

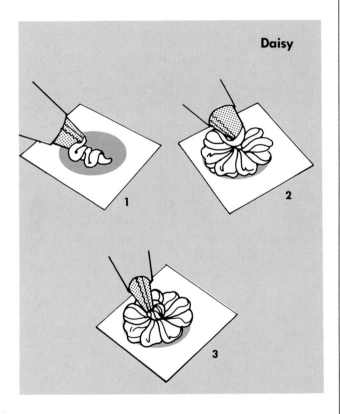

Daisy

8. To make sweet peas: Color remaining pink frosting a deeper pink. Using a ½-by-¹⁄₁₆-inch rose tip and holding pastry bag at 90-degree angle, with wide part of tip on pastry nail, press out frosting, raising tip slightly, then relaxing pressure to bring petal to a point at base (Sweet Pea: illustration 1). Repeat to make two side petals. Use a ¹⁄₁₆-inch small plain tip and green frosting to pipe base of flower (illustration 2). Repeat to make 12 sweet peas in all.

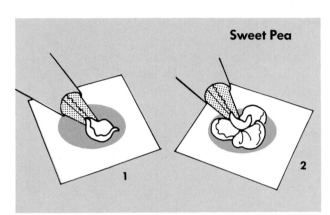

Sweet Pea

9. To make leaves: Hold pastry bag fitted with a ½-by-¹⁄₁₆-inch leaf tip at 45-degree angle and press out pale green frosting with a slight up-and-down motion. As you press out frosting, lift tip from waxed paper when you reach end of leaf, so that each leaf tapers to a point. Repeat to make 16 leaves in all.

Pound-Cake Ring

2¼ cups all-purpose flour
1½ teaspoons baking powder
¼ teaspoon salt
¾ cup (1½ sticks) butter or margarine, softened
1½ cups sugar
3 large eggs
1 teaspoon vanilla extract
½ teaspoon almond extract
½ cup milk

1. Preheat oven to 325°F. Grease well and flour a 12-cup tube pan. On waxed paper, combine flour with baking powder and salt; set aside.
2. In large bowl of electric mixer, at high speed, beat butter, sugar, eggs and extracts until light and fluffy—about 5 minutes—occasionally scraping side of bowl with rubber spatula.
3. At low speed, beat flour mixture (in fourths) into egg mixture alternately with milk (in thirds), beginning and ending with flour mixture. Beat just until smooth—about 1 minute.
4. Turn into prepared pan; bake 55 minutes or until cake tester inserted in center comes out clean. Cool, in pan, on wire rack 15 minutes. Turn out onto rack to cool completely.

Sensational Celebrations

Buttercream Frosting

¾ cup (1½ sticks) butter, softened
1 pkg (1 lb) confectioners' sugar
2 tablespoons milk
1 teaspoon vanilla extract

In small bowl, with electric mixer at low speed, blend butter and half of confectioners' sugar. Gradually add milk, vanilla and remaining sugar. Beat at medium speed until smooth and fluffy.

Favorite Birthday Cake
(pictured)

3 (8-inch) Devil's-Food-Cake Layers, recipe follows

Mocha-Butter Filling and Frosting

6 tablespoons hot milk
2 tablespoons instant coffee
2 tablespoons unsweetened cocoa
⅔ cup (1⅓ sticks) butter or margarine, softened
7 cups sifted confectioners' sugar
2 teaspoons vanilla extract

Chocolate-Sour-Cream Frosting

1 pkg (12 oz) semisweet chocolate pieces
1 cup sour cream
Dash salt

Candied lilacs (optional)
Decorator Icing, recipe follows

1. Prepare and bake the 3 Devil's-Food-Cake Layers.
2. Make Mocha-Butter Filling and Frosting: In large bowl, combine hot milk, coffee and cocoa; stir until coffee and cocoa are dissolved.
3. Add butter, confectioners' sugar and vanilla. With portable electric mixer or wooden spoon, beat mixture until smooth and fluffy. If filling seems too thick to spread, gradually beat in a little more hot milk. *Makes 2⅔ cups.*
4. Make Chocolate-Sour-Cream Frosting: Melt chocolate pieces in top of double boiler over hot water. Remove top of double boiler from hot water.
5. Add sour cream and salt. With rotary beater or portable electric mixer at medium speed, beat frosting until creamy and of spreading consistency.
6. To assemble cake: On plate, place a Devil's-Food-Cake layer, top side down; spread with 1 cup Mocha-Butter Filling. Add second layer, top side down. Spread with 1 cup Mocha-Butter Filling. Add third layer, top side up. Reserve remaining filling for decorating.
7. With spatula, frost cake with Chocolate-Sour-Cream Frosting.
8. To decorate: Put reserved filling into pastry bag with number-1 star tip. Make ruching as pictured. If desired, decorate with candied lilacs.

9. To write *Happy Birthday:* Make Decorator Icing. Use pastry bag with number-3 writing tip. *Makes 16 servings.*

Note: To make the mini birthday cake pictured on page 177, follow the recipe for Three (8-inch) Devil's-Food-Cake Layers, but make four 6-inch layers (using four 6-inch tier pans) and reduce baking time to 20 to 25 minutes. Assemble three layers according to the instructions beginning with Step 6. Freeze the fourth layer for snacking later.

Three (8-inch) Devil's-Food-Cake Layers

3 squares unsweetened chocolate
2¼ cups sifted cake flour
2 teaspoons baking soda
½ teaspoon salt
½ cup (1 stick) butter, softened
2½ cups firmly packed light-brown sugar
3 eggs
2 teaspoons vanilla extract
½ cup sour milk (see Note) or buttermilk
1 cup boiling water

1. Melt chocolate over hot, not boiling, water. Let cool.
2. Preheat oven to 350F. Grease well and flour three 8-by-1½-inch layer-cake pans.
3. Sift flour with soda and salt; set aside.
4. In large bowl of electric mixer, at high speed, beat butter, brown sugar, eggs and vanilla until light and fluffy—about 5 minutes—occasionally scraping side of bowl with rubber spatula.
5. At low speed, beat in chocolate.
6. Beat in flour mixture (in fourths), alternately with sour milk (in thirds), beginning and ending with flour mixture. Beat just until smooth—about 1 minute.
7. Beat in boiling water just until mixture is smooth. Batter will be thin.
8. Pour batter into prepared pans; bake 30 to 35 minutes or until surfaces spring back when gently pressed with fingertip.
9. Cool in pans 10 minutes. Remove from pans; cool thoroughly on wire racks. *Makes 3 (8-inch) layers.*

Note: To sour milk: Place 1½ teaspoons lemon juice or vinegar in measuring cup. Add milk to measure ½ cup. Let stand a few minutes before using.

Decorator Icing

1 egg white
1 cup confectioners' sugar
⅛ teaspoon cream of tartar

1. In small bowl of electric mixer, combine egg white, confectioners' sugar and cream of tartar.
2. Beat, at high speed, until icing is stiff enough to hold its shape.

Sensational Celebrations

Raggedy Ann Cake

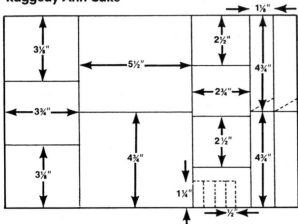

Raggedy Ann Cake
(pictured)

**1 pkg (1 lb, 2.25 oz or 1 lb, 2.5 oz) white-cake mix
    (two layers)**
**2 pkg (7.2-oz size) fluffy-white-frosting mix or 1 can
    (1 lb) vanilla frosting**
    Long wooden skewers
    Assorted food colors
1 tube (4¼ oz) pink decorator frosting
    Small gumdrops
    Small paintbrush
    Red licorice sticks and shoestring licorice

1. Preheat oven as package label directs. Generously grease and flour a 14½-by-11½-inch jelly-roll pan.
2. Prepare cake mix as package label directs; turn into prepared pan. Bake 30 to 35 minutes or until surface springs back when gently pressed with fingertip.
3. Let cool in pan on wire rack 5 minutes. Loosen edge of cake with sharp knife; turn out on wire rack; let cool completely.
4. Place on wooden board. With sharp knife, trim off all outside edges thinly to make sides of cake straight.
5. Cut cake into pieces, as shown in diagram.
6. If using frosting mix, prepare as package label directs. Use vanilla frosting directly from the can.
7. To assemble: On serving tray, place two 5½-by-4¾-inch pieces for skirt, put together with ¼ cup frosting.
8. Place three 3⅛-by-3¾-inch pieces of cake, put together with ¼ cup frosting, on top of skirt to form body. (To steady cake while assembling and decorating, insert wooden skewers between layers; remove before serving.)
9. Place three 2½-by-2¾-inch pieces of cake, put together with ¼ cup frosting, on body of doll to form head.

10. Trim one end of two 4¾-by-1⅛-inch strips of cake at a 45-degree angle, as diagram shows. Place flat on tray, angled end adjacent to skirt, to form doll's legs.
11. Place two remaining 4¾-by-1⅛-inch strips of cake against body of cake, at sides, to form arms.
12. From the one remaining piece of cake, cut four 1¼-by-½-inch rectangles to form shoes and hands; lean against ends of feet and arms.
13. With sharp knife, round off all top and bottom corners and sides of head and body sections of cake, so that head, chin, shoulders and waist take on tapered shape. For skirt, round off corners and sides of top portion only.
14. With red food color, tint 1 cup frosting a very delicate pink. Use to frost head, arms and hands.
15. Tint 2 tablespoons frosting black. Frost shoes black. (See Step 7, Zoo Express, page 199.)
16. Cover rest of doll with a thin layer of white frosting. With some of frosting, frost skirt, building frosting up into a gathered effect. (Dip spatula often in warm water.)
17. Frost body of doll, creating a blouse effect.
18. Place 2 to 3 tablespoons of frosting on top of each arm, forming a puffed-sleeve effect and blending in arm of doll to head portion.
19. Using star tip on tube of pink decorator icing, pipe a ruffle all around lower edge of skirt, bottom edges of puffed sleeves and around neck. Place sliced gumdrops about dress, polka-dot fashion.
20. Using small paintbrush dipped in red food color, paint each leg of doll with 5 or 6 red stripes, as shown in photograph on page 178, to form stocking effect.
21. Form eyes with 2 slices of black gumdrop. Highlight eyes with white icing. Form mouth and nose from tiny pieces of red gumdrop. With cotton swab dipped in diluted red color, brush on pink cheeks. Complete features—eyebrows, lashes, etc.—with paintbrush dipped in black food color.
22. To form doll's hair: Cut 7-inch red licorice sticks in half. With sharp scissors, cut up center of licorice and open flat; cut each flattened strip in half lengthwise. Form hair by cutting each flattened strip into three strands, not quite cutting through at top end. Beginning at top left side of head, place cut strands of licorice all around to top right side of head. To cover crown of head and create a bang effect, cut 25 to 30 one-inch strands of red licorice and place at random.
23. Make a sash around waist, cutting a piece of shoestring licorice to fit around front; repeat for back. Tie a bow of shoestring licorice at center back. *Makes about 12 servings.*

Zoo Express
(pictured)

1 **pkg (1 lb, 2.25 oz or 1 lb, 2.5 oz) yellow-cake mix (two-layer cake)**
4 **large spools (from thread)**
2 **pkg (15.4-oz size) creamy-white-frosting mix or 2 cans (1-lb size) vanilla frosting**
  Assorted food colors
2 **tablespoons unsweetened cocoa**
8 **round cookies for wheels**
1 **pkg white Life Savers**
6 **red gumdrops**
8 **animal cookies**
  Small paintbrush

1. Grease and flour a 13-by-9-by-2-inch baking pan. Prepare and bake cake mix as package directs. Reserve empty cake-mix box. Invert cake on wire rack to cool completely.
2. Meanwhile, cut off top and bottom ends of cake-mix box; then cut box in half crosswise. On a serving tray, place the two pieces of box together, with short sides of box touching. Trim boxes to width of cake—about 4 inches. Place a spool inside each end of each box half for support. This forms platform for cake.
3. If using frosting mix, prepare as package label directs. Use vanilla frosting directly from the can. Reserve ¾ cup and set aside. Color remaining frosting bright yellow, the color of a school bus.
4. Cut cooled cake in half lengthwise to make two (4¼-by-12½-inch) pieces of cake. Place one piece, flat side up, on box. Frost with ½ cup yellow frosting. Place remaining piece of cake, flat side down, on top of first layer. (If cake has rounded greatly in center during baking, combine layers so that cut side of one layer is placed on top of pan-edge side of other layer—this will even off any slant.) With sharp knife, trim off top front and back corners and edges to give a round, sloping appearance to front and back of bus.
5. Frost entire cake with a thin layer of yellow frosting to incorporate crumbs from cut surfaces of cake. Refrost cake and front and back sides of cake-mix box, using all remaining yellow frosting.
6. Combine cocoa with ⅓ cup reserved white frosting. Frost the cookie wheels. Place a white Life Saver in center of each wheel and position wheels against both sides of bus, as illustrated. Put remaining chocolate frosting in a small pastry bag with round writing tip. Letter in "ANIMAL EXPRESS" on top of bus. Complete bus, outlining four windows on each side of bus, front window, front grillwork and rear window. Place two red gumdrops on front of bus, for headlights, and four on rear of bus, for blinkers.
7. With remaining white frosting, tint 1 tablespoon gray,

1 tablespoon orange, 1 tablespoon light brown, 1 tablespoon dark brown, 1 teaspoon pink and leave 1 tablespoon white. Frost and decorate animal cookies as illustrated. (See Note.) To complete features on animals' faces, use a small paintbrush dipped in black food coloring. (If black food color is not available, combine equal amounts of red, green and blue food coloring to make a dark color.) Position animal cookies in bus windows, with a dab of frosting, as illustrated. *Serves 12.*

Note: Animals and wheels may be cut from colored construction paper and decorated with colored markers instead of using cookies, if preferred.

Hooty the Owl
(pictured)

1 **pkg (1 lb, 2.25 oz or 1 lb, 2.5 oz) white- or yellow-cake mix (two layers)**
  Wooden skewers
2 **pkg (7.2-oz size) fluffy-white-frosting mix or 1 can (1 lb) vanilla frosting**
  Assorted food colors
2 **round black gumdrops, flattened to size of penny**
  Small paintbrush

1. Preheat oven to 350F. Lightly grease and flour 2½-quart and 1½-quart heatproof bowls.
2. Prepare cake mix as package label directs. Turn 2½ cups batter into 1½-quart bowl; bake 35 minutes. Turn rest of batter into 2½-quart bowl; bake 40 minutes or until cake tester inserted in center comes out clean. Invert cakes on wire rack; let cool completely.
3. To assemble: Place larger cake, rounded side up, on serving tray; place small cake on top; secure with wooden skewers.
4. If using frosting mix, prepare one package at a time. If using vanilla frosting, use one-half for first coating. Frost cake all over with frosting to keep down crumbs.
5. Tint 1 tablespoon frosting orange, for beak. Tint 2 tablespoons yellow, for eyes.
6. Frost top layer, shaping owl's head. Apply ¼ cup of frosting on each side of head; pull up to points with spatula to resemble ears.
7. Swirl two large circles of white frosting, about 1½ inches in diameter, in center of face, for eyes. Place 1 tablespoon white frosting between eyes and pull out and down to resemble owl's beak.
8. Meanwhile, beginning at bottom layer of cake, apply remaining frosting in overlapping, featherlike

Sensational Celebrations

applications with tip of spatula. Repeat above procedure on top cake layer, being careful not to disturb eyes and beak.

9. Spread yellow frosting onto prepared circles on face of owl to form eyes. Place flattened gumdrops in center of each; dot with tiny drop of white frosting.

10. Spread orange icing over beak; allow to set. Draw 2 tiny black lines, one on each side of beak, with small brush dipped in black food color. With black color, thinned to gray with a little white frosting, paint three or four lines on owl's ears. Outline eyebrows in same manner. *Makes 12 to 16 servings.*

Happy-Birthday Hook and Ladder

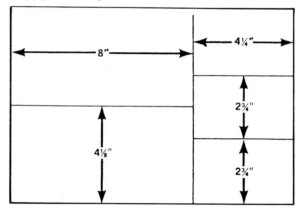

Happy-Birthday Hook and Ladder
(pictured)

1 pkg (1 lb, 2.25 oz or 1 lb, 2.5 oz) yellow- or chocolate-cake mix
5 large spools (from thread)
2 pkg (15.4-oz size) creamy-white-frosting mix or 2 cans (1-lb size) vanilla frosting
Long wooden skewers
1 tablespoon cocoa
6 round (2¼ inch) cookies
1 pkg white Life Savers
Red food color (use paste color)
4 white gumdrops
1 red maraschino cherry
1 pkg black shoestring licorice
Transparent tape
1 black licorice stick (7 inches)
2 wooden toothpicks

1. Prepare and bake cake as package label directs, using a 13-by-9-by-2-inch baking pan. (Reserve cake-mix box.) Bake 40 minutes or until surface springs back when gently pressed with fingertip. Let cake cool in pan on rack 5 minutes. Turn cake out on rack to cool completely.

2. On wooden board, with sharp knife, cut cake according to diagram. Cut off top and bottom of cake-mix box. Cut box in half crosswise. Lay the two pieces of box, short ends touching, on large serving tray. If necessary, trim sides of boxes to width of cake—approximately 4 inches. Insert spool into each end of boxes to support fire engine.

3. If using frosting mix, prepare as package label directs. Use vanilla frosting directly from can. With ⅓ cup frosting, put two 8-by-4⅛-inch pieces of cake together, flat sides touching. Place on top of cake-mix box, lining up back of cake with back of box.

4. Using ⅓ cup frosting, put three 2¾-by-4¼-inch pieces of cake together. Place on top of cake-mix box, lining up front of cake with front of box, so that cab and truck parts of fire engine are touching. Insert one or more wooden skewers through layers of cake to steady fire engine while decorating. (These are removed at serving time.)

5. Mix 1 tablespoon cocoa with 3 tablespoons frosting. Use to frost cookies, for wheels.

6. Place a white Life Saver in center of each wheel. Set aside until cake is frosted.

7. Place ½ cup frosting in small pastry bag with small star tip. Set aside.

8. Tint remaining frosting bright red. Frost entire fire engine with a thin coating. With remaining frosting, refrost fire engine and all visible parts of cake-mix box.

9. With star tip, outline border of the fire engine, the front windows and driver, the side doors, windows, pumps, gauges, ladder, etc. See photograph, page 179.

10. Place two dots of white icing on each side of top of cab; center a gumdrop on icing to form spotlights. Place a large dot of icing between spotlights and center maraschino cherry in icing to form revolving spotlight. Place two dots of icing on lower front of cab and place a white gumdrop on each dot to form headlights. Wind black shoestring licorice around large wooden thread spool. Secure loose ends of licorice with transparent tape to hold firmly. This spool forms the fire hose. Place fire hose on top of body of fire engine. Cut long black licorice stick in half to form two 3½-inch pieces. Place a toothpick into side of each piece of licorice at very tip end. Place the two pieces of licorice, side by side, on top of fire engine at rear, resting one end on cake and placing other end at a 45-degree angle, supported by toothpicks (see photograph). With frosting in pastry bag, make a straight line down each licorice stick and crisscross lines between the two licorice sticks to form the ladder. Arrange frosted wheels against sides of fire engine, as shown, *Makes 10 to 12 servings.*

Christening Brunch

(Planned for 8)

Grapefruit-Grenadine Sunrise*
Bacon Roses and Chived Eggs in Puff Pastry*
Lemon-Buttered Asparagus
Melon-Grape Mélange

Grapefruit-Grenadine Sunrise
(pictured)

¼ cup grenadine syrup
1½ quarts chilled grapefruit juice

Into each of eight 8- or 10-ounce stemmed cocktail glasses, spoon or pour 1½ teaspoons grenadine. Holding teaspoon in glass, right side up, ½ inch above grenadine, *slowly* pour ¾ cup grapefruit juice into bowl of spoon so that it trickles over, but does not mix with, grenadine. *Makes 8 servings.*

Bacon Roses and Chived Eggs in Puff Pastry
(pictured)

12 green onions
1 pkg (1 lb) sliced bacon

Puff-Pastry Shell
1 pkg (17¼ oz) frozen puff-pastry sheets
1 large egg, beaten with 1 teaspoon milk

Chived Eggs
12 large eggs
⅓ cup milk
½ teaspoon salt
Dash ground pepper
2 tablespoons butter or margarine
1 pkg (3 oz) cream cheese, cut into ½-inch pieces
2 tablespoons chopped chives

Chopped chives (optional)
Parsley sprigs

1. Make green-onion brushes: Cut white ends of green onions into 2-inch lengths, trimming roots. (Refrigerate green tops for use in other recipes.) At end

opposite root, make 1-inch-long cuts, ⅛ inch apart, through each onion piece. Place cut onions in bowl of ice water; refrigerate.

2. Preheat oven to 400F. Make bacon roses: Separate bacon slices and arrange in single layer in two 15½-by-10½-by-½-inch jelly-roll pans. Bake 10 to 15 minutes or until bacon begins to brown but is still limp; remove from oven. When bacon is cool enough to handle, loosely wrap each slice around index finger to form a flower shape; secure with toothpick. Discard fat in pans; place bacon roses in one pan; set aside.

3. Make Puff-Pastry Shell: Thaw puff pastry as package label directs. On lightly floured surface, with floured rolling pin, roll 1 sheet pastry to a 10-inch square; place pastry square in center of ungreased 15½ by 12-inch cookie sheet. Using fork, prick entire surface of pastry. Roll second pastry sheet as above. With sharp knife, cut an 8-inch square in center of sheet, leaving a 1-inch-wide frame around square. With pastry brush, brush entire top surface of uncut 10-inch square with egg-milk mixture. Carefully lift 1-inch-wide frame and place it on 10-inch square, aligning outer edges; refrigerate. Preheat oven to 400F. Using leaf-shape cutter or pastry wheel, cut 20 (2-inch-long) leaves from 8-inch square; remove excess dough from around leaves. With tip of knife, score lines in leaves to resemble veins, if desired. Brush egg mixture over top of pastry frame; place leaves diagonally on frame. Brush top of leaves with egg mixture. Bake 20 minutes or until shell is puffed and golden-brown.

4. Meanwhile, make Chived Eggs: In medium bowl, combine 12 eggs, the milk, salt and pepper. With wire whisk or fork, beat just until mixed. In large skillet, over medium-low heat, melt butter. Pour in egg mixture; cook, stirring occasionally as eggs begin to set on bottom. When eggs are almost cooked but still moist, add cream-cheese pieces and chives. Cook, stirring gently, until cream cheese is melted and eggs are cooked. Return bacon to oven; bake till browned; drain on paper towels.

5. Place pastry shell on serving platter. Spoon cooked eggs into shell. Remove toothpicks from bacon roses; arrange in center of eggs. Sprinkle additional chopped chives on eggs, if desired. Garnish with parsley sprigs and green-onion brushes. *Makes 8 servings.*

Recipes given for starred dishes.

Sensational Celebrations

Brunch Menu

(Planned for 8)

*Cranberry Spritzer**
*Valentine Quiche-Without-A-Crust**
Croissants   Preserves
*Chocolate-Strawberry Torte**
Coffee

Cranberry Spritzer

2 cups dry white wine, well chilled
2½ cups cranberry-juice cocktail, well chilled
1 bottle (28 oz) soda water, well chilled

1. Pour wine, cranberry juice and soda into a chilled 2-quart pitcher; stir just to combine.
2. Serve immediately in chilled wineglasses. *Makes 2 quarts.*

Valentine Quiche-Without-A-Crust

1 teaspoon butter or margarine
2 cups fresh-bread cubes
2 cups chopped onion
½ lb ham, sliced ¼ inch thick
3 cups grated natural Swiss cheese (12 oz)
6 eggs
2 tablespoons all-purpose flour
3 cups light cream or half-and-half
¼ teaspoon salt
Dash ground red pepper

1. Preheat oven to 350F. Butter a 10-inch ceramic quiche dish or an 11-inch pie plate, using ½ teaspoon butter.
2. Spread bread cubes on a baking sheet. Place in oven. Toast, stirring occasionally, until lightly browned—about 5 minutes. Spread in bottom of prepared dish.
3. Melt remaining ½ teaspoon butter in a large skillet. Sauté onion, stirring occasionally, until golden—3 to 5 minutes.
4. Using a 2-inch heart-shaped cookie cutter, cut 6 hearts from ham; set aside. Coarsely chop scraps of ham; sprinkle over bread in dish. Layer onion and cheese over ham.

Recipes given for starred dishes.

5. In a medium bowl, with rotary beater, beat eggs, flour, cream, salt and red pepper until well combined but not frothy.
6. Place baking dish on middle shelf of oven. Pour egg mixture into baking dish. Arrange ham hearts on top.
7. Bake 50 to 60 minutes or until top is golden and center is firm when gently pressed with fingertip. Let cool 10 minutes before cutting. *Makes 8 servings.*

Chocolate-Strawberry Torte

4 eggs
¾ cup sugar
1 teaspoon vanilla extract
1 cup ground pecans or walnuts
1 cup ground blanched almonds
3 sq (1-oz size) unsweetened chocolate, coarsely grated
2 tablespoons packaged dry bread crumbs
1 teaspoon baking powder
¼ teaspoon salt
1 pint strawberries, washed and hulled
¼ cup currant jelly, melted
½ cup chopped pecans or walnuts
1 cup heavy cream, whipped

1. Preheat oven to 350F. Grease and flour bottom of 9-inch springform pan.
2. In large bowl, with electric mixer at high speed, beat eggs and sugar until light and fluffy—5 minutes; beat in vanilla.
3. On sheet of waxed paper, combine ground nuts, chocolate, bread crumbs, baking powder and salt.
4. Add to egg mixture. With rubber spatula or wooden spoon, mix until well blended. Turn into prepared pan, spreading evenly.
5. Bake 30 to 35 minutes or until surface springs back when gently pressed with fingertip. Remove to rack; cool completely.
6. With spatula, carefully loosen torte from pan; remove torte to serving plate.
7. Toss berries with melted jelly. Arrange on top of torte. Garnish edge with chopped nuts. Serve with whipped cream. *Makes 8 servings.*

Brunch Menu

(Planned for 6)

Chilled White Wine
Eggs Tetrazzini With Spinach Twists*
Whole-Wheat Italian Bread
Sliced Oranges and Honeydew
With Cointreau*
Caffè Espresso With Lemon Twist

Eggs Tetrazzini With Spinach Twists

6 eggs
   Salt
1 pkg (16 oz) spinach twists (pasta)
¼ lb medium mushrooms
¼ cup (½ stick) butter or margarine
3 tablespoons all-purpose flour
2 cups milk
1 cup grated Swiss cheese
1 cup grated sharp Cheddar cheese
¼ cup grated Parmesan cheese
   Dash ground pepper

1. Place eggs in a medium saucepan; cover with water to 1 inch above them; bring rapidly to boiling. Take pan off heat; cover and let stand 20 minutes.
2. Bring 3 quarts salted water to boiling in a large saucepan. Add spinach twists. Boil, uncovered and stirring occasionally, 8 to 12 minutes. Drain very well; return to a dry saucepan.
3. Meanwhile, wash and slice mushrooms. Melt 1 tablespoon of the butter in a medium skillet. Add mushrooms; sauté, stirring occasionally, until golden. Add to drained pasta and toss until well combined. Cover and keep warm.
4. Meanwhile, melt remaining 3 tablespoons of butter in a medium saucepan. Remove from heat; stir in flour. Add ¼ cup milk and stir with wire whisk until smooth. Gradually beat in remaining milk. Bring to boiling over medium heat, stirring constantly until thickened.
5. Add Swiss cheese, Cheddar cheese, 2 tablespoons Parmesan cheese, ¼ teaspoon salt and the pepper; cook over low heat, stirring constantly, until sauce is blended and smooth. Keep warm.
6. Place eggs in cold water until they are cool enough to handle. Then peel and rinse them; slice eggs in half lengthwise.
7. Turn pasta into serving dish. Arrange eggs on top. Pour sauce over all. Sprinkle with remaining Parmesan cheese. Serve immediately. *Makes 6 servings.*

*Recipes given for starred dishes.

Sliced Oranges and Honeydew With Cointreau

3 large navel oranges, chilled
½ large honeydew melon, chilled
½ cup Cointreau or other orange liqueur

1. Peel oranges; slice crosswise. Peel honeydew; slice into ⅛-inch-thick crosswise slices. Cut orange slices into 2-inch pieces.
2. In a large chilled bowl, layer oranges and melon. Pour Cointreau over all. Refrigerate until serving. *Makes 6 servings.*

Brunch Menu

(Planned for 4 to 6)

Pecan-Oatmeal Pancakes*
Warm Maple Syrup
Bacon Curls
Sliced Fresh Pineapple and Kiwi
Irish Coffee

Pecan-Oatmeal Pancakes

1½ cups uncooked old-fashioned oatmeal
1 cup all-purpose flour
½ cup coarsely chopped pecans
2 tablespoons light-brown sugar
2 teaspoons baking powder
¼ teaspoon salt
1½ cups milk
2 eggs
2 tablespoons butter or margarine, melted
   Salad oil
   Butter
   Warm maple syrup

1. In a medium bowl, combine oatmeal, flour, pecans, brown sugar, baking powder and salt.
2. Combine milk, eggs and butter in a small bowl or 2-cup measuring cup. Beat with fork or wire whisk until well combined.
3. Pour the egg mixture over the dry ingredients. Stir just until they are combined.
4. Meanwhile, slowly heat griddle or heavy skillet. To test temperature, drop a little water onto hot griddle; water should roll off in drops.
5. Lightly oil griddle. Spoon on about ¼ cup batter for each pancake. Cook until bubbles form on surface and edges become dry. Turn; cook about 2 minutes longer or until underside is golden-brown. Serve immediately with butter and warm maple syrup. *Makes 16 (4-inch) pancakes.*

*Recipe given for starred dish.

CHAPTER

4

MAIN ATTRACTIONS: OUR BEST-LOVED ENTREES

♥

As the main course goes, so goes the entire meal: A wonderful entrée, cooked to perfection, gives the rest of the meal a fantastic flavor that lingers long after dessert. A main dish that misses the mark leaves a disappointing taste that even the most sensational accompaniments cannot completely erase. Such an integral component of a meal should not be left to mere chance. That's why we've filled this chapter with our very best collection of marvelous main dishes, each guaranteed to become the savory highlight of your dinner table. And as every McCall's recipe goes, so goes success.

Special Family Fare

Maybe it's to celebrate the great report card, the long-awaited promotion or just because you wanted to make something a little bit special. There are lots of reasons to treat your loved ones to the great taste of these scrumptious entrées. They're easy to prepare and sure to become favorites with the whole family. Recipes begin on page 212.

Left: When the accent is on Italian, these four main dishes speak the language deliciously. **Top left,** Pasta e Fagioli, a traditional thick soup made with kidney beans and macaroni shells — a meal in itself. **At top right,** Baked Stuffed Tufoli with a savory meat filling and rich tomato sauce. Pasta combines well with vegetables, too. **At bottom right,** ziti with tomato sauce and fresh broccoli. And, **at far left,** a steaming platter of cheese-topped spaghetti with broiled eggplant.

Above: Fruit adds a succulent sweetness to this family-fare trio. **Clockwise, from top left:** Poached and peppered peach halves add pizzazz to this glazed, broiled ham steak; chicken quarters are browned and cooked in a fruit sauce made from green-pepper and peach slices, chopped tomatoes and peach nectar; and spareribs are enhanced with a tantalizing sweet-and-spicy sauce made by simmering fresh red plums. *Recipes begin on page 215.*

Left: Plunge into these cold pasta dishes for light, delectable refreshment. **At top:** Half-moon spinach and egg ravioli are filled with sweet Italian sausage, then tossed with a red-wine vinaigrette and a primavera combination of asparagus, mushrooms and cherry tomatoes. **Below:** Pasta shells peek out from under mussels that have been steamed and then filled with a sauce verte. **In the foreground,** a variation on the classic antipasto salad: Radiatori pasta is dressed with olive oil, vinegar and spices, then combined with peppers, mushrooms, provolone, salami, garbanzo beans and olives. *Recipes begin on page 213.*

Above: Everyone will love these classic Swedish meatballs, tradition-ally spiced with dillweed, allspice, nutmeg and cardamom and baked in a delicate light-cream sauce. *See recipe on page 217.*

Left: The secret to great Italian dishes is in the sauce. Our Italian-Sausage Lasagne starts with a wonderfully spiced homemade sauce that is layered between al dente noodles and a parsley-cottage-cheese mix. Thinly sliced mozzarella cheese, sliced and sautéed Italian sausage and Parmesan cheese bake into the luscious top layer of this hot-and-hearty meal. *See recipe on page 216.*

Special Family Fare

continued from page 207

Pasta e Fagioli
Macaroni and Beans
(pictured)

¼ **cup salad or olive oil**
1 **clove garlic, crushed**
1 **cup chopped onion**
1 **can (1 lb) Italian tomatoes, undrained**
1 **teaspoon salt**
¼ **teaspoon ground pepper**
½ **teaspoon dried oregano leaves**
2 **tablespoons chopped parsley**
1 **tablespoon salt**
1½ **quarts boiling water**
½ **pkg (7- or 8-oz size) shell macaroni, elbow macaroni or other tubular pasta (2 cups cooked)**
1 **can (15 oz) red kidney beans or cannellini beans, undrained**
    Grated Parmesan cheese

1. In hot oil in 5-quart Dutch oven or heavy kettle, sauté garlic and onion, stirring, until golden—about 5 minutes.
2. Add tomatoes, 1 teaspoon salt, the pepper, oregano and parsley. Simmer, covered, 30 minutes; mash tomatoes.
3. Meanwhile, cook macaroni: In large kettle, bring salted water to a rapid boil. Add macaroni. Bring back to boiling. Stirring occasionally with long fork to prevent sticking, cook, uncovered, just until tender—7 to 10 minutes (do not overcook); drain.
4. Add macaroni and beans to tomato mixture, stirring to combine.
5. Simmer 5 minutes or until thoroughly hot. Serve in individual bowls. Sprinkle with Parmesan cheese. *Makes 4 to 6 servings.*

♥

Pasta With Broccoli Sauce
(pictured)

2 **cups Tomato Sauce, recipe follows**
1½ **lb fresh broccoli**
    Boiling water
    Salt
½ **pkg (1-lb size) ziti or other tubular pasta**
½ **cup grated Parmesan cheese**

1. Make Tomato Sauce.
2. Prepare broccoli. Trim stem end; wash thoroughly; cut into 1-inch pieces.
3. Place broccoli in 6-quart saucepan. Add 6 cups boiling water and 1 teaspoon salt. Cook, covered, 10 minutes or until tender. Drain. Add to Tomato Sauce while sauce is cooking the last 10 minutes.

4. In large kettle, bring three quarts of water and 1 tablespoon salt to rapid boil. Add ziti; bring back to boiling. Stirring occasionally with long fork to prevent sticking, cook, uncovered, just until tender— about 12 minutes; do not overcook.
5. Drain in colander or sieve; do not rinse.
6. Turn into heated serving dish. Pour broccoli sauce over ziti. Sprinkle with Parmesan cheese. *Makes 4 servings.*

Baked Stuffed Tufoli
(pictured)

4 **cups Tomato Sauce, recipe follows**
2 **tablespoons salt**
6 **quarts boiling water**
½ **pkg (1-lb size) tufoli (20) or manicotti**

Filling
¼ **cup salad or olive oil**
1 **cup chopped onion**
1 **clove garlic, crushed**
1 **lb ground chuck**
½ **lb ground veal**
1 **pkg (10 oz) frozen chopped spinach, thawed, drained and finely chopped**
2 **tablespoons chopped parsley**
1 **teaspoon dried oregano leaves**
1 **teaspoon salt**
¼ **teaspoon ground pepper**
1 **pkg (8 oz) mozzarella cheese, cut in ½-inch cubes**
1 **pkg (8 oz) mozzarella cheese, thinly sliced crosswise**
½ **cup grated Parmesan cheese**

1. Make Tomato Sauce.
2. In large kettle, add 2 tablespoons salt to boiling water. Add tufoli; return to boiling. Boil 10 to 15 minutes or until almost tender. Drain; lay flat on tray to cool.
3. Meanwhile, make Filling: In hot oil in large skillet, sauté onion and garlic until tender—about 5 minutes. Add beef and veal; brown lightly, stirring, about 15 minutes.
4. Remove from heat. Add spinach, parsley, oregano, salt, pepper and cubed mozzarella. Mix well.
5. Preheat oven to 375F. With small spoon, spoon meat mixture into tufoli from each end.
6. Pour 1 cup Tomato Sauce in bottom of 13-by-9-by-2-inch baking dish or shallow, oval baking dish.
7. Arrange tufoli in Tomato Sauce. Pour rest of Tomato Sauce over top. Cover with foil. Bake 25 minutes.
8. Remove from oven; remove foil. Place slice of mozzarella on each tufoli (as pictured). Sprinkle with Parmesan cheese. Bake 10 minutes or until cheese is melted. *Makes 8 to 10 servings.*

Special Family Fare

Spaghetti and Eggplant
(pictured)

4 cups Tomato Sauce, recipe follows
3 eggplants (1-lb size)
   Salt
6 quarts boiling water
1 pkg (1 lb) spaghetti
¾ cup (1½ sticks) butter or margarine, melted
½ cup grated Parmesan cheese

1. Make Tomato Sauce.
2. Wash eggplants; do not peel. Cut off stem ends; cut lengthwise into slices—about ¾ inch thick.
3. Sprinkle with 2 teaspoons salt; arrange in a colander set on a tray; let stand 1 hour to allow all excess liquid to drain.
4. In large kettle, add 2 tablespoons salt to boiling water. Bring to rapid boil. Add spaghetti; place one end in boiling water and gradually coil in rest as it softens.
5. Bring back to boiling. Stirring occasionally with a long fork to prevent sticking, cook, uncovered, just until tender—about 7 to 10 minutes; do not overcook.
6. Drain in colander or sieve; do not rinse. In large bowl, toss spaghetti with ¼ cup melted butter. To keep spaghetti warm, place bowl in kettle with 2 inches simmering water.
7. Wipe eggplant slices dry, using paper towels.
8. Place in bottom of broiler pan. Brush on both sides with remaining melted butter. Broil, 4 inches from heat, 4 minutes on each side or until golden-brown.
9. To serve: Heat Tomato Sauce to boiling. Arrange eggplant slices, overlapping, inside edge of large warm platter.
10. Turn spaghetti into center of platter, mounding. Spoon sauce around spaghetti. Sprinkle Parmesan cheese over spaghetti. *Makes 8 servings.*

Tomato Sauce

1 can (2 lb, 3 oz) Italian tomatoes
¼ cup olive or salad oil
1 cup finely chopped onion
1 clove garlic, crushed
1 can (6 oz) tomato paste
1½ cups water
2 parsley sprigs
½ tablespoon salt
2 teaspoons sugar
1 teaspoon dried oregano leaves
½ teaspoon dried basil leaves
¼ teaspoon ground pepper

1. Purée undrained Italian tomatoes in electric blender or press through sieve with juice.
2. In hot oil in large saucepan, sauté onion and garlic until golden-brown—about 5 minutes.
3. Add puréed tomato, tomato paste, 1½ cups water, the parsley, salt, sugar, oregano, basil and pepper; mix well.
4. Bring to boiling; reduce heat and simmer, covered, 1 hour, stirring occasionally. Cook, uncovered, ½ hour longer, stirring occasionally. *Makes 4½ cups.*

Note: Freeze any unused Tomato Sauce for another time.

Mussels With Sauce Verte
(pictured)

1½ dozen mussels

Sauce Verte
  1 cup mayonnaise
  ½ cup chopped spinach
  ⅓ cup chopped parsley
  ⅓ cup chopped watercress
  1 tablespoon snipped fresh chives
  1 tablespoon snipped fresh dill
  2 teaspoons dried tarragon leaves
  1 tablespoon lemon juice
    Dash salt

  ½ clove garlic, crushed
  ½ pkg (1-lb size) medium shells or other pasta
  ½ cup Italian-style salad dressing

1. Inspect mussels, discarding any that are not tightly closed. Scrub well under cold running water to remove sand and seaweed. With a sharp knife, trim off the "beard" around edges. Let soak 1 to 2 hours in cold water.
2. Meanwhile, make Sauce Verte: Combine all ingredients in blender or food processor and process until smooth. Turn into a small bowl; refrigerate, covered. *Makes 1¼ cups.*
3. Lift mussels from water and place in a colander. Rinse with cold water; let drain.
4. Place mussels in large skillet; add ½ cup water and garlic.
5. Cook, covered, over high heat 5 to 8 minutes. Shake skillet frequently so mussels will cook uniformly.
6. With slotted utensil, remove mussels to dish; refrigerate, covered, 1 hour.
7. Meanwhile, cook pasta shells according to package directions; drain. Toss with Italian dressing. Refrigerate 1 hour.

Special Family Fare

8. To serve: Spoon 1 teaspoon Sauce Verte on top of each mussel in shell. Reserve remaining sauce. Turn pasta shells onto serving platter. Mound filled mussels in the middle. Pass reserved sauce. *Makes 6 appetizer servings.*

Antipasto Salad Platter
(pictured)

Dressing
½ cup olive or salad oil
¼ cup lemon juice
1 teaspoon salt
¼ teaspoon freshly ground black pepper
⅛ teaspoon crushed red pepper
1 clove garlic, crushed
1 tablespoon snipped fresh basil or 1 teaspoon dried basil leaves

1 tablespoon salt
1 tablespoon salad oil
8 oz radiatori or other pasta
½ cup cubed green pepper
½ cup cubed red pepper
4 medium mushrooms, washed and sliced
¼ lb provolone, cubed
1 can (1 lb, 4 oz) garbanzos, drained
¼ lb sliced salami (slices cut into quarters)
¼ cup small black pitted olives
2 tablespoons chopped parsley

1. Make Dressing: In jar with tight-fitting lid, combine oil, lemon juice, 1 teaspoon salt, the black and red peppers, garlic and basil; shake until well combined.
2. Cook radiatori: In large kettle, bring 3 quarts water, the salt and salad oil to rapid boil. Add pasta; bring back to boiling. Stirring occasionally with long fork to prevent sticking, cook, uncovered, just until tender—about 7 to 8 minutes. Do not overcook. Drain well; do not rinse.
3. Turn into large bowl; add dressing; toss to combine. Cool completely.
4. To radiatori mixture, add green and red peppers, sliced mushrooms, provolone, garbanzos, salami, olives and parsley; toss lightly to combine. Turn into serving bowl; refrigerate, covered, 1 hour. Toss well before serving. *Makes 8 servings.*

Half-Moon Ravioli Primavera
(pictured)

2 sweet Italian sausages
1 medium onion, coarsely chopped
1 slice whole-wheat bread
¼ teaspoon dried oregano leaves
¼ teaspoon dried basil leaves
1 egg
1 recipe Egg Pasta, recipe follows (see Note)
1 recipe Spinach Pasta, recipe follows (see Note)
   Salt
½ lb fresh asparagus
¼ cup red-wine vinegar
3 tablespoons lemon juice
⅔ cup olive oil
1 teaspoon sugar
2 cloves garlic, pressed
½ lb medium mushrooms
½ box cherry tomatoes (½ pt)

1. Remove sausage meat from skins. In a medium skillet, sauté sausage and onion until sausage is cooked through—5 to 7 minutes.
2. Combine sausage, onion, bread, oregano, basil and egg in processor fitted with chopping blade. Process until smooth. Or chop sausage, onion and bread, a little at a time, in blender and combine with oregano, basil and egg in a medium bowl.
3. Prepare Egg Pasta. Roll out one-fourth to make a 14-by-10-inch rectangle. Cut into rounds, using a 2-inch plain or fluted cookie cutter. Spoon ½ teaspoon sausage filling onto each round. Moisten half of edge of each round; fold over and press edges together with a fork to make half-moon ravioli.
4. Repeat with one-fourth of Spinach Pasta. (Remaining dough may be rolled out, folded between pieces of floured waxed paper, tightly wrapped and frozen for use at a later time. Scraps from cutting ravioli may be finely chopped and frozen for use as pastina or in soup.)
5. Cook egg and spinach ravioli together in boiling, salted water as directed for Egg Pasta. Wash asparagus well; trim off ends and pare lower part of stems with vegetable parer. Slice diagonally to make 2-inch pieces; add to pasta for last 5 minutes. Drain well.
6. In a large bowl, combine vinegar, lemon juice, olive

Special Family Fare

oil, 1 teaspoon salt, the sugar and garlic. Add pasta and asparagus; toss to coat well.

7. Wash and slice mushrooms. Wash cherry tomatoes and cut in half. Add to pasta. Toss; refrigerate, covered, until thoroughly chilled—at least 4 hours. *Makes 8 servings.*

Note: You may substitute 48 packaged frozen small ravioli for Egg and Spinach Pastas. Start with Step 5.

Egg Pasta

3 cups all-purpose flour
½ teaspoon salt
4 eggs
1 tablespoon salad or olive oil
2 to 3 tablespoons lukewarm water
   Salt
   Salad oil

1. Sift flour with salt into medium bowl.
2. Make a well in center. Add eggs and oil. Pour water in gradually and mix with fork until well combined. Dough will be stiff. Form into a ball. (See Note.)
3. Turn out on lightly floured wooden board. Knead dough until it is smooth and elastic—about 15 minutes. Cover with bowl; let rest at least 30 minutes (this makes it easier to roll out). *Makes 1½ pounds.*
4. To shape: Divide dough into four parts. Keep covered with bowl until ready to roll out or refrigerate in plastic bags.
5. On lightly floured pastry cloth or board, roll each part into a rectangle about 16 by 14 inches and about ¹⁄₁₆ inch thick.
6. Work quickly, because dough dries out. From long side, roll up loosely as for jelly roll.
7. With thin sharp knife, cut roll crosswise, ⅛ inch wide for fettuccine. For lasagne, cut the rolled dough into strips 2 inches wide, 6 inches long. For wide noodles (tagliatelle), cut into strips ¾ inch wide. For narrow noodles, cut ¼ inch wide.
8. Unroll noodles and wind loosely around fingers. For fresh pasta, cook immediately or freeze in plastic bags for a week.
9. To dry pasta, arrange on ungreased cookie sheets;

let dry overnight. Store pasta in a covered glass jar in a cool place.

10. To cook pasta: In large kettle, bring 3 quarts of water and 1 tablespoon each of salt and salad oil to rapid boil. Add pasta; bring back to boiling; stirring occasionally with long fork to prevent sticking, cook, uncovered, just until tender—3 to 5 minutes for fresh pasta, 7 to 10 minutes for dried. (Do not thaw frozen pasta.) Do not overcook. Drain well; do not rinse.

Note: For food processor, place all ingredients in processor container fitted with the steel blade. Process about 1 minute or just until mixture leaves sides of container. Continue with Step 3.

Spinach or Broccoli Pasta

1 pkg (10 oz) frozen chopped spinach or broccoli
3 cups all-purpose flour
½ teaspoon salt
2 eggs
1 tablespoon salad or olive oil

Cook spinach according to package directions; drain well. Purée in food processor or blender. Follow directions for making Egg Pasta, adding puréed spinach along with eggs and oil and omitting water. (If dough seems sticky, add more flour to board during kneading.) *Makes 1½ pounds.*

Peppered Peaches With Ham
(pictured)

3 large (8-oz size) ripe peaches, peeled, halved and pitted
2 tablespoons lemon juice
2 cups water
⅔ cup sugar
1 teaspoon dry mustard
   1½-lb fully cooked ham steak, cut 1 inch thick
2 tablespoons green peppercorns, packed in brine, drained and chopped
   Parsley sprigs (optional)

1. In large bowl, place peach halves; sprinkle with lemon juice.

Special Family Fare

2. In medium saucepan, combine water and sugar. Over high heat, bring to boiling; stir frequently with a slotted spoon until sugar is dissolved. Reduce heat; add peach halves; simmer, uncovered, 10 minutes, turning peach halves over after 5 minutes. Remove saucepan from heat; with slotted spoon, remove peaches and place, cut side up, on plate.
3. Add 1 teaspoon dry mustard to the liquid remaining in saucepan. Over medium-high heat, cook, uncovered, until the liquid is reduced to ½ cup. Remove saucepan from heat.
4. Preheat broiler. Place ham steak on broiler rack over pan; brush with peach syrup. Broil, 4 to 5 inches from heat, about 8 minutes. Turn; brush with syrup; broil 8 minutes more.
5. Meanwhile, brush cut side of peach halves with syrup; sprinkle with green peppercorns. Place, cut side up, on broiler rack with ham steak during the last 5 minutes of cooking.
6. To serve: Place ham steak and peach halves on serving platter. Garnish with parsley sprigs, if desired. *Makes 6 servings.*

Braised Chicken With Peaches
(pictured)

1 (3-lb) broiler-fryer, quartered
1 tablespoon butter or margarine
1 tablespoon salad oil
1 medium green pepper, stemmed, seeded and cut into ¼-inch strips
1 medium onion, chopped
2 medium tomatoes, coarsely chopped
1 cup unsweetened peach nectar
1 tablespoon soy sauce
⅛ teaspoon ground pepper
2 large (8-oz size) ripe peaches
1 tablespoon cornstarch

Cooked rice (optional)

1. Rinse chicken under cold water; pat dry with paper towels.
2. In large skillet, heat butter and oil; add pepper strips. Over medium heat, cook, stirring occasionally with slotted spoon, 5 minutes. Remove strips to bowl; set aside.
3. Place chicken in same skillet. Over medium heat, cook until golden-brown on both sides—about 10 minutes. Add onion and half of chopped tomato; cook 1 minute. Stir in ¾ cup peach nectar, the soy sauce and pepper. Reduce heat; simmer, covered, until chicken is fork-tender—30 minutes.
4. Meanwhile, peel peaches; cut in half lengthwise; dis-

card pits. Slice each peach half into eight wedges; set aside.
5. With slotted spoon, transfer chicken pieces to serving platter; keep warm. In small bowl, stir cornstarch into remaining ¼ cup peach nectar until dissolved. Stirring constantly, add cornstarch mixture to sauce in skillet; bring to boiling; cook 1 minute. Add reserved chopped tomato, pepper strips and peach wedges; cook until heated through—about 3 minutes. Pour sauce mixture over chicken. Serve hot with cooked rice, if desired. *Makes 4 servings.*

Italian-Sausage Lasagne
(pictured)

2 tablespoons salad oil
½ lb sweet or hot Italian sausage (3 links)
½ cup finely chopped onion
1 clove garlic, crushed
2 tablespoons sugar
   Salt
1½ teaspoons dried basil leaves
½ teaspoon fennel seed
¼ teaspoon ground pepper
¼ cup chopped parsley
1 can (1 lb, 12 oz) Italian-style tomatoes, undrained
1 can (6 oz) tomato paste
½ cup water
12 curly lasagne noodles (¾ of 1-lb pkg)
1 container (1 lb) cottage cheese
1 egg
6 tablespoons grated Parmesan cheese
¼ lb mozzarella cheese, thinly sliced

1. In hot oil in 5-quart Dutch oven, over medium heat, sauté sausage, onion and garlic, turning, until lightly browned—10 minutes. Remove sausage.
2. Add sugar, 1 tablespoon salt, the basil, fennel seed, pepper and half the parsley; mix well. Add tomatoes, tomato paste and ½ cup water, mashing tomatoes with wooden spoon. Bring to boiling; reduce heat; cover and simmer, stirring occasionally, until thick—1½ hours.
3. In 8-quart kettle, bring 3 quarts water and 1 tablespoon salt to boiling. Add lasagne, two or three at a time. Return to boiling; boil, uncovered, stirring occasionally, 10 minutes or just until tender. Drain in colander; rinse under cold water. Dry lasagne on paper towels.
4. Preheat oven to 375F. In medium bowl, combine cottage cheese, egg, remaining parsley and ½ teaspoon salt; mix well.
5. Slice sausage on the diagonal into ½-inch slices.

Special Family Fare

6. In bottom of 13-by-9-by-2-inch baking dish, spoon 1½ cups sauce. Layer with six lasagne, lengthwise and overlapping, to cover. Spread with half of cottage-cheese mixture. Spoon 1½ cups sauce over cheese; sprinkle with 2 tablespoons Parmesan. Repeat layering, starting with six lasagne and ending with 1½ cups sauce sprinkled with Parmesan. Spread with remaining sauce; top with mozzarella and sliced sausage and sprinkle with 2 tablespoons Parmesan. Cover with foil, tucking around edge.

7. Bake 25 minutes; remove foil; bake, uncovered, 25 minutes longer or until bubbly. Cool 15 minutes before serving. *Makes 10 servings.*

Plum-Glazed Spareribs
(pictured)

Plum Sauce, recipe follows
4 lb pork spareribs, cut into 2- or 3-rib sections
1 onion, quartered
2 teaspoons salt
¼ teaspoon ground pepper
   Red plums for garnish (optional)
   Watercress (optional)

1. Make Plum Sauce. Use one jar for glazing the ribs.
2. To parboil spareribs: In a large kettle or saucepot, place rib sections, onion, 2 teaspoons salt and ¼ teaspoon pepper. Add water to cover; over high heat, bring to boiling. Reduce heat and simmer, covered, 45 minutes. Drain rib sections, discarding liquid. (See Note.)
3. Prepare outdoor grill for barbecuing, or preheat indoor grill or broiler. Grill ribs, 6 inches above medium coals, or broil, 5 inches from heat, turning occasionally, until ribs are fork-tender—about 15 minutes. To glaze: Brush ribs with Plum Sauce; turn; cook 2 minutes. Repeat to glaze other side of ribs.
4. To make plum "feather" garnish: Cut plums lengthwise into quarters; discard pits. Rest each plum quarter on one cut surface. With sharp knife, cut three V-shaped wedges, ¼ inch apart, parallel to cut surfaces (see photograph). With fingers, push wedges out slightly to resemble a feather.
5. Transfer ribs to platter; garnish with plum "feathers" and watercress. Serve ribs with sauce on the side, if desired. *Makes 6 servings.*

Note: Ribs may be simmered the day before or several hours ahead and kept refrigerated until ready to cook. Increase broiling time to reheat the ribs before glazing with plum sauce.

Plum Sauce

3 lb ripe red plums, unpeeled
2 cloves garlic, minced
1 medium onion, chopped
1 cup cider vinegar
1 teaspoon crushed red pepper
1 teaspoon ground ginger
1 teaspoon ground coriander
½ teaspoon ground allspice
½ teaspoon salt
1 cup granulated sugar
1 cup firmly packed light-brown sugar

1. Cut plums in half lengthwise; discard pits. Cut plum halves into slices ½ inch thick.
2. In 5-quart Dutch oven, combine plums, minced garlic, chopped onion, 1 cup vinegar, the red pepper, ginger, coriander, allspice and salt.
3. Over medium heat, stirring occasionally, bring to boiling. Continue to boil, stirring frequently, 30 minutes; remove from heat.
4. To purée: Carefully ladle hot plum mixture into food mill or large strainer placed over a bowl. Press plum pulp through; discard skins. Return plum purée to Dutch oven.
5. Add 1 cup granulated sugar and 1 cup light-brown sugar; over medium heat, bring to boiling, stirring constantly. Continue to boil, stirring frequently to prevent sticking, until mixture is thick and smooth—about 30 minutes.
6. Ladle into four hot, sterilized 8-ounce canning jars and seal. Cool; label with date. Store in a cool, dark place. Plum Sauce may be used as a glaze on chicken, pork or ham or as a condiment with cooked poultry or pork. *Makes 4 (8-ounce) jars.*

Swedish Meatballs
(pictured)

2 eggs, slightly beaten
1 cup milk
½ cup dry bread crumbs
3 tablespoons butter or margarine
½ cup finely chopped onion
1 lb ground chuck
¼ lb ground pork
1¾ teaspoons salt
¾ teaspoon dried dillweed
¼ teaspoon ground allspice
⅛ teaspoon ground nutmeg
⅛ teaspoon ground cardamom
3 tablespoons all-purpose flour
⅛ teaspoon ground pepper
1 can (10½ oz) condensed beef broth, undiluted
½ cup light cream or half-and-half
   Fresh dill sprigs (optional)

Special Family Fare

1. In a large bowl, combine the eggs, milk and dry bread crumbs.
2. In large skillet, heat 1 tablespoon butter. Sauté chopped onion until soft—about 5 minutes. Lift out with slotted spoon. Add to bread-crumb mixture, along with ground chuck and ground pork, 1½ teaspoons salt, ¼ teaspoon dillweed, the allspice, nutmeg and cardamom. With a wooden spoon or your hands, mix well to combine.
3. Refrigerate, covered, for 1 hour.
4. Shape meat mixture into meatballs, each about 1 inch in diameter.
5. Preheat the oven to 325F.
6. In remaining hot butter, sauté meatballs, about half at a time, until browned all over. Remove the meatballs to a 2-quart casserole as they are browned.
7. Remove the skillet from heat. Pour off drippings. Measure 2 tablespoons drippings, adding more butter if necessary. Pour back into skillet; add flour, the remaining ¼ teaspoon salt and the pepper, stirring together to make a smooth mixture.
8. Gradually stir in beef broth; bring mixture to boiling, stirring constantly. Add cream and remaining ½ teaspoon dillweed. Pour over meatballs in casserole.
9. Bake, covered, 30 minutes. Garnish top of meatballs with fresh dill sprigs, if desired. *Makes 6 servings.*

Pesto Sauce for Spaghetti

¼ **cup (½ stick) butter or margarine, softened**
¼ **cup grated Parmesan cheese**
½ **cup finely chopped parsley**
 1 **clove garlic, crushed**
 1 **teaspoon dried basil leaves**
½ **teaspoon dried marjoram leaves**
¼ **cup olive or salad oil**
¼ **cup finely chopped walnuts or pine nuts**

1. With wooden spoon, cream butter, Parmesan, parsley, garlic, basil and marjoram until well blended. Or you may combine these ingredients in a blender and proceed with Step 2.
2. Gradually add oil, beating constantly. Add nuts; mix well. Toss with hot spaghetti to coat well. *Makes enough for 8 ounces spaghetti.*

Meat-And-Mushroom Sauce for Spaghetti

 2 **tablespoons olive or salad oil**
 2 **cloves garlic, sliced**
¼ **lb fresh mushrooms, sliced**
½ **lb ground pork**
½ **lb ground veal**
 1 **can (2 lb) Italian tomatoes, undrained**
½ **can (6-oz size) tomato paste**
 2 **teaspoons sugar**
 3 **teaspoons salt**
¼ **teaspoon ground pepper**

1. In hot oil in large heavy skillet or saucepan, sauté garlic just until golden; lift out garlic and discard.
2. To oil, add mushrooms, pork and veal; cook, stirring occasionally, 10 minutes.
3. Add tomatoes, tomato paste, sugar, salt and pepper; bring to boiling; reduce heat; cover and simmer, stirring occasionally, 1 hour. *Makes 6 cups sauce.*

Spinach Soup With Tortellini

1½ **lb marrowbones, cracked**
 1 **cup chopped onion**
 1 **bay leaf**
 4 **black peppercorns**
¼ **teaspoon salt**
    Water
 3 **cans (10½-oz size) condensed beef broth, undiluted**
 1 **cup chopped carrot**
 1 **cup chopped celery**
 2 **tablespoons chopped parsley**
    Tortellini, recipe follows (see Note)
½ **lb fresh spinach leaves**
    Chopped parsley
    Parmesan cheese

1. Scrape marrow (fat inside bones) into a 5-quart Dutch oven. Melt marrow over medium heat and sauté onion, stirring, until golden—about 5 minutes.
2. Add marrowbones, bay leaf, peppercorns and salt. Add water to beef broth to make 8 cups; add to Dutch oven. Cover and bring to boiling; lower heat and simmer, covered, 1 hour. Drain; remove and discard marrowbones. Skim off fat.

Special Family Fare

3. Add carrot, celery and parsley. Return soup to boiling; reduce heat; simmer 20 minutes. Add 24 tortellini; cook over medium heat, stirring occasionally, 10 minutes.
4. Prepare spinach: Cut off root ends; wash several times; drain.
5. During last 5 minutes of cooking, add spinach leaves. Serve sprinkled with parsley and Parmesan cheese. *Makes 8 servings (8 cups).*

Note: Or use 24 frozen packaged tortellini; do not thaw.

Tortellini

Filling
½ **lb chicken livers**
2 **tablespoons butter or margarine**
¼ **cup chopped onion**
2 **tablespoons Parmesan cheese**
½ **teaspoon dried basil leaves**
¼ **teaspoon salt**
   Dash ground pepper
1 **egg**

   Egg Pasta, recipe page 90

1. Make Filling: Wash chicken livers; drain on paper towels. Cut each in half.
2. In hot butter in large skillet, sauté onion and chicken livers about 5 minutes.
3. Turn chicken-liver mixture into food processor or blender; add Parmesan, basil, salt, pepper and egg; blend until smooth.
4. Prepare Egg Pasta. On lightly floured pastry cloth or board, roll a fourth of the dough at a time, 1/16 inch thick.
5. Cut into rounds with a 2½-inch cookie cutter or small drinking glass. Wet edges; place ½ teaspoon filling on each round. Fold the dough over the filling; press the edges together to seal. You now have a semicircle. Wrap the piece of dough around your finger and press ends together. Use in Spinach Soup as directed above. To serve with other recipes, cook in boiling salted water until just tender. *Makes 80 tortellini.*

Note: You may freeze any leftover tortellini before cooking.

Sardine Sauce for Spaghetti

2 **tablespoons salad or olive oil**
1 **clove garlic, pressed**
1 **medium onion, finely chopped**
1 **can (1 lb) Italian tomatoes, undrained**
½ **can (8-oz size) tomato paste**
1 **cup water**
1 **teaspoon sugar**
¼ **teaspoon salt**
   Dash ground pepper
½ **teaspoon dried oregano leaves**
1 **tablespoon chopped parsley**
1 **can (3¾ oz) sardines in tomato sauce**

1. In hot oil in large skillet, sauté garlic and onion, stirring, 5 minutes or until tender.
2. Add tomatoes, tomato paste, water, the sugar, salt, pepper, oregano and parsley; mix well. Bring to boiling; reduce heat; cover and simmer, stirring occasionally, 45 minutes.
3. Gently remove bones from sardines. Add sardines in tomato sauce to tomato mixture; simmer, covered, 5 minutes. *Makes 2⅔ cups, enough for 8 ounces spaghetti.*

Greek Salad With Macaroni

Dressing
¼ **cup salad oil**
2 **tablespoons lemon juice**
2 **tablespoons wine vinegar**
1 **teaspoon dried oregano leaves**
½ **teaspoon salt**
⅛ **teaspoon ground pepper**

1 **pkg (8 oz) elbow macaroni or other pasta**
1 **cup green-pepper strips, ⅛ inch wide**
1 **large tomato, halved lengthwise and thinly sliced**
½ **cup sliced green onion**
½ **lb feta cheese, cubed**
½ **cup pitted black olives**
2 **tablespoons snipped fresh dill or 1 teaspoon dried dillweed**

1. Make Dressing: In jar with tight-fitting lid, combine oil, lemon juice, vinegar, oregano, salt and pepper; shake until well combined.

Special Family Fare

2. Cook elbow macaroni as package label directs; drain; turn into large bowl; add dressing; toss to combine. Cool completely.
3. To macaroni mixture, add green pepper, tomato, green onion, feta cheese, black olives and dill; toss lightly to combine. Turn into serving bowl; refrigerate, covered, 1 hour. Toss well before serving. *Makes 8 servings.*

Old-Fashioned Split-Pea Soup

  1 **pkg (1 lb) dried, split green peas**
  7 **cups water**
2½ **lb smoked ham hocks or smoked neck bones**
  2 **cans (13¾- or 14½-oz size) chicken broth**
  1 **medium onion, chopped**
  2 **large carrots, pared and sliced**
  2 **stalks celery, sliced**
  2 **parsley sprigs, chopped**
  1 **clove garlic, minced**
  1 **bay leaf**
 ⅛ **teaspoon dried thyme leaves**
 ⅛ **teaspoon ground pepper**

1. In 5-quart Dutch oven or kettle, over high heat, bring all ingredients to boiling. Reduce heat to low; simmer, covered, 1½ hours, adding more water if too thick.
2. Discard bay leaf and remove ham hocks from soup; cool. Cut off any meat and skin from bones; chop meat and skin if desired; return to soup. Discard the bones. Over low heat, reheat soup, covered, 15 minutes or until hot. *Makes about 2½ quarts (10 1-cup servings).*

Deviled-Crab-And-Scallop Casserole

¼ **cup (½ stick) butter or margarine**
¼ **cup finely chopped onion**
  3 **tablespoons all-purpose flour**
¼ **teaspoon salt**
  1 **teaspoon bottled thick steak sauce**
½ **teaspoon Worcestershire sauce**
    Dash hot red-pepper sauce
  1 **cup light cream or half-and-half**
⅓ **cup milk**
½ **cup dry sherry**
  1 **lb sea scallops, quartered**
  2 **cans (7½-oz size) king-crab meat**

Topping
  1 **tablespoon butter or margarine, melted**
¼ **cup packaged seasoned dry bread crumbs**

1. Preheat oven to 375F.
2. In ¼ cup hot butter in medium saucepan, sauté onion until golden—about 5 minutes. Remove from heat.
3. Stir in flour, salt, steak sauce, Worcestershire, red-pepper sauce, cream and milk.
4. Bring to boiling, stirring; reduce heat and simmer 1 minute longer. Remove from heat.
5. Stir in sherry and scallops.
6. Drain crabmeat, removing any cartilage. Break crabmeat into large pieces; add to scallop mixture.
7. Turn into a 1½-quart casserole.
8. Make Topping: Combine butter with crumbs. Sprinkle over top.
9. Bake 25 to 30 minutes or until mixture is bubbly and heated through. Nice served with lemon-buttered fresh asparagus. *Makes 6 servings.*

Old-Fashioned Chicken and Dumplings

    4-lb roasting chicken
    Water
½ **cup chopped onion**
  2 **teaspoons salt**
  1 **bay leaf**
  6 **black peppercorns**
  1 **large carrot, pared and sliced**

Parsley Dumplings
  1 **cup all-purpose flour**
1½ **teaspoons baking powder**
½ **teaspoon salt**
½ **cup milk**
  1 **large egg**
  2 **tablespoons chopped parsley**
  1 **tablespoon salad oil**
  3 **tablespoons all-purpose flour**

1. Place chicken and giblets in 6-quart Dutch oven along with 5 cups water. Add onion, 2 teaspoons salt, the bay leaf, peppercorns and carrot. Bring to boiling over high heat; reduce heat; simmer, covered, 1 hour or till tender. Remove Dutch oven from heat; remove chicken and giblets to bowl to cool.
2. Meanwhile, make Parsley Dumplings: In medium bowl, sift together 1 cup flour, the baking powder and salt. In 1-cup measuring cup, measure milk; with fork, stir in egg, parsley and oil until well combined. Pour all at once into flour mixture, mixing with fork until dry ingredients are moistened; set aside.
3. Strain broth and skim off fat. Measure broth—there should be 5 cups; add water if there is not enough. Return broth to Dutch oven. (If there is too much broth, boil, uncovered, to reduce to 5 cups.)

Special Family Fare

4. In small bowl, place flour; gradually whisk in 3 table-spoons water until smooth. Stir flour mixture into broth in Dutch oven. Bring to boiling; boil 1 minute.
5. Drop tablespoonfuls of parsley-dumpling batter into gently boiling broth, making 18 dumplings in all. Cook, uncovered, over low heat 10 minutes. Cover tightly; cook 10 minutes longer.
6. Meanwhile, cut chicken into serving-size pieces. Or bone and skin chicken, then cut into chunks. Add cut-up chicken and giblets to Dutch oven. Cook 5 minutes or until heated through. Serve chicken and dumplings with gravy. *Makes 6 servings.*

Chilled Sole Platter

6 medium (4-oz size) fresh fillets of sole or flounder

Herbed Yogurt Sauce
1 container (8 oz) plain low-fat yogurt
¼ cup chopped parsley
¼ cup chopped green onion
¼ teaspoon salt
⅛ teaspoon ground white pepper
⅓ cup mayonnaise

1 small cucumber, unpeeled
4 nectarines, unpeeled, halved, pitted and cut into 1-inch chunks
2 parsley sprigs

1. In large skillet, place a wire rack that fits on bottom; add water to just below rack. Fold fish fillets in half; place on pie plate or heatproof plate; place plate on rack; cover. Over medium-high heat, bring to boiling; reduce heat; simmer 8 to 10 minutes or just until fish feels firm to the touch.
2. With wide spatula, transfer fish to dish; refrigerate until chilled.
3. Meanwhile, make Herbed Yogurt Sauce: In blender container, combine one-fourth of the yogurt, ¼ cup parsley, the green onion, salt and pepper; blend until smooth.
4. In small bowl, with wire whisk, blend mayonnaise and remaining yogurt until smooth. Add yogurt-herb mixture, whisking just until well mixed; refrigerate.
5. Cut cucumber in half lengthwise; with spoon, remove and discard seeds. Trim ends; cut each half crosswise, on the diagonal, into slices ⅛ inch thick.

6. To serve: Place nectarine chunks on chilled platter; arrange fish fillets on nectarines. Spoon 2 table-spoons sauce over each fillet. Garnish with cucumber and parsley. Pass remaining sauce. *Makes 6 servings.*

Turkey Cutlets With Apricots

2 turkey-breast tenderloins (about 1¼ lb) or 8 slices turkey breast
⅓ cup all-purpose flour
2 tablespoons butter or margarine
2 tablespoons salad or olive oil
1 shallot, minced, or 1 tablespoon minced white part of green onion
1 cup chicken broth or 1 chicken-flavor bouillon cube, dissolved in 1 cup hot water
½ cup white wine
½ cup heavy cream
¾ teaspoon curry powder
¼ teaspoon ground white pepper
4 large apricots, unpeeled, halved and pitted, each half cut into 3 wedges

1. With sharp knife held parallel to cutting board, split each turkey tenderloin in half horizontally to make 4 thinner tenderloins. Cut each in half crosswise to make 8 pieces in all. (If using slices, omit Step 1.)
2. Put turkey pieces or slices between sheets of waxed paper. Using a meat mallet or side of a heavy saucer, gently pound each to a ¼-inch-thick cutlet. Place flour on waxed paper and use to coat cutlets.
3. In large skillet, heat 1 tablespoon butter and 1 table-spoon oil. Over medium-high heat, sauté 4 cutlets at a time until lightly browned on both sides. Transfer to serving platter; keep warm. Repeat with remaining cutlets, adding remaining butter and oil.
4. Pour off and discard all but 1 teaspoon of the fat from skillet. In skillet, sauté shallot, stirring, about 30 seconds. Add chicken broth, wine, cream, curry powder and pepper. Over high heat, cook, stirring constantly, until sauce is thickened and coats a spoon—about 5 minutes. Add apricot wedges; cook, stirring occasionally, just until apricots are hot—about 1 minute. Remove from heat; pour sauce over turkey cutlets. Serve immediately. *Makes 4 servings.* ∎

Classic Company Dinners

♥   ♥   ♥

Our dinner classics are all time-honored favorites. Each represents the highest standard of culinary excellence, so there's never a need to worry about the success of the meal...and there's never a surprise when all who partake feel compelled to offer words of praise for a superb dining experience. The recipes for our classics, plus sensational menus, begin on page 227.

———

Left: Three resplendent roasts. **Clockwise, from left:** Succulent herbed capon rests on a bed of ripe strawberries, green grapes and zigzag kiwi halves; apple-apricot-sausage-stuffed crown roast of pork is garnished with celery-stick curls and whole apricots; fresh-snipped parsley and other herbs envelop the crumb-coated leg of lamb, beautifully enhanced by mint-jelly-filled lemon baskets.

223

Above: A perfect mix of fresh herbs is the secret behind this sophisticated sirloin. A marjoram-basil-thyme butter fills shallow slits in the sirloin top, which is spread with mustard and wine, then broiled rare to medium. A sprinkling of tarragon, parsley and chives, and this French-inspired specialty is ready to serve with a delightful Béarnaise sauce. *See recipe on page 230.*

Right: Ham can be cooked in a variety of glorious ways. Its rich flavor blends wonderfully with spices and fruit sauces, as evidenced by this clove-studded baked ham, basted with dry red wine and glazed with apricot preserves and a candied-orange-petal daisy. *See recipe on page 231.*

Our Old-Fashioned Roast Turkey brings back the wonderful taste of yesteryear with each succulent bite. With its classic bread stuffing, giblet gravy and sweet garnish of broiled peaches, it continues to delight us with a welcome touch of Americana. *See recipe on page 232.*

Classic Company Dinners

continued from page 223

Menu

Cream-Of-Spinach Soup*
Roast Capon With Tarragon*
Mushroom Rice Pilaf*   *Fresh Asparagus*
Whole-Wheat Italian Bread
Chilled Pears With Raspberry Sauce*
Ladyfingers
Coffee   Chilled Chablis

Cream-Of-Spinach Soup

 1 **pkg (10 oz) frozen chopped spinach**
¼ **cup chopped onion**
⅓ **cup sliced celery**
¼ **teaspoon salt**
⅛ **teaspoon ground pepper**
⅛ **teaspoon ground nutmeg**
 1 **bay leaf**
   Water
 2 **cans (10¾ oz) condensed chicken broth, undiluted**
 2 **tablespoons butter or margarine**
 2 **tablespoons all-purpose flour**
1½ **cups light cream or half-and-half**
½ **cup heavy cream, whipped**

1. In 3-quart saucepan, combine spinach, onion, celery, salt, pepper, nutmeg and bay leaf. Add water to chicken broth to make 3 cups; add to spinach mixture. Bring to boiling; reduce heat and simmer, covered, until spinach is defrosted and tender—about 5 minutes.
2. Drain; reserve broth. Purée vegetables in blender or food processor with half of reserved broth.
3. In large saucepan, melt butter; remove from heat; add flour, stirring until smooth. Gradually add remaining broth, stirring until mixture boils.
4. Add puréed vegetables and cream. Continue stirring until soup is hot and well blended—5 minutes. Top each serving with a spoonful of whipped cream. *Makes 8 servings (6 cups).*

*Recipes given for starred dishes.

Roast Capon With Tarragon
(pictured)

 5½-**to 6-lb ready-to-cook capon or roasting chicken**
   Salt
   Ground pepper
½ **cup (1 stick) butter or margarine, softened**
 1 **tablespoon lemon juice**
 1 **tablespoon chopped chives**
 1 **tablespoon chopped parsley**
 1 **clove garlic, crushed**
1½ **teaspoons chopped fresh tarragon or ½ teaspoon dried tarragon leaves**
 1 **onion, sliced**
 2 **carrots, pared and sliced**
 1 **stalk celery, sliced**

Gravy
 1 **can (10¾ oz) condensed chicken broth, undiluted**
½ **cup cold water**
 3 **tablespoons all-purpose flour**

Fruit Garnish
 3 **kiwi, peeled and cut in half, zigzag fashion**
½ **lb green grapes**
½ **pint strawberries, washed**
   Watercress sprigs

1. Preheat oven to 400F.
2. Wash capon well, inside and out, under cold water. Pat dry, inside and out, with paper towels. Sprinkle inside with 1 teaspoon salt and ¼ teaspoon pepper. Rinse giblets; set aside.
3. In small bowl, with portable electric mixer or wooden spoon, beat butter with lemon juice, chives, parsley, garlic, tarragon, ½ teaspoon salt and ⅛ teaspoon pepper until well blended.
4. With fingers, carefully loosen skin from breast meat. Spread 2 tablespoons butter mixture over breast meat, under skin, on each side. Tie legs together; fold wing tips under back. Spread 1 tablespoon butter mixture over capon. Insert meat thermometer inside thigh at thickest part.
5. Place onion, carrot, celery and giblets (except liver) in shallow roasting pan. Set capon on vegetables.
6. Roast, uncovered, 1 hour. Reduce oven to 325F; roast 1 to 1¼ hours, basting occasionally with remaining butter mixture, until meat thermometer registers 185F and leg moves easily at joint.

Classic Company Dinners

7. Remove capon to heated platter. Remove string. Let stand 20 minutes.
8. Meanwhile, make Gravy: Pour undiluted chicken broth into roasting pan; bring to boiling, stirring to dissolve brown bits. Strain into a 4-cup measure; skim off and discard fat.
9. In small saucepan, stir water into flour to dissolve flour. Stir in chicken broth. Bring to boiling, stirring constantly until thickened; reduce heat; simmer 5 minutes. Add salt and pepper, if necessary.
10. Garnish capon with Fruit Garnish, as pictured. Pass gravy. *Makes 8 servings.*

Mushroom Rice Pilaf

¼ cup (½ stick) butter or margarine
1½ cups converted white rice
2 chicken-bouillon cubes, crumbled
¾ teaspoon salt
¼ teaspoon ground pepper
    Dash dried thyme leaves
1½ cups chopped fresh mushrooms
3½ cups boiling water
    Chopped parsley

1. Preheat oven to 375F.
2. Melt butter in 1½-quart flameproof casserole. Add rice and sauté, stirring, until lightly browned—about 10 minutes.
3. Add bouillon cubes, salt, pepper, thyme, mushrooms and boiling water; mix well.
4. Bake, tightly covered, 40 minutes or until rice is tender and liquid is absorbed.
5. To serve: Fluff up pilaf with a fork and turn out on serving platter. Sprinkle with chopped parsley. *Makes 8 servings.*

Chilled Pears With Raspberry Sauce

2 cans (1-lb size) pear halves
2 pkg (10-oz size) frozen raspberries, thawed
1 tablespoon cornstarch
½ cup currant jelly

1. Drain pears, reserving liquid. Refrigerate pears.
2. Drain raspberries, reserving liquid. Add enough pear liquid to raspberry liquid to make 2 cups.
3. In small saucepan, blend liquid with cornstarch. Bring to boiling over medium heat, stirring constantly; boil 5 minutes. Stir in jelly until melted. Remove from heat; add raspberries. Refrigerate, covered.
4. To serve: Turn pear halves into serving bowl. Pour raspberry sauce over them. *Makes 8 servings.*

Menu

Herring in Sour Cream*
Crown Roast of Pork With
Fruit Stuffing*
Buttered Broccoli With Baby Carrots
Sliced Tomatoes With Endive
Assorted Hot Rolls
Orange, Banana and Pineapple Ambrosia*
Coffee   Beaujolais

Herring in Sour Cream

3 cans (6-oz size) matjes-herring fillets or 4 matjes-herring fillets
1 large onion
36 black peppercorns
3 bay leaves
1¼ cups sour cream
⅓ cup dry white wine

1. Rinse fillets in cold water; drain; dry on paper towels. Cut crosswise into 1-inch pieces. Then slice onion into thin rings.
2. In large bowl, layer onion rings, peppercorns, bay leaves and herring.
3. Combine sour cream and wine. Pour over herring mixture; stir gently to combine ingredients.
4. Refrigerate, covered, 8 hours or overnight. *Makes 8 appetizer servings.*

   Note: Herring in Sour Cream may be stored, covered, in refrigerator 3 days.

Crown Roast of Pork With
Fruit Stuffing
(pictured)

6-lb crown roast of pork (14 ribs)
    Salt
    Ground pepper
1 cup water
¼ cup white vinegar

Stuffing
¼ cup (½ stick) butter or margarine
2 sweet Italian sausages (¼ lb)
½ cup thinly sliced celery
½ cup chopped onion
1 cup diced, pared tart apple
½ cup chopped dried apricots
2 cups bread cubes (¼-inch)
1 teaspoon dried sage leaves

3 tablespoons all-purpose flour
    Celery Garnish, recipe follows
1 can (1 lb, 13 oz) whole apricots, drained (optional)
    Watercress (optional)

*Recipes given for starred dishes.

Classic Company Dinners

1. Preheat oven to 400F. Wipe pork with damp paper towels.
2. Combine 1 teaspoon salt and ¼ teaspoon pepper; rub meat well with mixture. Press piece of foil down into center of crown roast.
3. Place roast in shallow roasting pan without rack. Roast, uncovered, 15 minutes.
4. Reduce oven to 350F. Combine water and vinegar; pour into pan with roast. Cover tightly with foil. Roast 1 hour and 45 minutes.
5. Meanwhile, prepare Stuffing: In hot butter in medium skillet, sauté sausage (remove casing and cut up sausage), celery and onion, stirring, until onion is golden—about 5 minutes.
6. In a large bowl, combine sausage mixture, apple, apricot, bread cubes, sage, ½ teaspoon salt and ⅛ teaspoon pepper; mix well.
7. Remove roast from oven. Remove foil. Spoon stuffing into center cavity, mounding. Cover stuffing with 10-inch square of foil. Return roast to oven; roast 45 minutes. Place roast on heated platter; keep warm while making gravy.
8. Make gravy: Strain drippings in roasting pan. Pour off fat from top, reserving 2 tablespoons. Return the 2 tablespoons fat to roasting pan. Stir flour into fat until smooth. Stir in drippings (about 2 cups); bring to boil; reduce heat; simmer, stirring, about 3 minutes or until thickened.
9. Before serving, secure Celery Garnish with toothpicks between bones, as pictured. Garnish with apricots and watercress, if desired. Pass gravy. *Makes 10 servings.*

Celery Garnish

12 (1½-inch) pieces of celery

1. With paring knife, cut thin slices, ½ inch long, at one end of celery pieces.
2. Place immediately in ice water to curl ends. Before using, drain well on paper towels.

Orange, Banana and Pineapple Ambrosia

4 large navel oranges
1 can (1 lb, 4 oz) pineapple chunks, in pineapple juice
2 tablespoons orange juice
4 medium bananas
2 tablespoons confectioners' sugar
1 can (3½ oz) flaked coconut

1. Peel oranges; remove white membrane. Cut oranges crosswise into ⅛-inch-thick slices.

2. Drain pineapple, saving juice. Combine the pineapple juice with the orange juice; set aside.
3. Peel bananas. Cut on the diagonal into ⅛-inch-thick slices.
4. In attractive serving bowl, layer half the orange slices; sprinkle with 1 tablespoon confectioners' sugar. Layer half the banana slices and half the pineapple; sprinkle with half the coconut.
5. Repeat layering. Pour juice mixture over top.
6. Refrigerate several hours or until well chilled. *Makes 10 servings.*

Menu
Chilled Cream-Of-Tomato Soup
With Fresh Dill*
Parsley Leg of Lamb*
Mint Jelly in Lemon Baskets*
Fresh Peas and New Potatoes
Tossed Green Salad   Warm French Bread
Strawberries Jubilee*
Coffee   Cabernet Sauvignon

Chilled Cream-Of-Tomato Soup

1 can (1 qt, 14 oz) tomato juice, chilled
3 tablespoons lemon juice
1 cup sour cream
Fresh dill sprigs

1. Blend tomato juice, lemon juice and sour cream in blender. Chill until very cold.
2. To serve: Serve in chilled serving dishes; garnish with fresh dill sprigs. *Makes 8 servings (6 cups).*

Parsley Leg of Lamb
(pictured)

6- to 7-lb leg of lamb
1½ teaspoons salt
¼ teaspoon ground pepper
1 cup chopped onion
1 cup sliced carrot
White wine
1½ cups fresh-bread crumbs
¾ cup chopped parsley
1 clove garlic, crushed
¼ cup brown mustard
½ cup (1 stick) butter or margarine, melted
2 tablespoons all-purpose flour
1 cup chicken broth
Parsley
Lemon Baskets, recipe follows

*Recipes given for starred dishes.

Classic Company Dinners

1. Preheat oven to 350F.
2. Wipe lamb with paper towels. Rub surface with salt and pepper.
3. Place lamb in shallow roasting pan without rack. Sprinkle chopped onion and carrot around roast. Insert meat thermometer in thickest part of meat, away from bone and fat.
4. Add 1 cup white wine. Roast, uncovered, basting occasionally with pan juices, 2 hours.
5. Meanwhile, in medium bowl, combine bread crumbs, chopped parsley and garlic; toss lightly to combine.
6. Remove roast from oven; let cool about 15 minutes.
7. Spread mustard over surface of lamb. Firmly pat crumb mixture into mustard. Pour butter over bread crumbs.
8. Return roast to oven and continue roasting, uncovered, about 30 minutes or until meat thermometer registers 160F for medium-well done or 170F to 180F for well done.
9. Remove lamb to heated platter. Let roast stand 20 minutes for easier carving.
10. Make gravy: Pour fat into a measuring cup. Return 2 tablespoons fat to roasting pan. Stir in flour to make a smooth paste. Add broth and ½ cup white wine.
11. Bring to boiling, stirring. Simmer 3 minutes or until slightly thickened. Strain; discard vegetables. Makes 1½ cups.
12. Before serving, garnish platter with parsley and Lemon Baskets. Pass gravy. *Makes 10 servings.*

Lemon Baskets

4 lemons
1 jar (12 oz) apple-mint jelly, chilled

1. Insert 2 toothpicks, ¼ inch apart, in center of lemon.
2. With sharp knife, cut lemon halfway, on each side of toothpick, to make handle. On each side, cut away top half of lemon. Scoop out pulp from under handle and from inside basket. Scallop handle, as pictured, if desired.
3. Cut jelly into ½-inch cubes; arrange in baskets.

Strawberries Jubilee

2 boxes (1-pt size) strawberries
½ cup strawberry jam
¼ cup sugar
Brandy
8 vanilla or strawberry ice-cream balls

1. Wash berries gently; remove hulls. If large, slice in half lengthwise. Set aside in bowl.
2. In small saucepan, combine strawberry jam, sugar and ½ cup brandy. Simmer, uncovered, until slightly thickened—15 minutes. Pour over strawberries in bowl. Let stand several hours.
3. To serve, add 2 tablespoons brandy to strawberries; reheat gently; turn into metal serving bowl. (Or reheat strawberries in a chafing dish.) In small saucepan, heat 2 tablespoons brandy just until vapor begins to rise; ignite and pour into strawberries. Serve, flaming, over ice cream. *Makes 8 servings.*

Menu

Steak With Mustard and Herbs*
Béarnaise Sauce*
Baked Potatoes
Steamed Green Beans With Almonds
Hot Sour-Dough Rolls
Green Salad With Cherry Tomatoes
Chilled Peach Halves Served in Champagne
Coffee

Steak With Mustard and Herbs
(pictured)

¼ cup (½ stick) butter or margarine, softened
1 teaspoon dried marjoram leaves
1 teaspoon dried basil leaves
1 teaspoon dried thyme leaves
1 teaspoon cracked black pepper
4½- to 5-lb sirloin steak, 1½ inches thick
6 tablespoons dry mustard
3 tablespoons dry white wine
1 to 2 tablespoons finely chopped fresh tarragon
1½ to 2½ tablespoons finely chopped parsley
1 to 2 tablespoons finely chopped chives
Béarnaise Sauce, recipe follows

*Recipes given for starred dishes.

Classic Company Dinners

1. In small bowl, combine softened butter with marjoram, basil and thyme, rubbing dried herbs between fingers while blending in. Add ¼ teaspoon pepper.
2. With point of sharp knife, make ½-inch-deep cuts in steak, 1½ inches apart.
3. Fill each cut with ¼ teaspoon herb butter, reserving the rest of the herb butter.
4. In small bowl, combine mustard, remaining pepper and the wine to form a paste.
5. Spread mustard paste smoothly on both sides of steak. Place steak on waxed paper; allow to stand, uncovered, at room temperature 1 to 1½ hours before broiling.
6. Place steak, herb-butter side down, on broiler rack. Broil steak, 2 to 3 inches from heat, 8 minutes on first side or until mustard paste is brown and crusty. Turn steak and broil 3 minutes.
7. Remove steak from broiler; spread surface with remaining herb butter and sprinkle with 1 tablespoon fresh tarragon combined with 1½ tablespoons parsley and 1 tablespoon chives. Return steak to broiler and continue to broil about 4 minutes longer or until steak is cooked rare to medium.
8. To serve, place on steak board. Sprinkle with remaining fresh herbs, if desired. Slice steak on the diagonal, ¼ inch thick. Serve with Béarnaise Sauce. *Makes 6 to 8 servings.*

Béarnaise Sauce
(pictured)

¼ **cup tarragon vinegar**
¼ **cup dry white wine**
1 **tablespoon finely chopped fresh tarragon or**
    1 teaspoon dried tarragon leaves
1 **tablespoon chopped fresh chives**
2 **tablespoons chopped parsley**
¼ **teaspoon dried basil leaves**
¼ **teaspoon dried thyme leaves**
¼ **teaspoon dried marjoram leaves**
1 **tablespoon finely chopped shallot**
3 **egg yolks**
½ **cup (1 stick) butter or margarine**

1. In small saucepan, combine vinegar, wine, tarragon, chives, parsley, basil, thyme, marjoram and shallot; over medium heat, bring just to boiling. Reduce heat

and simmer, uncovered, until the liquid is reduced to ¼ cup—8 to 10 minutes.
2. Strain mixture into top of double boiler. With wire whisk or rotary beater, beat in egg yolks. Cook over hot, not boiling, water, beating constantly until mixture begins to thicken.
3. Beat in the butter, 1 tablespoon at a time, beating well after each addition. Keep warm. (Add just enough cold water to hot water in bottom of double boiler to make it lukewarm. Set double-boiler top with the sauce over the lukewarm water and set aside, covered.) Beat again just before serving. Serve with steak. *Makes 1 cup.*

Menu

Jellied Consommé
Baked Ham With Candied-Orange Daisy*
Baked Sweet Potatoes   Buttered Spinach
Belgian Endive Salad   Corn Muffins
Angel Food Cake à la Mode
Coffee   Sparkling Rosé Wine

Baked Ham With Candied-Orange Daisy
(pictured)

10- to 12-lb fully cooked bone-in ham (see Note)
1 **cup sliced onion**
2 **bay leaves, crushed**
¼ **cup firmly packed light-brown sugar**
4 **parsley sprigs**
    Whole cloves
3 **black peppercorns**
2 **cups dry red or white wine**

Glaze
½ **cup firmly packed light-brown sugar**
½ **cup apricot preserves**
1 **tablespoon prepared mustard**

    Candied-Orange Petals, recipe follows
1 **candied red cherry**

1. Preheat oven to 325F. Place ham, fat side up, in shallow roasting pan. Arrange onion and crushed bay

*Recipe given for starred dish.

Classic Company Dinners

leaves on ham; sprinkle with ¼ cup brown sugar, the parsley, 6 whole cloves and the peppercorns. Insert meat thermometer in center of thickest part, away from bone.

2. Pour wine around ham. Cover pan tightly with foil. Bake, basting with a baster every 30 minutes with wine in pan, about 3 to 3½ hours or until meat thermometer registers 140F. (To baste, remove ham from oven; take off foil.)

3. Make Glaze: In small saucepan, combine brown sugar, apricot preserves and mustard; cook over medium heat, stirring, just until sugar is dissolved.

4. Remove ham from oven. Turn oven temperature to 400F. Remove ham from roasting pan; take out meat thermometer. Pour off all fat and drippings. Return ham to roasting pan. With sharp knife, carefully remove any skin and excess fat. To score, make diagonal cuts in fat (do not cut into meat) ¼ inch deep and 1¼ inches apart.

5. Insert a clove in each diamond; brush half of glaze over ham; bake 10 minutes.

6. Brush with rest of glaze; bake 10 minutes longer.

7. Arrange 8 Candied-Orange Petals on ham; secure with whole cloves. Place candied cherry in center. For easy slicing, let ham stand 20 minutes. *Makes 16 to 18 servings.*

Note: Smoked ham labeled "fully cooked" needs only to be heated to an internal temperature of 140F on the meat thermometer. "Cook-before-eating" smoked ham should be heated to an internal temperature of 160F.

Candied-Orange Petals

1 **medium-size navel orange**
  Water
¾ **cup sugar**
1 **tablespoon light corn syrup**

1. With sharp paring knife, make 8 sections on skin of orange, being careful not to cut too deep. Carefully remove skin.

2. In small saucepan, cover peel with 1½ cups cold water. Bring to boiling; simmer, uncovered, 15 minutes. Drain; trim peel to simulate petals.

3. In small saucepan, combine sugar, corn syrup and ¾ cup water. Bring to boiling, stirring until sugar is dissolved.

4. Add peel; simmer in syrup 15 minutes or until glazed and transparent. Remove peel from syrup to rack to drain. *Makes 8 petals.*

Menu

Old-Fashioned Roast Turkey*
Bread Dressing*   *Giblet Gravy*
Broiled Peach Halves*
Buttered Cauliflower and Green Beans
Hot Corn-Bread Squares
Warm Deep-Dish Cranberry-Apple Pie
Vanilla Ice Cream
Milk   Coffee

Old-Fashioned Roast Turkey
(pictured)

12-lb ready-to-cook turkey
Bread Dressing, recipe follows
½ **cup (1 stick) margarine, melted**
Salt
Ground pepper
Giblet gravy
Broiled Peach Halves, recipe follows (optional)

1. Remove giblets and neck from turkey; wash; set aside. Wash turkey inside and out. Pat dry with paper towels. Remove and discard excess fat.

2. Make Bread Dressing. Preheat oven to 325F.

3. Spoon some of dressing into neck cavity of turkey. Bring skin of neck over back; fasten with poultry pin.

4. Spoon remaining dressing into body cavity; do not pack. Insert 4 or 5 poultry pins at regular intervals. Lace cavity with twine; tie.

5. Bend wing tips under body or fasten to body with poultry pins. Tie ends of legs together. Insert thermometer in inside of thigh at thickest part, not touching bone.

6. Place turkey on rack in shallow roasting pan. Brush with some of margarine; sprinkle with salt and pepper.

*Recipes given for starred dishes.

Classic Company Dinners

7. Roast uncovered, brushing occasionally with remaining margarine and pan drippings, about 4½ hours or until meat thermometer registers 185F. Leg joints should move freely. When turkey begins to turn golden, cover with a square of margarine-soaked cheesecloth or a loose tent of foil.
8. While turkey roasts, cook giblets and neck to use in your favorite recipe for giblet gravy.
9. Place turkey on heated platter; remove cheesecloth or foil, twine and poultry pins. Let stand 20 to 30 minutes before carving. Garnish with Broiled Peach Halves. Make gravy. *Makes 16 servings.*

Bread Dressing

12 cups fresh white-bread cubes
½ cup chopped parsley
1 tablespoon poultry seasoning
2 teaspoons salt
½ teaspoon ground pepper
½ cup (1 stick) margarine
3 cups chopped celery
1 cup chopped onion

1. In large bowl, combine bread cubes, parsley, poultry seasoning, salt and pepper; toss to mix well.
2. In hot margarine in medium skillet, sauté celery and onion until golden—7 to 10 minutes.
3. Add to bread mixture; toss lightly until well mixed. *Makes 12 cups, enough to stuff a 12- to 16-pound turkey.*

Broiled Peach Halves

¼ cup (½ stick) margarine, melted
¼ cup firmly packed light-brown sugar
1 large can (1 lb, 14 oz) peach halves, drained

1. In small bowl, mix margarine and brown sugar.
2. Arrange peach halves, hollow side up, on broiler tray. Spoon sugar mixture in center of each peach half. Broil, 4 inches from heat, just until sugar is melted.

Menu

Chilled Tomato Juice
Shrimp and Crabmeat au Gratin*
Buttered Broccoli Spears   Steamed Rice
Lettuce Wedges With Oil-And-Vinegar Dressing
Hot Parker House Rolls
Lemon Sherbet With Blueberries
Coffee   Chilled White Wine

*Recipe given for starred dish.

Shrimp and Crabmeat au Gratin

1 lb shrimp, shelled and deveined
1 pkg (9 oz) frozen artichoke hearts
¼ cup (½ stick) butter or margarine
½ lb fresh mushrooms, sliced lengthwise through the stem
1 clove garlic, crushed
2 tablespoons finely chopped shallots
¼ cup all-purpose flour
½ teaspoon ground pepper
1 tablespoon snipped fresh dill (optional)
¾ cup milk
1 pkg (8 oz) sharp Cheddar cheese, grated
⅔ cup dry white wine
2 cans (7½-oz size) king-crab meat
2 tablespoons cornflake crumbs
½ tablespoon butter or margarine

1. Cook shrimp in salted, boiling water to cover for 3 minutes or just until shrimp are pink. Drain.
2. Cook artichoke hearts as package label directs. Drain.
3. Preheat oven to 375F. In 2 tablespoons hot butter in a skillet, sauté sliced mushrooms for 5 minutes.
4. In 2 tablespoons butter in a saucepan, sauté garlic and the chopped shallot 5 minutes. Remove from heat.
5. Stir in the flour, pepper and dill; then stir in milk.
6. Bring to boiling, stirring; remove from heat. Add half of the cheese; stir until it is melted. Stir in the wine.
7. Drain crabmeat; remove cartilage; flake. In a 2-quart casserole, combine the sauce, crabmeat, shrimp, artichokes, mushrooms and rest of cheese; mix lightly.
8. Sprinkle with cornflake crumbs; dot with butter.
9. Bake 30 minutes or until the mixture is bubbly and the cornflake crumbs are browned. *Makes 6 servings.*

Menu

Hot Consommé
Ducklings à l'Orange*
Wild and White Rice
Green Peas, French Style
Green Salad   Warm French Bread
Cheese and Green Grapes
Coffee   Beaujolais

Ducklings à l'Orange

2 (5-lb size) ready-to-cook ducklings, quartered (see Note)
½ cup Burgundy
Orange Sauce, recipe follows
1 cup orange marmalade
Orange peel (see Orange Sauce, recipe follows)

*Recipe given for starred dish.

Classic Company Dinners

1. Preheat oven to 425F.
2. Remove giblets and necks from ducklings; set livers aside for Orange Sauce. Wash ducklings well under running water; drain; dry.
3. Place duckling pieces, skin side up, on rack in large, shallow roasting pan. Pour Burgundy over duckling.
4. Roast, uncovered, 30 minutes. Reduce oven temperature to 375F, and roast 1½ hours, removing fat from the roasting pan with a baster every half hour. Meanwhile, make Orange Sauce.
5. Spread duckling with orange marmalade. Roast 10 minutes longer.
6. Remove to heated platter. Spoon some of sauce over top; garnish with reserved orange peel, cut in thin strips. *Makes 8 servings.*

   Note: If using frozen duckling, let thaw completely.

Orange Sauce

5 large oranges
⅓ cup (⅔ stick) butter or margarine
Livers from ducklings, above
⅓ cup brandy
½ tablespoon minced garlic
¼ cup all-purpose flour
1½ tablespoons catsup
2 teaspoons meat-extract paste (see Note)
Dash ground pepper
1½ cans (10¾-oz size) condensed chicken broth, undiluted
¾ cup Burgundy
½ cup orange marmalade

1. Grate peel from 2 oranges, to measure 4 tablespoons. Set aside. Using a vegetable knife or other sharp knife, cut thin ½-inch-wide strips of peel from 1 orange. Cut strips lengthwise into thin julienne. Set aside for garnish. Squeeze the peeled oranges and reserve 1 cup of juice. Holding the remaining oranges over bowl to catch juice, peel with sharp knife; remove sections; set aside.
2. In 3 tablespoons hot butter in medium skillet, brown duckling livers well. Remove pan from heat.

3. In small saucepan, heat brandy slightly. Ignite; slowly pour over livers. When flames subside, remove livers; set aside.
4. Add remaining butter, 4 tablespoons grated peel and the garlic to skillet; sauté 3 minutes. Remove from heat; stir in flour, catsup, meat-extract paste and pepper until well blended. Gradually stir in broth, Burgundy, marmalade and reserved orange juice.
5. Bring to boiling, stirring constantly. Reduce heat and simmer, stirring occasionally, 15 minutes.
6. Meanwhile, chop livers. Add to sauce, along with orange sections. Heat gently. *Makes 2 cups.*

   Note: Do not use liquid meat extract.

Salmon Steaks Poached in White Wine

6 salmon steaks (2¼ lb)
4 tablespoons (½ stick) butter or margarine
1 teaspoon salt
2 shallots, finely chopped
1 tablespoon lemon juice
2 bay leaves, quartered
½ cup American Sauterne or dry white wine
1½ tablespoons all-purpose flour
2 tablespoons heavy cream
Chopped parsley

1. Preheat oven to 400F. Wash salmon steaks; dry on paper towels.
2. Spread 2 tablespoons butter in medium baking dish. Place fish in dish; sprinkle with salt, shallot, lemon juice and bay leaves. Add Sauterne.
3. Cover dish with foil; bake 20 minutes. Baste steaks with liquid in dish; bake, covered, 15 minutes longer or just until fish flakes easily with fork.
4. Carefully remove fish from baking dish and drain well. Strain liquid; measure 1 cup, adding more Sauterne, if necessary.
5. Arrange steaks on heatproof serving platter or return to baking dish; keep warm.
6. Melt remaining butter in small saucepan; remove from heat. Stir in flour until smooth. Gradually stir

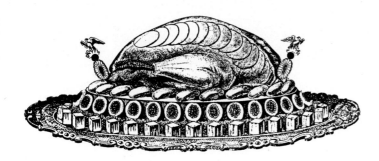

Classic Company Dinners

in reserved fish liquid; cook over medium heat, stirring, until thick. Stir in cream.

7. Pour sauce over salmon steaks. Run under broiler 3 to 5 minutes or till golden-brown. Sprinkle with parsley. *Makes 6 servings.*

Fillets of Sole With Mussels

  3 **dozen mussels**
  4 **lb fillets of sole or flounder**
⅓ **cup lemon juice**
  2 **teaspoons salt**
¼ **teaspoon ground white pepper**
  8 **tablespoons (1 stick) butter or margarine**
  1 **small bay leaf**
1½ **cups dry white wine**
½ **cup finely chopped shallot**
  6 **tablespoons all-purpose flour**
  2 **cups light cream or half-and-half**
  2 **sprigs parsley**
  2 **tablespoons chopped parsley**

1. Discard any mussels that are not tightly closed. Scrub well with brush, under cold running water, to remove sand and seaweed. Using kitchen shears, cut off beards. In large bowl, soak mussels in cold water to cover 2 hours.
2. Place mussels in colander; rinse well under running water; drain.
3. Preheat oven to 350F. Rinse sole fillets under running water; pat dry with paper towels. Dip each fillet into lemon juice and roll dark side inside.
4. In buttered 13-by-9-by-2-inch baking pan, arrange rolled fillets in single layer. Sprinkle with 1 teaspoon salt and ⅛ teaspoon pepper. Dot fillets with 2 tablespoons butter; add bay leaf; pour ½ cup wine over all.
5. Bake, uncovered, 20 minutes or until fish flakes easily when tested with a fork.
6. With slotted spatula, lift fillets to a large serving platter. Cover with foil; keep warm. Reserve 1½ cups fish stock, discarding bay leaf.
7. In 4 tablespoons hot butter in large saucepan, sauté

¼ cup chopped shallot over medium heat, stirring, 3 to 5 minutes. Remove from heat; stir in flour and the remaining salt and pepper. Add reserved fish stock and the cream, stirring until smooth. Cook over medium heat, stirring constantly, until mixture comes to boiling. Reduce heat; simmer 3 minutes. Strain sauce and return to saucepan; keep warm.

8. Meanwhile, in 2 tablespoons hot butter in large skillet, sauté ¼ cup chopped shallot 5 minutes. Add parsley sprigs, 1 cup wine and the drained mussels. Cook, covered, over high heat 5 to 8 minutes or until shells open. Shake pan frequently to cook mussels uniformly. Remove from heat; discard parsley sprigs; keep warm.
9. Drain off any liquid from sole. Pour hot fish sauce over sole. Arrange 12 well-drained mussels, still in shells, at random on the platter. Pile remaining mussels with broth in a deep serving dish. Sprinkle all with chopped parsley. *Makes 6 to 8 servings.*

Tarragon Cornish Hens

  2 **(1½-lb size) fresh or frozen Cornish hens**
½ **cup (1 stick) butter or margarine**
½ **teaspoon dried tarragon leaves**
  1 **pkg (1 lb, 8 oz) frozen potato wedges with skins**
  2 **cups frozen cut green beans**
½ **teaspoon salt**
¼ **teaspoon ground pepper**

1. Thaw hens if frozen. Remove giblets and necks from hens; wash; wrap and freeze for use in other recipes. Wash hens; pat dry with paper towels; with kitchen scissors or knife, split in half lengthwise.
2. Preheat oven to 400F. In 13-by-9-by-2-inch baking dish, melt butter in oven. Remove dish and stir in tarragon. Place hen halves in butter, turning to coat all sides. Bake hens, skin side down, 15 minutes.
3. Remove dish from oven; turn hens; scatter frozen potato wedges and beans around hens, tossing to coat with butter. Sprinkle vegetables and hens with salt and pepper. Bake 30 minutes longer or until hens are tender. *Makes 4 servings.* ∎

Easy, Exciting, Everyday Meals

♥   ♥   ♥

What's for supper? How about one of these tantalizing main dishes that put an end to boring, everyday meals? Some, like savory Baked Pork and Stuffing, go from start to finish in about 30 minutes. Others, like chunky Beef-And-Vegetable Stew, slow-cook to capture every succulent drop of flavor. They're all wonderfully delicious and terrifically easy to prepare... because we know that's how you like them, and that's what you expect from us. Recipes begin on page 246.

Clockwise from top left: In this Puffy Omelet With Zucchini Sauce, zucchini is simmered, topped with a frothy egg mixture, then skillet-baked so it's lighter than air; a mix of flaked tuna and tartar sauce is shaped, breaded and browned, then elegantly adorned with sautéed asparagus and packaged hollandaise sauce to become Tuna Patties Hollandaise; Salisbury Steak Skillet Supper combines a plump beef patty with mushroom gravy, canned potato slices and Italian green beans; Chicken With Spanish Rice is an all-in-one-skillet dish spiced with frozen artichoke hearts, olives, onion, oregano and a prepared rice mix; and a packaged creamy noodle mix is swirled with sautéed chicken livers and green peas to create Chicken-Livers Stroganoff in just 20 minutes.

237

JOHN PAUL ENDRESS

Above: Cut-up cooked chicken is batter-fried to a crispy perfection and served with a quick mushroom-pimiento sauce in this Chicken Croquettes entrée. *See recipe on page 248.*

Right: These individual potpies of chunky chicken, onions, carrots and celery are covered with a crust so flaky it begs to be broken for the first delicious bite. *See recipe on page 249.*

Above: Our Favorite Meat Loaf is wrapped in bacon and brushed with a blend of chili sauce, brown sugar and mustard for a smoky, sweet flavor. *See recipe on page 250.*

Left: Hamburger — that versatile standby — goes exotic in Sweet-And-Pungent Meatballs With White Rice. Ground beef, diced water chestnuts, soy sauce and ginger shape into meatballs; vinegar, brown sugar, molasses, pineapple chunks, kumquats and cornstarch thicken into a translucent sauce. Add green-pepper strips and cherries, then serve atop hot white rice. *See recipe on page 251.*

This crock of Beef-And-Vegetable Stew is brimming with beef chunks, potato halves, whole carrots and onions that slow-simmer in a delicate tomato broth laced with herbs till they are moist and tender. *See recipe on page 252.*

244

Easy, Exciting, Everyday Meals

continued from page 237

Tuna Patties Hollandaise
(pictured)

2 cans (6½-oz size) tuna, drained
2 large eggs
2½ cups fresh whole-wheat bread crumbs
   (about 5 slices)
¼ cup bottled tartar sauce
½ teaspoon dried, minced onion flakes
⅛ teaspoon ground pepper
4 tablespoons salad oil
1 pkg (10 oz) frozen asparagus spears, thawed
1 pkg (⅞ or 1 oz) hollandaise-sauce mix
   Lemon peel and quartered lemon slices (optional)

1. In medium bowl, with fork, flake tuna; stir in eggs, 1½ cups bread crumbs, the tartar sauce, onion flakes and pepper; mix well. Place remaining crumbs on waxed paper. Coat ¼ cup tuna mixture with crumbs. Shape into a 3-inch patty; set aside on waxed paper. Repeat with remaining tuna mixture and crumbs to make 8 patties in all.
2. In medium skillet, over medium heat, heat 2 tablespoons oil. Cook patties, 4 at a time, until lightly browned—about 3 minutes on each side. Drain on paper towels; cover; keep warm.
3. With paper towel, wipe skillet clean. In same skillet, heat remaining oil. Sauté asparagus until just heated through—about 5 minutes. Remove. In same skillet, prepare hollandaise-sauce mix as label directs. (If using 1-ounce package, increase water to 1 cup.)
4. To serve: Arrange tuna patties and asparagus over hollandaise in skillet. Garnish with lemon peel and lemon slices. *Makes 4 servings.*

Chicken With Spanish Rice
(pictured)

1 tablespoon salad oil
   3-lb broiler-fryer, cut into eight pieces
½ cup frozen or fresh chopped onion
1 clove garlic, minced
1 can (14½ or 16 oz) stewed tomatoes
½ teaspoon dried oregano leaves
½ cup water
1 pkg (4.6 oz) Spanish-rice mix
1 pkg (9 oz) frozen artichoke hearts
¼ cup pimiento-stuffed olives, halved crosswise
   (about 10)

1. In large skillet, over medium-high heat, heat oil; cook chicken pieces, skin side down, until browned—about 10 minutes. Add onion; cook 5 minutes more. Stir in garlic; cook 1 minute more. Add tomatoes and oregano, breaking up tomatoes with spoon if necessary. Reduce heat; simmer, covered, 15 minutes.
2. Uncover skillet; turn chicken pieces. Add water, rice mix, artichoke hearts and olives. Stir and cook 10 minutes longer or until rice is tender. *Makes 4 servings.*

Chicken-Livers Stroganoff
(pictured)

1 lb chicken livers
2 tablespoons salad oil
1 large onion, quartered and sliced
½ teaspoon dried rosemary leaves, crumbled
¼ teaspoon salt
   Dash ground pepper
1½ cups water
½ cup milk
1 pkg (4.3 oz) noodles-and-stroganoff-sauce mix
1 pkg (10 oz) frozen green peas
1 cherry tomato, quartered (optional)
   Fresh rosemary (optional)

1. Cut chicken livers into halves; remove veins and any fat. Dry on paper towels. In large skillet, over medium-high heat, heat oil; add chicken livers, onion, rosemary, salt and pepper. Sauté, stirring frequently with slotted spoon, until chicken livers are firm but slightly pink inside and onion is translucent—about 4 minutes. Remove chicken livers and onion to small bowl; cover and keep warm.
2. Add 1½ cups water and the milk to same skillet; stir to dissolve any browned bits. Stir in noodles-and-sauce mix and peas; bring to boiling; reduce heat and simmer, uncovered, 5 minutes. Return chicken livers and onion to skillet; simmer mixture until heated through—about 2 minutes. Garnish with cherry-tomato quarters and rosemary. *Makes 4 servings.*

Puffy Omelet With Zucchini Sauce
(pictured)

6 large eggs
1 tablespoon olive or salad oil
½ cup frozen or fresh chopped green pepper
½ cup frozen or fresh chopped onion
1 clove garlic, minced
1 can (14½ or 16 oz) cut zucchini in Italian-style
   tomato sauce
1 can (8 oz) tomato sauce
¼ teaspoon cream of tartar
½ cup shredded mozzarella cheese (2 oz)

1. Preheat oven to 350F. Separate eggs, placing whites in large bowl and yolks in small bowl. In 10-inch skillet with ovenproof handle, over medium-high heat,

Easy, Exciting, Everyday Meals

heat oil. Reserve 1 tablespoon chopped pepper; sauté the remaining pepper, the onion and garlic until tender—about 2 minutes. Stir in zucchini with its sauce and tomato sauce; bring to boiling. Reduce heat; simmer, uncovered, 5 minutes.

2. With portable electric mixer at high speed, beat egg whites and cream of tartar until stiff peaks form; set aside. With same beaters, beat egg yolks until thick and lemon-colored. Fold beaten yolks into egg-white mixture until no white streaks remain.

3. In center of skillet, sprinkle mozzarella over zucchini and sauce. Pour egg mixture over cheese. Bake 20 minutes or until omelet is set and golden. Sprinkle reserved green pepper over top. *Makes 4 servings.*

Salisbury Steak Skillet Supper
(pictured)

¼ cup packaged dry bread crumbs
1 large egg
¼ cup catsup
½ teaspoon salt
1 lb ground beef round
1 tablespoon salad oil
1 can (10½ oz) condensed golden-mushroom soup, undiluted
¼ cup dry white wine
1 can (1 lb) whole new potatoes, drained and sliced, or sliced potatoes, drained
1 pkg (9 oz) frozen Italian green beans

1. In medium bowl, with fork, combine bread crumbs, egg, catsup and salt until well blended; mix in ground beef. Shape into a large patty about 1 inch thick.

2. In large skillet, over medium-low heat, heat oil; brown beef patty, or Salisbury steak, on each side. Meanwhile, in small bowl, mix soup and wine. Drain excess fat from skillet.

3. Add soup mixture, potato and frozen green beans around beef patty in skillet. Cover and simmer 10 minutes longer, stirring vegetables once during cooking. *Makes 4 servings.*

Baked Pork and Stuffing
(pictured)

1 pkg (6 or 8 oz) corn-bread stuffing mix
2 tablespoons butter or margarine
8 (½ inch thick) boneless center-cut pork chops or 1 lb boneless pork loin, cut into ½-inch slices
3 cups water
½ pkg (2.5- or 2.6-oz size) onion-soup mix (1 env) or 1 pkg (1.9 oz) French-onion-soup mix
1 pkg (1 lb) frozen broccoli, cauliflower and carrots
½ cup milk
1 tablespoon all-purpose flour

1. In 13-by-9-by-2-inch oval baking dish or 2½- to 3-quart shallow casserole, sprinkle dry stuffing mix on bottom. (If using 6-ounce package, toss stuffing with contents of seasoning packet.) In skillet, over medium-high heat, melt butter. Sauté pork until browned—about 3 minutes on each side. Remove pork; drain on paper towels.

2. Preheat oven to 350F. Add water, onion-soup mix and frozen vegetables to same skillet; cover; bring just to boiling. With slotted spoon, remove vegetables; arrange around edge of baking dish. Remove 1¾ cups liquid from skillet; pour over vegetables and stuffing. Overlap browned pork on top of stuffing in center of dish. Cover with foil and bake 15 to 20 minutes.

3. Meanwhile, in 1-cup measuring cup or small bowl, stir milk and flour until smooth. Stir into liquid remaining in skillet. Over medium heat, bring mixture to boiling, stirring until thickened. Serve sauce with pork chops. *Makes 4 servings.*

Reuben Casserole
(pictured)

1 pkg (1 lb) sauerkraut
½ cup bottled Thousand Island salad dressing
½ cup frozen or fresh chopped green pepper
¼ cup frozen or fresh chopped onion
½ teaspoon caraway seeds
1 can (12 oz) corned beef
1 pkg (8 oz) rectangular slices Swiss cheese
4 large, oval slices rye bread
4 teaspoons prepared Dijon-style mustard

1. Preheat oven to 375F. In large strainer or colander, rinse sauerkraut under cold water and squeeze out excess liquid; place in large bowl. Using two forks, toss sauerkraut with salad dressing; then add green pepper, onion and caraway seeds. Stir until mixture is well combined. Cut corned beef into 1-inch cubes; add to sauerkraut mixture; toss lightly to mix.

2. Grease a 12-by-8-by-2-inch baking dish or 2-quart shallow casserole. Reserve 1 slice cheese; place one-third of corned-beef mixture on bottom; cover with half of remaining cheese slices. Repeat layering of corned-beef mixture and cheese; spread remaining corned-beef mixture on top.

3. Cut each slice of rye bread crosswise into three equal triangles and spread one side of each with mustard. Reserve the 4 triangles from center of bread; arrange 8 triangles, crust side up, around edge of casserole, placing mustard side toward center of dish and tucking triangles well into corned-beef mixture. Cover casserole loosely with foil. Bake 20 minutes.

Easy, Exciting, Everyday Meals

4. Cut remaining slice of cheese in half crosswise; cut each half diagonally to make 4 triangles in all. Place a cheese triangle on top of each reserved bread triangle. Remove foil from casserole; overlap reserved cheese-bread triangles on top of casserole; bake 10 minutes longer or until bread points begin to brown slightly. *Makes 4 servings.*

Quick Beef Stew
(pictured)

1   lb beef cube steaks
1   pkg (1 lb) frozen French-cut green beans, cauliflower and carrots
1   can (10¼ oz) beef gravy
½   cup frozen chopped onion or ½ teaspoon dried, minced onion flakes
1   tablespoon Worcestershire sauce
¼   teaspoon dried thyme leaves
⅛   teaspoon ground pepper
1   cup dry instant-mashed-potato flakes or granules (if using the powdered form, use only ⅓ cup)
1   cup boiling water
½   cup shredded Cheddar cheese (2 oz)
2   tablespoons milk

1. Preheat oven to 350F. Cut beef cube steaks into 1-inch squares. In 10-inch round baking dish or 1-quart shallow casserole, combine beef, frozen vegetables, gravy, onion, Worcestershire sauce, thyme and pepper; mix well.
2. In small bowl, place instant-potato flakes; stir in boiling water, Cheddar cheese and milk until potato is smooth and fluffy. Drop tablespoonfuls of potato mixture in rows on top of beef mixture. Bake 25 to 30 minutes or till mixture is bubbling and potato is lightly browned. *Makes 4 servings.*

Note: To cook stew in a microwave oven, prepare as directed, using a microwave-safe casserole or dish, but do not add potato mixture on top. Microwave, uncovered, on HIGH 10 minutes, stirring after 5 minutes. Add potato mixture; microwave on HIGH 5 minutes longer. If desired, sprinkle potato with paprika before serving.

Chicken Croquettes With Mushroom Sauce
(pictured)

3   tablespoons butter or margarine
1   small onion, finely chopped
⅓   cup all-purpose flour
1   cup milk
    Salt and pepper to taste
1   large egg yolk
2   cups finely chopped, cooked chicken or turkey
2   tablespoons chopped parsley
1½ cups packaged dry bread crumbs
1   large egg
¼   cup water
    Mushroom Sauce, recipe follows
    Salad oil or shortening for deep-frying

1. In medium saucepan, over medium heat, melt butter. Add onion; sauté 2 minutes. Remove from heat. Mix in flour. Gradually stir in milk. Return to heat; bring to boiling, stirring. Reduce heat to low; simmer, stirring occasionally, 10 minutes or until very thick. Add salt and pepper to taste.
2. Remove saucepan from heat. Stir in egg yolk until well blended; return to heat; cook, stirring, 2 minutes longer. Stir in chicken and parsley; mix well. Spread mixture in a 13-by-9-by-2-inch baking dish; cover. Refrigerate 1½ hours or until chilled.
3. Divide chilled mixture into eight portions. With hands, shape each portion into cone-shape croquettes. (A cone-shape ice-cream scoop may be used.) Place bread crumbs on waxed paper; roll each croquette in bread crumbs, coating completely. Refrigerate on tray 1 hour.
4. In small bowl, with fork, beat egg with ¼ cup water. Dip each croquette in beaten egg; reroll in crumbs. Refrigerate 30 minutes longer. Meanwhile, make Mushroom Sauce; keep warm.
5. In deep-fat fryer or 5-quart, heavy Dutch oven, heat 3 inches oil to 300F on deep-frying thermometer. With slotted spoon, gently drop three or four croquettes into hot oil. Fry, turning frequently, until golden-brown—3 to 4 minutes. Remove with slotted spoon; drain on paper towels. Keep warm in 275F oven while frying remaining croquettes. Serve with Mushroom Sauce. *Makes 4 servings.*

Easy, Exciting, Everyday Meals

Mushroom Sauce

2 tablespoons butter or margarine
¼ lb mushrooms, cut in ¼-inch slices
½ cup milk
1 can (10¾ oz) condensed creamy-chicken-mushroom
**   or cream-of-mushroom soup, undiluted**
1 tablespoon chopped pimiento

In medium skillet, over medium heat, melt butter. Add mushrooms; sauté 3 minutes. Stir in milk, undiluted soup and chopped pimiento; mix well. Reduce heat to low; simmer, uncovered, until hot. *Makes 2 cups sauce.*

Savory Chicken Potpies
(pictured)

5- to 5½-lb roasting chicken, cut up (see Note)
1 large onion, peeled and quartered
3 leafy celery tops
3 parsley sprigs
1 teaspoon salt
10 black peppercorns
1 bay leaf
2 cups water

Pastry

2 cups all-purpose flour
1 teaspoon salt
¾ cup shortening or ⅔ cup lard
4 to 6 tablespoons ice water

1 lb small carrots, pared and sliced into ½-inch
**   pieces**
½ pkg (1-lb size) frozen pearl onions
2 large celery stalks, sliced on diagonal into ¼-inch
**   pieces**
¾ cup milk
½ cup all-purpose flour
¾ teaspoon poultry seasoning
½ teaspoon salt
¼ teaspoon ground pepper
1 large egg yolk, beaten with 1 tablespoon water

1. In 6- or 8-quart kettle, place chicken (freeze giblets for soup stock). Add quartered onion, celery tops, parsley, 1 teaspoon salt, the peppercorns, bay leaf and 2 cups water. Over high heat, bring to boiling. Reduce heat and simmer, covered, about 1 hour or until chicken is tender.

2. Meanwhile, make Pastry: In medium bowl, stir 2 cups flour and 1 teaspoon salt together. With pastry blender or two knives, using a short, cutting motion, cut in shortening until mixture resembles coarse cornmeal.

3. Sprinkle ice water, 1 tablespoon at a time, over all of pastry mixture, tossing lightly with fork after each addition and pushing dampened portion to side of bowl; sprinkle only dry portion remaining. (Pastry should be just moist enough to hold together, not sticky.) Shape into a ball; flatten and wrap in plastic wrap; refrigerate until ready to use.

4. Remove chicken from kettle to bowl; cool until easy to handle. Remove and discard skin and bones from chicken. Cut chicken meat into 1-inch pieces, to make 4 to 5 cups.

5. Strain stock into a large saucepan; bring to boiling. Add carrot, pearl onions and celery. Cook, covered, 5 to 10 minutes or until vegetables are just tender.

6. In a 2-cup measuring cup, measure milk; whisk in flour, poultry seasoning, ½ teaspoon salt and the pepper until smooth. Stir into vegetable-stock mixture; bring to boiling, stirring constantly. Reduce heat; boil 1 minute. Add cut-up chicken to saucepan, mixing well. Divide mixture among six 1⅓-cup casseroles or individual baking dishes.

7. Preheat oven to 400F. Remove pastry from refrigerator. On lightly floured surface, cut pastry into six equal pieces. Form each piece into a ball; flatten and evenly roll each piece to a circle the same diameter as the top of a casserole. Cut a cross (about 1½ inches crosswise and lengthwise) in center of each pastry circle.

8. With pastry brush dipped in water, lightly moisten edges of casseroles. Place pastry circles on top of each casserole. With tip of knife, lift up and turn back the four points in center of pastry, exposing the pie filling. With dinner fork, firmly press the edge of pastry to casseroles. Place the casseroles on a large baking tray or a rimmed cookie sheet.

9. Bake 30 minutes or until filling is bubbly. Remove from oven. Brush crusts with egg-yolk mixture. Return to oven. Bake 5 minutes longer or until pastry is golden-brown. *Makes 6 servings.*

Note: Or use 2 (2½- to 3-pound size) broiler-fryers, and cook about 45 minutes.

Easy, Exciting, Everyday Meals

Our Favorite Meat Loaf
(pictured)

  6 slices bacon
  3 large eggs
½ cup milk
  1 teaspoon salt
¼ teaspoon ground pepper
¼ teaspoon dried thyme leaves
¼ teaspoon ground nutmeg
  Dash ground cloves
  1 cup soft white-bread crumbs
  2 lb ground beef or 1 lb beef plus ½ lb each ground pork and veal
½ cup chopped green onion
  2 tablespoons chopped parsley
  2 tablespoons chopped celery leaves (optional)
  1 clove garlic, minced
⅓ cup chili sauce
  1 tablespoon light-brown sugar
½ teaspoon dry mustard
  Watercress sprigs (optional)
  Cooked green peas (optional)

1. In medium skillet, over medium heat, sauté bacon until partially cooked but not browned. Drain on paper towels; set aside. Preheat oven to 350F.
2. In a large bowl, with fork, lightly beat eggs with milk, salt, pepper, thyme, nutmeg and cloves. Stir in bread crumbs; let stand 5 minutes.
3. To egg mixture, add beef, green onion, parsley, celery leaves and garlic. Stir until well mixed. Transfer beef mixture to a foil-lined 12-by-8-inch baking pan. With hands, press and shape mixture into a 10-by-4-inch loaf. Arrange bacon diagonally on top of loaf. Bake 45 minutes.
4. Meanwhile, in small bowl, combine chili sauce, brown sugar and mustard; stir to blend. Remove meat loaf from oven. Brush sauce over meat loaf. Return to oven; bake 15 minutes longer.
5. To serve: Transfer meat loaf to warm serving platter. Garnish with watercress. Serve with cooked green peas, if desired. *Makes 8 servings.*

Mashed Potatoes
(pictured)

  2 lb (6 medium) potatoes, pared and cut into 2-inch cubes
  Water
½ cup milk
  2 tablespoons butter or margarine
½ teaspoon salt
  Dash ground white pepper
  Brown Gravy, recipe follows

1. Place potato in medium saucepan with 1 inch water. Over high heat, bring to boiling. Reduce heat to low; cook, covered, until tender—about 15 minutes. Drain in colander. (If desired, save cooking water for soup stock.)
2. In same saucepan, heat milk, butter, salt and pepper just until butter melts. Return potato to pan. Using potato masher or portable electric mixer, mash potato until light and fluffy. Keep warm.
3. Make Brown Gravy; serve over potato. *Makes 8 servings.*

Brown Gravy
(pictured)

¼ cup water
  3 tablespoons all-purpose flour
  1 can (10½ oz) condensed beef broth (bouillon), undiluted

In small saucepan, gradually add water to flour, whisking until smooth. Add beef broth; whisk until well combined. Over medium-high heat, bring to boiling, stirring constantly. Boil 30 seconds. Serve over mashed potatoes. *Makes 1⅓ cups.*

Cassoulet With Knockwurst

  2 quarts water
  1 pkg (1 lb) dried white Great Northern beans
  1 clove garlic, crushed
  1 cup sliced onion
1½ teaspoons salt
  4 whole cloves
  1 can (8 oz) tomato sauce
½ teaspoon dried thyme leaves
  2 bay leaves
  1 pkg (16 oz) knockwurst, cut lengthwise into quarters to make long strips

1. In a 4-quart kettle, bring 2 quarts water to boiling. Add beans; return to boiling; boil 2 minutes. Remove from heat and let stand 1 hour.
2. Add garlic, onion, salt and cloves; bring to boiling. Reduce heat and simmer, covered, 1 hour or until tender, not mushy. Remove and discard cloves.
3. Stir in tomato sauce, thyme, bay leaves and knockwurst. Cover and simmer 45 minutes longer or until beans are tender.
4. Turn into warm serving dish. *Makes 8 servings.*

Easy, Exciting, Everyday Meals

Sweet-And-Pungent Meatballs With White Rice
(pictured)

Meatballs
    1 slice white bread
       Water
 1 ½ lb ground chuck
    1 teaspoon salt
  ¼ teaspoon ground ginger
    1 teaspoon soy sauce (see Note)
  ¼ teaspoon hot red-pepper sauce
    1 can (5 oz) water chestnuts, drained and diced

    2 tablespoons salad or olive oil

Sauce
  ¼ cup cider vinegar
  ½ cup water
  ¾ cup canned, condensed beef bouillon, undiluted
    1 tablespoon catsup
    1 tablespoon soy sauce (see Note)
    1 tablespoon molasses
  ¼ cup firmly packed light-brown sugar
    1 can (13 ¼ oz) frozen pineapple chunks, thawed and drained
  ½ cup preserved kumquats, drained
    2 tablespoons cornstarch
  ¼ cup water
  ½ cup green-pepper strips, 2 inches long
  ⅓ cup watermelon-pickle rounds, drained
    6 maraschino cherries

       Cooked white rice
       Soy sauce

1. Make Meatballs: Soak bread in water; then squeeze dry. In large bowl, combine bread, chuck, salt, ginger, 1 teaspoon soy sauce, the red-pepper sauce and water chestnuts. Toss lightly just to combine. Gently shape into 20 meatballs.
2. In hot oil in large skillet, sauté meatballs, turning, until nicely browned all over. Remove from heat and set aside.
3. Make Sauce: In another large skillet or Dutch oven, combine vinegar, ½ cup water, the bouillon, catsup, 1 tablespoon soy sauce, the molasses, brown sugar, pineapple chunks and kumquats; mix well. Bring to boiling.
4. Meanwhile, dissolve cornstarch in ¼ cup water; stir into boiling mixture. Boil, stirring, 2 minutes or until mixture is thickened and translucent.
5. Add browned meatballs, pepper strips, watermelon pickle and cherries; stir to combine. Cook just until heated through.
6. Serve over hot boiled rice; pass soy sauce. *Makes 5 or 6 servings.*

Note: Different brands of soy sauce vary slightly in strength. It may be necessary to use a little more or less, depending on the brand.

Mushroom Sauce for Hamburgers

    3 tablespoons butter or margarine
    3 tablespoons all-purpose flour
    1 can (10 ½ oz) condensed beef bouillon, undiluted
  ½ teaspoon salt
  ¼ teaspoon ground pepper
    1 can (6 oz) sliced mushrooms, undrained
  ¼ cup Burgundy

1. Melt butter in a small saucepan. Remove from heat. Stir in flour until smooth. Cook over low heat, stirring, until mixture turns golden-brown—about 5 minutes.
2. Gradually add bouillon, stirring. Add salt and pepper; cook, stirring occasionally, 5 minutes longer or until thickened.
3. Stir in mushrooms and wine; heat through. *Makes about 2 cups.*

Bordelaise Sauce for Hamburgers

    2 tablespoons butter or margarine
    1 shallot, finely chopped
    1 clove garlic, finely chopped
    1 onion slice
    2 carrot slices
       Parsley sprig
    6 black peppercorns
    1 whole clove
    1 bay leaf
    2 tablespoons all-purpose flour
    1 cup canned, condensed beef bouillon, undiluted
  ¼ teaspoon salt
  ⅛ teaspoon ground pepper
  ⅓ cup Burgundy
    1 tablespoon finely chopped parsley

1. In hot butter in medium skillet, sauté shallot, garlic, onion and carrot slices with parsley sprig, peppercorns, clove and bay leaf until onion is golden — about 3 minutes. Remove from heat.
2. Stir in flour until smooth. Cook over very low heat, stirring, until flour is lightly browned — about 5 minutes. Remove from heat.
3. Gradually stir in bouillon; bring to boiling over medium heat, stirring constantly. Reduce heat; simmer, uncovered, stirring occasionally, 10 minutes.
4. Strain; discard vegetables. Add the salt, pepper, Burgundy and parsley; reheat slowly. *Makes 1 cup.*

Easy, Exciting, Everyday Meals

Spaghetti With Eggplant Sauce and Meatballs

Meatballs, recipe follows

Eggplant Sauce

¼ **cup salad oil**
1 **eggplant (1 to 1½ lb), unpared and cut in 1-inch cubes**
½ **cup finely chopped onion**
1 **clove garlic, crushed**
2 **tablespoons fresh parsley, chopped**
1 **can (16 oz) tomatoes**
1 **can (6 oz) tomato paste**
½ **cup dry red wine**
1 **teaspoon dried oregano leaves**
1 **teaspoon salt**
1 **teaspoon sugar**

1 **lb thin spaghetti, cooked as label directs**
2 **tablespoons grated Parmesan cheese**

1. Make Meatballs.
2. Make Eggplant Sauce: In a 5-quart Dutch oven, heat oil over medium heat. Add eggplant cubes, onion, garlic and parsley; cook in oil until onion is transparent and tender—5 minutes.
3. Stir in tomatoes, tomato paste, wine, oregano, salt and sugar; break up tomatoes with fork; add meatballs. Reduce heat; cover and simmer 45 minutes, stirring occasionally.
4. Serve over drained spaghetti, sprinkled with grated Parmesan. *Makes 8 servings.*

Meatballs

1 **egg**
¼ **cup milk**
2 **slices whole-wheat bread, crumbled**
½ **lb ground beef**
¼ **cup finely chopped onion**
¼ **cup finely chopped green pepper**
1 **tablespoon chopped parsley**
1 **clove garlic, crushed**
½ **teaspoon salt**
   Dash ground pepper
2 **tablespoons salad oil**

1. In medium bowl, beat egg slightly. Add milk and bread; mix well. Let stand 5 minutes.
2. Add rest of meatball ingredients; mix until well blended.
3. Shape into 24 balls—1 inch in diameter.
4. In 2 tablespoons oil in 5-quart Dutch oven, sauté meatballs, turning until browned—about 10 minutes. Remove from Dutch oven. Set aside.

Beef-And-Vegetable Stew
(pictured)

3 **lb beef for stew**
6 **tablespoons salad oil**
1 **cup chopped onion**
1 **cup chopped green pepper**
1 **cup sliced celery**
   Water
1 **can (10½ oz) condensed beef broth, undiluted**
1 **can (8 oz) tomato sauce**
2 **tablespoons chopped parsley**
1 **clove garlic, finely chopped**
1 **tablespoon salt**
¼ **teaspoon ground pepper**
⅛ **teaspoon dried thyme leaves**
1 **bay leaf**
6 **small potatoes, pared and halved (about 2 lb)**
6 **medium carrots, pared (about ¾ lb)**
6 **small white onions, peeled**
1 **to 2 tablespoons all-purpose flour**
1 **tomato, cut in wedges (optional)**

1. Cut beef into 1-inch pieces. In hot oil in Dutch oven, over medium heat, brown one-third meat at a time (just enough to cover bottom of pan) until browned on all sides. Remove as browned.
2. Add chopped onion, green pepper and celery to Dutch oven and sauté until tender—about 8 minutes. Return beef to pan.
3. Add ½ cup water, the beef broth, tomato sauce, parsley, garlic, salt, pepper, thyme and bay leaf; bring to boiling. Reduce heat; simmer, covered and stirring several times, 1¼ hours.
4. Add potato, carrots and onions. Simmer, covered, 1 hour longer or until meat and vegetables are tender. Remove from heat; skim off fat.

Easy, Exciting, Everyday Meals

5. Mix flour with 2 tablespoons water. Stir into beef mixture. Arrange tomato wedges, skin side up, on top; simmer, covered, 10 minutes. *Makes 6 servings.*

♥

Black-Eyed Peas With Sweet-And-Sour Pork

1 teaspoon salad oil
½-lb boneless pork loin, rib end, cut into thin slices (see Note)
1 medium onion, sliced
1 pkg (1 lb) dried black-eyed peas
Water
Salt
¼ teaspoon ground pepper
½ teaspoon dried basil leaves
1 large green pepper, cut into ¼-inch-wide strips
1 can (8 oz) pineapple chunks in juice
2 tablespoons sugar
2 tablespoons cornstarch
½ teaspoon ground ginger
2 tablespoons vinegar
2 teaspoons soy sauce

1. In hot oil in 4-quart Dutch oven, sauté pork strips, turning with tongs, until browned on all sides. Add onion; sauté, stirring, until golden—3 to 5 minutes.
2. Rinse peas well; drain. Add to pork, along with 5½ cups water, 1 tablespoon salt, the pepper and basil. Bring to boiling; reduce heat; simmer gently, covered, stirring occasionally, 45 minutes or until peas are tender.
3. Place green-pepper strips and ½ teaspoon salt in center of pork mixture. Simmer, covered, until peppers are just fork-tender—about 7 minutes.
4. Make sauce: Drain pineapple, pouring juice into a 2-cup measure. Add water to measure 1½ cups. Cut pineapple chunks in half.
5. In a small saucepan, combine sugar, cornstarch and ginger; mix well. Gradually stir in reserved juice, vinegar and soy sauce. Bring to boiling, stirring; boil 2 minutes. Pour over green pepper in Dutch oven. Turn into serving dish, with pork and vegetables in center surrounded by black-eyed peas. *Makes 8 servings.*

Note: To make pork easier to slice thinly, place in freezer long enough to chill thoroughly.

♥

Belgian Beef Stew

¼ cup all-purpose flour
2½ teaspoons salt
½ teaspoon ground pepper
2 lb beef chuck, cut in 1-inch cubes
½ cup salad oil
2 lb onions, peeled and sliced
1 clove garlic, crushed
1 can (12 oz) light beer
1 tablespoon soy sauce
1 tablespoon Worcestershire sauce
1 tablespoon bottled steak sauce
2 bay leaves
½ teaspoon dried thyme leaves
2 lb potatoes, pared and quartered
1 pkg (10 oz) frozen peas
2 tablespoons chopped parsley

1. Combine flour, salt and pepper. Use to coat chuck well.
2. In ¼ cup hot oil in Dutch oven or kettle, sauté onion and garlic until onion is tender—8 to 10 minutes. Remove and set aside.
3. Heat remaining oil in Dutch oven. Add chuck and brown well on all sides. (If necessary, brown the meat in two batches; don't crowd pan.)
4. Add onion and garlic to Dutch oven, along with beer, soy sauce, Worcestershire, steak sauce, bay leaves and thyme; mix well.
5. Bring mixture to boiling. Reduce heat and simmer, covered, 1½ hours.
6. Add potato; simmer, covered, 20 minutes or until potato is tender.
7. Add peas; simmer, covered, 8 minutes longer or just until tender.
8. To serve: Turn stew into serving dish. Garnish with the chopped parsley. *Makes 6 servings.*

Easy, Exciting, Everyday Meals

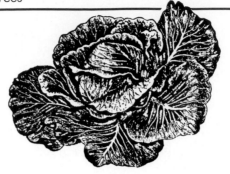

Chicken-And-Noodle Fricassee

3-lb roasting chicken, cut up
2 tablespoons butter or oil
2 celery stalks, cut up
1 teaspoon salt
¼ teaspoon ground pepper
1 teaspoon dried sage leaves
2 cups water
2 large carrots, pared and halved lengthwise
2 medium potatoes (1 lb), pared and quartered
2 medium onions, peeled and quartered
1 pkg (8 oz) wide noodles
¼ cup all-purpose flour
¼ cup water
Chopped parsley

1. Wash chicken pieces and pat dry with paper towels. In 6-quart Dutch oven, sauté chicken in butter until golden-brown. Add celery, salt, pepper and sage. Sauté, stirring, 3 minutes.
2. Add 2 cups water; bring to boiling; reduce heat and simmer, covered, 30 minutes.
3. Add carrot; cook 10 minutes. Add potato and onion; simmer, covered, until tender — 15 minutes.
4. Meanwhile, cook noodles in salted water as package label directs. Drain.
5. Stir flour into ¼ cup water to dissolve. Remove ½ cup hot chicken broth; stir into flour mixture. Gently stir into Dutch oven. Bring to boiling.
6. To serve: Fold in noodles. Simmer, uncovered, 5 minutes. Remove to serving dish. Sprinkle with parsley. *Makes 6 servings.*

Venetian Liver With Vegetables

1½ lb beef liver, sliced 1 inch thick
¼ cup all-purpose flour
1½ teaspoons salt
¼ teaspoon ground pepper
¼ cup (½ stick) butter or margarine
¼ cup salad oil
1 lb onions, thinly sliced
½ teaspoon dried sage leaves
¼ cup dry white wine
1 tablespoon lemon or lime juice
2 tablespoons chopped parsley
2 pkg (10-oz size) frozen broccoli spears

1. With paper towels, pat liver dry. Cut into strips ¼ inch wide (see Note).
2. On sheet of waxed paper, combine flour, salt and pepper. Roll liver in mixture, coating well.
3. In large skillet, heat butter and 2 tablespoons oil. Sauté liver strips, turning frequently, until lightly browned on all sides — 5 minutes. Remove; set aside.
4. Add remaining oil to skillet. Sauté onion slices, stirring frequently, until golden — 10 minutes. Add sage. Cook, covered, over low heat 5 minutes.
5. Combine liver with onion, tossing lightly. Cook, covered, over low heat 5 minutes.
6. Add white wine and lemon juice; bring to boiling, stirring, until liver and onion are glazed — about 2 minutes. Sprinkle with chopped parsley. Garnish with broccoli spears, cooked according to package directions. *Makes 8 servings.*

Note: To make liver easier to slice thinly, place in freezer long enough to chill thoroughly.

Lima-Bean Chili

1 pkg (1 lb) dried baby lima beans
5 cups cold water
Salt
½ lb ground chuck
2 medium onions, sliced
1 to 1½ tablespoons chili powder
1 can (16 oz) stewed tomatoes
1 can (8 oz) tomato sauce
⅛ teaspoon ground pepper
½ teaspoon sugar
¼ cup catsup
½ cup grated Cheddar cheese (2 oz)
2 tablespoons chopped green pepper

1. Rinse beans thoroughly; drain. Cover with 5 cups cold water. Refrigerate, covered, overnight.
2. Next day, turn beans and liquid (do not drain) into a 4-quart kettle or Dutch oven; add 1 teaspoon salt. Bring to boiling; reduce heat, cover and simmer gently,

Easy, Exciting, Everyday Meals

stirring occasionally, 45 minutes or until tender, not mushy.

3. In a large, heavy skillet, over medium heat, sauté ground chuck, stirring until browned.
4. Add onion and chili powder; cook, stirring, about 5 minutes or until onion is tender.
5. Add to beans, along with stewed tomatoes, tomato sauce, pepper, sugar, catsup and 1 teaspoon salt.
6. Cover and simmer slowly, stirring occasionally, about 20 minutes.
7. Turn into a 2-quart casserole; garnish with grated cheese and green pepper. *Makes 8 servings.*

German Meatballs With Red Cabbage

```
 1   egg
½   cup soft bread crumbs
1½  lb ground chuck
 1   can (8 oz) sauerkraut, drained and chopped
 1   can (1 lb, 4 oz) apple slices, drained and chopped
 2   tablespoons grated onion
     Salt
     Ground pepper
¼   teaspoon dried marjoram leaves, crumbled
 4   strips bacon, diced
 1   head (1½ lb) red cabbage, chopped
½   cup chopped onion
½   teaspoon caraway seed
 1   cup canned chicken broth
 2   tablespoons red-wine vinegar
 1   tablespoon sugar
```

1. In medium bowl, beat egg well. Add bread crumbs, chuck, ¼ cup sauerkraut, ¾ cup chopped apple, the grated onion, 1 teaspoon salt, ½ teaspoon pepper and the marjoram; mix until well blended. Shape into 20 meatballs.
2. In 4-quart Dutch oven, fry bacon until crisp. Remove and set aside. In hot drippings, brown meatballs on all sides. Remove; set aside.
3. In Dutch oven, combine remaining sauerkraut and chopped apple, the cabbage, chopped onion, caraway

seed, chicken broth, vinegar, sugar, ¼ teaspoon salt and ⅛ teaspoon pepper; stir until well blended. Bring to boiling, covered.

4. Arrange meatballs on top of cabbage; cook over low heat, covered, 30 minutes or until cabbage is tender.
5. To serve, sprinkle with crisp bacon bits. *Makes 5 to 6 servings.*

Frankfurter-And-Potato Pie

```
 6   large potatoes (3 lb)
½   pkg (10-oz size) piecrust mix
 3   tablespoons all-purpose flour
½   cup grated Cheddar cheese
 1   large onion, sliced
½   lb frankfurters (5), cut on diagonal
 1   tablespoon margarine
 1   clove garlic, crushed
1½  teaspoons salt
¼   teaspoon ground pepper
⅛   teaspoon ground nutmeg
 1   cup milk
½   cup light cream or half-and-half
```

1. Pare potatoes; slice very thin. Cover with cold water in a large bowl.
2. Prepare piecrust mix as package label directs. Preheat oven to 350F.
3. Toss flour with cheese.
4. Drain potato thoroughly. Layer in a greased 8-cup, round, shallow baking dish with sliced onion, cheese mixture, frankfurters, margarine, garlic, salt, pepper and nutmeg. Top layer should be potato. Pour milk over potato.
5. Roll out pastry to a 13-inch circle for round dish. Fit over potato mixture; turn under and flute edges. Cut four slits in pastry to allow steam to escape. Brush with 1 or 2 tablespoons cream.
6. Bake 1 hour or until pastry is golden-brown and potato is done. Remove from oven; pour remaining cream through vents into pie. Let stand 15 minutes before serving. *Makes 8 servings.* ■

CHAPTER

5

FRESH-FROM-THE-GARDEN FAVORITES

❧

Crisp green beans that snap with delight; ruby red tomatoes oozing juicy goodness; sparkling white cauliflower, firm and crunchy—these are but a few of nature's freshest and tastiest gifts. They grow in vast patchwork fields, in backyard gardens and on small apartment terraces all across America. The farmers and gardeners who plant, nurture and harvest this tender bounty realize the same pride and appreciation that rewarded our Colonial settlers and the Indians before them. We've been cultivating our own recipe garden of fresh-vegetable favorites and we proudly share them in this chapter. From savory main dishes to hearty soups and perky salads, each boasts the classic, fresh taste of homegrown Americana.

Summer Vegetable Specials

Summer bursts forth with a glorious bounty of wonderfully ripe vegetables to enjoy fresh-picked plain or in our selection of succulent recipes, each of which is a tasty celebration of nature's goodness. Two delightful examples are **at left**: boiled new potatoes tossed with a buttery, fresh lemon-mint dressing and tender young green beans ready for a drizzle of our favorite hollandaise sauce. Recipes for all of our summer specials begin on page 267.

259

Vegetables can be prepared in an almost infinite variety of ways. Pictured here are some eye-catching combinations! The Spinach-Pasta-And-Cheese Loaf, **near right,** is marbled with carrots and red pepper and served with a tangy cheese sauce; **above right** sits Fresh Corn Custard made from corn-off-the-cob, eggs, cheese and green pepper; **below it** is Bagwell's Vegetable Terrine with Sun-Dried-Tomato Sauce, a chicken base studded with red peppers, asparagus, radishes, green beans and carrots, then coated with spinach leaves and served with chunky tomato sauce. *Recipes begin on page 267.*

Help yourself to our full-of-fresh-flavor meals. **Opposite at top** is Spaghetti Squash Primavera, a mouth-watering medley of sautéed vegetables served with a creamy Parmesan cheese sauce. **Below** is Corn-Filled Roulade With Roasted-Pepper Sauce, a heavenly rolled soufflé touched with a spiced red-pepper topping. Tomato-Mussel Pasta, **this page at top,** tosses mini lasagne noodles with ripe plum tomatoes and mussels fresh from the sea. And for a South-of-the-Border treat, try our Chimichangas With Cherry-Tomato Salsa, fried-chicken tortillas served with zesty salsa, melted cheese and guacamole. *Recipes begin on page 268.*

GEORGE RATKAI/PAUL DOME

Above: Zucchini and yellow squash are among summer's most versatile and bountiful vegetables. Their delicate flavor and colorful character make them sensational ingredients in a multitude of dishes such as this Squash Creole, **top,** which can go from garden to table in about 25 minutes. *See recipe on page 273.*

Right: Summer vegetables become magnificent appetizers and light meals. **At top left,** tender petals of zucchini and summer squash circle a creamy, rich Squash-Cheese Tart. **Below it** are delightful Oriental Wrapped Vegetables With Plum Sauce, crunchy bundles encased in omelets and tied with green-onion strips. Salmon-Cucumber Mousse, **at top right,** is a majestic triple-layered beauty sparked with hot-pepper sauce and fresh dill. Fresh corn-off-the-cob flavors the pair **below it:** Southern-style Corn Cakes With Caviar and cheesy Corn Custard in Pepper Cups. *Recipes begin on page 271.*

IRWIN HOROWITZ

Savor a taste of the garden with this beautiful Gift-Wrapped Summer Pâté. It's studded with peppers, carrots and green beans, then cleverly wrapped in zucchini and yellow squash and topped with a carrot bow. *See recipe on page 274.*

Summer Vegetable Specials

continued from page 259

New Potatoes With Fresh Mint
(pictured)

3 lb new potatoes
   Salt
½ cup (1 stick) butter or margarine
2 to 3 tablespoons lemon juice
2 tablespoons chopped fresh mint
   Mint sprigs (optional)

1. Scrub potatoes. Pare a strip of peel about ½ inch wide around center of each potato. Place in medium saucepan; add 1 teaspoon salt and water to cover potatoes.
2. Bring to boiling; reduce heat; cook, covered, 20 minutes or until potatoes are tender. Drain. Return to heat, shaking pan, to dry potatoes.
3. Melt butter in small saucepan. Add lemon juice, chopped mint and ½ teaspoon salt. Pour over potatoes; toss until potatoes are well coated.
4. Turn potatoes into heated serving bowl. Garnish with mint sprigs, if desired. *Makes 8 servings.*

Green Beans Hollandaise
(pictured)

2 lb fresh young green beans
½ teaspoon salt
   Boiling water
4 tablespoons (½ stick) butter or margarine, melted
   Hollandaise Sauce, recipe follows, or
   ¼ cup mayonnaise mixed with
   1 tablespoon lemon juice

1. Wash beans in cold water; drain. Trim ends.
2. Place in large, heavy saucepan. Add salt and boiling water to 1 inch below top of beans. Cook, covered, 20 minutes or until tender.
3. Drain well. Return to saucepan and toss with melted butter. Turn into heated serving bowl. Serve with Hollandaise Sauce or mayonnaise-lemon mixture. *Makes 6 to 8 servings.*

Hollandaise Sauce
(pictured)

2 egg yolks
¼ cup (½ stick) butter or margarine, melted
¼ cup boiling water
1½ tablespoons lemon juice
¼ teaspoon salt
   Dash ground red pepper

1. In top of double boiler, with wire whisk or fork, slightly beat egg yolks.
2. Slowly stir in the melted butter. Gradually add boiling water, beating constantly.
3. Cook, stirring, over hot water (water in double-boiler base should not touch pan above) just until thickened.
4. Remove double-boiler top from hot water. Gradually beat lemon juice, salt and red pepper into sauce.
5. Cover and keep hot over warm water until serving. *Makes about ⅔ cup.*

Spinach-Pasta-And-Cheese Loaf
(pictured)

2 lb fresh spinach or 2 pkg (10-oz size) frozen chopped spinach
2 tablespoons grated Parmesan cheese
4 tablespoons (½ stick) butter or margarine
½ cup chopped onion
1 cup light cream or half-and-half
1 teaspoon salt
½ teaspoon sugar
   Dash ground pepper
   Dash ground nutmeg
4 eggs
½ cup fresh bread crumbs (2 slices)
½ cup grated Swiss or Gruyère cheese (2 oz)
1½ cups cooked elbow macaroni
1½ cups cooked carrot (in ½-inch cubes)
1 cup cubed red pepper (in ½-inch cubes)
   Cheese Sauce, recipe follows

1. Wash spinach; remove and discard large stems. Place in large kettle with just the water clinging to leaves. Cook, covered, tossing with a fork once or twice, 5 minutes or until spinach is just tender. Drain very well. Chop coarsely. (If using frozen spinach, cook as package label directs; drain very well.)
2. Preheat oven to 350F. Grease well a 9-by-5-by-2¾-inch loaf pan; line bottom with a strip of aluminum foil; dust with Parmesan cheese.
3. In hot butter in large saucepan, sauté onion until tender—about 5 minutes. Add spinach, cream, salt, sugar, pepper and nutmeg; heat just to boiling. Remove from heat.
4. In a large bowl, beat eggs slightly. Add bread crumbs and Swiss cheese; gradually stir in spinach mixture, macaroni, carrot and red pepper.
5. Turn into prepared pan. Set pan in larger baking pan on oven rack; pour water into pan to depth of 1½ inches. Place a piece of waxed paper over top of pan.
6. Bake 35 to 40 minutes or until knife inserted in center of spinach mixture comes out clean.
7. Loosen mold around edge with a small spatula. Invert onto heated serving platter. Serve with Cheese Sauce. *Makes 8 servings.*

Summer Vegetable Specials

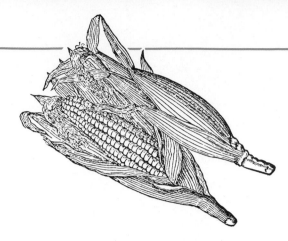

Cheese Sauce
(pictured)

2   **tablespoons butter or margarine**
2   **tablespoons all-purpose flour**
½   **teaspoon dry mustard**
¾   **teaspoon salt**
     Dash ground white pepper
     Dash ground red pepper
1   **cup light cream or half-and-half**
1   **cup grated sharp Cheddar cheese (¼ lb)**

1. In small saucepan, slowly melt butter (do not brown); remove from heat. Stir in flour, mustard, salt, white pepper, red pepper and cream until smooth.
2. Bring to boiling, stirring until thickened. Reduce heat; add cheese. Cook, stirring, until cheese is melted and mixture is smooth. *Makes 1½ cups.*

Fresh-Corn Custard
(pictured)

1   **tablespoon butter or margarine**
2   **tablespoons chopped green pepper**
2   **cups fresh corn, cut from cob**
3   **eggs**
½   **lb natural Cheddar cheese, grated**
¼   **cup all-purpose flour**
½   **teaspoon salt**
⅛   **teaspoon ground white pepper**
1   **tablespoon sugar**
     Dash ground nutmeg
2   **tablespoons butter or margarine, melted**
2   **cups light cream or half-and-half**
6   **Italian tomatoes, halved**
6   **strips green pepper, 2 inches long**

1. In 1 tablespoon hot butter in a small skillet, sauté chopped green pepper just until tender—about 2 minutes.
2. Preheat oven to 325F. Lightly grease a 1½-quart, shallow baking dish.
3. In a large bowl, combine corn, eggs, cheese and green pepper; mix well.
4. In a small bowl, combine flour, salt, pepper, sugar and nutmeg. Stir into corn mixture.
5. Add butter and cream; mix well. Pour into prepared baking dish. Arrange tomatoes and green-pepper

strips around edge, as pictured. Set baking dish in a pan set on oven rack; pour hot water to 1-inch depth around baking dish.

6. Bake, uncovered, 1 hour and 10 minutes or until custard is firm and knife inserted in center comes out clean. Serve hot. *Makes 8 servings.*

Spaghetti Squash Primavera
(pictured)

1   **medium spaghetti squash (about 3 lb)**
½   **lb medium zucchini**
½   **lb broccoli**
1   **small red pepper**
¼   **lb snow peas**
2   **tablespoons olive oil**
1   **shallot, minced**
1   **cup (½ pint) heavy cream**
¼   **cup (½ stick) butter or margarine**
     Grated Parmesan cheese
¼   **teaspoon salt**
     Dash freshly ground black pepper

1. With fork, prick surface of spaghetti squash. Place in large kettle; cover with cold water. Bring to boiling; reduce heat. Simmer, covered, 50 to 55 minutes or until squash is tender when pierced with fork.
2. Meanwhile, cut zucchini diagonally into ¼-inch-wide slices. Cut broccoli into flowerets. (Save stalks to use in another recipe.) Remove and discard stem, ribs and seeds from red pepper. Cut pepper lengthwise into ¼-inch-wide strips. Trim ends and remove strings from snow peas.
3. Drain spaghetti squash; cool slightly. Cut in half lengthwise; scrape out and discard seeds. With fork, scrape down squash lengthwise, carefully separating meat into strands; set aside.
4. In large skillet, heat oil. Over medium heat, sauté zucchini, broccoli, red pepper and shallot 3 to 5 minutes. Stir occasionally. Add snow peas; cook 1 minute longer. Remove vegetables from heat; set aside.
5. In small saucepan, heat cream and butter just until mixture begins to boil. Stir in ¾ cup Parmesan cheese, salt and pepper; toss with spaghetti squash. Spoon onto platter; arrange vegetables in center. Serve with additional Parmesan, if desired. *Makes 6 servings.*

Summer Vegetable Specials

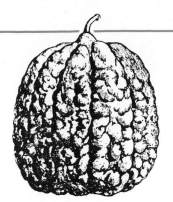

Bagwell's Vegetable Terrine With Tomato Sauce
(pictured)

Recipe from Chef Yves Memoret, Bagwell's, Hyatt Regency, Waikiki, Honolulu, Hawaii.

Salt
7 small carrots, pared
7 thin stalks asparagus, washed
¼ lb green beans, washed
1 large red pepper, washed
1 thin daikon (Japanese white radish) or 2 white turnips
1 bunch fresh spinach
Olive oil
¾ cup broccoli flowerets
1 tablespoon chopped parsley
¾ lb boneless, skinless chicken breasts, cut in chunks
2 egg whites
1 teaspoon dried tarragon leaves
¼ teaspoon ground nutmeg
⅛ teaspoon ground pepper
2¼ cups heavy cream
Tomato Sauce, recipe follows
Assorted raw vegetables (optional)

1. Bring 1½ inches salted water to boiling in a large skillet. Simmer carrots, covered, 5 minutes. Trim asparagus and green beans. Add to skillet; cover and set aside 5 minutes.
2. Discard seeds from red pepper and slice into ½-inch strips. Peel daikon or turnips and cut into julienne slices. Add to skillet; cover and set aside no more than 5 minutes longer.
3. Remove and discard stems from spinach. Wash leaves carefully and blanch in boiling hot water until leaves are just flexible but haven't lost their color. Drain well.
4. Generously coat a 9-by-5-by-2¾-inch loaf pan with olive oil; line with spinach leaves, leaving some of leaves hanging over edge. Preheat oven to 300F.
5. Combine broccoli, parsley, chicken and egg whites in processor fitted with chopping blade. Process until smooth. Add tarragon, nutmeg, 1¼ teaspoons salt, the pepper and half of cream. Process until well combined. Gradually add remaining cream.
6. Drain reserved vegetables well. Spread a little chicken mixture in the bottom of prepared pan. Make a layer

of red pepper. Continue layering vegetables, alternating with chicken mixture, using asparagus, daikon, green beans and carrots in that order.
7. Fold spinach leaves over mixture, adding more, if necessary, to cover. Brush with oil; cover with foil. Set pan into a shallow baking dish set on oven rack. Pour boiling water around pan to measure 1 inch. Bake 1 hour and 15 minutes.
8. Cool terrine completely. To serve, pour off liquid; unmold and serve in slices surrounded by Tomato Sauce. If desired, garnish top with raw vegetables, as pictured. *Makes 12 servings.*

Tomato Sauce

1 lb ripe regular or plum tomatoes
3 tablespoons red-wine vinegar
½ cup olive oil
1 drop hot red-pepper sauce
¼ teaspoon Worcestershire sauce
Dash ground pepper
½ teaspoon salt
½ teaspoon chopped fresh tarragon leaves or ¼ teaspoon dried tarragon leaves

1. Blanch tomatoes in boiling water; remove skins and stems. Cut in quarters.
2. In blender or food processor, combine vinegar, olive oil, red-pepper sauce, Worcestershire, pepper, salt and tarragon. Blend until smooth.
3. Add tomato and blend just until tomato is chopped. Refrigerate.

Avocado Halves au Naturel

4 large ripe avocados (about 3 lb), chilled
2 tablespoons lemon juice
Salad greens
½ cup bottled Italian-style salad dressing

1. Cut avocados in half lengthwise. Remove pits; do not peel. Sprinkle exposed surfaces with lemon juice. Arrange on greens on 8 individual salad plates.
2. Shake dressing well. Pour into hollows of avocado halves. *Makes 8 servings.*

Summer Vegetable Specials

Chimichangas With Cherry-Tomato Salsa
(pictured)

Cherry-Tomato Salsa

- 1 **container (1 pint) cherry tomatoes, quartered**
- 1 **small red onion, chopped**
- 1 **to 2 medium pickled, hot jalapeño chiles, stemmed, seeded and finely chopped**
- 2 **tablespoons chopped cilantro**

Guacamole

- 1 **large ripe avocado, peeled, seeded and chopped**
- 1 **medium clove garlic, minced**
- 1 **medium pickled, hot jalapeño chile, stemmed, seeded and finely chopped**
- 2 **tablespoons lemon juice**
- 1 **tablespoon olive or salad oil**
- ½ **teaspoon salt**

Chimichangas

- ¼ **cup salad oil**
- 1 **large green pepper, chopped**
- 1 **large onion, chopped**
- 2½ **cups shredded, cooked chicken (1 whole breast with ribs, about 1¼ lb) (see Note)**
- ¼ **to ½ cup chicken broth**
- 1½ **teaspoons salt**
- 8 **(10-inch) flour tortillas**

  Salad oil
- ½ **cup shredded Cheddar cheese (2 oz)**
- ½ **cup shredded Monterey Jack cheese (2 oz)**
  Sour cream

1. Make Cherry-Tomato Salsa: In small bowl, combine salsa ingredients. Cover; set aside at room temperature up to 3 hours.
2. Make Guacamole: In bowl, with back of fork, mash avocado to desired consistency. Blend in remaining ingredients; cover with plastic wrap till ready to serve.
3. Make Chimichangas: In large skillet, heat oil. Over medium heat, sauté pepper and onion until soft. Stir in chicken, 1 cup salsa, enough chicken broth to moisten and the salt; set aside.
4. Preheat oven to 250F. Wrap tortillas in foil and heat until slightly soft—about 5 minutes. Place a scant ½ cup chicken mixture at one end of a tortilla, in a mound about 5 inches long. (Keep other tortillas wrapped while filling each one.) Roll tortilla around mixture, folding edges toward center. Secure end with 2 wooden picks. Repeat with remaining tortillas and filling.
5. In large, deep skillet, heat 1 inch oil; fry Chimichangas until golden-brown and crisp, turning once. Drain on paper towels; remove wooden picks. Place on baking sheet.
6. Spread 1 cup salsa evenly over fried tortillas; sprinkle with cheeses. Heat under broiler until cheese

melts. Serve with Guacamole and sour cream; pass remaining salsa. *Makes 4 servings (8 Chimichangas).*

Note: To prepare chicken: In 3-quart saucepan, place chicken breast in 2 cups water. If desired, add 1 small onion, quartered, and several leafy celery tops. Over high heat, bring mixture to boiling. Reduce heat; simmer, covered, about 45 minutes or until chicken is tender. Remove chicken to bowl; cool until easy to handle. Remove and discard skin and bones from chicken. Shred meat with 2 forks or cut into slivers.

Corn-Filled Roulade With Roasted-Pepper Sauce
(pictured)

Roasted-Pepper Sauce, recipe follows

Roulade

- 1 **cup fresh corn kernels (from 2 large ears)**
- 1¼ **cups milk**
- 6 **large eggs**
- ⅓ **cup (⅔ stick) butter or margarine**
- ⅓ **cup all-purpose flour**
- ½ **teaspoon salt**
  Dash ground red pepper
- ½ **cup grated Parmesan cheese (2 oz)**
- ¼ **teaspoon cream of tartar**

Filling

- 2 **tablespoons butter or margarine**
- 1 **cup fresh corn kernels (from 2 large ears)**
- 1 **small green pepper, chopped (¾ cup)**
- 1 **small red pepper, chopped (¾ cup)**
- ½ **cup chopped green onion**
- ¼ **teaspoon freshly ground pepper**
- ⅓ **cup grated Parmesan cheese (about 1½ oz)**

1. Prepare Roasted-Pepper Sauce through Step 5.
2. Make Roulade: Place 1 cup corn kernels in food processor or blender; add 2 tablespoons milk; process about 3 minutes or until mixture is smooth.
3. Separate eggs, placing whites in small bowl of electric mixer and yolks in large bowl. Let whites come to room temperature—about 20 minutes. Grease bottom of 15½-by-10½-by-1-inch jelly-roll pan; line with waxed paper; grease lightly.
4. Preheat oven to 350F. In medium saucepan, melt ⅓ cup butter. With wire whisk, stir in flour, salt and pepper until smooth. Gradually stir in remaining milk and puréed corn. Bring to boiling, stirring constantly. Reduce heat; simmer, stirring, until very thick—about 1 minute. Stir in ½ cup Parmesan cheese; remove from heat. With wire whisk, beat egg yolks until blended. Gradually stir in corn mixture. Cool about 15 minutes.

Summer Vegetable Specials

5. With portable electric mixer at high speed, beat whites with cream of tartar until stiff peaks form when beaters are slowly raised. Fold one-third of whites into corn mixture. Carefully fold in remaining whites until no white streaks remain.

6. Spread corn mixture evenly in prepared pan. Bake 20 minutes or until surface is puffed and firm when pressed with fingertip.

7. Meanwhile, make Filling: In hot butter in large skillet, sauté corn and peppers 3 to 4 minutes or until soft. Stir in green onion, pepper and Parmesan cheese, mixing well. Keep warm. Complete Step 6 of Roasted-Pepper Sauce.

8. When Roulade is done, with metal spatula, loosen edges from sides of pan. Invert on a dish towel; gently peel off waxed paper.

9. Spread surface with filling to within 1 inch of edge. From long side, roll up, jelly-roll fashion, grasping edge of towel to assist in rolling; place Roulade, seam side down, on heated serving plate. Spoon some Roasted-Pepper Sauce over Roulade; pass remaining sauce. *Makes 6 servings.*

Roasted-Pepper Sauce

  1 **lb (3 medium) red bell peppers or 1 jar (7 oz) roasted red peppers (see Note)**
  1 **tablespoon olive or salad oil**
  ⅓ **cup chopped onion**
  1 **large clove garlic, minced**
  ¼ **teaspoon crushed red-pepper flakes**
  ¾ **cup heavy cream**
  ½ **teaspoon salt**
  ¼ **teaspoon ground white pepper**

1. Preheat broiler. Place peppers on baking sheet. Broil, 4 to 6 inches from heat, 20 to 25 minutes, turning frequently until all sides are charred and blistered. Remove peppers from broiler; place in paper bag, twisting top to seal. Allow peppers to stand 20 minutes.

2. Meanwhile, heat oil in a medium skillet; add chopped onion, minced garlic and red-pepper flakes; sauté 2 to 3 minutes or until onion is soft. Remove from heat and set aside.

3. Place cream in heavy saucepan; bring to boiling over medium-high heat, stirring constantly; boil until cream is reduced to ½ cup—about 3 to 4 minutes. Remove pan from heat; set aside.

4. Place peppers on cutting board; cut each in half lengthwise. Remove and discard stems, ribs and seeds; peel and discard skin from peppers.

5. Place peppers and onion mixture in processor or blender. Purée until mixture is very smooth—about 3 minutes (if using blender, purée half at a time).

6. Return purée mixture to skillet and boil over medium-high heat, stirring constantly, 3 minutes. Stir in reduced cream, salt and pepper.

Note: If using prepared roasted peppers, omit Step 1 and Step 4. Drain peppers and proceed as above.

Squash-Cheese Tart
(pictured)

1¼ **to 1½ cups all-purpose flour**
  1 **pkg fast-rising or regular dry yeast**
  1 **teaspoon sugar**
  ¾ **teaspoon salt**
  ½ **cup water (120 to 130F)**
    Olive oil
  ¾ **lb medium zucchini**
  ½ **lb medium yellow summer squash**
  2 **medium onions, chopped (about 1½ cups)**
  ¼ **teaspoon dried rosemary leaves, crushed**
  1 **cup shredded Jarlsberg cheese (4 oz)**
    Tomato rose (optional)

1. In large bowl, combine ¾ cup flour, the yeast, sugar and ½ teaspoon salt; mix well. With portable electric mixer at low speed, beat in water and 1 tablespoon oil until smooth. With wooden spoon, mix in enough remaining flour to make a stiff, not sticky, dough.

2. On lightly floured board, knead dough until smooth and elastic—about 5 minutes. Place dough in greased bowl and turn dough over to bring up greased side. Cover dough with towel and let rise in a warm place (85F), free from drafts, 30 minutes.

3. Cut zucchini and yellow summer squash diagonally into ¼-inch-wide slices. In a medium saucepan, bring 2 inches water to boiling. Add the zucchini and yellow-squash slices and cook 1 minute. Drain vegetables and rinse with cold water; drain again.

4. In medium skillet, heat 1 tablespoon oil. Over medium heat, sauté the chopped onions until golden; stir in remaining ¼ teaspoon salt and the rosemary and set aside. Preheat oven to 450F. Grease two 8-inch fluted tart pans with removable bottoms.

5. Divide dough in half. On lightly floured surface, roll each half into a 9-inch circle. Place each in a prepared pan; trim edges. Lightly brush surfaces with oil. With fork, prick bottoms. Bake crusts 10 minutes or just until lightly golden; remove from oven.

6. Fill each crust with onion mixture and cheese, dividing evenly. Arrange overlapping zucchini slices around edge of crust and yellow squash in center. Lightly brush squash with oil. Bake 10 minutes. Garnish with tomato rose, if desired. Cut each tart into 8 wedges. *Makes 2 tarts (16 appetizer servings).*

Summer Vegetable Specials

Tomato-Mussel Pasta
(pictured)

 2   dozen medium mussels (about 2 lb)
¾   cup olive oil or salad oil
 4   large green onions, chopped
¼   lb fresh mushrooms, sliced (about ¾ cup)
 2   lb fresh plum tomatoes, seeded and chopped
       (4 cups)
½   cup fresh basil leaves, chopped
½   cup Calamata or other ripe olives, pitted and
       quartered
 3   medium cloves garlic, minced
⅛   teaspoon crushed red-pepper flakes
⅛   teaspoon freshly ground black pepper
 1   pkg (1 lb) mafalade or mini-lasagne pasta
⅓   cup grated Parmesan cheese
 2   tablespoons chopped parsley

1. Check mussels, discarding any that are not tightly closed. Scrub well under cold running water to remove sand and seaweed. With a sharp knife, trim off the beards around edges. Let soak 1 to 2 hours in cold water. Lift mussels from water and place in colander. Rinse with cold water; drain.
2. In large skillet, heat oil. Over medium heat, sauté onions and mushrooms until onions are soft. Add mussels, tomatoes, basil, olives, garlic and red and black peppers; cover and cook 5 minutes or until mussels open.
3. Meanwhile, cook pasta as package label directs; drain; place in large serving bowl. Toss pasta with mussels in tomato sauce and cheese. Sprinkle with parsley. *Makes 6 servings.*

Salmon-Cucumber Mousse
(pictured)

       2-lb boneless fresh-salmon fillet or 3 cans (7½ oz
       each) red salmon, drained
 2   env unflavored gelatine
 1   cup cold water
 1   cup mayonnaise
 1   container (8 oz) plain low-fat yogurt
¼   cup minced onion
 2   tablespoons lemon juice
 1   teaspoon hot red-pepper sauce
1¼   teaspoons salt
 1   cup finely chopped, unpared Kirby cucumber
 2   tablespoons snipped fresh dill
 1   cup (½ pint) heavy cream
 2   small unpared Kirby cucumbers
       Dill sprig (optional)

1. In large skillet or steamer with ½ inch water, place wire or steaming rack (rack should be just above water). Place fresh salmon on rack; cover. Over high heat, bring to boiling. Reduce heat; simmer about 10 minutes or until salmon flakes when pierced with a fork. Remove salmon from pan; refrigerate until completely chilled.
2. In small saucepan, sprinkle gelatine over water; let soften 1 minute. Over low heat, cook, stirring occasionally, just until gelatine is dissolved. (Or, in small bowl, sprinkle gelatine over water; let soften 1 minute. Microwave on HIGH 1 minute or until gelatine is dissolved.) Pour ½ cup gelatine into medium bowl and remaining gelatine into large bowl; cool to room temperature—about 20 minutes.
3. Meanwhile, remove and discard skin from cooked or canned salmon. With fingers, finely flake salmon (about 3 cups).
4. Into large bowl of gelatine, stir ½ cup each mayonnaise and yogurt, 2 tablespoons minced onion, the lemon juice, red-pepper sauce and 1 teaspoon salt; mix well. Add salmon, stirring until mixed; refrigerate. Into medium bowl of gelatine, stir the remaining ½ cup each mayonnaise and yogurt, 2 tablespoons onion, ¼ teaspoon salt, the chopped cucumber and snipped dill; mix well; refrigerate. Stir both mixtures occasionally until thickened—about 20 minutes.
5. Meanwhile, in small bowl, whip cream just until stiff peaks form when beaters are raised. Fold half of whipped cream into thickened salmon mixture, then remaining half into cucumber mixture. Spoon half of salmon mixture into 9-inch springform pan, spreading evenly. Carefully spoon all of cucumber mixture onto salmon layer in pan, spreading to cover evenly. Spoon remaining salmon mixture onto cucumber layer, spreading to cover evenly. Cover pan with foil or plastic wrap; refrigerate until completely chilled—several hours or overnight.
6. To serve: Slice cucumbers crosswise into very thin rounds. Run thin-bladed knife around edge of salmon-cucumber mousse to loosen; remove side of springform pan. Place mousse on serving plate. Arrange cucumber slices, overlapping, to decorate edge of mousse. Garnish with dill sprig. *Makes 16 servings.*

Cream-Of-Leek Soup

¼   cup (½ stick) butter or margarine
 2   cups chopped, washed leeks
 2   cans (10¾-oz size) condensed cream-of-potato soup
 4   cups milk

1. Melt butter in a large saucepan. Add leeks; sauté, stirring, until tender—5 minutes.

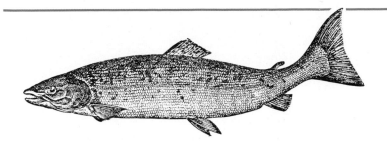

Summer Vegetable Specials

2. Blend soup and 1 cup milk in electric blender, at high speed, 1 minute or until smooth. Add to leeks with remaining milk.
3. Heat over medium heat, stirring occasionally, just until soup comes to boiling. *Makes 6 servings.*

Squash Creole
(pictured)

2 lb small yellow squash or zucchini
1 tablespoon butter or margarine
½ cup chopped green onion
1 teaspoon salt
Dash ground pepper
1 can (1 lb) stewed tomatoes

1. Wash squash or zucchini. Cut them crosswise, on the diagonal, into slices ½ inch thick.
2. In hot butter in a large skillet, sauté chopped green onion until it is tender—about 3 minutes. Add the sliced squash, salt and pepper; toss together lightly.
3. Cook, covered, over low heat, about 15 minutes or just until squash is tender. Add the stewed tomatoes and toss to combine. Cook, covered, 1 minute longer or until mixture is heated through. *Makes 8 servings.*

Oriental Wrapped Vegetables With Plum Sauce
(pictured)

Plum Sauce, recipe follows
1 large red pepper
1 large yellow pepper
½ daikon (Oriental radish) or 1 white turnip
1 medium carrot (8 inches long)
20 snow peas (2 oz)
2 heads romaine
8 strips (9 inches each) from green-onion tops

Egg Wrappers
5 large eggs
3 tablespoons water
Salad oil

1. Three hours or day ahead, make Plum Sauce.
2. Day of serving, prepare vegetables: Halve peppers lengthwise (save half of each for other use). Discard ribs and seeds from pepper halves; trim off rounded ends, making a 4-inch length of pepper. With sharp knife, cut pepper halves lengthwise into strips about ⅛ inch wide. Divide red-pepper strips into 4 equal bunches and divide yellow-pepper strips into 4 equal bunches.
3. Pare daikon and carrot; cut into 4-inch-long strips as for peppers. Divide each into 4 equal bunches.
4. Remove stem end and strings from snow peas. Cut into 4-by-⅛-inch strips, as for other vegetables, and divide into 4 bunches.
5. Wash romaine. Select 20 of the largest green leaves. Trim each leaf into a 6-by-4-inch rectangle: Use upper part of leaf to avoid thick part of lower rib, and cut the 4-inch width across the rib. Reserve trimmings for salad.
6. Arrange 1 bunch of red-pepper strips on one end of a prepared romaine leaf, lining up 4-inch length of strips with 4-inch length of romaine; roll up firmly to enclose pepper strips; secure end with wooden pick. Repeat with remaining 3 bunches of red-pepper strips. Continue rolling all prepared vegetable bunches in romaine (20 rolls in all).
7. Bring 1 inch of water to boiling in a large skillet, Dutch oven or wok. Arrange vegetable rolls in a steamer, placing carrot, daikon and snow-pea rolls on bottom; place red- and yellow-pepper rolls on top of other bundles. Place green-onion strips on top of vegetable rolls. Place steamer over boiling water; cover; steam 5 minutes. Immediately plunge steamer into a large pan containing ice water to stop cooking. Drain; set aside.
8. Prepare Egg Wrappers: In medium bowl, combine eggs, water and 1 tablespoon oil; beat vigorously with wire whisk to blend well. Brush bottom of a skillet or crêpe pan that measures 7 inches on *bottom* with oil. Pour a scant ¼ cup egg mixture into skillet, tipping pan to allow egg to cover bottom completely. Cook over medium heat until egg is completely set. With broad spatula, carefully loosen edge of cooked egg; remove to plate; cover with waxed paper. Repeat, making 3 more egg rounds and covering each with waxed paper as it is removed from pan.
9. To assemble: Remove picks from vegetable rolls. Trim two opposite sides of each egg round to make

Summer Vegetable Specials

a 7-by-4-inch wrapper. Arrange a carrot and a dai-kon roll side by side in center of wrapper, lining up the 4-inch length of wrapper with the vegetable rolls; place a snow-pea roll and red-pepper roll on top of first two rolls; place a yellow-pepper roll on top of last two rolls. Bring one end of wrapper up and over vegetable rolls; bring other end up and overlap ends. Repeat to make 4 vegetable bundles in all.

10. To serve, trim ends of bundles. Cut each egg-wrapped bundle of vegetables in half crosswise. Wrap a green-onion strip around each bundle, tying ends in single knot. Arrange vegetable rolls, cut side up, on serving plate. Serve with Plum Sauce. *Makes 8 appetizer-size vegetable rolls.*

Plum Sauce

 2 jars (4 oz each) strained plums
¼ cup light sesame oil
⅓ cup red-wine vinegar
 2 teaspoons soy sauce
 1 teaspoon powdered five-spice seasoning (see Note)
½ cup chopped daikon (Oriental radish) or white turnip

In small bowl, combine all ingredients. Cover and refrigerate at least 3 hours or overnight to allow flavors to blend. *Makes 1½ cups.*

Note: Five-spice powder is available in Oriental food stores.

Corn Custard in Pepper Cups
(pictured)

 8 small (4-oz each) red peppers
 2 tablespoons butter or margarine
¼ cup chopped onion
¼ cup chopped green pepper
 2 tablespoons all-purpose flour
 2 teaspoons sugar
¼ teaspoon salt
⅛ teaspoon ground white pepper
 Dash ground nutmeg
 2 large eggs
 1 cup fresh corn kernels (from 2 large ears)
 1 cup shredded Cheddar cheese (4 oz)
 1 cup light cream or half-and-half

1. With sharp knife, cut a slice from top of each red pepper. Carefully remove and discard ribs and seeds from peppers. Stand each pepper upright in a 2½-inch muffin-pan cup; set aside.
2. In hot butter in small skillet, sauté onion and green pepper until tender—about 2 minutes.
3. Preheat oven to 325F. On waxed paper, combine flour, sugar, salt, white pepper and nutmeg. In a medium bowl, beat eggs; stir in corn, Cheddar cheese and onion mixture; blend well. Stir in flour mixture until well blended. Stir in cream.
4. Pour scant ½ cup corn mixture into each of prepared red peppers. Bake 1 hour and 10 minutes or until corn custard is firm and knife inserted in center comes out clean. *Makes 8 appetizer or side-dish servings.*

Gift-Wrapped Summer Pâté
(pictured)

Pâté
 1 lb sweet Italian sausage
 2 lb fresh or frozen, thawed ground turkey
¼ cup brandy
¼ cup chopped shallots
1½ teaspoons salt
 1 teaspoon dried thyme leaves
½ teaspoon dried rosemary leaves, crushed
½ teaspoon coarsely ground black pepper
 2 large eggs
¼ lb green beans, trimmed and cut into ½-inch pieces
 2 medium carrots, pared and cut into ½-inch pieces
 1 small red pepper, cut into ½-inch pieces
½ cup packaged dry bread crumbs

Vegetable Wrapping
 3 large carrots (1½-inch diameter), pared
 2 medium zucchini, unpared
 2 medium yellow summer squash, unpared
 Curly leaf lettuce
¼ cup Dijon-style mustard
¼ cup mayonnaise
 Crackers (optional)
 Mustard (optional)

1. Make Pâté: Remove sausage from casings. In large bowl, combine sausage, turkey, brandy, chopped shallots, salt, thyme, rosemary and pepper; mix well. Add eggs and green-bean, carrot and red-pepper pieces; mix well. Add bread crumbs; mix well.
2. Preheat oven to 350F. Place an 8-by-2½-inch spring-form pan or a 9-by-5-by-3-inch loaf pan on foil-cov-

Summer Vegetable Specials

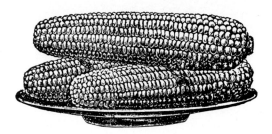

ered jelly-roll pan (needed to catch meat juices). Place meat mixture in pan, pressing slightly to pack evenly. Cover with foil, leaving a ½-inch space between meat mixture and foil. Cut 4 slits in foil to vent. Bake 1 hour and 45 minutes; remove from oven; let rest 20 minutes to cool slightly. Remove side of springform pan, letting excess meat juices run onto foil-lined pan. With wide spatula, lift pâté off bottom of springform pan and place on large plate or tray. (If using loaf pan: With pot holders, tip pan to pour off excess meat juices. Invert loaf pan onto plate to release pâté; remove pan.) Refrigerate until completely chilled— several hours or overnight. (Pâté can be made up to 1 week ahead.)

3. Remove pâté from refrigerator 30 minutes before serving. Meanwhile, make Vegetable Wrapping: In large skillet, bring 1½ inches water to boiling. Add carrots; simmer, covered, until tender—about 10 minutes. Using tongs, remove carrots from water and place in bowl of ice water to stop cooking; dry on paper towels. With sharp knife, cut zucchini and yellow squash lengthwise into ¼-inch-thick slices. Place zucchini slices in same simmering water; cook until tender—about 2 minutes. Remove and place in bowl of ice water to stop cooking; dry well on paper towels. Repeat with yellow-squash slices.

4. Arrange lettuce on serving plate; place pâté on lettuce. In small bowl, combine mustard and mayonnaise; mix well. With flat icing spatula, spread mustard mixture evenly on top and side of pâté. Place zucchini and yellow-squash slices, alternating and slightly overlapping them, on pâté, with wide ends on side and narrow ends on top of pâté.

5. With sharp knife or vegetable parer, cut carrots lengthwise into 15 (1/16-inch-thick) slices. Trim eight slices 8 inches long and seven slices 6 inches long. Place the eight 8-inch slices, spoke fashion, on pâté (one end of each slice in center). Lift opposite end of each slice up and over to meet in center, forming loops. Make a loop with each of six 6-inch carrot slices, placing each on one of the longer loops on pâté. Curl remaining carrot slice around two fingers; place in center of bow; secure with wooden picks.

6. Serve pâté at room temperature, with crackers and additional mustard, if desired. (Remove wooden picks before serving.) *Makes 16 servings.*

Corn Cakes With Caviar
(pictured)

    2 cups fresh corn kernels (from 4 large ears)
    ⅓ cup milk
    ⅓ cup yellow cornmeal
    ⅓ cup all-purpose flour
    2 teaspoons baking powder
    ½ teaspoon salt
    ¼ teaspoon freshly ground pepper
    ¼ cup (½ stick) butter or margarine, melted
    2 large eggs
    1 large egg yolk
    ¼ cup finely chopped green onion
       Salad oil
    1 container (8 oz) crème fraîche or sour cream
    1 jar (2 oz) black lumpfish caviar
    1 jar (2 oz) red lumpfish caviar

1. Place 1 cup corn kernels in food processor or blender; add 2 tablespoons milk. (If using blender, blend half at a time.) Process until almost smooth.
2. In medium bowl, stir together cornmeal, flour, baking powder, salt and pepper. Make well in center; add puréed corn, remaining 1 cup corn kernels, the remaining milk, butter, eggs, yolk and green onion. With wooden spoon, blend well.
3. Brush griddle or nonstick skillet lightly with oil; heat until a drop of water sprinkled on surface sizzles. Spoon 1 rounded tablespoon batter onto griddle for each cake. Cook several at a time, not letting cakes touch, 1½ to 2 minutes per side. Remove; repeat with remaining batter.
4. To serve: Arrange corn cakes, slightly overlapping, on salad plates. Spoon crème fraîche on top of each cake; top with black and red caviar. Serve immediately. *Makes 24 corn cakes.*

Baked Spiced Rhubarb

    4 cups rhubarb, cut in 1-inch pieces (about 2 lb) or
       2 pkg (1-lb size) frozen rhubarb in syrup
    1 cup sugar
       1-inch cinnamon stick
    4 whole cloves

Summer Vegetable Specials

1. Preheat oven to 400F.
2. Place rhubarb in a 2-quart casserole. Sprinkle with sugar; add cinnamon and cloves. If using frozen rhubarb, place frozen fruit in a 10-by-8-by-2-inch baking dish. Sprinkle with only ¼ cup sugar; add spices.
3. Bake, covered, 10 minutes. Stir gently to dissolve sugar and baste fruit with syrup. Bake 15 minutes longer or until rhubarb is tender but not mushy.
4. Let stand, covered, on wire rack until cool. *Makes 4 to 6 servings.*

Two-Tone Summer Squash Loaf

1 lb zucchini
1 lb yellow summer squash
   Salt
1 bunch watercress
4 tablespoons (½ stick) butter
½ cup chopped shallots
   Freshly ground pepper
⅔ cup heavy cream
5 eggs
1 cup grated cheese (a combination of Swiss, Cheddar and Parmesan)
   Boiling water

1. Trim, wash and dry the zucchini and yellow squash; grate separately. Sprinkle with salt and drain in separate colanders for 30 minutes.
2. Wash the watercress; discard the heavy stems; chop the leaves. Once the squashes have drained, squeeze to remove excess moisture.
3. Combine the zucchini and watercress. In a sauté pan, heat 2 tablespoons of the butter and cook half the shallots until wilted. Add the zucchini and watercress and sauté until heated through—4 to 5 minutes. Season with salt and pepper to taste. Remove from pan to a medium bowl and set aside.
4. In same sauté pan, melt 2 tablespoons butter and cook the remaining shallots until wilted. Add the yellow squash and cook 4 to 5 minutes. Season with salt and pepper to taste and remove from pan to a medium bowl.
5. Mix ⅓ cup of the cream into each squash mixture. Beat the eggs and add half of them to each bowl.

6. Preheat oven to 375F. Butter a 1½-quart, 9-by-5-by-2¾-inch loaf pan and line with buttered waxed paper. Spread half the zucchini mixture in the bottom of the pan and sprinkle with one-third of the cheese. Gently spread on half the yellow squash without disturbing the lower layer. Sprinkle on another third of the cheese. Repeat the layering once, ending with the yellow squash. Place the loaf pan into a larger baking dish and pour boiling water halfway up the side of the loaf pan.
7. Bake for 15 minutes; lower the heat to 350F and bake another 30 minutes or until the loaf is firm. Remove and let rest in the pan for 15 to 20 minutes before turning out onto a serving dish. *Serves 8.*

Fresh-Vegetable 'Pizza'

½ bunch fresh broccoli
   Salt
1 tablespoon butter or margarine
1½ cups sliced onion
12 eggs
½ teaspoon dried basil leaves
2 cloves garlic, pressed
⅛ teaspoon ground pepper
2 medium tomatoes
1 cup grated Cheddar cheese (4 oz)

1. Wash broccoli; trim into flowerets. Peel and coarsely chop stems. Cook 5 minutes, covered, in 1 cup lightly salted boiling water; drain well.
2. Preheat oven to 350F. Rub a 14-inch pizza pan with 1 teaspoon butter. In medium skillet, melt remaining butter and sauté the sliced onion until tender—about 5 minutes.
3. In a large bowl, beat eggs until frothy. Stir in basil, garlic, 1 teaspoon salt and the pepper. Fold in chopped broccoli stems and sautéed onion. Turn into prepared pan.
4. Wash tomatoes. Cut into eighths. Arrange tomato and broccoli flowerets on egg mixture. Sprinkle with cheese. Bake 15 minutes or until eggs are set and lightly browned. Cut into wedges to serve. *Makes 6 servings.*

Summer Vegetable Specials

Creamed-Spinach Ring

2 **lb fresh spinach or 2 pkg (10-oz size) frozen chopped spinach**
   Grated Parmesan cheese
4 **tablespoons (½ stick) butter or margarine**
½ **cup chopped onion**
1 **cup light cream or half-and-half**
1 **teaspoon salt**
½ **teaspoon sugar**
   Dash ground pepper
   Dash ground nutmeg
4 **eggs**
½ **cup fresh bread crumbs (2 slices)**
⅓ **cup grated Swiss or Gruyère cheese**
   Boiling water
   Lemon-Glazed Carrots, recipe follows

1. Wash spinach; remove and discard large stems. Place in large kettle with just the water clinging to leaves. Cook, covered, tossing with a fork once or twice, 5 minutes or until spinach is just tender. Drain very well. Chop coarsely. If using frozen spinach, cook as package label directs; drain very well.
2. Preheat oven to 350F. Grease a 4½-cup ring mold well and dust with grated Parmesan cheese.
3. In hot butter in large saucepan, sauté onion until tender—about 5 minutes. Add spinach, cream, salt, sugar, pepper and nutmeg; heat just to boiling. Remove from heat.
4. In large bowl, beat eggs slightly. Add bread crumbs and Swiss cheese; gradually stir in spinach mixture.
5. Turn into prepared mold. Set mold in baking pan on oven rack; pour boiling water into pan to depth of 1½ inches. Place a piece of waxed paper over top of mold.
6. Bake 30 to 35 minutes or until knife inserted in center of spinach mixture comes out clean.
7. Loosen mold around edge with a small spatula. Invert onto heated serving plate. Fill center of ring with Lemon-Glazed Carrots. *Makes 6 to 8 servings.*

Lemon-Glazed Carrots

1 **lb carrots**
   Salt
   Boiling water
3 **tablespoons butter or margarine**
2 **tablespoons sugar**
4 **thin slices lemon**

1. Wash carrots; pare; cut diagonally into 1-inch pieces.
2. Place in medium saucepan with enough salted boiling water to cover; simmer, covered, 15 minutes or until tender. Drain.
3. Melt butter in heavy medium-size skillet. Stir in sugar; add lemon slices and carrot; cook over medium heat, stirring occasionally, until carrot is glazed. *Makes 4 servings.*

Spaghetti Squash With Fresh-Spinach Sauce

1 **spaghetti squash (2¾ to 3 lb)**
   Boiling water

Fresh-Spinach Sauce

1 **lb fresh spinach**
¼ **cup salad oil**
2 **tablespoons butter or margarine**
1 **large onion**
2 **cloves garlic, pressed**
½ **teaspoon dried basil leaves**
¼ **teaspoon salt**
   Grated Parmesan cheese

2 **tablespoons coarsely chopped walnuts**

1. Wash spaghetti squash; cut in half lengthwise; remove seeds. Pierce skin with fork. Set halves, skin side down, in a large pot with a cover. Add boiling water to measure 2 inches. Cover; return to boiling; reduce heat to simmer; cook 30 minutes or until tender.
2. Meanwhile, make Fresh-Spinach Sauce: Remove stems from spinach and wash leaves thoroughly; drain; chop coarsely.
3. Heat oil and butter in a medium skillet. Peel and slice onion; add to skillet with the garlic. Sauté until golden—3 minutes. Add spinach, basil and salt. Cover; reduce heat and simmer until spinach has just wilted—5 minutes.
4. Drain squash. Run a fork over inside of cooked squash to release strands. Place on a warm platter. Stir ¼ cup Parmesan cheese into the spinach mixture. Spoon over spaghetti squash. Top with nuts. Serve with more Parmesan cheese. *Makes 4 servings.*

GEORGE RATKAI

Autumn's Harvest of Vegetable Favorites

With the cooler weather comes heartier eating and sensational seasonal vegetables that we've harvested into a ravishing repertoire of recipes sure to warm the spirit and tempt the tastebuds. Pictured here are the luscious fresh vegetables of fall, each with a specially prepared stuffing that makes an old favorite taste new again. **At near left** is Eggplant Creole in Shell with a stuffing made from the pulp of the eggplant, ground chuck, onion, pepper, celery, tomatoes and hot red-pepper sauce for zing. **Below it** are Savory Stuffed Turnips filled with broccoli, mushrooms and garlic in beef broth. Continuing **clockwise**: Baked Acorn Squash With Squash-And-Apple Filling sweetened with brown sugar and cinnamon; Stuffed Red Cabbage filled with a delicious meatloaf-like mixture; and, **at top**, Chili-Stuffed Squash. Recipes for these and more cool-weather favorites begin on page 284.

Baskets of the season's favorite fresh vegetables and fruits fill this roadside stand with their fantastic just-picked flavor. We found room to include two samples of their bountiful good taste. Crisp 'n' juicy apples, pears and grapes team up with citrus fruit to create this sparkling Jellied Winter Fruit Bowl ringed with snowy flaked coconut. Pumpkin-pie spice, butter and brown sugar bake into tender-cooked butternut and acorn squash in this platter of Glazed Winter Squash. *See recipes on pages 286 and 287.*

From New England down to the grand Old South, hearty bean dishes have been cooked and served for generations. Good cooks like dried beans not only for their rich, mellow taste but also for the way they take on a myriad of subtle flavorings. Bake them with honey, toss them with pasta or brew them into a soup. Pictured **clockwise from top right:** White Beans, Country Style with tomatoes, garlic and herbs; Hearty Vegetable-Bean Soup with kielbasa; and Black-Eyed Beans With Ham. *Recipes begin on page 286.*

Autumn's Harvest

continued from page 279

Stuffed Red Cabbage
(pictured)

     1 head (3 lb) leafy red cabbage
        Boiling water
     1 quart ice water
     3 tablespoons butter or margarine
    ½ cup finely chopped onion
     2 tablespoons finely chopped parsley
    ¾ lb ground beef chuck
    ¼ lb ground pork
    ⅔ cup cooked white rice
     1 egg, slightly beaten
     2 teaspoons Worcestershire sauce
  1½ teaspoons salt
    ⅛ teaspoon ground pepper
    ½ teaspoon ground allspice
     1 slice bacon
     2 cans (10½-oz size) beef consommé, undiluted
     1 tablespoon dark corn syrup
     2 tablespoons all-purpose flour
        Few drops liquid gravy seasoning (optional)

1. Wash cabbage. In 8-quart kettle, cover cabbage with 4 quarts boiling water; boil, covered, 5 minutes. Lift out with two slotted spoons; cool. With knife, remove six outer leaves; plunge into ice water; drain; reserve. Return head of cabbage to boiling water. Cover; boil 20 minutes. Drain.
2. Make filling: In 1 tablespoon butter in small skillet, sauté onion and parsley. In medium bowl, combine sautéed vegetables, meats, rice, egg, Worcestershire, salt, pepper, allspice and ½ cup boiling water; toss with fork.
3. With sharp knife, trim core to make cabbage stand level. Carefully fold back four outer leaves. Cut 5-inch circle in center of cabbage top.
4. With serrated knife, remove cabbage from circled area, leaving cavity 3 inches deep. Shell should be 1 inch thick.
5. Fill cavity with filling, mounding slightly. Crush 12-inch square of foil over meat; fold four outer leaves around foil. Place folded bacon under base; tie with string.
6. In 5-quart Dutch oven, combine the consommé, corn syrup and 1 cup boiling water. Place cabbage in liquid. Cover; simmer 1 hour or until fork-tender. Place large fork under string; lift to hot platter. Fold back outer leaves; remove foil and string. Reserve liquid.
7. Make sauce: In a medium saucepan, melt 2 tablespoons butter. Remove pan from heat; stir in flour until smooth. Stir in 1¾ cups reserved cooking liquid and the gravy seasoning. Return to heat; bring to boiling, stirring until thickened. Brush meat with some sauce. Dip reserved cabbage leaves into hot sauce. Fold around cabbage. To serve, cut in wedges; pass sauce. *Makes 8 servings.*

Eggplant Creole in Shell
(pictured)

     1 large eggplant (about 2 lb)
     2 tablespoons lemon juice
    ½ lb ground beef chuck
     2 cloves garlic, crushed
    ¼ cup finely chopped onion
    ¼ cup finely chopped green pepper
    ¼ cup finely chopped celery
     1 can (1 lb) tomatoes, undrained
     1 teaspoon salt
    ¾ teaspoon dried thyme leaves
    ¼ teaspoon hot red-pepper sauce
    ½ cup Grapenuts
        Grated Parmesan cheese

1. Wash eggplant. Score and remove skin from six ¾-inch diagonal bands on eggplant (see picture).
2. Cut a 2½-inch slice from top of eggplant. Slice a ¼-inch slice from bottom to give eggplant a firm base to stand on. With a long-handled spoon, scoop out pulp, leaving ½-inch-thick shell. Dice pulp.
3. Brush inside and outside of shell and lid with lemon juice. Wrap in foil. Keep warm in low oven.
4. In large skillet, sauté beef with garlic until brown; drain off any fat. Add onion, green pepper, diced eggplant and celery; cook over low heat about 5 minutes.

Autumn's Harvest

5. Stir in tomatoes, salt, thyme, red-pepper sauce and Grapenuts. Simmer 5 minutes.

6. Set eggplant shell on a warm serving platter; spoon meat mixture into it. Sprinkle top with Parmesan cheese.

7. To serve, spoon Eggplant Creole from shell. Pass more Parmesan cheese. Nice with buttered rice. *Makes 6 servings.*

   Note: Eggplant shell may be cut up and cooked another time.

Chili-Stuffed Squash
(pictured)

1¼ **lb ground beef round**
1 **cup chopped onion**
1 **green pepper, coarsely chopped**
2 **cloves garlic, pressed**
½ **teaspoon crushed red-pepper flakes**
1 **tablespoon chili powder**
1 **teaspoon ground cumin**
¼ **teaspoon dried oregano leaves**
1¼ **teaspoons salt**
1 **can (1 lb) red kidney beans, undrained**
1 **can (1 lb) whole tomatoes, undrained**
1 **pkg (10 oz) frozen whole-kernel corn**
1 **can (8 oz) tomato sauce**
1 **winter squash or pumpkin (about 8 lbs)**
 Salad oil

1. In large heavy skillet, over medium heat, sauté ground beef, stirring occasionally to keep beef in small chunks, until red color disappears. Pour off fat.

2. Add onion, green pepper, garlic, crushed red pepper, chili powder, cumin, oregano and salt; mix well. Cook, stirring, until onion and green pepper are tender.

3. Add beans, tomatoes, corn and tomato sauce; stir to mix well, breaking up tomatoes with fork. Cover and simmer slowly, stirring occasionally, until thickened and flavors are blended—about 45 minutes.

4. Meanwhile, cut off top of squash. Remove seeds and fibers from center. Remove any pulp attached to top. Preheat oven to 350F.

5. Place squash on a rimmed cookie sheet or shallow baking pan. Fill squash with chili. (If there is too much filling for squash, spoon extra hot chili around it for serving.) Replace lid. Brush surface of squash with oil. Bake until squash is tender—about 70 minutes. To serve, spoon chili into soup plates. Scoop out meat of squash and mound some in center of each serving. *Makes 8 servings.*

Baked Acorn Squash With Squash-And-Apple Filling
(pictured)

1 **large acorn squash (2½ lb)**
1 **small acorn squash (1½ lb)**
1 **large cooking apple**
 Butter or margarine
2 **tablespoons light-brown sugar**
 Salt
 Pepper
 Dash ground cinnamon

1. Preheat oven to 375F. Scrub squash; make a small slit in each. Place in a large baking pan and bake until large squash is tender—about 1 hour and 15 minutes.

2. Pare, core and slice apple; cut slices into thirds. Place in a small saucepan with 2 tablespoons water. Cover and simmer until just tender—3 to 5 minutes. Drain well.

3. Remove squash from oven. Cut small squash in half. Scoop out and discard seeds; spoon pulp into a medium bowl. Cut a thin slice from one end of large squash. Set up on cut end. Trim a 2-inch piece off top. Scoop squash from pieces removed; add to bowl.

4. Add 1 tablespoon butter and the sugar to squash. Beat with portable electric mixer until light and fluffy. Fold in apple.

5. Scoop seeds from large squash. Sprinkle cavity with salt and pepper; dot with butter. Spoon whipped squash mixture into large squash, mounding on top. Sprinkle top with cinnamon.

6. To serve, cut into six wedges. *Makes 6 servings.*

Autumn's Harvest

Savory Stuffed Turnips
(pictured)

6 large white turnips (2 lb)
 Boiling water
 Salt
¼ cup (½ stick) butter or margarine
 1 cup chopped broccoli, fresh or frozen
¼ lb mushrooms, washed and chopped
 1 clove garlic, crushed
½ cup chicken broth
 2 tablespoons chopped parsley

1. Wash and pare turnips. Cut thin slice off root and stem ends. In 1 inch boiling, salted water in large saucepan, cook turnips 20 to 25 minutes or just until tender; drain. Cool slightly. With a spoon, scoop out centers, leaving ½-inch shell. Finely chop centers; reserve.
2. Preheat oven to 350F. Butter a 1½-quart baking dish.
3. In hot butter in 10-inch skillet, over medium heat, sauté broccoli, mushrooms, garlic and ½ teaspoon salt, stirring, about 5 minutes. Remove from heat. Add chopped turnip; mix well.
4. Spoon into shells, dividing evenly. Place in buttered baking dish. Pour chicken broth around turnips.
5. Bake, covered with foil, 20 to 25 minutes or until hot. Remove from oven. Sprinkle with parsley. *Makes 6 servings.*

Jellied Winter Fruit Bowl
(pictured)

3 cups boiling water
 1 pkg (3 oz) orange-flavored gelatin
 1 pkg (3 oz) lemon-flavored gelatin
 1 large apple
 1 ripe winter pear
 1 large grapefruit
 2 medium oranges
 1 cup Tokay grapes
¼ cup sugar
¼ cup orange juice
½ cup flaked coconut

1. Pour boiling water over both flavors of gelatin in medium bowl, stirring until dissolved. Refrigerate until syrupy—about 1 hour.
2. Meanwhile, prepare fruit and place in large bowl: Pare and quarter apple; cut crosswise into thin slices. Pare and quarter pear; cut lengthwise into thin slices. Peel and section grapefruit. Peel oranges and slice into ¼-inch-thick slices. Cut the grapes in half and remove seeds.
3. Sprinkle fruit with sugar; add orange juice. Toss gently until combined; set aside.
4. Add chilled gelatin to fruit; stir gently until well blended.
5. Refrigerate until firm—at least 4 hours. At serving time, sprinkle coconut around edge of bowl. *Makes 8 to 10 servings.*

White Beans, Country Style
(pictured)

1 lb dried Great Northern white beans (2 cups)
 4 teaspoons salt
¼ teaspoon ground pepper
 2 cloves garlic, pressed
 2 bay leaves
 6 tablespoons (¾ stick) butter or margarine
 2 onions, finely chopped (about 2 cups)
 1 green pepper, finely chopped (about 1 cup)
 1 can (1 lb) tomatoes, undrained
 1 teaspoon dried oregano leaves
¼ cup finely chopped parsley
 Tomato wedges (optional)
 Bay leaves (optional)

1. Cover beans with cold water; refrigerate, covered, overnight.
2. Next day, drain beans; turn into a 4- or 5-quart Dutch oven; cover with 5 cups cold water. Add the salt, pepper, garlic and bay leaves. Bring to boiling; reduce heat; simmer, covered, 1 hour or until beans are tender. Stir several times during cooking. Drain. Turn beans back into Dutch oven. Preheat oven to 350F.
3. Meanwhile, in a large skillet, heat 4 tablespoons butter; sauté chopped onion until golden—about 5 minutes. Add green pepper, tomatoes, oregano and parsley; cook 5 more minutes.

Autumn's Harvest

4. Stir vegetable mixture and remaining 2 tablespoons butter into drained beans. Bake, covered, 1 hour and 15 minutes; bake, uncovered, 15 minutes longer. If desired, garnish top with tomato wedges and bay leaves. *Makes 6 servings.*

Hearty Vegetable-Bean Soup
(pictured)

½ lb dried Great Northern white kidney beans
1½ lb zucchini
3 medium white turnips (1 lb)
1 large potato
6 medium carrots (1 lb)
2 celery stalks with leaves
2 onions
  Water
1 onion, studded with 4 whole cloves
1 bay leaf
1 can (1 lb, 1 oz) whole tomatoes, undrained
1 tablespoon dried basil leaves
⅛ teaspoon crushed red pepper flakes
1½ tablespoons salt
  1-lb kielbasa, in one piece
2 tablespoons olive or salad oil
2 tablespoons chopped parsley

1. Day before, cover beans with cold water; refrigerate, covered, overnight.
2. Next day, drain beans in colander; rinse under cold water.
3. Prepare vegetables: Dice zucchini; pare and dice turnips and potato. Pare carrots; slice thinly; slice celery. Coarsely chop 2 onions.
4. Turn beans into a 6-quart Dutch oven with 6½ cups water; bring to boiling over medium heat.
5. Add prepared vegetables and remaining ingredients, except kielbasa, oil and parsley. Bring back to boiling; reduce heat and simmer, covered, 2½ hours or until beans are tender; add about ½ cup water during cooking, if necessary. Add whole kielbasa last half hour of cooking.
6. To serve, remove and discard onion with cloves and the bay leaf. Cut up kielbasa; return to soup. Stir in oil. Taste for seasoning. Sprinkle with parsley. *Makes 4½ quarts.*

Glazed Winter Squash
(pictured)

2 butternut or acorn squash (about 1½ lb each) or 4 pieces (about 4-inch pieces) Hubbard squash (2¼ lb)
3 tablespoons butter or margarine, melted
¾ teaspoon salt
¼ teaspoon pumpkin-pie spice (see Note)
3 tablespoons dark-brown sugar

1. Preheat oven to 400F.
2. If using butternut or acorn squash, cut in half lengthwise; remove seeds. Place whichever variety is used cut side down in shallow roasting pan. Pour water to ½-inch depth around squash.
3. Bake 35 to 40 minutes or until tender. Pour off water. Turn squash cut side up.
4. Combine butter, salt and spice; brush on squash. Sprinkle with brown sugar.
5. Bake 10 minutes more or until sugar is melted. *Makes 4 servings.*

Note: You may substitute ⅛ teaspoon each of ground nutmeg and ground cinnamon for pumpkin-pie spice.

Black-Eyed Beans (Peas) With Ham
(pictured)

1 lb black-eyed beans (peas)
  1-lb to 1½-lb smoked pork butt
  Salt
2 bay leaves
1 medium onion, studded with 4 whole cloves
2 tablespoons butter or margarine
2 tablespoons salad oil
1 cup chopped onion
½ cup chopped celery
1 teaspoon dried thyme leaves
⅛ teaspoon ground pepper
6 tablespoons light-brown sugar
¼ cup water
1 can (1 lb) whole tomatoes, undrained
½ cup dry red wine
  Chopped parsley

Autumn's Harvest

1. Cover beans with cold water; refrigerate, covered, overnight.
2. Next day, place pork butt in 8-quart kettle; cover with 5 cups water, 1 tablespoon salt, bay leaves and whole onion studded with cloves. Bring to boiling; reduce heat and simmer, covered, 1 hour.
3. Drain beans; add to kettle with pork. Bring to boiling; reduce heat and simmer, covered, 1 hour or until beans are tender.
4. Meanwhile, in hot butter and oil, sauté onion, celery and thyme, stirring, 5 minutes. Add 1 teaspoon salt, the pepper, ¼ cup brown sugar and ¼ cup water. Bring to boiling; reduce heat to very low and simmer (mixture should barely bubble), uncovered, stirring occasionally, 20 minutes.
5. Preheat oven to 350F. Drain beans, reserving liquid. Slice pork butt.
6. In 3-quart casserole, combine beans and tomatoes; stir in onion-celery mixture and red wine; mix well. Arrange pork slices across top. Bake, covered, ½ hour, adding a little bean liquid if necessary. Sprinkle top with 2 tablespoons brown sugar; bake, uncovered, 30 minutes longer. Sprinkle with parsley. *Makes 8 servings.*

Old-Fashioned Baked Beans

1½ lb dried Great Northern white beans (3 cups)
2 quarts water
¾ lb salt pork
1 medium onion
1 teaspoon salt
¼ cup firmly packed light-brown sugar
2 teaspoons dry mustard
1 cup light molasses

1. Wash beans, discarding imperfect ones. Cover beans with 2 quarts cold water; refrigerate, covered, overnight.
2. Next day, drain beans. Turn into 6-quart kettle; cover with 2 quarts cold water.
3. Bring to boiling; reduce heat; simmer, covered, 30 minutes. Drain, reserving liquid.

4. Preheat oven to 300F.
5. Trim rind from salt pork. Cut pork almost through at half-inch intervals.
6. Place onion in bottom of 4-quart bean pot or casserole. Add beans; bury salt pork, cut side down, in center of beans.
7. Heat reserved bean liquid to boiling.
8. Mix remaining ingredients. Stir in 1 cup boiling bean liquid. Pour over beans. Add boiling liquid just to cover beans—about 1½ cups.
9. Bake, covered, 6 hours. Stir once every hour so beans will cook evenly. If they seem dry after stirring, add a little hot bean liquid or water.
10. To brown top of beans, remove cover for last half hour of baking time. *Makes 8 servings.*

Baked Beans, New York Style

1 lb dried Great Northern white beans (2 cups)
¼ lb salt pork, diced
1 large onion, chopped
¾ cup firmly packed light-brown sugar
½ cup catsup
1 teaspoon dry mustard
1 teaspoon salt
1 tablespoon Worcestershire sauce
1 cup boiling water
¼ lb salt pork, cut in strips

1. Cover beans with cold water; refrigerate, covered, overnight.
2. Next day, drain beans. Cover with cold water; bring to boiling; reduce heat and simmer gently just until skins start to burst. Drain.
3. Preheat oven to 275F.
4. Turn beans into a 3-quart casserole; add diced salt pork, onion, sugar, catsup, mustard, salt, Worcestershire and boiling water; mix well. Arrange strips of salt pork over top.
5. Bake, covered, 6 hours; uncover during last hour, adding more water if beans become dry. *Makes 8 servings.*

Autumn's Harvest

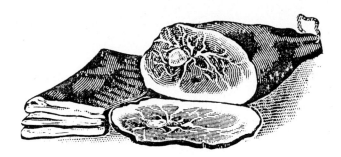

Honey-Baked Beans

 2 cups dried lima beans (1 lb)
    Water
 ¼ lb sliced bacon, diced
 1 teaspoon salt
1½ teaspoons dry mustard
 1 teaspoon ground ginger
 ¾ cup honey
 1 medium onion, peeled and studded with 3 whole
    cloves
 1 cup sliced onion

1. Wash beans; drain. In large saucepan, cover beans with water; refrigerate, covered, overnight.
2. Next day, over medium heat, cook beans in same water, uncovered, until tender and skins burst. Drain, reserving liquid.
3. In 2½-quart casserole, place half of bacon, the beans and remaining ingredients, combined with ½ cup bean liquid. Cover with rest of bacon.
4. Bake, covered, 1½ hours or until tender. During last half hour, remove cover to brown. (Add more bean liquid during cooking if necessary.) *Makes 8 servings.*

Baked Beans au Gratin

    Boiling water
 1 lb dried Great Northern white beans (2 cups)
 1 onion studded with 3 whole cloves
    Bouquet garni (see Note)
    Salt
 2 tablespoons butter or margarine
 1 onion, finely chopped
 1 can (16 oz) tomatoes, undrained
 1 clove garlic, crushed
 1 can (10¾ oz) condensed chicken broth, undiluted
 ½ cup heavy cream
 ¼ teaspoon ground pepper
 1 cup fresh white-bread crumbs
 2 tablespoons butter or margarine, melted

1. In large saucepan, pour enough boiling water over beans just to cover; bring to boiling; boil 2 minutes. Set aside, covered, 2 hours.

2. Drain beans; turn into a heavy, 5-quart Dutch oven along with onion studded with cloves, bouquet garni and 1 teaspoon salt. Add enough water just to cover the beans (about 1 quart); bring to boiling; reduce heat and simmer, covered, until tender—1½ to 2 hours. Drain, discarding onion and bouquet garni.
3. Meanwhile, in a large saucepan, heat 2 tablespoons butter; sauté chopped onion until golden—several minutes. Add tomatoes and garlic; cook, stirring, several minutes more. Stir in chicken broth and cream, blending well; simmer a few minutes. Meanwhile, preheat oven to 375F.
4. Stir in drained beans, 1 teaspoon salt and pepper, mixing just until combined. Turn into a 12-by-8-by-2-inch baking dish or 3-quart au-gratin dish.
5. Toss bread crumbs with melted butter; sprinkle over top of beans; bake, uncovered, 30 minutes or until hot and crumbs are browned. *Makes 8 to 10 servings.*

   Note: Bouquet garni: 1 sprig parsley, 1 bay leaf, ½ teaspoon dried thyme leaves tied in a cheesecloth bag.

Yellow-Split-Pea Soup With Ham Hocks

 1 lb quick-cooking, split yellow or green peas
    (2 cups)
 3 quarts water
 ⅛ lb salt pork or bacon, coarsely chopped
    (about ⅓ cup)
 ½ cup coarsely chopped green onion
1½ cups coarsely chopped celery
 1 cup coarsely chopped onion
 4 (8-oz size) smoked ham hocks
 2 parsley sprigs
 1 bay leaf
 ⅛ teaspoon dried rosemary leaves
    Salt
 1 tablespoon chopped parsley

1. In a 6-quart kettle, combine peas and water. Bring to boiling; reduce heat and simmer, covered, 45 minutes.
2. Meanwhile, in small skillet, sauté salt pork several minutes. Add green onion, celery and onion; sauté,

Autumn's Harvest

stirring, until onion is golden—takes about 5 minutes.

3. Wipe ham hocks with damp paper towels. Add to kettle along with salt pork and sautéed vegetables, parsley sprigs, bay leaf, rosemary and 1 teaspoon salt. Bring back to boiling; reduce heat and simmer, covered, 2 hours or until ham hocks are tender and meat begins to fall off bones. Remove from heat.
4. With slotted utensil, lift out ham hocks to cool. Remove meat from the bones; discard the skin, fat and bones.
5. If necessary, skim fat from soup. Put soup with vegetables through coarse sieve, puréeing vegetables.
6. Pour back into kettle. Add meat from ham hocks; reheat slowly, stirring occasionally, until heated through. Add salt to taste; heat the soup 5 minutes longer.
7. Sprinkle with the chopped parsley. *Makes about 3 quarts.*

Cranapple-Stuffed Squash

2 (1½-lb size) butternut squash
2 cooking apples (Granny Smith)
1 tablespoon cornstarch
¼ cup apple juice or cider
¼ cup firmly packed light-brown sugar
2 tablespoons butter or margarine
Salt
Ground pepper
1 cup fresh cranberries, washed

1. Preheat oven to 375F.
2. Scrub squash; cut in half lengthwise; remove seeds. Arrange, cut side down, in shallow baking pan. Surround with ½ inch hot water. Bake 30 minutes.
3. Prepare apples: pare, core and coarsely chop.
4. In a medium saucepan, stir cornstarch into apple juice, mixing until smooth. Add brown sugar, butter, dash salt, dash pepper, apple and cranberries. Bring mixture to boiling, stirring constantly. Reduce heat; simmer, covered, 10 minutes or until apple is tender and sauce is thickened.
5. Turn squash cut side up; bake 30 minutes longer or until fork-tender. Remove squash from oven. Scoop out centers of squash, leaving ½ inch around edge. Sprinkle inside of shells with dash each salt and pepper. Chop squash; add to filling.
6. Over low heat, stir until heated through. Spoon filling into cavities of squash, dividing evenly. To serve: Cut each squash in half lengthwise. *Makes 8 servings.*

White Beans With Pasta

1 lb dried Great Northern white beans (2 cups)
Water
Salt
1 cup shell macaroni
¼ cup olive or salad oil
2 cloves garlic, crushed
½ cup chopped onion
2 tablespoons chopped fresh parsley
1 can (8 oz) tomato sauce
1 teaspoon dried savory leaves
½ teaspoon dried thyme leaves
¼ teaspoon ground pepper
½ pkg (8-oz size) American-cheese slices, halved
Chopped parsley

1. Cover beans with cold water; refrigerate, covered, overnight.
2. Next day, drain beans, reserving liquid; turn beans and 6 cups liquid into a 3-quart Dutch oven; add 1 teaspoon salt. Bring to boiling; reduce heat and simmer, covered, 2 hours or until tender; if necessary, add 1 cup water during cooking; drain.
3. A half hour before beans are done, in medium saucepan, bring to boiling 3 cups water and 1 teaspoon salt. Add macaroni; cook until tender—about 15 minutes; drain.
4. In hot oil in medium skillet, sauté garlic, onion and parsley 1 minute. Add tomato sauce, savory, thyme, 2 teaspoons salt and the pepper. Cook, uncovered, over medium heat until onion is tender—about 5 minutes.
5. To serve, turn beans and macaroni into a 2-quart shallow casserole; stir in tomato mixture. Arrange cheese slices over top of beans in a circle. Run under broiler a few minutes to melt cheese. Sprinkle top with chopped parsley. *Makes 8 servings.*

Kidney-Bean-And-Tuna Salad

2 cans (1-lb, 4-oz size) white kidney beans
¼ cup wine vinegar
¼ cup chopped parsley
3 green onions, chopped
¼ cup salad oil
1 teaspoon salt
Dash ground pepper
1 can (7 oz) tuna, drained and broken into large pieces
2 hard-cooked eggs, quartered
Crisp lettuce
Chopped parsley (optional)

Autumn's Harvest

1. Drain kidney beans; turn into medium bowl.
2. Add vinegar, parsley, onion, oil, salt and pepper; stir gently to mix well.
3. Refrigerate, covered, to chill well—at least 2 hours.
4. To serve, toss gently with tuna and egg. Line salad bowl with lettuce. Turn salad into bowl. Sprinkle with chopped parsley, if desired. *Makes 6 servings.*

Cream-Of-Pumpkin Soup

 2 tablespoons butter or margarine
 ½ lb yellow onions, thinly sliced
 ½ tablespoon all-purpose flour
 1 can (10¾ oz) condensed chicken broth, undiluted
 1 can (1 lb) pumpkin
 2 cups milk
 1 cup heavy cream
 1 teaspoon salt
 ⅛ teaspoon ground pepper
 ¼ teaspoon ground ginger
 ⅛ teaspoon ground cinnamon
 Ground nutmeg

1. In hot butter in 6-quart Dutch oven, sauté onion, stirring occasionally, 10 minutes or until tender. Remove from heat.
2. Stir flour into onion; gradually stir in chicken broth. Bring to boiling; reduce heat; simmer, covered, 10 minutes.
3. Ladle mixture into electric blender. Blend, covered, at high speed one minute or until completely smooth.
4. Return to Dutch oven; blend in pumpkin with wire whisk until mixture is smooth. Add milk, ½ cup cream, the salt, pepper, ginger, cinnamon and ⅛ teaspoon nutmeg; beat with wire whisk to blend.
5. Heat soup slowly over medium heat just to boiling; reduce heat, cover and simmer 15 minutes, stirring occasionally.
6. Meanwhile, beat remaining cream just until stiff.
7. Serve soup hot. Garnish each serving with a spoonful of whipped cream; sprinkle with a little more nutmeg. *Makes 6 servings (1½ quarts).*

Butternut-Squash Soup

 1 butternut squash, about 3 lb (see Note)
 2 cans (10¾-oz size) condensed chicken broth, undiluted
 ¼ teaspoon salt
 Dash ground white pepper
 1 cup heavy cream
 ¼ teaspoon ground nutmeg

1. Preheat oven to 400F. Bake whole squash about 1 hour or until tender when pierced with a fork.
2. Let squash cool slightly. Cut in half lengthwise; discard seeds. With a spoon, scoop squash pulp from the skin.
3. In electric blender, combine half of squash pulp and 1 can broth; blend at low speed until well combined, then at high speed until smooth. Turn into bowl. Repeat with remaining squash and broth. Stir in salt and pepper.
4. Refrigerate soup, covered, overnight.
5. At serving time, heat squash mixture just to boiling. Gradually stir in ½ cup cream; cook slowly until heated through. Taste for seasoning, adding more salt and pepper if necessary.
6. Meanwhile, beat remaining cream just until stiff.
7. Serve soup very hot. Garnish each serving with a spoonful of whipped cream; sprinkle with nutmeg. *Makes 6 servings.*

 Note: Or use 3 packages (12-ounce size) frozen winter squash, partially thawed.

Pumpkin-Spice Cake

 1 cup seedless raisins
 ½ cup muscat raisins
 1 cup walnuts
 2 cups sifted all-purpose flour
 2 teaspoons baking soda
 ½ teaspoon salt
 2 teaspoons ground cloves
 2 teaspoons ground cinnamon
 1 teaspoon ground ginger
 4 eggs
 2 cups sugar
 1 cup salad oil
 1 can (1 lb) pumpkin
 Cream-Cheese Frosting, recipe follows

1. Preheat oven to 350F. Grease well a 13-by-9-by-2-inch baking pan. Coarsely chop raisins and walnuts.
2. Sift flour with baking soda, salt, cloves, cinnamon and ginger into large bowl. Add raisins and walnuts; toss lightly to combine.
3. In large bowl of electric mixer, at high speed, beat eggs until thick and yellow. Gradually beat in sugar until thick and light. At low speed, beat in oil and pumpkin to blend well. Gradually stir in flour mixture until well blended.
4. Turn into prepared pan. Bake 50 minutes or until surface springs back when gently pressed with fingertip.
5. Let cool completely in pan placed on wire rack.

Autumn's Harvest

6. To serve, loosen edge with spatula. Invert on cake plate. Frost with Cream-Cheese Frosting. Cut into squares. *Makes 12 servings.*

   Note: This cake improves in flavor if it is stored a day or two in refrigerator.

Cream-Cheese Frosting

1 **pkg (8 oz) cream cheese, softened**
1 **tablespoon butter or margarine**
1 **teaspoon vanilla extract**
1 **lb confectioners' sugar**

1. In medium bowl, with electric mixer at medium speed, beat the cream cheese with butter and vanilla until creamy.
2. Add confectioners' sugar; beat until light and fluffy. Spread thickly over top of cake; make decorative swirls with knife. *Makes 2½ cups.*

Brandied Pumpkin Flan

¾ **cup sugar**

Pumpkin Custard

1 **cup canned or cooked pumpkin**
1 **cup milk**
1 **cup light cream or half-and-half**
6 **eggs**
½ **cup sugar**
½ **teaspoon salt**
2 **teaspoons vanilla extract**
⅓ **cup brandy**

2 **tablespoons brandy**

1. In a large, heavy skillet, over medium heat, cook ¾ cup sugar until it melts and forms a light-brown syrup. Stir to blend.
2. Immediately pour syrup into a heated 8¼-inch, round, shallow baking dish. Holding dish with pot holders, quickly rotate to cover bottom and side completely with syrup. Set aside.
3. Preheat oven to 325F.
4. Make Pumpkin Custard: In medium saucepan, combine pumpkin, milk and cream, stirring until well blended. Heat over low heat until bubbles form around edge of pan.
5. In large bowl, with portable electric mixer or rotary beater, beat eggs slightly. Add sugar, salt and vanilla. Gradually stir in the hot milk mixture and ⅓ cup brandy. Pour into prepared baking dish.
6. Set dish in shallow pan; pour boiling water to a depth of ½ inch around dish.
7. Bake 50 to 60 minutes or until silver knife inserted in center comes out clean. Let custard cool; refrigerate overnight.
8. To serve: Run small spatula around edge of dish to loosen. Invert on shallow serving dish; shake gently to release. The caramel acts as sauce. At the table, warm 2 tablespoons brandy slightly; ignite and quickly pour over flan. *Makes 8 servings.*

Butternut-Squash Pie

Filling

3 **eggs, slightly beaten**
½ **cup sugar**
½ **cup maple or maple-flavored syrup**
½ **teaspoon ground cinnamon**
½ **teaspoon ground ginger**
½ **teaspoon salt**
2 **pkg (12-oz size) thawed frozen winter squash, undrained**
1 **cup light cream or half-and-half**

9-inch unbaked pie shell with high, fluted edge
½ **cup heavy cream, whipped**
Maple syrup

1. Preheat oven to 400F.
2. Make Filling: In large bowl, combine eggs, sugar, maple syrup, spices, salt, squash and light cream. Beat, with portable electric mixer or rotary beater, until mixture is smooth.
3. Turn most of filling into unbaked pie shell. Place on lowest shelf of oven; pour in rest of filling. Bake 55 to 60 minutes or until filling is set in center when pie is gently shaken.
4. Let cool on wire rack. Serve pie slightly warm or cold. Garnish with whipped-cream rosettes drizzled with maple syrup. *Makes 8 servings.*

Autumn's Harvest

Pumpkin Pie, New Orleans Style

- **2 cups milk**
- **½ cup sugar**
- **4 eggs**
- **1 can (1 lb) pumpkin**
- **½ cup light molasses (New Orleans style)**
- **2 tablespoons butter or margarine, melted**
- **¼ teaspoon salt**
- **⅛ teaspoon ground nutmeg**
- **⅛ teaspoon ground cloves**
- **⅛ teaspoon ground ginger**
- **⅛ teaspoon ground allspice**
- **10-inch unbaked pie shell with high, fluted edge**
- **Chilled whipped cream**

1. Preheat oven to 350F. In medium bowl, combine milk, sugar and eggs. Beat with rotary beater just to combine.
2. In another bowl, combine pumpkin, molasses, melted butter, salt and spices; mix well. Fold in custard mixture until well combined. Turn into prepared pie shell.
3. Bake 1 hour and 20 minutes or until crust is golden and pumpkin mixture seems firm.
4. Let cool slightly on wire rack. Serve slightly warm or cold; pass whipped cream. *Makes 10 servings.*

Baked Acorn Squash

- **4 (1-lb size) acorn squash**
- **4 tablespoons (½ stick) butter or margarine**
- **2 tablespoons coarsely grated orange peel**
- **2 tablespoons coarsely grated lemon peel**
- **2 tablespoons orange juice**
- **2 tablespoons lemon juice**
- **2 tablespoons sherry**
- **Salt**

1. Preheat oven to 350F. Cut squash in half; remove seeds and strings. Place, skin side up, in buttered 15-by-10-by-1-inch baking pan.
2. Bake until tender—40 minutes; remove from oven. Turn squash halves over and prick flesh with fork. Dot each with ½ tablespoon butter. Sprinkle each with ¾ teaspoon mixed orange and lemon peel.

3. In small bowl, combine orange juice, lemon juice and sherry. Spoon mixture over squash and into holes in center. Sprinkle each with a little salt.
4. Return to oven and bake 15 to 20 minutes longer, basting once or twice with liquid in center. *Makes 8 servings.*

Baked Acorn Squash With Cranberries

- **2 (1-lb size) acorn squash**
- **2 tablespoons butter or margarine, melted**
- **2 teaspoons salt**
- **½ cup canned whole-cranberry sauce**
- **1 teaspoon ground cinnamon**
- **¼ cup firmly packed light-brown sugar**

1. Preheat oven to 400F. Scrub squash; cut in half. With spoon, remove seeds and strings.
2. Arrange squash halves, cut side down, in shallow baking pan. Add hot water, ½ inch deep. Bake 40 minutes.
3. Pour off liquid from baking pan. Turn squash cut side up. Brush inside of each with ½ tablespoon butter; then sprinkle with ½ teaspoon salt.
4. Combine cranberry sauce with cinnamon and brown sugar; mix well. Divide evenly into squash halves.
5. Bake 30 minutes longer. *Makes 4 servings.*

Braised Red Cabbage

- **1 can (10¾ oz) condensed chicken broth, undiluted**
- **6 quarts thinly sliced red cabbage (4 to 4½ lb)**
- **4 oz salt pork, diced**
- **1 cup chopped onion**
- **1 cup firmly packed brown sugar**
- **1 cup apple juice or cider**
- **½ cup white-wine vinegar**
- **1 tablespoon salt**
- **¼ teaspoon ground pepper**

1. In a Dutch oven, slowly bring undiluted chicken broth to boiling. Add cabbage; cook over low heat, covered, 1 hour.

Autumn's Harvest

2. Sauté salt pork in skillet until very crisp. Remove with slotted spoon. Sauté onion in hot drippings until tender—about 5 minutes.
3. Add brown sugar, apple juice, vinegar, salt, pepper and sautéed onion to red cabbage. Simmer, uncovered, stirring occasionally, 1 hour. Add salt pork and simmer ½ hour longer or until cabbage is tender. *Makes 10 servings.*

Squash Hawaiian

    3 cups mashed, cooked Hubbard squash or 2 pkg
       (12-oz size) frozen winter squash
    1 can (9 oz) crushed pineapple
    6 tablespoons (¾ stick) butter or margarine
    2 tablespoons brown sugar
 1 ½ teaspoons salt
   ¼ teaspoon ground pepper

1. Heat fresh mashed squash (thaw and heat frozen squash according to package directions) in a saucepan.
2. Drain pineapple, reserving juice. When squash is hot, add butter, drained pineapple, sugar, salt and pepper; beat hard until well mixed. Then beat in just enough of the reserved pineapple juice (1 or 2 tablespoons) to make squash light and fluffy. Serve hot. *Makes 6 servings.*

Pumpkin Bread

 1⅔ cups all-purpose flour
    1 teaspoon baking soda
   ¼ teaspoon baking powder
   ¾ teaspoon salt
   ½ teaspoon ground cloves
   ½ teaspoon ground cinnamon
   ½ teaspoon ground nutmeg
   ½ teaspoon ground allspice
 1 ½ cups sugar
   ½ cup salad oil
    2 eggs
    1 cup canned pumpkin

1. Preheat oven to 350F. Lightly grease and flour a 9-by-5-by-3-inch loaf pan.
2. On a sheet of waxed paper, sift flour with baking soda, baking powder, salt and spices.
3. In medium bowl, wiith portable electric mixer, beat sugar with oil until smooth. Beat in eggs, one at a time, until smooth.
4. Stir in pumpkin and the flour mixture until well combined. Turn into prepared pan.
5. Bake 60 to 65 minutes or until cake tester inserted in center comes out clean. Let cool on wire rack 10 minutes.
6. Loosen edges with spatula. Turn out of pan; cool completely. Serve thinly sliced. Nice with tea or coffee. *Makes 1 loaf.*

Baked Acorn Squash With Meat Filling

    3 (1-lb size) acorn squash
   ⅓ cup (⅔ stick) butter or margarine
    1 clove garlic, split
    2 medium onions, chopped (1¼ cups)
    1 lb ground chuck
    1 can (1 lb) whole tomatoes, drained
    2 cups cooked white rice
 1¼ teaspoons dried oregano leaves
 1 ½ teaspoons salt
   ¾ cup grated sharp Cheddar cheese

1. Preheat oven to 375F.
2. Scrub squash. Cut in half lengthwise; remove seeds and stringy fibers.
3. Arrange, cut side down, in shallow baking pan. Surround with ½ inch hot water. Bake 30 minutes.
4. Meanwhile, in hot butter in large skillet, sauté garlic until golden. Lift out and discard. Add onion; sauté, stirring, until golden. Add chuck. Break up into small pieces with fork. Cook 5 to 8 minutes or until meat is lightly browned. Add drained tomatoes, rice, oregano and salt; mix well.
5. Fill each squash half with one cup mixture. Sprinkle each with 2 tablespoons grated cheese. Bake, uncovered, 20 minutes longer. Run under broiler several minutes to brown top. *Makes 6 servings.*

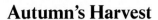

Autumn's Harvest

Whipped Potatoes and Rutabagas

1½- lb rutabaga
3¼ teaspoons salt
2 lb potatoes
⅛ teaspoon ground pepper
½ cup (1 stick) butter or margarine, melted
¼ cup light cream or half-and-half
Chopped parsley

1. Wash rutabaga; pare. Cut into 1-inch cubes—you should have 4 cups cubes.
2. In 1 inch boiling water with 1 teaspoon salt in medium saucepan, simmer rutabaga, covered, about 30 minutes or until it is very tender. Drain.
3. Meanwhile, pare potatoes. Cut into 1-inch cubes—you should have 4 cups cubes.
4. In 1 inch boiling water with 1¼ teaspoons salt in large saucepan, simmer potato, covered, 20 minutes or until tender. Drain.
5. In the large saucepan, combine rutabaga with potato. Place over low heat several minutes, shaking pan occasionally to dry vegetables. Remove from heat.
6. Add remaining teaspoon salt, the pepper and melted butter to vegetables. Mash with potato masher or beat with portable electric mixer until mixture is smooth and well combined.
7. Place over low heat. Gradually add cream, beating constantly with mixer or wire whisk. Continue to beat until mixture is very fluffy and heated through.
8. Pile into serving dish; sprinkle with chopped parsley. *Makes 6 to 8 servings.*

Baked Onions

8 medium yellow onions (2 lb)
4 chicken-bouillon cubes
3 tablespoons butter or margarine, melted
½ teaspoon paprika
Dash ground pepper

Crumb Topping

½ cup packaged dry bread crumbs
2 tablespoons butter or margarine, melted
½ teaspoon salt
⅛ teaspoon dried thyme leaves

1. Peel onions. Place in large saucepan, along with bouillon cubes and 2 quarts water; bring to boiling. Reduce heat; simmer, covered, 30 minutes or until onions are tender. Drain.
2. Preheat oven to 400F.
3. Place 3 tablespoons butter, the paprika and pepper in a shallow baking pan. Add onions; toss to coat well with butter. Bake 10 minutes.
4. Meanwhile, make Crumb Topping: In small bowl, combine crumbs, butter, salt and thyme. Sprinkle over tops of onions. Bake 10 minutes longer. *Makes 8 servings.*

Glazed Carrots and Onions

1 lb carrots, pared
Boiling water
1 teaspoon salt
1 lb small white onions, peeled

Glaze

¼ cup firmly packed light-brown sugar
1 teaspoon cornstarch
1½ tablespoons water
2 tablespoons butter or margarine
⅛ teaspoon ground nutmeg
1½ tablespoons lemon juice

1. Slice carrots, on the diagonal, into 1½-inch-thick pieces.
2. In 1 inch boiling water and the salt in 3-quart saucepan, bring carrot and onions to boiling.
3. Reduce heat; simmer, covered, 20 to 25 minutes or just until vegetables are tender. Drain well.
4. Meanwhile, make Glaze: In medium saucepan, combine sugar and cornstarch. Gradually stir in water to make a smooth mixture. Add butter, nutmeg and lemon juice.
5. Bring to boiling, stirring constantly; boil 5 minutes, stirring occasionally, until mixture is thick and translucent.
6. Add vegetables to glaze. Cook, uncovered, a few minutes, turning gently so they become glazed on all sides. *Makes 4 servings.*

Salads With Style

Salads, considered by some to be a ho-hum intermission before or after an entrée, have shed their lackluster image to become one of the more exciting and imaginative aspects of meals today. One look at this As-You-Like-It Salad bears this out. It's a savory selection of, **clockwise from top:** sprouts, zucchini squash, enoki and domestic mushrooms, summer squash, sprouts, tofu slivers, Chinese cabbage and, at center, a sliced black turnip, all on red-leaf and Bibb lettuce. Drizzle with our Soy-Vinaigrette Dressing or Creamy Blue-Cheese Dressing. Recipes for all of our salads begin on page 303.

GEORGE RATKAI/PAUL DOME

These three beautiful salads are perfect for entertaining. They offer make-ahead ease and all promise to tastefully accent your entire table. **At far left,** a tender head of cauliflower, marinated in herbs, is at the center of our Fiesta Salad Platter, which is artfully edged with Boston lettuce, tomato slices and marinated green beans. A dressing of mayonnaise and chopped green herbs is served alongside. **Below it,** cherry tomatoes fill the center and thin overlapping cucumber slices encircle this shimmering Crisp Cucumber Aspic, which folds grated cucumber and celery into a tangy lemon gel sparked with horseradish and dill. **At right** is refreshing Gazpacho-Salad Mold With Sliced Avocados, a classic combination of chunky tomatoes, cucumber, green pepper and onion that's been a favorite for years. *Recipes begin on page 303.*

299

This attractively composed salad of crisp raw vegetables and succulent cooked shrimp is designed for dipping into our Light Onion Dip, a mix of plain yogurt, cottage cheese and onion-soup mix with a dash of chili powder. At only 13 calories per delicious tablespoon, this streamlined version of the popular onion-soup-sour-cream party dip will become a favorite to serve with all of your salads. *See recipe on page 305.*

At top: Tossed Salad With Avocado is a sophisticated combination of romaine lettuce, red-onion rings and wedges of ripe avocado gently tossed with delicate White-Wine French Dressing. *See recipe on page 305.*

Bottom: Crisp, torn leaves of fresh spinach and escarole share the bowl with sliced cucumber and radishes in this Tossed Green Salad, dressed with a mix of garlic, cumin, tarragon vinegar and olive oil. *See recipe on page 306.*

Salads With Style

continued from page 297

As-You-Like-It Salad
(pictured)

Red-leaf lettuce
Bibb lettuce
Enoki mushrooms
Domestic cultivated mushrooms, thinly sliced through the stem
Yellow summer squash, thinly sliced
Assorted sprouts
Chinese cabbage, sliced across the head
Zucchini, thinly sliced
Black turnip, thinly sliced
Tofu slivers

Soy-Vinaigrette Dressing, recipe follows
Creamy Blue-Cheese Dressing, recipe follows

1. Wash lettuce in tepid water; dry on paper towels or spin in a salad dryer. Store in plastic bags, refrigerated, until cold and crisp.
2. Prepare all other vegetables and tofu and store, refrigerated, in separate plastic bags or containers.
3. Make salad dressings.
4. At serving time, line a chilled plate with the lettuce, alternating the leaves for color. Arrange the prepared vegetables and tofu on the platter as pictured. Serve salad dressings in bowls to be used as desired.

Note: No quantities have been given for the ingredients in this composed salad. You may add other vegetables, such as lightly blanched snow peas, carrot circles or broccoli flowerets, or substitute as you like with available produce.

Soy-Vinaigrette Dressing

⅓ **cup peanut or corn oil**
⅓ **cup cider vinegar**
⅓ **cup water**
2 **tablespoons light soy sauce**
2 **tablespoons minced green onion**
1 **tablespoon honey**
½ **teaspoon dry mustard**

Combine all ingredients in jar with a tight-fitting lid. Shake vigorously. Refrigerate until ready to serve. Shake again before using. *Makes about 1¼ cups.*

Creamy Blue-Cheese Dressing

¼ **lb blue or Roquefort cheese**
1 **cup sour cream**
¼ **cup mayonnaise or cooked salad dressing**
¼ **cup sherry**
¼ **cup wine vinegar**
1 **tablespoon grated onion**
½ **teaspoon salt**
¼ **teaspoon garlic powder**
¼ **teaspoon paprika**

1. Coarsely crumble blue cheese into medium bowl. Add remaining ingredients, stirring until well blended.
2. Refrigerate, covered, until well chilled—at least 1 hour. *Makes about 2 cups.*

Fiesta Salad Platter
(pictured)

Green Mayonnaise
1 **cup mayonnaise or cooked salad dressing**
2 **tablespoons lemon juice**
2 **tablespoons chopped parsley**
1 **tablespoon chopped chives**
1 **tablespoon chopped watercress**

1 **large head cauliflower (2½ lb)**
Boiling water
1 **cup milk**
1 **teaspoon salt**
1 **bottle (8 oz) herb-flavored oil-and-vinegar dressing**
2 **pkg (9-oz size) frozen whole green beans or 2 cans (15½-oz size) whole green beans**
1 **tablespoon butter or margarine**
½ **cup day-old bread cubes**
Boston lettuce
2 **large tomatoes, sliced (1 lb)**
Pimiento
Dill sprigs

1. Make Green Mayonnaise: In small bowl, combine mayonnaise, lemon juice, parsley, chives and watercress; mix well. Refrigerate, covered, overnight.
2. Wash cauliflower and leave whole. Remove and discard heavy stem and any outer leaves, if necessary. Place in large kettle; cover with boiling water. Add

Salads With Style

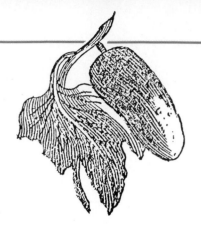

milk and salt; boil gently, uncovered, 30 minutes or just until stem of cauliflower is tender. Drain; then let cool 10 minutes. Place, stem end up, in bowl; pour herb dressing over cauliflower. Refrigerate, covered, overnight.

3. Several hours before serving, cook frozen green beans as package label directs. Drain. (If using canned beans, drain well.) Drain cauliflower, reserving dressing. Place beans in shallow dish with reserved dressing. Refrigerate, covered, along with cauliflower, until needed.

4. In hot butter in small skillet, sauté bread cubes until golden-brown. Set aside.

5. To serve: Drain beans. Place cauliflower, stem end down, in center of large platter; place lettuce leaves around edge. Alternate green beans and tomato slices on lettuce leaves. Garnish the beans with bread cubes and the cauliflower with bits of pimiento and dill sprigs. Pass Green Mayonnaise. *Makes 8 to 10 servings.*

Crisp Cucumber Aspic
(pictured)

2 cups boiling water
1 pkg (6 oz) or 2 pkg (3-oz size) lemon-flavored gelatin
⅓ cup white-wine vinegar
¼ teaspoon salt
　Green food color
2 medium cucumbers, pared and grated (2 cups)
½ cup finely chopped celery
1 to 2 tablespoons prepared horseradish
1 tablespoon grated onion
2 teaspoons snipped fresh dill
　About 20 paper-thin slices cucumber
2 pint boxes cherry tomatoes, washed
　Crisp salad greens
½ pint sour cream

1. In medium bowl, pour boiling water over gelatin; stir until dissolved. Stir in vinegar, salt and few drops green food color.

2. Set in bowl of ice, stirring occasionally, until mixture is consistency of unbeaten egg white—about 35 minutes.

3. Fold in grated cucumber, celery, horseradish, onion and dill until well blended. Turn into 5½-cup ring mold that has been rinsed in cold water and lined with the thin cucumber slices.

4. Refrigerate until firm—at least 3 hours.

5. To unmold: Run a small spatula around edge of mold. Invert over platter; place a hot, damp dishcloth over inverted mold and shake gently to release.

6. Fill center with tomatoes. Garnish edge with salad greens. Pass sour cream. *Makes 8 servings.*

Gazpacho-Salad Mold With Sliced Avocados
(pictured)

3 env unflavored gelatine
1 can (1 pt, 2 oz) tomato juice
⅓ cup red-wine vinegar
1 teaspoon salt
　Hot red-pepper sauce
2 medium tomatoes, peeled and diced (1¼ cups)
1 large cucumber, pared and diced (1½ cups)
1 medium green pepper, diced (¾ cup)
¼ cup finely chopped red onion
1 tablespoon chopped chives
3 large ripe avocados (about 2¼ lb)
　Lemon juice
⅓ cup bottled oil-and-vinegar dressing
　Watercress

1. In medium saucepan, sprinkle gelatine over ¾ cup tomato juice to soften. Place over low heat, stirring constantly, until gelatine is dissolved. Remove from heat.

2. Stir in remaining tomato juice, the vinegar, salt and few drops red-pepper sauce. Set in bowl of ice, stirring occasionally, until mixture is consistency of unbeaten egg white—about 15 minutes.

3. Fold in tomato, cucumber, green pepper, onion and chives until well combined. Pour into 1½-quart mold that has been rinsed in cold water.

4. Refrigerate until firm—at least 6 hours.

5. To unmold: Run a small spatula around edge of mold. Invert over serving platter; place a hot, damp dishcloth over inverted mold and shake gently to release. Refrigerate.

Salads With Style

6. Just before serving, peel and slice avocados. Brush with lemon juice. Arrange the avocado slices around the molded salad and pour dressing over them. Garnish with watercress. *Makes 6 servings.*

Light Onion Dip
(pictured)

- 1 **cup yogurt**
- 1 **cup low-fat cottage cheese**
- 3 **tablespoons dry onion-soup mix**
- ¼ **teaspoon chili powder**

1. In medium bowl, combine yogurt and cottage cheese until well blended. Stir in the dry onion-soup mix and chili powder.
2. Refrigerate the dip, covered, 3 hours to chill well and to let flavor develop.
3. Arrange on tray with an assortment of crisp vegetables and chilled shrimp. *Makes 2 cups dip.*

Tossed Salad With Avocado
(pictured)

White-Wine French Dressing
- 2 **tablespoons white-wine vinegar**
- 2 **tablespoons lemon juice**
- ½ **cup salad oil**
- 1 **teaspoon salt**
- ½ **teaspoon ground pepper**
- 1 **teaspoon sugar**
- ¼ **teaspoon dry mustard**
- 1 **clove garlic**

Salad
- 1 **large head romaine lettuce**
- 1 **small red onion**
- 1 **large ripe avocado**

1. Make White-Wine French Dressing: Combine all dressing ingredients in jar with a tight-fitting lid; shake vigorously. Refrigerate until ready to use.
2. Prepare salad ingredients: Wash lettuce and dry leaves on paper towels or spin in a salad dryer. Tear dried leaves into bite-size pieces and store in a plastic bag to chill thoroughly.

3. Peel red onion; slice and separate into rings. Store, covered, in the refrigerator until serving time.
4. When ready to serve, turn greens and onion rings into a chilled salad bowl. Remove garlic from dressing and discard. Shake dressing well and pour about three-fourths of it over salad.
5. Peel avocado; remove pit and slice fruit into sixths. Arrange over greens and drizzle slices with remaining dressing. Toss gently and serve at once on chilled plates. *Makes 6 servings.*

Molded Shrimp Salad

- 2 **env unflavored gelatine**
- 1½ **cups cold water**
- 1½ **cups skim-milk yogurt**
- 1 **cup low-calorie mayonnaise**
- ½ **cup chili sauce**
- 2 **tablespoons lemon juice**
- 2 **tablespoons finely chopped green onion**
- 1 **teaspoon salt**
- ¼ **teaspoon dried tarragon leaves**
- 2 **lb shelled, deveined shrimp, cooked**
- ½ **cup chopped celery**
  Lettuce

1. Sprinkle gelatine over cold water in medium saucepan; let soften—about 5 minutes. Bring to boiling, stirring until gelatine is dissolved.
2. Set pan in a bowl of ice cubes until gelatine is cold; stir once or twice.
3. Add yogurt, mayonnaise, chili sauce, lemon juice, onion, salt and tarragon to gelatine; mix until well blended. Refrigerate or place over ice, stirring occasionally, until mixture is consistency of unbeaten egg white.
4. Set aside and refrigerate 8 shrimp for garnish. Cut remaining shrimp into ¼-inch pieces. Add chopped shrimp and celery to yogurt mixture; mix well. Turn into a chilled 2-quart mold or 8 individual molds.
5. Refrigerate until set—about 6 hours or overnight.
6. To serve: Unmold onto crisp lettuce. Garnish edge with whole shrimp. *Makes 8 servings.*

Salads With Style

Tossed Green Salad
(pictured)

½ teaspoon salt
¼ teaspoon freshly ground pepper
⅛ teaspoon ground cumin seed
1 small clove garlic, minced
2 tablespoons tarragon vinegar
6 tablespoons olive oil
1 quart crisp, torn escarole leaves
1 quart crisp, torn spinach leaves, heavy stems removed
1 small unpared cucumber, thinly sliced
½ cup thinly sliced radishes

1. Put the salt, pepper, cumin and garlic into a wooden salad bowl. Mash the garlic and seasonings with the back of a wooden spoon until the garlic disappears.
2. Stir the vinegar into the seasonings; add the oil, beating with a fork until dressing is smooth.
3. Arrange the crisp, dry greens on top of the dressing; cover with foil or plastic wrap and refrigerate until serving time. Do not toss.
4. Refrigerate the sliced cucumber and radish separately.
5. At serving time, add the cucumber and radish to the greens. Toss the salad gently and serve immediately on chilled plates. *Serves 4 to 6.*

Salad of Spring Greens

2 heads Bibb lettuce
2 Belgian endives
½ lb fresh spinach
½ lb dandelion greens
¼ bunch watercress

1 tablespoon snipped chives
1 tablespoon fresh tarragon sprigs
½ cup bottled Italian-style salad dressing

1. Separate leaves of lettuce and endives. Remove stems from spinach. Remove coarse stems from dandelion greens and watercress. Wash all greens thoroughly in cold water. Drain well; lay on paper or linen towel to dry or spin in a salad dryer. Place in crisper several hours or overnight.
2. Into large salad bowl, break lettuce, endive, spinach and dandelion greens into bite-size pieces; divide watercress into sprigs.
3. In small jar, combine chives, tarragon and dressing; shake well. Drizzle over greens.
4. Toss greens until evenly coated. Serve immediately. *Makes 6 servings.*

Guacamole Mold

2 medium-size ripe tomatoes, peeled and seeded
2 ripe avocados (about 1 lb each)
2 tablespoons lemon juice
¼ cup chopped green pepper
½ cup finely chopped onion
1 teaspoon seasoned salt
⅛ teaspoon ground pepper
1 teaspoon chili powder
1 cup sour cream
1 cup mayonnaise or cooked salad dressing
3 env unflavored gelatine
1 cup cold water
Parsley sprigs

1. In large bowl, crush tomatoes with potato masher.
2. Halve avocados crosswise; discard pits; peel avocados. Slice into tomatoes. Crush to blend well. (Tomatoes and avocados may be puréed in a food processor fitted with the steel blade.)
3. Add lemon juice, green pepper, onion, seasoned salt, pepper, chili powder, sour cream and mayonnaise. Mix to blend well.
4. Meanwhile, sprinkle gelatine over cold water in small saucepan; let stand 5 minutes to soften.
5. Place saucepan over low heat, stirring until gelatine is dissolved. Refrigerate until consistency of unbeaten egg white—about 20 minutes.
6. Stir gelatine into avocado mixture to combine well.
7. Turn into a 1½-quart melon mold. Refrigerate until firm—4 hours —or overnight.
8. To unmold: Run a small spatula around edge of mold. Invert over platter; shake gently to release. If necessary, place a hot, wet dishcloth over bottom of mold; shake again to release.
9. Garnish with parsley. *Makes 6 to 8 servings.*

Cucumber-Yogurt Dressing

1 large cucumber
1 cup yogurt
2 tablespoons finely chopped fresh mint
½ teaspoon salt
Mixed salad greens

1. Pare cucumber; quarter lengthwise. Cut each quarter crosswise into thin slices.
2. In medium bowl, combine yogurt, cucumber, mint and salt; mix well.
3. Refrigerate, covered, 1 hour to blend flavors.
4. Serve over mixed salad greens. *Makes 6 servings (2 cups), ⅓ cup per serving.*

Salads With Style

Crab Salad

- **2 cans (7½-oz size) king-crab meat, drained**
- **½ cup low-calorie mayonnaise**
- **2 tablespoons chopped parsley**
- **2 tablespoons snipped chives**
- **1 teaspoon Worcestershire sauce**
- **½ teaspoon lemon juice**
- **1 cup diced, pared cucumber**
- **Crisp lettuce cups**
- **4 hard-cooked eggs, sliced**

1. If necessary, remove cartilage from crabmeat.
2. In medium bowl, combine mayonnaise, parsley, chives, Worcestershire and lemon juice; mix well. Add crabmeat and cucumber; toss.
3. Refrigerate, covered, until well chilled—about 1 hour.
4. To serve: Arrange lettuce cups on 4 serving plates. Fill with salad. Garnish with sliced egg. *Makes 4 servings.*

Shrimp-And-Tomato Aspic

- **1 bay leaf**
- **2 teaspoons salt**
- **¼ cup white vinegar**
- **½ teaspoon pickling spice**
- **1 lb deveined, shelled raw shrimp**
- **1 env unflavored gelatine**
- **1 teaspoon sugar**
- **1⅔ cups tomato juice**
- **2 tablespoons red-wine vinegar**
- **3 tablespoons lemon juice**
- **2 tablespoons finely chopped chives**
- **Crisp salad greens**

1. In medium saucepan, combine 3½ cups water with bay leaf, salt, white vinegar and pickling spice. Bring to boiling.
2. Add shrimp; bring back to boiling; reduce heat and simmer, uncovered, 5 minutes. Drain shrimp.
3. Set aside 4 of the shrimp for garnish. Coarsely chop rest of the shrimp; set aside.
4. In small saucepan, combine gelatine and sugar. Stir in 1 cup tomato juice; stir, over low heat, to dissolve gelatine. Pour into medium bowl.
5. Add rest of tomato juice, the red-wine vinegar and lemon juice. Refrigerate until consistency of unbeaten egg white—about 1½ hours.
6. Fold chopped shrimp and chives into gelatine mixture. Turn into a 3½-cup mold. Refrigerate until firm—3 hours—or overnight.
7. To unmold: Run a small spatula around edge of mold.

Invert over platter; shake gently to release. If necessary, place a hot, wet dishcloth over bottom of mold; shake again to release.
8. Garnish with salad greens and reserved whole shrimp. *Makes 4 to 6 servings.*

Summer-Fruit Salad With Blue-Cheese Dressing

Blue-Cheese Dressing

- **½ cup mayonnaise or cooked salad dressing**
- **¼ cup bottled herb dressing**
- **½ cup crumbled blue cheese**
- **2 tablespoons milk**
- **2 tablespoons lemon juice**

- **3 fresh pears**
- **2 tablespoons lemon juice**
- **3 navel oranges**
- **1 pint box blueberries**
- **1 pint box large strawberries, unhulled**
- **Crisp iceberg lettuce**
- **4 cups honeydew-melon balls**

1. Make Blue-Cheese Dressing: In small bowl, combine mayonnaise, herb dressing, blue cheese, milk and 2 tablespoons lemon juice. Beat until well combined.
2. Refrigerate dressing, covered.
3. Pare pears; halve; core. Dip pears in lemon juice. Peel oranges, removing any white membrane; cut each orange crosswise into 6 slices. Wash blueberries and strawberries; drain. Refrigerate fruit until ready to use.
4. To serve: Arrange lettuce leaves on 6 chilled salad plates. Place pear halves, cut side up, on lettuce; spoon blueberries evenly over pears.
5. Arrange 3 orange slices and ⅔ cup melon balls around pear on each plate. Garnish with strawberries.
6. Serve dressing over salad. *Makes 6 servings.*

Molded Fruit-And-Ginger Salad

- **1 can (13½ oz) pineapple chunks**
- **Boiling water**
- **1 pkg (6 oz) orange-pineapple-flavored gelatin**
- **1 pkg (1 lb) frozen cantaloupe and honeydew-melon balls, thawed and drained**
- **¼ cup finely chopped, crystallized ginger**
- **Parsley sprigs**

1. Drain pineapple chunks, reserving ⅔ cup syrup.
2. Pour 2⅓ cups boiling water over gelatin in large

Salads With Style

bowl, stirring to dissolve gelatin. Add reserved pine-apple syrup.

3. Refrigerate until the consistency of unbeaten egg white—about 1 hour.
4. Fold in fruit and ginger. Turn into a 4½-cup mold. Refrigerate until firm—2 to 3 hours.
5. To unmold: Run a small spatula around edge of mold. Invert over platter; shake gently to release. If necessary, place a hot, wet dishcloth over bottom of mold; shake again to release. Garnish with parsley. *Makes 4 to 6 servings.*

Our Best Perfection Salad

2 env unflavored gelatine
¼ cup sugar
½ teaspoon salt
1 chicken-bouillon cube, dissolved in 1½ cups boiling water
⅓ cup tarragon-wine vinegar
½ cup lemon juice
1¼ cups cold water
1 pkg (10 oz) frozen peas and carrots
1 cup canned whole-kernel corn, drained
1 cup finely shredded green cabbage
Crisp salad greens

1. In large bowl, combine gelatine with sugar and salt. Add hot bouillon, stirring until the gelatine is dissolved.
2. Stir in vinegar, lemon juice and cold water.
3. Refrigerate until consistency of unbeaten egg white—about 1½ to 2 hours.
4. Meanwhile, cook peas and carrots as package label directs; drain. Refrigerate until ready to use.
5. Gently fold all of the vegetables except salad greens into gelatine mixture. Turn into a 1½-quart mold or into a 9-by-5-by-3-inch loaf pan. Refrigerate until firm—3 to 4 hours.
6. To unmold: Run a small spatula around edge of mold. Invert over platter; shake gently to release. If necessary, place a hot, wet dishcloth over bottom of mold; shake again to release.
7. Garnish with salad greens. *Makes 4 to 6 servings.*

Tossed Zucchini Salad

⅓ cup salad or olive oil
2 tablespoons lemon juice
2 tablespoons white-wine vinegar
1 teaspoon sugar
2 teaspoons chopped parsley
¾ teaspoon salt
¼ teaspoon ground pepper
3 medium zucchini (1 lb)
2 large red Delicious apples (1 lb)
1 cup sliced red onion
1 green pepper, washed and coarsely chopped (1 cup)
1 cup celery, sliced thinly on the diagonal
½ cup sliced radishes
Crisp salad greens

1. In large bowl, combine salad oil, lemon juice, vinegar, sugar, parsley, salt and pepper; mix well.
2. Wash zucchini; cut into quarters lengthwise; slice into ½-inch pieces.
3. Wash and quarter apples; remove cores; do not pare. Cut apple into ½-inch pieces.
4. Add zucchini, apple, onion, green pepper, celery and radish slices to dressing in large bowl; mix well.
5. Refrigerate, covered, 1 to 2 hours to chill well.
6. To serve: Line bowl with salad greens; turn zucchini mixture into center, mounding. *Makes 8 to 10 servings.*

Peach-Currant-Salad Mold

1 can (1 lb, 13 oz) cling-peach halves
1 cup boiling water
1 pkg (3 oz) peach-flavored gelatin
2 tablespoons currant jelly
2 tablespoons orange marmalade
2 tablespoons toasted, slivered almonds
Crisp salad greens

1. Drain peaches, reserving 1 cup syrup.
2. Pour boiling water over gelatin, stirring to dissolve gelatin. Add reserved syrup from peaches.
3. Pour 3 tablespoons gelatin mixture into each of 6 (6-oz) custard cups. Refrigerate until firm—about 15 minutes.

Salads With Style

4. Refrigerate remaining gelatin mixture until consistency of unbeaten egg white—about 1 hour.
5. In small bowl, combine currant jelly, marmalade and almonds. Place 1 tablespoon mixture on top of set gelatin in each custard cup.
6. Invert a peach half over jelly mixture in each custard cup.
7. Pour rest of gelatin mixture over peaches. Refrigerate until firm—about 2 hours—or overnight.
8. To unmold: Run a small spatula around edge of cups. Invert over serving plate; shake gently to release. If necessary, place a hot, wet dishcloth over bottom of cups; shake again to release.
9. Garnish with salad greens. Nice served with ham or turkey. *Makes 6 servings.*

Curried-Chicken-Salad Mold

2 env unflavored gelatine
Water
1 can (10¾ oz) condensed cream-of-chicken soup, undiluted
1 chicken-bouillon cube, dissolved in 1 cup boiling water
2 tablespoons lemon juice
1½ teaspoons curry powder
1 cup coarsely chopped, cooked chicken
¼ cup chopped pimiento
¼ cup sweet-pickle relish, drained
4 pimiento-stuffed olives, sliced
Watercress sprigs

1. In large bowl, sprinkle gelatine over ½ cup cold water; let stand 5 minutes to soften.
2. In small saucepan, heat chicken soup with 1 cup water. Add gelatine, stirring until gelatine is dissolved.
3. Remove from heat. Stir in bouillon and lemon juice.
4. Blend curry with 1½ tablespoons cold water, stirring to dissolve curry. Stir into gelatine mixture.
5. Refrigerate until consistency of unbeaten egg white—about 1½ to 2 hours.
6. Fold in chicken, pimiento and pickle relish. Turn into a 5-cup mold.
7. Refrigerate until firm—2 to 3 hours—or overnight.
8. To unmold: Run a small spatula around edge of mold.

Invert over platter; shake to release. If necessary, place a hot, wet dishcloth over bottom of mold; shake again to release.
9. To serve, garnish with sliced olives and watercress sprigs. *Makes 4 to 6 servings.*

Crab-And-Cucumber Mold

¼ cup white-wine vinegar
¼ cup lemon juice
¼ cup cold water
1 env unflavored gelatine
1 cup sour cream
1 can (7½ oz) crabmeat, drained and flaked
¼ cup diced pimiento
1 cup pared, diced cucumber
Watercress sprigs

1. In small saucepan, combine vinegar, lemon juice and cold water. Sprinkle gelatine over surface; let stand 5 minutes to soften.
2. Stir, over low heat, to dissolve gelatine. Remove from heat. Stir in sour cream.
3. Refrigerate until consistency of unbeaten egg white—about 30 minutes.
4. Stir in rest of ingredients except watercress. Turn into a 3-cup ring mold. Refrigerate until firm—3 to 4 hours.
5. To unmold: Run a small spatula around edge of mold. Invert over platter; shake gently to release. If necessary, place a hot, wet dishcloth over bottom of mold; shake again to release.
6. To serve, garnish with watercress sprigs. *Makes 4 servings.*

Raspberry-Cheese Mold

1 pkg (10 oz) frozen raspberries, thawed
1 cup boiling water
1 pkg (6 oz) raspberry-flavored gelatin
1 cup (8 oz) cream-style cottage cheese
½ cup mayonnaise
⅓ cup lemon juice
Crisp salad greens

Salads With Style

1. Drain raspberries, reserving ½ cup juice.
2. Pour boiling water over gelatin in medium bowl; stir to dissolve gelatin. Add reserved raspberry juice.
3. Refrigerate until consistency of unbeaten egg white—about 1 hour.
4. In electric blender (or with portable electric mixer), at low speed, blend cottage cheese, mayonnaise and lemon juice until smooth.
5. Beat in chilled gelatin mixture. With spoon, fold in raspberries.
6. Pour into a 1-quart mold. Refrigerate until firm—2 to 3 hours.
7. To unmold: Run a small spatula around edge of mold. Invert over platter; shake gently to release. If necessary, place a hot, wet dishcloth over bottom of mold; shake again to release.
8. Garnish with salad greens. *Makes 4 to 6 servings.*

Pineapple-And-Cottage-Cheese Salad Ring

1 can (1 pt, 2 oz) pineapple juice
⅓ cup mayonnaise or cooked salad dressing
1 can (1 lb, 4½ oz) crushed pineapple
  Water
2 env unflavored gelatine
¼ cup lemon juice
¼ cup sugar
⅛ teaspoon salt
  Few drops yellow food color
1 cup finely chopped celery
1 cup creamed cottage cheese
  Crisp salad greens

1. Mix ¼ cup pineapple juice with the mayonnaise. Refrigerate, covered, until needed. Pour remaining juice into 1-quart measure; add syrup drained from crushed pineapple and water, if necessary, to make 3 cups liquid.
2. In medium saucepan, sprinkle gelatine over 1 cup pineapple liquid to soften. Then place over low heat, stirring constantly, until gelatine is dissolved. Remove gelatine mixture from heat; add remaining pineapple liquid, the lemon juice, sugar, salt and yellow food color, stirring until the sugar is dissolved.

3. Turn into bowl. Refrigerate until mixture is consistency of unbeaten egg white—about 1 hour.
4. Fold in crushed pineapple, celery and cottage cheese. Turn into 1½-quart ring mold that has been rinsed in cold water.
5. Refrigerate until firm enough to unmold—several hours or overnight.
6. To serve: Run a small spatula around edge of mold. Invert over platter; place a hot, damp dishcloth over inverted mold and shake gently to release. Garnish with salad greens. Place mayonnaise mixture in cup in center of mold. *Makes 6 to 8 servings.*

Curried-Chicken-And-Fresh-Fruit Salad

Curry Mayonnaise
½ cup mayonnaise or cooked salad dressing
1 tablespoon chopped, preserved ginger in syrup
2 teaspoons curry powder
1 teaspoon grated onion
½ teaspoon salt
½ cup heavy cream, whipped

3 cups cubed, cooked chicken or turkey
¼ cup bottled oil-and-vinegar dressing
2 cups fresh pineapple in 1-inch chunks; or 1 can (1 lb, 4½ oz) pineapple chunks, drained
1½ cups diced, pared apple (1 large)
1½ cups seedless green grapes
¼ cup chutney
¼ cup chopped green pepper
  Crisp lettuce
  Watercress sprigs (optional)

1. Make Curry Mayonnaise: In small bowl, combine mayonnaise, ginger, curry powder, onion and salt; mix until well blended. Fold in cream just until combined. Refrigerate, covered, until needed.
2. In large bowl, combine chicken and oil-and-vinegar dressing; toss until well coated. Refrigerate, covered, at least 2 hours.
3. Add pineapple, apple, grapes, chutney and green pepper to chicken; mix well. Gently fold in curry mayonnaise until well blended.
4. Refrigerate, covered, until chilled—about 2 hours.

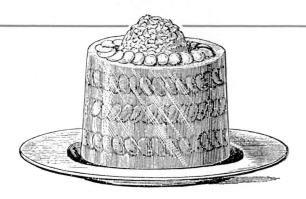

Salads With Style

5. To serve: Arrange lettuce leaves on platter. Mound salad in center. If desired, garnish with watercress sprigs. *Makes 6 to 8 servings.*

Winter-Salad Mold

2 env unflavored gelatine
¾ cup cold water
1 can (6 oz) frozen grapefruit-juice concentrate, undiluted
3 ice cubes
1 can (1 lb) grapefruit sections, undrained
½ cup diced celery
½ cup diced, unpared red apple
Crisp salad greens

1. Sprinkle gelatine over cold water in medium saucepan; let stand 5 minutes to soften. Over low heat, stir until gelatine is dissolved.
2. Remove from heat. Add grapefruit juice and ice cubes; stir until ice is dissolved.
3. Add grapefruit, celery and apple. Turn into a 1-quart mold. Refrigerate until firm—2 to 3 hours.
4. To unmold: Run a small spatula around edge of mold. Invert over platter; shake gently to release. If necessary, place a hot, wet dishcloth over bottom of mold; shake again to release. Garnish with salad greens. *Makes 6 servings.*

Apple-Mint Mold

½ cup boiling water
1 pkg (3 oz) lime-flavored gelatin
¼ cup lime juice
1 cup canned applesauce
⅛ teaspoon peppermint extract
½ cup coarsely chopped walnuts
Crisp salad greens

1. Pour boiling water over gelatin in medium bowl, stirring to dissolve gelatin. Add lime juice. Refrigerate until consistency of unbeaten egg white—about 30 minutes.
2. Fold in applesauce, peppermint extract and walnuts, combining well.

3. Turn into a 2-cup mold.
4. Refrigerate about 2 hours or until firm.
5. To unmold: Run a small spatula around edge of mold. Invert over platter; shake gently to release. If necessary, place a hot, wet dishcloth over bottom of mold; shake again to release. Garnish with salad greens. Nice served with lamb. *Makes 6 servings.*

Chef's Salad Deluxe

Cheese Dressing
½ cup salad oil
¼ cup mayonnaise or cooked salad dressing
1 jar (5 oz) sharp-cheese spread
3 tablespoons white vinegar
1 teaspoon Worcestershire sauce
½ teaspoon paprika
¼ teaspoon salt

3 bacon slices, halved
4 frankfurters
1 medium head iceberg lettuce, torn into bite-size pieces
½ small green pepper, cut into thin strips
1 tomato, cut into wedges
½ medium red onion, sliced into thin rings

1. Make Cheese Dressing: In small bowl, combine oil, mayonnaise, cheese spread, vinegar, Worcestershire, paprika and salt. Beat with portable electric mixer until well blended. Refrigerate, covered, until well chilled—about 2 hours.
2. Meanwhile, in medium skillet, sauté bacon until crisp. Drain bacon well on paper towels, reserving 1 tablespoon drippings.
3. Halve frankfurters lengthwise; cut each half into quarters.
4. In reserved bacon drippings, sauté frankfurters 5 minutes, stirring occasionally; drain.
5. Refrigerate bacon, frankfurters and remaining salad ingredients until well chilled.
6. Just before serving, turn lettuce into a large salad bowl; arrange bacon, frankfurters, green pepper, tomato and onion attractively over lettuce.
7. Toss salad to mix well. Serve with Cheese Dressing. *Makes 6 servings.*

A CELEBRATION OF DELICIOUS DESSERTS

America has always had a love affair with sweets. After all, they go hand-in-hand with all kinds of celebrations and as joyous finales to meals. In bringing you this classic collection of desserts, we searched and tasted our way through our recipe archives to carefully select these best-loved favorites. Included are a fruits-and-berries bonanza of juicy pies, tortes and soufflés; a spectacular array of fabulously rich cakes; and a frozen fantasy of ice-cream creations that will melt in your mouth. Now that's worth celebrating!

Fabulous 'n' Fruity Delights

● ● ●

In the wonderful world of desserts, few ingredients match the versatility of fruits. Their juicy goodness can be puréed into soufflés, baked into pies, simmered into sauces and glazed onto cakes. Here is a glorious showing of luscious, ripe-for-the-tasting desserts made with our country's native berries. Frozen Raspberry Soufflé, **center,** is rich with cream, eggs and puréed fruit and crowned with raspberry glaze. **At far left** is Strawberry-Blueberry Dessert Cake, a crumb-topped batter with a brightly glazed cap of berries. **Below it,** Raspberries Sabayon in Cookie Shells makes an elegant presentation. Finally, **in the foreground,** tart cherries and almond cream peek out from under a lattice-work crust in Cherry-Cream Pie. The recipes for all of our fruited treats begin on page 326.

315

The elegant crystal dish, **opposite page,** holds a treasure trove of summer's fresh red currants, tiny and tart. **On this page,** a trio of beautiful red-currant creations: **At top,** Currant Bavarian Torte with its luscious rum-flavored filling, chocolate-crumb crust and sweet currant glaze mounded inside a ruffle of cream; **below it,** warm cream-cheese-filled Devonshire Crêpes With Currant Sauce; and **at left,** Lattice Currant Pie, baked till the juices bubble, then dusted with confectioners' sugar. *Recipes begin on page 328.*

Blackberries, like most of their kin, are available both wild and cultivated. Handfuls of soft, ripe blackberries, **above,** fill this colorful country mug with their subtle, fresh-picked flavor and deep luster. They're also the crowning glory in our nut-encrusted Blackberry Tart, **left,** with a puff-pastry shell and velvety custard center. Juicy, red raspberries make a sweet substitute for the blackberries. *See recipe on page 331.*

From orchards all over the country comes America's favorite fruit in a crunchy variety of tastes, colors and recipe applications. In this Lemon Mousse With Blueberries, **below,** ladyfingers embrace a smooth, spirited mousse mixture that's mounded high with glazed fresh berries and fluted with whipped cream. **On opposite page,** tart Granny Smiths are ideal for this Strasbourg Apple Tart, a single-crusted sensation that's further enhanced with a rich, creamy custard partway through the baking. *See recipes on pages 330 and 331.*

Fresh, juicy lemons contribute their tangy juices and grated peel to create this old-fashioned Lemon-Meringue Pie that's so gossamer, it seems to float off the plate. **Below,** you'll recognize a classic taste of Americana, Strawberry Shortcake: Individual home-made biscuits are split to hold a generous portion of plump, sweetened, ruby red strawberries, then dolloped with fresh cream. *See recipes on pages 332 and 336.*

VICTOR SCOCOZZA

Clockwise from top right: Tangerine Mousse With Kiwi Sauce is a show-off dessert that's light, airy and surprisingly simple to make; raspberry jam and a tart lemon-custard filling alternate with layers of flaky puff pastry in our elegant almond-studded Lemon-Raspberry Napoleon; sweet heart-shaped biscuits top this Mixed-Fruit Cobbler—a mélange of canned fruits that bakes till lightly browned and bubbly; Orange-Coconut Cheesecake is a smooth blend of cheeses and citrus fruit generously sprinkled with toasted coconut; and Chocolate-Banana Parfait layers homemade liqueur-laced chocolate pudding with crumbled cookies and soft, sweet chunks of banana. *Recipes begin on page 333.*

Fabulous 'n' Fruity Delights

continued from page 315

Frozen Raspberry or Strawberry Soufflé
(pictured)

3   egg whites
Sugar
½   cup water
¼   teaspoon cream of tartar
Dash salt
1   pkg (10 oz) frozen raspberries or strawberries, thawed, or 1 pint fresh raspberries or strawberries, hulled
3   egg yolks
Few drops of red food color (optional)
1½   cups heavy cream
½   cup heavy cream, whipped stiff

Glaze (optional)
1   pkg (10 oz) frozen raspberries or strawberries, thawed
1   tablespoon cornstarch

1. Prepare a 1½-quart soufflé dish: Fold 26-inch-long piece of waxed paper lengthwise into thirds. Lightly butter one side. With string, tie collar (buttered side in) around soufflé dish to form a 2-inch rim above top.
2. In small bowl of electric mixer, let egg whites warm to room temperature—about 1 hour.
3. In a 1-quart saucepan, combine ½ cup sugar with water; cook over low heat, stirring, until sugar is dissolved.
4. Bring to boiling over medium heat; boil without stirring, uncovered, to 236F on candy thermometer or until syrup spins a 2-inch thread when dropped from spoon.
5. Meanwhile, at high speed, beat egg whites with cream of tartar and salt just until stiff peaks form when beaters are slowly raised.
6. Pour hot syrup in thin stream over egg whites, beating constantly until mixture forms stiff peaks when beaters are raised. Chill bowl over ice cubes.
7. Purée 1 package thawed berries, or the pint of fresh berries, in food processor. Makes 1 cup.
8. In top of double boiler, combine ¾ cup puréed berries, the egg yolks, food color and ¾ cup sugar; mix well.

9. Cook over hot, not boiling, water (water should not touch bottom of double-boiler top), stirring constantly, until mixture thickens—12 to 15 minutes.
10. Remove pan from hot water. Chill over ice cubes, stirring occasionally, until cold—about 30 minutes.
11. In large bowl, whip 1½ cups cream until stiff. With wire whisk or rubber spatula, fold the cooled berry custard and rest of purée into whipped cream; then fold in meringue. Turn into prepared soufflé dish. Freeze until firm—several hours or overnight.
12. Remove paper collar. Place the whipped cream in pastry bag with number-6 star tip. Pipe edge decoratively. Refrigerate.
13. Make Glaze, if desired: Drain berries well, reserving ½ cup liquid.
14. In a small saucepan, combine the reserved liquid and the cornstarch; blend until smooth.
15. Over medium heat, bring to boiling, stirring; boil 1 minute. Remove from heat; cool completely. Stir until smooth; fold in berries.
16. Spoon glaze in center of soufflé. Refrigerate. *Makes 8 servings.*

Strawberry-Blueberry Dessert Cake
(pictured)

Crumb Topping
¼   cup all-purpose flour
1   teaspoon sugar
2   teaspoons butter or margarine
½   teaspoon vanilla extract

Cake
1½   cups sifted cake flour
1¼   teaspoons baking powder
¼   teaspoon salt
½   cup (1 stick) butter or margarine, softened
1   cup sugar
2   eggs
1   teaspoon vanilla extract
½   cup milk

½   pint strawberries, washed, hulled and halved
¼   cup blueberries, washed
2   tablespoons currant jelly, melted
½   cup heavy cream, whipped (optional)

Fabulous 'n' Fruity Delights

1. Preheat oven to 350F. Grease well and flour an 8-inch springform pan.
2. Prepare Crumb Topping: In small bowl, with fork, blend together flour, 1 teaspoon sugar, 2 teaspoons butter and ½ teaspoon vanilla until mixture resembles coarse crumbs.
3. Make Cake: Sift cake flour with baking powder and salt; set aside. In large bowl of electric mixer, at high speed, beat butter and sugar until light. Add eggs, one at a time, beating well after each addition. Add vanilla. Continue beating, occasionally scraping side of bowl with rubber spatula, until light and fluffy—about 2 minutes.
4. At low speed, beat in flour mixture (in fourths) alternately with milk (in thirds), beginning and ending with flour mixture. Beat just until smooth—about 1 minute.
5. Pour batter into prepared pan; sprinkle with Crumb Topping.
6. Bake 40 to 45 minutes or until surface springs back when gently pressed with fingertip. Remove to rack to cool 10 minutes. Remove ring from pan.
7. Arrange strawberries and blueberries in center of cake, as pictured. Brush fruit with melted currant jelly. Serve with whipped cream, if desired. *Makes 8 servings.*

Raspberries Sabayon in Cookie Shells
(pictured)

Sabayon Sauce
4 egg yolks
2 tablespoons sugar
¼ cup Grand Marnier
⅓ cup heavy cream, whipped

2 pint boxes red raspberries, washed and drained
5 or 6 Cookie Shells, recipe follows

1. Make Sabayon Sauce: In top of double boiler, with electric mixer at medium speed, beat egg yolks until

thick. Gradually beat in sugar; beat until mixture is light and soft peaks form when beaters are slowly raised.
2. Place double-boiler top over simmering water (water in bottom should not touch base of top). Slowly beat in Grand Marnier; continue beating until mixture is fluffy and mounds—takes about 5 minutes.
3. Remove double-boiler top from hot water; set in ice water. Beat the custard mixture until cool. Gently fold in whipped cream.
4. Refrigerate sauce, covered.
5. Spoon berries into Cookie Shells. Stir sauce; pass or spoon over fruit. *Makes 5 or 6 servings.*

Cookie Shells

¼ cup (½ stick) butter, softened
⅓ cup sugar
2 egg whites
⅛ teaspoon vanilla extract
½ cup sifted all-purpose flour

1. Combine butter and sugar in medium bowl of electric mixer. Beat until smooth and fluffy.
2. Add egg whites, one at a time, beating well after each addition. At low speed, beat in vanilla and flour.
3. Preheat oven to 350F. Make one cookie shell at a time. Grease a 7-inch round in the center of a cookie sheet.
4. Measure 3 tablespoons cookie batter onto round. Spead to make a 7-inch round, using greased round as a guide.
5. Bake one cookie at a time, 6 minutes, until edges are lightly browned.
6. Meanwhile, invert several glasses with 2½-inch bottoms. Cut 2½-inch squares in foil; grease well; fit over glasses.
7. Remove cookie from oven. Loosen edge of cookie with spatula. Invert onto a prepared glass. Press cookie edges in toward glass with hand, making a flute between each finger. Set aside to cool.

Fabulous 'n' Fruity Delights

8. Repeat with remaining dough. Remove only one cookie from oven at a time and work quickly to prevent cracking.

9. When cookies are cool, turn right side up, and peel off foil. Wrap tightly and store in a cool dry place. Best used within two weeks. *Makes 5 or 6 cookie shells.*

Cherry-Cream Pie
(pictured)

1 pkg (10 or 11 oz) piecrust mix

Cream Filling
  1 pkg (3¼ oz) vanilla-pudding-and-pie-filling mix
  2 egg yolks, slightly beaten
1½ cups milk
  1 teaspoon almond extract

Cherry Filling
  4 cups pitted fresh red cherries or 2 cans (1-lb size) tart red cherries, packed in water
  1 cup sugar
½ cup all-purpose flour
⅛ teaspoon salt
  2 tablespoons butter or margarine
¼ teaspoon almond extract
    Few drops red food color (optional)

¼ cup currant jelly, melted
  1 egg yolk
  2 teaspoons water

1. Prepare piecrust mix as package label directs. Form into a ball. On a lightly floured pastry cloth or floured surface, roll two-thirds of pastry into a 12-inch round. Use to line a 9-inch pie plate; refrigerate with rest of pastry.

2. Make Cream Filling: Prepare pudding mix as package label directs, adding 2 egg yolks and the milk. When pudding is cooked, stir in 1 teaspoon almond extract. Pour into a bowl; place sheet of waxed paper directly on surface. Set in bowl of ice cubes to chill—about 30 minutes.

3. Make Cherry Filling: If using fresh cherries, add ¼ cup water and heat gently, stirring, until mixture

comes to boiling. Drain liquid, reserving ¾ cup. (Add water if necessary.) If using canned cherries, drain cherries, reserving ¾ cup liquid.

4. In small bowl, combine sugar, flour and salt; stir into cherry liquid in saucepan. Bring to boiling, stirring constantly. Reduce heat and simmer 5 minutes. Mixture will be thickened. Stir in butter. Stir in almond extract and food color. Add cherries; place in a larger bowl of ice cubes to chill—30 minutes; stir occasionally.

5. Preheat oven to 400F. Spread Cream Filling in bottom of pie shell. Spoon Cherry Filling over Cream Filling. Pour currant jelly over the top.

6. Roll out rest of pastry to form a 10-inch round. With knife or pastry wheel, cut into 12 strips ¼ inch wide. Slightly moisten rim of pie shell. Arrange six strips across jelly; press ends to rim of shell; trim the ends, if necessary.

7. Arrange the rest of strips at right angles to the first strips to form a lattice. Bring overhang of the pastry up over ends of strips; crimp edge decoratively. Mix egg yolk with 2 teaspoons water; brush on lattice, not edge.

8. Bake 40 to 45 minutes or until crust is golden. Remove to wire rack to cool; serve warm. *Makes 8 servings.*

Devonshire Crêpes With Currant Sauce
(pictured)

Crêpes
1½ cups milk
1⅔ cups all-purpose flour
  2 tablespoons salad oil
  3 eggs

Devonshire Filling
  2 pkg (8-oz size) cream cheese, softened at room temperature
¾ cup sour cream
¼ cup confectioners' sugar
  2 tablespoons lemon juice

    Currant Sauce, recipe follows
    Confectioners' sugar

Fabulous 'n' Fruity Delights

1. Make Crêpes: In medium bowl, with rotary beater or portable electric mixer, beat milk with flour and salad oil until smooth. Add eggs; beat until mixture is well combined.
2. Slowly heat a 7-inch skillet until a little water sizzles when dropped on it. Brush pan lightly with salad oil. Pour about ¼ cup batter into skillet, tilting pan so batter covers bottom completely.
3. Cook until lightly browned on underside. Loosen edge; turn; cook until browned on other side. Remove from pan; cool on wire rack; then stack with waxed paper between crêpes. Repeat with rest of batter to make 18 crêpes. Lightly brush pan with oil before making each.
4. Make Devonshire Filling: In medium bowl, combine all filling ingredients; beat with portable electric mixer until smooth. *Makes 3 cups.*
5. Spread 2 tablespoons filling on each crêpe. Fold each in half, then in half again. Arrange on ovenproof serving platter. Keep warm in low oven.
6. Make Currant Sauce. Spoon warm sauce over crêpes. Sprinkle with confectioners' sugar. *Makes 8 servings.*

Currant Sauce

 1 **cup red currants**
 ½ **cup sugar**
 1 **tablespoon cornstarch**
 ½ **cup water**
 ¼ **cup currant jelly**

1. Wash and stem currants.
2. In small saucepan, combine sugar and cornstarch. Add water.
3. Over medium heat, bring to boiling, stirring constantly. Boil 1 minute.
4. Add currants and the currant jelly; stir just until jelly is melted. Remove from heat. Serve warm over Devonshire Crêpes. *Makes 1¼ cups.*

Currant Bavarian Torte
(pictured)

1¼ **cups crushed chocolate wafers**
 ¼ **cup melted butter or margarine**

Rum Bavarian
 1 **env unflavored gelatine**
 ¼ **cup granulated sugar**
 ¼ **cup all-purpose flour**
    Dash salt
 5 **egg yolks**
 1 **cup milk**
 ¼ **cup rum**
 2 **egg whites, stiffly beaten**
 1 **cup heavy cream, chilled**
 2 **tablespoons confectioners' sugar**
 1 **teaspoon vanilla extract**

    Currant Glaze, recipe follows
 ½ **cup heavy cream**
 2 **tablespoons confectioners' sugar**

1. Lightly grease a 9-inch springform pan. In small bowl, combine crumbs and butter; mix well. Press into bottom of pan; refrigerate.
2. Make Rum Bavarian: In small, heavy saucepan, mix gelatine, granulated sugar, flour and salt; mix well.
3. In small bowl, beat egg yolks with milk and rum. Add to gelatine mixture; cook over medium heat, stirring constantly with wire whisk, until mixture thickens and comes to boiling.
4. Pour into medium bowl; set bowl in pan of ice and water; let stand, stirring occasionally, until cool—about 8 to 10 minutes. Fold in beaten egg whites.
5. Beat 1 cup heavy cream with 2 tablespoons confectioners' sugar until stiff; fold into gelatine mixture, mixing until smooth. Stir in vanilla. Turn into prepared pan, spreading evenly.
6. Refrigerate until firm—3 hours or overnight. Make Currant Glaze.
7. Before serving, remove side of springform pan. Spoon glaze over torte, mounding slightly in center.
8. In chilled bowl, combine heavy cream and confectioners' sugar. Beat with electric mixer until stiff.
9. Turn cream into pastry bag with number-5 tip. Make ruching around edge, as pictured. Refrigerate until ready to serve. *Makes 12 servings.*

Fabulous 'n' Fruity Delights

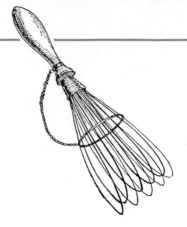

Currant Glaze

1½ **cups red currants**
½ **cup sugar**
1 **tablespoon cornstarch**
¼ **cup water**
2 **tablespoons currant jelly**

1. Wash and stem currants; drain well.
2. In small saucepan, combine sugar and cornstarch. Add water.
3. Over medium heat, bring to boiling, stirring constantly. Boil 1 minute.
4. Add currants and currant jelly; stir just until jelly is melted. Remove from heat. Cool completely.

Lemon Mousse With Blueberries
(pictured)

1 **pkg (3 oz) ladyfingers**

Lemon Mousse
1 **env unflavored gelatine**
¾ **cup granulated sugar**
2 **egg yolks**
⅓ **cup lemon juice**
¼ **cup water**
2 **tablespoons grated lemon peel**
2 **tablespoons Cointreau**
2 **egg whites at room temperature (¼ cup)**
1 **cup heavy cream, whipped stiff**

Glazed Blueberries
2 **cups fresh blueberries**
¼ **cup granulated sugar**
1 **tablespoon cornstarch**
¼ **cup water**
½ **cup heavy cream**
2 **tablespoons confectioners' sugar**

1. Lightly grease 1-quart soufflé dish. Split ladyfingers; arrange around side of mold vertically, rounded side against the mold.

2. Make Lemon Mousse: In top of double boiler, combine gelatine with ¼ cup granulated sugar.
3. In small bowl, with mixer at high speed, beat egg yolks until thick. Gradually beat in ¼ cup granulated sugar, beating until thick. Add lemon juice and ¼ cup water; mix until blended. Stir into gelatine mixture; mix well.
4. Cook, stirring constantly, over boiling water until gelatine dissolves and mixture is thickened—about 15 minutes. Remove from hot water; add lemon peel and Cointreau. Turn into a bowl set in another bowl of ice cubes; let stand, stirring occasionally, 10 minutes or until mixture mounds when dropped from a spoon.
5. In a small bowl, with mixer at high speed, beat egg whites until soft peaks form when beaters are slowly raised. Gradually beat in ¼ cup granulated sugar, beating until stiff peaks form when beaters are raised.
6. With whisk, using an under-and-over motion, fold gelatine mixture into egg whites; then fold whipped cream into gelatine. Turn into soufflé dish. Refrigerate 3 hours or overnight.
7. Make Glazed Blueberries: Mash ½ cup blueberries. In small saucepan, combine granulated sugar and cornstarch; add water and crushed blueberries, stirring until blended.
8. Over low heat, bring to boiling, stirring until mixture is thickened and translucent. Remove from heat. Stir in remaining blueberries; refrigerate.
9. To serve: Mound blueberries on top of mousse. Combine heavy cream and confectioners' sugar; beat until stiff. Turn into pastry tube with number-5 tip; pipe ruching around edge of dish, as pictured. *Makes 8 servings.*

Lattice Currant Pie
(pictured)

1 **pkg (11 oz) piecrust mix**
3 **cups red currants (1½ pints)**
1½ **cups granulated sugar**
¼ **cup quick-cooking tapioca**
  Dash salt
¼ **teaspoon almond extract**
  Confectioners' sugar

Fabulous 'n' Fruity Delights

1. Preheat oven to 400F.
2. Prepare pastry as package label directs. Shape pastry into a ball; divide in half.
3. On lightly floured surface, roll out half of pastry into an 11-inch circle; use to line 8-inch pie plate. Refrigerate along with rest of pastry.
4. Wash and stem currants; drain well.
5. In medium bowl, combine granulated sugar, tapioca and salt; add currants and almond extract; toss lightly until berries are coated with mixture. Turn currant mixture into pastry-lined pie plate, mounding in center.
6. Roll other half of pastry into a 10-inch circle. With knife or pastry wheel, cut eight ¾-inch strips.
7. Moisten edge of pie with cold water. Arrange three pastry strips across filling; press ends to rim. Place three more strips across first ones at right angles to make a lattice; press to rim. Trim edge.
8. Place remaining two strips around edge; press lightly.
9. Bake 30 to 40 minutes or until crust is golden and juice bubbles through.
10. Cool on wire rack. Before serving, sprinkle confectioners' sugar over the lattice and edge of pie. *Makes 8 servings.*

Note: For Lattice Currant-Raspberry Pie, use 2 cups red currants and 1 cup raspberries, washed and drained.

Blackberry Tart
(pictured)

½ pkg (17½-oz size) frozen puff pastry

Custard Filling

2 tablespoons granulated sugar
1 tablespoon cornstarch
1 cup milk
1 egg yolk
½ teaspoon vanilla extract

1 cup blackberries, washed and drained
2 tablespoons currant jelly, melted
1 cup confectioners' sugar
3 to 4 teaspoons milk
½ cup chopped walnuts or pecans

1. Remove puff pastry from freezer. Let stand at room temperature 20 minutes to thaw.
2. Preheat oven to 400F.
3. Unfold one sheet of pastry (two in a package); refreeze remaining sheet for later use.
4. With sharp knife, cut six ¾-inch strips from long side. The 10-by-4½-inch pastry rectangle is the base. Place on cookie sheet; prick all over with fork.
5. Brush edges with water; place a strip on each side of the rectangle. Cut a third strip into two pieces to fill in the ends. Place on narrow side of rectangle. Repeat with remaining strips of pastry to make a triple thickness of pastry around the edge.
6. Bake 15 to 20 minutes or until golden-brown. Remove to wire rack to cool.
7. Make Custard Filling: Combine granulated sugar and cornstarch. Gradually add to 1 cup milk, stirring constantly.
8. Cook, stirring, over medium heat until mixture starts to boil. Remove from heat; stir in egg yolk. Return to heat; cook, stirring, until custard is thick. Add vanilla. Chill over bowl of ice cubes.
9. To serve: Spoon custard into center of tart, spreading evenly. Arrange blackberries on top. Spoon melted jelly over berries.
10. In small bowl, mix confectioners' sugar and milk. Frost sides of tart and sprinkle with nuts. *Makes 6 servings.*

Note: Raspberries may be substituted for blackberries.

Strasbourg Apple Tart
(pictured)

1 pkg (11 oz) piecrust mix
2½ lb tart cooking apples
¾ cup sugar
1 teaspoon ground cinnamon
4 egg yolks
½ cup heavy cream

1. Make pastry as package label directs for a 9-inch pie shell. On lightly floured surface, roll out into an 11-inch circle. Use to line a 9-inch pie plate. Fold under

Fabulous 'n' Fruity Delights

edge of crust and press into an upright rim, about 1 inch high, to make a substantial edge. Flute decoratively. Refrigerate.

2. Preheat oven to 350F.
3. Pare and core apples; slice into eighths. Arrange apple slices in pie shell in an attractive pattern. Sprinkle with ½ cup sugar combined with the cinnamon.
4. Bake 30 minutes. Meanwhile, in small bowl, beat together egg yolks, cream and remaining ¼ cup sugar.
5. Remove pie from oven. Pour egg-yolk mixture over the apple; return to oven. Bake 35 minutes or until apple is tender and topping turns golden-brown. Serve slightly warm. *Makes 8 servings.*

Lemon-Meringue Pie
(pictured)

Flaky Pastry, recipe follows, or 9-inch baked pie shell

Lemon Filling
- ¼ cup cornstarch
- 3 tablespoons all-purpose flour
- 1¼ cups sugar
- ¼ teaspoon salt
- 2 cups water
- 4 egg yolks, slightly beaten
- ½ cup lemon juice
- 1 tablespoon grated lemon peel
- 1 tablespoon butter

Meringue
- 4 egg whites
- ¼ teaspoon cream of tartar
- ½ cup sugar

1. Prepare and bake Flaky Pastry; cool completely before filling.
2. Make Lemon Filling: In medium saucepan, combine cornstarch, flour, sugar and salt, mixing well. Gradually add 2 cups water, stirring until smooth.
3. Over medium heat, bring to boiling, stirring occasionally; boil 1 minute.
4. Remove from heat. Quickly stir some of hot mixture into egg yolks. Return to hot mixture; stir to blend.

5. Return to heat; cook over low heat 5 minutes, stirring occasionally.
6. Remove from heat. Stir in lemon juice, lemon peel and butter. Pour into pie shell.
7. Preheat oven to 400F.
8. Make Meringue: In medium bowl, with portable electric mixer at medium speed, beat egg whites with cream of tartar until frothy.
9. Gradually beat in sugar, 2 tablespoons at a time, beating after each addition. Then beat at high speed until stiff peaks form when beaters are slowly raised.
10. Spread over Lemon Filling, carefully sealing to edge of crust and swirling top decoratively.
11. Bake 7 to 9 minutes or until meringue is golden-brown. Let pie cool completely on wire rack—2½ to 3 hours. *Makes 8 servings.*

Flaky Pastry

- 1 cup all-purpose flour
- ½ teaspoon salt
- ⅓ cup plus 1 tablespoon shortening or ⅓ cup lard
- 2½ to 3 tablespoons ice water

1. In medium bowl, combine flour and salt. With pastry blender or 2 knives, using a short cutting motion, cut in shortening until mixture resembles coarse cornmeal.
2. Quickly sprinkle ice water, 1 tablespoon at a time, over pastry mixture, tossing lightly with fork after each addition and pushing dampened portion to side of bowl; sprinkle only dry portion remaining (pastry should be just moist enough to hold together, not sticky).
3. Shape pastry into a ball; flatten to 1-inch thickness; refrigerate at least 30 minutes or several hours.
4. On lightly floured surface, roll out pastry to 11-inch circle. Fold rolled pastry in half; carefully transfer to 9-inch pie plate, making sure fold is in center. Unfold pastry and fit carefully into pie plate. Do not stretch pastry.

Fabulous 'n' Fruity Delights

5. Fold under edge of crust and press into upright rim. Crimp decoratively. Prick entire surface evenly with fork. Refrigerate 30 minutes.
6. Preheat oven to 450F. Bake pie shell 8 to 10 minutes or until golden-brown. Cool completely on wire rack before filling. *Makes one 9-inch shell.*

Tangerine Mousse With Kiwi Sauce
(pictured)

    2   env unflavored gelatine
2½   cups cold water
    1   can (6 oz) frozen tangerine-juice concentrate, partially thawed
    1   tablespoon lemon juice
    1   cup frozen whipped topping with real cream, thawed

Kiwi Sauce
    4   medium kiwi fruit
    2   tablespoons confectioners' sugar

    Tangerine sections (optional)

1. In small saucepan, sprinkle gelatine over ½ cup cold water; let gelatine soften 1 minute. Over low heat, heat just until gelatine is dissolved; remove from heat. (Or use microwave oven; see Note.)
2. In medium bowl, combine tangerine juice, lemon juice and remaining cold water; stir until blended. Add gelatine mixture; stir to mix. Set bowl in large bowl of ice water. Stir tangerine mixture frequently until it begins to thicken and is the consistency of unbeaten egg whites—about 10 minutes. Remove bowl from ice water.
3. Using whisk, fold whipped topping into tangerine mixture until no white streaks remain and pour into 1-quart mold. Refrigerate until firm—at least 3 hours.
4. Meanwhile, make Kiwi Sauce: Pare kiwi and cut into 1-inch pieces. In food processor or electric blender, process or blend kiwi and confectioners' sugar just till smooth. (If desired, add more sugar to taste.) Chill sauce until ready to serve.

5. To unmold and serve: Loosen mousse around edge of mold with small spatula; shake mold gently. Dip mold in bowl or pan of warm water 5 seconds; dry mold with towel. Invert rimmed serving plate over mold; hold mold and plate; invert. Shake mold to release mousse; remove mold. Spoon some sauce around mousse; garnish with tangerine sections. Pass remaining sauce. *Makes 8 servings.*

Note: To dissolve gelatine in microwave oven: In glass measuring cup, sprinkle gelatine over ½ cup cold water; let stand 1 minute. Microwave at HIGH 15 seconds; stir. Microwave at HIGH 25 seconds longer; stir again.

Chocolate-Banana Parfait
(pictured)

⅓   cup sugar
    2   tablespoons cornstarch
    2   tablespoons unsweetened cocoa
⅛   teaspoon salt
1½   cups milk
    2   large egg yolks, lightly beaten
¼   cup cocoa-flavored cream liqueur
    1   tablespoon butter or margarine
    3   medium bananas
½   cup chocolate cookie crumbs
½   cup frozen whipped topping with real cream, thawed

1. In medium saucepan, combine sugar, cornstarch, cocoa and salt. Gradually stir in milk and yolks until well blended. Over medium heat, cook, stirring constantly, until mixture thickens and comes to a boil. Reduce heat; simmer, stirring, 30 seconds. Remove from heat; stir in cream liqueur and butter. Transfer chocolate pudding to medium bowl; press plastic wrap onto surface of pudding; refrigerate until cold.
2. Just before serving, assemble parfaits: Peel bananas; from widest part of one banana, cut a 1-inch crosswise section; roll section in cookie crumbs to coat; set aside. Cut leftover banana and other bananas

Fabulous 'n' Fruity Delights

lengthwise in quarters; then cut crosswise into ¼-inch pieces. In each of four parfait glasses, alternately layer chocolate pudding, remaining crumbs and banana pieces, dividing evenly. Top with whipped topping. Cut crumb-coated banana section crosswise into four slices. Place a banana slice on each parfait. *Makes 4 servings.*

Mixed-Fruit Cobbler
(pictured)

Biscuit Topping
- **2** cups all-purpose flour
- **2** tablespoons sugar
- **1** tablespoon baking powder
- **½** teaspoon salt
- **6** tablespoons (¾ stick) cold unsalted butter, cut into ½-inch slices
- **½** cup light cream or half-and-half

Fruit Filling
- **1** can (1 lb, 13 oz) peach slices, drained
- **1** can (1 lb, 13 oz) pear slices, drained
- **1** can (1 lb, 5 oz) cherry-pie filling
- **1** tablespoon finely minced, crystallized ginger
- **1** teaspoon grated lemon peel
- **1** large egg, lightly beaten with ½ teaspoon water

1. Make Biscuit Topping: In food-processor bowl or a medium bowl, combine flour, sugar, baking powder, salt and butter. With processor, turn machine on and off quickly several times until mixture resembles coarse cornmeal. (For mixing in bowl, use short cutting motions with pastry blender or two knives.) Add cream to flour mixture, processing or stirring just until dry ingredients are moistened and dough forms a ball. Press dough to 1-inch thickness; wrap in plastic wrap; refrigerate 20 minutes.

2. Meanwhile, make Fruit Filling: In bowl, combine peaches, pears, pie filling, ginger and lemon peel; stir to mix well. Pour into 12-by-9-inch (2½-quart), shallow, oval baking dish. Preheat oven to 375F.

3. On lightly floured surface, with floured rolling pin, roll dough to a 12-inch circle ¼ inch thick. With 3-inch heart or round biscuit cutter, cut 12 biscuits from dough. Place biscuits on fruit mixture; brush biscuit tops with egg mixture. Bake 30 minutes or until biscuits are lightly browned and Fruit Filling is bubbling. (Trimmings from biscuits can be baked separately and eaten as snacks.) Serve warm or at room temperature. *Makes 12 servings.*

Orange-Coconut Cheesecake
(pictured)

- **½** pkg (15-oz size) refrigerated ready-to-bake piecrusts (1 crust)
- **1** large navel orange
- **1** pkg (8 oz) cream cheese, softened
- **1** container (15 oz) part-skim ricotta cheese
- **1** can (8.5 oz) or 1 cup (from 15- or 16-oz size) cream of coconut
- **3** large eggs
- **½** cup flaked or shredded coconut, toasted (see Note)

1. Preheat oven to 450F. Unfold piecrust as package label directs; press out fold lines; patch any cracks; sprinkle crust with flour and roll to a 12-inch circle. Invert piecrust into a 9- or 10-inch fluted cake pan with removable bottom (or into 9-inch pie plate). Press crust against bottom and side of pan (or, in pie plate, fold crust edge under to make a ½-inch-high rim and crimp decoratively). Place pan or pie plate on cookie sheet; bake 7 minutes or just until crust begins to brown.

2. Meanwhile, grate 1 teaspoon peel from orange; reserve orange for garnish. In bowl, with portable electric mixer at medium speed, beat cream cheese and ricotta cheese until smooth. Beat in cream of coconut and orange peel; add eggs, one at a time, beating just until they are blended. Remove cookie sheet with crust from oven and reduce oven temperature to 350F. Pour cheese filling into crust; carefully return to oven. Bake 50 minutes or until cheesecake is puffed and center is set but still soft. (If needed, cover loosely

Fabulous 'n' Fruity Delights

with foil after 30 minutes to prevent overbrowning.) Cool cheesecake on wire rack. Refrigerate at least 1 hour.

3. Before serving: With sharp knife, cut off and discard all remaining peel and white part from reserved orange. Carefully cut along each membrane to remove orange sections. Remove side of pan from the cheesecake; place cake on serving plate. Sprinkle coconut evenly over top. Garnish with orange sections. *Makes 10 servings.*

Note: To toast flaked or shredded coconut, heat in heavy skillet, stirring frequently until lightly browned. Or toast the coconut in a baking pan in 350F oven, stirring occasionally, about 15 minutes or until coconut is lightly browned.

Fresh-Peach Ice Cream

    2 lb fresh, ripe peaches
    3 tablespoons lemon juice
 1½ cups granulated sugar
    2 eggs, separated
    2 tablespoons confectioners' sugar
    1 cup heavy cream

1. Set refrigerator control at coldest temperature.
2. Reserve 2 peaches for garnish. Peel remaining peaches; halve and remove pits. Place peach halves in large bowl with lemon juice; crush with potato masher.
3. Stir in granulated sugar.
4. In medium bowl, with portable electric mixer, beat egg whites with confectioners' sugar until soft peaks form.
5. In small bowl, beat egg yolks well.
6. Fold yolks gently into whites, using wire whisk or rubber spatula.
7. Whip cream until it holds soft peaks; fold gently into egg mixture.
8. Fold in crushed peaches. Pour into 1-quart ice-cube tray or 8-inch square pan.
9. Freeze until firm around edges.

10. Transfer to bowl; beat with portable electric mixer until smooth and creamy. Return to tray.
11. Freeze until firm.
12. To serve: Peel and slice reserved peaches. Use to garnish servings. *Makes 6 servings (1 quart).*

Lemon-Raspberry Napoleon
(pictured)

Lemon Filling
 ⅓ cup granulated sugar
    3 tablespoons cornstarch
 ¼ teaspoon salt
 1⅓ cups milk
    2 large egg yolks
 ¼ cup fresh or frozen lemon juice, thawed
    1 tablespoon butter or magarine

 ½ pkg (17¼-oz size) frozen puff pastry (1 sheet)
 ⅓ cup seedless raspberry jam
    1 cup frozen whipped topping with real cream, thawed
      Confectioners' sugar
 ½ cup sliced natural almonds

1. Make Lemon Filling: In medium saucepan, combine granulated sugar, cornstarch and salt; stir to mix. Gradually add milk, stirring until smooth. Over medium heat, bring milk mixture to boiling, stirring constantly; remove from heat.
2. In small bowl, combine egg yolks and lemon juice; beat lightly. Add about one-third of the hot milk mixture to yolk mixture, stirring until blended. Stir yolk mixture into milk mixture remaining in saucepan. Over low heat, cook, stirring, 1 to 2 minutes without boiling; stir in butter until melted. Transfer Lemon Filling to medium bowl; press plastic wrap onto surface of filling; refrigerate until cold.
3. Meanwhile, thaw puff pastry as package label directs. Preheat oven to 400F. On lightly floured surface, with floured rolling pin, roll puff-pastry sheet to a 15-by-12-inch rectangle. With sharp knife, cut pastry into three 12-by-5-inch strips. Place strips on ungreased cookie sheets. Using fork, prick entire surface of each strip to prevent uneven puffing.

Fabulous 'n' Fruity Delights

4. Bake pastry strips 10 minutes or until lightly browned. (If strips begin to puff unevenly during baking, press surfaces lightly with metal spatula to release air.) Cool pastry strips completely on cookie sheets on wire racks.

5. Spread half of jam on each of two cooled pastry strips. Fold ½ cup whipped topping into Lemon Filling until no white streaks remain. Spread half of Lemon Filling evenly on each jam-covered pastry strip. On serving plate, place one strip, filling side up; top with second strip, filling side up; press layers together gently. Invert remaining pastry strip and place on top of filled layers. Chill 30 minutes.

6. Before serving, sift confectioners' sugar to lightly cover top of Napoleon. With metal spatula, spread remaining whipped topping on sides; press almonds on whipped topping to cover sides. Using spatula or blunt edge of knife, draw edge through sugar to score top. With serrated knife, cut into slices; serve immediately. *Makes 10 servings.*

Blackberry Flummery

2 cups blackberries
½ cup hot water
1 cup sugar
  Dash salt
⅛ teaspoon ground cinnamon
3 tablespoons water
2 tablespoons cornstarch
  Heavy cream (optional)

1. Wash and carefully pick over blackberries. In medium saucepan, combine blackberries, hot water, sugar, salt and cinnamon. Bring to boiling point; reduce heat and simmer, uncovered, about 5 to 8 minutes.

2. Add 3 tablespoons water to cornstarch, stirring to make a smooth paste. Blend into hot blackberry mixture; cook, stirring, until slightly thickened and translucent—3 to 5 minutes.

3. Cool completely. Then refrigerate in covered bowl to chill—2 hours.

4. Serve cold, with heavy cream, if desired. *Makes 6 servings.*

Fresh-Berry Cobbler

4 cups blueberries, strawberries, blackberries or raspberries, washed and hulled
⅔ cup sugar
½ teaspoon lemon juice
2 tablespoons butter or margarine
1½ cups packaged buttermilk-biscuit mix
3 tablespoons butter or margarine, melted
1 egg, slightly beaten
½ cup milk
  Whipped cream or ice cream

1. Preheat oven to 400F. Grease well a 10-by-6½-by-2-inch baking dish.

2. Toss berries lightly with sugar and lemon juice. Place in baking dish. Dot with 2 tablespoons butter.

3. In medium bowl, combine biscuit mix, melted butter, egg and milk. Lightly mix with fork just until combined. With a spoon, drop dough over fruit.

4. Bake 30 to 35 minutes or until top is golden-brown. Serve warm with whipped cream or ice cream. *Makes 6 servings.*

Individual Strawberry Shortcakes
(pictured)

2 pints fresh strawberries, washed and hulled
¼ cup sugar (or more to taste)

Shortcake

2 cups all-purpose flour
¼ cup sugar
1 tablespoon baking powder
½ teaspoon salt
½ cup (1 stick) butter or margarine, cut into chunks
⅔ cup milk

2 tablespoons unsalted butter or margarine, softened
½ cup heavy cream, whipped stiff

1. Slice strawberries into medium bowl; toss with ¼ cup sugar. Refrigerate. Preheat oven to 425F.

2. Make Shortcake: In large bowl, combine flour, sugar, baking powder and salt. With pastry blender or two knives, using a short cutting motion, cut in ½ cup butter until mixture resembles coarse cornmeal.

Fabulous 'n' Fruity Delights

3. In center of mixture, make a well; pour in milk. Mix with fork until flour is moistened. (Dough will be lumpy.)
4. Turn dough out onto floured pastry cloth; knead dough 8 to 10 times or until smooth. Roll dough ½ inch thick. With floured, 2¾-inch round cookie cutter, cut out four or five shortcakes. Lightly press remaining pieces of dough together; reroll and cut more to get six shortcakes in all. Place shortcakes 1 inch apart on ungreased cookie sheet. Bake 11 to 13 minutes or until light golden.
5. Split warm shortcakes horizontally. Place bottom halves, cut side up, on dessert plates. Spread with butter; spoon on half of strawberries, dividing evenly; top with other shortcake halves; spoon remaining strawberries on tops. Garnish with whipped cream. Serve immediately. *Makes 6 servings.*

Note: For quick shortcakes, use prepared biscuit mix; make and bake as label directs.

Frozen Lemon-Yogurt Pie

1 can (14 oz) sweetened condensed milk (not evaporated milk)
1 container (8 oz) plain low-fat yogurt
1 teaspoon grated lemon peel (optional if using frozen juice)
½ cup fresh or thawed, frozen lemon juice
1 cup (½ pint) heavy cream
1 pkg (6 oz) ready-to-fill butter-flavored piecrust
2 thin lemon slices, quartered (optional)

1. In medium bowl, combine condensed milk, yogurt and lemon peel and juice.
2. In small bowl, with portable electric mixer, beat cream until soft peaks form. Fold half of the whipped cream into lemon mixture until no white streaks remain; pour into piecrust. Freeze pie at least 3 hours or overnight. Cover remaining whipped cream with plastic wrap; refrigerate.
3. Just before serving, with wire whisk, re-whip remaining whipped cream just until stiff peaks form. Garnish pie with whipped cream and quartered lemon slices. *Makes 8 servings.*

Fondant-Dipped Strawberries

2 pint boxes large strawberries

<u>Fondant</u>
2½ cups confectioners' sugar
3 tablespoons lemon juice
2 tablespoons light corn syrup

1. Wash strawberries gently; drain well on paper towels. Leave hulls and stems on.
2. In top of double boiler, combine confectioners' sugar, lemon juice and corn syrup. Cook, stirring, over hot water until mixture is smooth and shiny and thin enough to coat strawberries. Remove from heat; keep warm over hot water.
3. Holding each strawberry by the stem, dip into fondant, covering berry. Place dipped berries, hull end down, 2 inches apart on racks placed on cookie sheets.
4. Let strawberries dry on racks at least 1 hour before serving. (Strawberries can be dipped in the morning for serving later in the day, but do not leave overnight.) *Makes about 30.*

Pineapple-Ginger Cake

1 pkg (18¼ to 18½ oz) yellow-cake mix (see Note)
1 can (1 lb, 4 oz) crushed pineapple in juice
  Water
1¼ teaspoons ground ginger
2 tablespoons butter or margarine
¼ cup lightly packed brown sugar
1 can (3½ oz) flaked coconut (1⅓ cups)

1. Preheat oven to temperature directed on cake-mix package label. Grease and flour a 13-by-9-by-2-inch baking pan. In strainer held over a 2-cup measuring cup, drain pineapple, pressing with back of spoon; set aside pineapple. Add enough water to pineapple juice to equal the amount of liquid needed in cake-mix package directions. Prepare cake mix as label directs, adding 1 teaspoon ginger. Pour batter into prepared pan; bake as directed.
2. About 5 minutes before cake is done, in small saucepan, melt butter; add brown sugar, coconut, drained pineapple and remaining ginger; stir till well mixed.

Fabulous 'n' Fruity Delights

When cake is done, remove from oven; turn oven to broil. Using a fork, spread pineapple mixture over surface of hot cake.

3. Broil with top of cake 4 inches from heat, turning pan if necessary, until topping is evenly browned—about 2 minutes. Serve cake warm or cold. *Makes 12 servings.*

    Note: Yellow-cake mix with pudding can be used.

Fresh Strawberries in Port

2 pint boxes fresh strawberries
½ cup sugar
1 cup red or white port wine
Sweetened whipped cream (optional)

1. Gently wash strawberries in cold water; drain and hull.
2. In medium bowl, gently toss strawberries with sugar. Add wine.
3. Refrigerate at least 2 hours, stirring occasionally.
4. If desired, top individual servings with sweetened whipped cream. *Makes 6 servings.*

Floating-Heart Cherries Jubilee

3 pints strawberry or vanilla ice cream

Cherries Jubilee
1 can (1 lb, 14 oz) pitted Bing cherries
1 tablespoon cornstarch
⅓ cup cherry, apricot or other fruit brandy
⅓ cup brandy or Curaçao

1. Line a 1½- to 2-quart heart mold with plastic wrap. Let ice cream stand at room temperature 15 minutes to soften slightly.
2. Pack ice cream firmly into mold. Freeze until serving. Then turn out into a serving dish with deep sides.
3. Make Cherries Jubilee: Drain cherries, reserving syrup. In 10-inch skillet, combine syrup and cornstarch; stir until smooth. Add cherry brandy; bring to boiling, stirring; boil 2 minutes. Stir in cherries; heat through.

4. Just before serving, heat brandy just until bubbles form around edge of pan and vapor begins to rise. Do not overheat. Ignite with match. Pour into cherry mixture.
5. Pour Cherries Jubilee around ice-cream mold. Serve over ice cream. *Makes 8 to 10 servings.*

Four-Fruit Flan With Lemon Sherbet

Cookie Shell
2¼ cups sifted all-purpose flour
¾ teaspoon baking powder
¼ teaspoon salt
⅔ cup (1⅓ sticks) butter or margarine, softened
1 cup sugar
1 egg
¾ teaspoon vanilla extract

3 pints lemon sherbet
3 fresh peaches
6 fresh apricots
½ lb green grapes
1 pint box blueberries or raspberries
Sugar
Mint leaves

1. Make Cookie Shell: Preheat oven to 400F. Line a 15½-by-10½-by-1-inch jelly-roll pan with foil, letting foil extend over ends about 1 inch; grease foil well. Sift flour, baking powder and salt; set aside.
2. In large bowl, with portable electric mixer at medium speed, beat butter with sugar, egg and vanilla until smooth and fluffy.
3. With wooden spoon, stir in half of flour mixture until blended. Add remaining flour mixture; mix until well blended. Refrigerate, covered, 1 hour. Press evenly over bottom and sides of prepared pan.
4. Bake 10 to 12 minutes or until golden-brown. Let cool completely.
5. Let sherbet soften slightly. Spread evenly over cookie shell.
6. Freeze, covered, until very firm—several hours or overnight.
7. Shortly before serving, wash all fruit and drain well. Peel peaches; cut each in sixths and toss with a little sugar. Cut apricots and grapes in half.

Fabulous 'n' Fruity Delights

8. Remove flan from freezer. Lift out of pan; remove foil. Arrange on serving tray, board or plate.
9. Drain peach wedges; place in a row diagonally across flan. Place two rows of grape halves, then a row of apricot halves, on each side of peach row. Fill corners with berries. Garnish center of peach row with several berries and one or two mint leaves. Serve immediately. *Makes 12 servings.*

Coeur à la Crème

- **2 pkg (8-oz size) cream cheese**
- **½ cup sugar**
- **1 cup heavy cream, whipped**
  Strawberries and Raspberries, recipe follows

1. Line a pretty, heart-shaped mold (about 6 inches in diameter and about 2 inches deep) with dampened cheesecloth, completely covering bottom and side of mold.
2. In medium bowl, let cream cheese stand at room temperature to soften—about 1 hour.
3. With wooden spoon, beat cheese with sugar until smooth. Beat in whipped cream, a small amount at a time, until mixture is light and smooth.
4. Turn into prepared mold, filling evenly. Smooth top with spatula. Refrigerate, covered, overnight or until well chilled.
5. To serve, turn into a serving dish with a rim. Surround with Strawberries and Raspberries. *Makes 8 or more servings.*

Note: This is a rather rich dessert; servings should be small.

Strawberries and Raspberries

- **1 pkg (10 oz) quick-thaw frozen strawberries, thawed**
- **1 pkg (10 oz) quick-thaw frozen raspberries, thawed**
  Water
- **1 tablespoon cornstarch**
- **¼ cup kirsch**

1. Drain fruits, reserving juice. Add water to juice to measure 1¾ cups.

2. In small saucepan, combine cornstarch and juice, mixing until smooth. Bring to boiling over medium heat, stirring constantly. Reduce heat and cook 5 minutes or until thickened and translucent. Let cool.
3. Add strawberries, raspberries and kirsch. Refrigerate, covered, overnight. *Makes 2½ cups.*

Banana-Cream Pie

Flaky Pastry, page 332, or 9-inch baked pie shell

Filling

- **⅔ cup granulated sugar**
- **¼ cup cornstarch**
  Dash salt
- **2½ cups milk**
- **3 large egg yolks**
- **1 tablespoon butter or margarine**
- **1 teaspoon vanilla extract**

- **2 medium bananas**
- **½ cup heavy cream (see Note)**
- **2 tablespoons confectioners' sugar**

1. Prepare Flaky Pastry.
2. Make Filling: In medium saucepan, combine granulated sugar, cornstarch and salt; mix well. Gradually stir in milk, mixing until smooth. Over medium heat, bring to boiling, stirring constantly; boil 1 minute, stirring. Remove from heat.
3. In small bowl, lightly beat egg yolks. Stir half of hot mixture into yolks, mixing well; pour yolk mixture into saucepan. Bring back to boiling, stirring. Cook 30 seconds longer. Into medium bowl, pour hot filling; stir in butter and vanilla. Cover surface with plastic wrap or waxed paper; refrigerate until cold.
4. To assemble: Pour half of filling into pie shell. Slice bananas into ¼-inch-thick rounds. Arrange banana slices evenly over filling. Cover with remaining filling.
5. In medium bowl, with portable electric mixer at medium speed, beat cream and confectioners' sugar until soft peaks form. Spoon whipped cream onto pie, swirling attractively to cover surface. Chill well. *Makes 8 servings.*

Note: If you like a higher topping, increase heavy cream to 1 cup and confectioners' sugar to 4 tablespoons. ▪

GEORGE RATKAI

The Grandest Cakes of All

❦ ❦ ❦

No matter how you slice them, these grand cakes offer a tiny taste of heaven with each scrumptious forkful. Each one is resplendently rich, handsomely adorned (we include decorating instructions, so don't worry) and divinely tempting. **At lower left** is an exquisite Dobos Torte, named for the Hungarian chef commissioned to create it. Eight layers of sponge cake are stacked with chocolate buttercream, then topped with a caramel layer that's been cut into wedges while hot. **At top**, raspberry-filled Chocolate-Truffle Cake is frosted with buttercream and crowned with creamy nut jewels of chocolate-sprinkled truffles. Recipes and instructions begin on page 346.

Above: Delicate chocolate curls accentuate this elegant pair. Devil's-Food Rum Cake, **at top,** is three layers of chocolate cake and rum-flavored cream covered with curls and sprinkled with confectioners' sugar. **Below it,** twin layers of fudge cake sandwich a creamy cocoa mousse in this fabulous Chocolate-Mousse Cake enveloped in Chocolate-Sour-Cream Frosting. *Recipes begin on page 349.*

Left: Circles of glistening cherries and sliced almonds top this ruffled Neapolitan Chocolate Cake, its layers separated by sweet almond cream and covered with cocoa frosting and chopped almonds. *See recipe on page 348.*

All chocolate lovers will delight in this dramatic duo. **Above,** triangles of mint candy radiate from atop this Crème-De-Menthe Chocolate Cake layered with a hint of the sweet liqueur itself and spread with a rich Dark-Chocolate Frosting. Chopped walnuts edge this Chocolate-Sundae Cake, **right,** that's four layers high, filled with cream, combed with Chocolate Frosting and dotted with frosting-dipped cherries sprinkled with nuts. *See recipes on pages 350 and 352.*

344

Say "I love you" with this beautiful Lemon-Strawberry Gâteau, a light and airy heart-shaped chiffon cake topped with fresh strawberries that nestle within a latticework of whipped-cream frosting. *See recipe on page 351.*

The Grandest Cakes of All

continued from page 341

Dobos Torte
(pictured)

8 Sponge-Cake Layers, recipe follows

<u>**Chocolate Buttercream**</u>
2 pkg (6-oz size) semisweet chocolate pieces
¾ lb (3 sticks) unsalted butter, softened
3 cups sifted confectioners' sugar
3 egg yolks

   Caramel Layer, recipe follows
¼ cup sifted unsweetened cocoa (optional)

1. Make cake layers as directed; cool.
2. Make Chocolate Buttercream: Melt chocolate over hot, not boiling, water; remove from heat; cool.
3. In small bowl, with portable electric mixer, beat butter with confectioners' sugar until light and fluffy. Add egg yolks, one at a time, beating until very light and fluffy. Place bowl in large bowl of ice. Gradually beat in chocolate; continue beating until stiff enough to spread.
4. On cake plate, put seven layers together with about ⅓ cup buttercream between each two. Reserve eighth layer. Frost around side of cake; reserve about ½ cup buttercream for later. Refrigerate.
5. Make Caramel Layer and cut as directed. Arrange wedges on top layer of cake, all around, spacing evenly. Tip each one slightly at an angle, as pictured, by placing a dot of reserved buttercream underneath. Frost around outside edge of caramel layer. Make frosting dot in center.
6. If desired, make design around side: Using a 2½- to 3-inch biscuit cutter, mark semicircles around bottom half of cake. Carefully apply cocoa around bottom half, as pictured. Refrigerate until serving. *Makes 12 servings.*

Sponge-Cake Layers
(for Dobos Torte)

8 eggs
1½ cups sifted cake flour
1½ teaspoons baking powder
½ teaspoon salt
1½ cups sugar
2 teaspoons vanilla extract

1. Day before: About 1 hour ahead, let eggs warm to room temperature.
2. Preheat oven to 400F. With waxed paper, line bottom of four 9-inch layer-cake pans; grease paper well (not sides). Sift flour, baking powder and salt onto a sheet of waxed paper.
3. In large mixer bowl, at high speed, beat eggs until thick; then add sugar gradually, continuing to beat until very thick and light.
4. Using rubber spatula or wire whisk, fold in flour mixture and vanilla. Turn into pans, using about 1¾ cups batter for each pan and spreading batter evenly. Bake 10 minutes or until surfaces spring back when gently pressed with fingertip.
5. Cool slightly; carefully turn out of pans; remove waxed paper at once; cool completely.
6. To split layers: Halfway up side of cake layer, all the way around, insert toothpicks. Using these as a guide, with long, sharp knife, carefully split layer. Remove picks. Repeat for other layers.

Caramel Layer

1 cup sugar
½ cup water
¼ teaspoon cream of tartar
   Reserved cake layer (from Dobos Torte)

1. In medium skillet, combine sugar, ½ cup water and the cream of tartar; stir to combine. Bring to boiling, stirring. Continue cooking just until mixture turns a golden-amber color—no longer. Remove from heat; turn into a cold skillet to prevent further cooking. Stir until bubbles are gone.
2. Place a large sheet of foil in a 9-inch cake pan, extending over edge. Grease well. Place reserved top cake layer in pan.
3. Pour caramel over cake layer evenly. Let stand 1 minute. Working quickly, using a large knife dipped in boiling water, make 12 grooves in caramel partway through. Then cut through completely with buttered scissors, separating wedges as they are cut.

Chocolate-Truffle Cake
(pictured)

   Chocolate-Cake Layers, recipe follows
12 Chocolate Truffles, recipe follows
   Chocolate Buttercream, recipe follows

¾ cup raspberry jam
   Chocolate sprinkles

1. Make Chocolate-Cake Layers as directed; cool.
2. Prepare Chocolate Truffles; store as directed.

The Grandest Cakes of All

3. Prepare Chocolate Buttercream.
4. To assemble cake: Place one Chocolate-Cake Layer on cake plate and spread with raspberry jam. Place second layer on top and spread with 1 cup Chocolate Buttercream. Top with third layer.
5. Set aside ¾ cup buttercream for decoration. With remaining buttercream, frost side and top of cake.
6. Swirl decorating comb around side and top of cake to create grooved effect, if desired.
7. Place the reserved buttercream in pastry bag fitted with a number-30 star tip.
8. Decorate cake with Chocolate Truffles, chocolate sprinkles and buttercream, as pictured. *Makes 12 servings.*

Chocolate-Cake Layers
(for Chocolate-Truffle Cake)

1   **cup unsweetened cocoa**
2   **cups boiling water**
2¾ **cups sifted all-purpose flour**
2   **teaspoons baking soda**
½   **teaspoon salt**
½   **teaspoon baking powder**
1   **cup (2 sticks) butter or margarine, softened**
2½ **cups sugar**
4   **eggs**
1½ **teaspoons vanilla extract**

1. In medium bowl, combine cocoa with boiling water, mixing with wire whisk until smooth. Cool completely.
2. Sift flour with baking soda, salt and baking powder onto a sheet of waxed paper. Preheat oven to 350F. Grease well and lightly flour three 9-by-1½-inch layer-cake pans.
3. In large bowl, with portable electric mixer at high speed, beat butter, sugar, eggs and vanilla, scraping bowl occasionally, until light—about 5 minutes.
4. At low speed, beat in flour mixture (in fourths) alternately with cocoa mixture (in thirds), beginning and ending with flour mixture. Do not overbeat.

5. Pour batter into pans, dividing evenly; smooth top. Bake 25 to 30 minutes or until surfaces spring back when gently pressed with fingertip.
6. Cool in pans 10 minutes. Carefully loosen sides with spatula; remove from pans; cool on wire racks. *Makes 3 (9-inch) cake layers.*

Chocolate Truffles

½   **cup walnuts**
3   **squares (1-oz size) semisweet chocolate**
2   **tablespoons heavy cream**
⅔   **cup confectioners' sugar**
1   **tablespoon Grand Marnier, Cointreau or rum**
⅓   **cup chocolate sprinkles**

1. Grind nuts in a blender or food processor. Line bottom of a 9-by-5-by-3-inch loaf pan with waxed paper.
2. In small heavy saucepan, combine chocolate and cream. Heat over low heat just until chocolate is melted. Remove from heat.
3. In medium bowl, combine nuts and sugar. With wooden spoon, stir until combined. Stir in chocolate mixture and liqueur to combine well.
4. Turn into prepared pan. Refrigerate until firm. Shape into 30 round balls. Roll in chocolate sprinkles. Store, covered, in refrigerator until ready to use. *Makes about 30 pieces.*

Chocolate Buttercream

¾   **lb (3 sticks) butter, softened**
2   **cups sifted confectioners' sugar**
3   **egg yolks, unbeaten**
1   **pkg (6 oz) semisweet chocolate pieces**

1. With portable electric mixer at medium speed, beat butter until fluffy.
2. Gradually beat in confectioners' sugar; then beat in egg yolks, one at a time, beating until very fluffy.

The Grandest Cakes of All

3. In top of double boiler, melt chocolate pieces over hot, not boiling, water; remove from heat to cool completely.
4. Then beat chocolate into butter mixture, beating until of spreading consistency.

Neapolitan Chocolate Cake
(pictured)

3 (9-inch) Dark-Chocolate-Cake Layers (see Note)

Cream Filling
1 cup heavy cream, chilled
¼ cup confectioners' sugar
½ teaspoon almond extract

Cocoa-Cream Frosting
¾ cup light cream or evaporated milk, undiluted
⅓ cup (⅔ stick) butter, softened
¼ teaspoon salt
½ cup sifted unsweetened cocoa
2 teaspoons vanilla extract
6 cups sifted confectioners' sugar

½ cup sliced, unblanched almonds
1 jar (4 oz) candied red cherries
½ oz semisweet chocolate, shaved

1. Make 3 (9-inch) Dark-Chocolate-Cake Layers; cool.
2. Make Cream Filling: Beat heavy cream with ¼ cup confectioners' sugar and the almond extract just until stiff; refrigerate.
3. Make Cocoa-Cream Frosting: In small saucepan, heat cream until bubbles form around edge of pan. Let cool slightly.
4. In medium bowl, combine butter, salt, cocoa, vanilla, the hot cream and 3 cups confectioners' sugar.
5. With wooden spoon or portable electric mixer at medium speed, beat mixture until smooth.
6. Gradually add remaining sugar, beating until smooth and fluffy. If frosting seems too thick to spread, gradually beat in a little chilled cream.
7. To assemble cake: Set aside 1⅓ cups Cocoa-Cream Frosting for decorating. Chop half of sliced almonds (save 65 slices for top of cake). Chop half of cherries (save 14 for top).

8. On cake plate, place a Dark-Chocolate-Cake Layer, top side down; spread with half of Cream Filling. Sprinkle with half of chopped cherries and shaved chocolate.
9. Add second layer, top side down; spread with rest of Cream Filling; top with rest of chopped cherries and chocolate.
10. Add third layer, top side up. To frost: With metal spatula, frost side first, covering whipped cream; use rest of frosting on top. Cover side with chopped, sliced almonds.
11. To decorate: Following picture on page 342, with reserved frosting, make a shell border on top, using a pastry bag fitted with a number-4 star tip. Make a circle of sliced almonds; then make a shell border on the other side of almonds. Slice 11 cherries in half and arrange in a circle inside border.
12. Pipe on another smaller circle of shell border; arrange remaining sliced almonds and make another shell border, with the three whole cherries in the center. Pipe a border around the bottom. Refrigerate until serving. *Makes 16 servings.*

Note: Use 2 packages chocolate-cake mix, making four (9-inch) layers. Freeze one for later use. Or make recipe for Dark-Chocolate-Cake Layers, below.

Three (9-inch) Dark-Chocolate-Cake Layers

1 cup unsifted, unsweetened cocoa
2 cups boiling water
2¾ cups sifted all-purpose flour
2 teaspoons baking soda
½ teaspoon salt
½ teaspoon baking powder
1 cup (2 sticks) butter, softened
2½ cups sugar
4 eggs
1½ teaspoons vanilla extract

1. In medium bowl, combine cocoa with boiling water, mixing with wire whisk until smooth. Cool completely. Onto a sheet of waxed paper, sift flour with soda, salt and baking powder.

The Grandest Cakes of All

2. Preheat oven to 350F. Grease well and lightly flour three 9-by-1½-inch layer-cake pans.
3. In large bowl, with portable electric mixer at high speed, beat butter, sugar, eggs and vanilla, scraping bowl occasionally, until light—about 5 minutes.
4. At low speed, beat in flour mixture (in fourths) alternately with cocoa mixture (in thirds), beginning and ending with flour mixture. Do not overbeat.
5. Pour batter into pans, dividing evenly; smooth tops. Bake 25 to 30 minutes or until surfaces spring back when gently pressed with fingertip. Cool in pans 10 minutes.
6. Carefully loosen sides with spatula; remove from pans; cool on racks. *Makes 3 (9-inch) cake layers.*

Devil's-Food Rum Cake
(pictured)

3 (8-inch) Devil's-Food-Cake Layers (see Note)

Rum-Whipped-Cream Filling and Frosting

2 cups heavy cream, chilled
1 cup sifted confectioners' sugar
3 tablespoons golden rum

Chocolate Buttercream

½ cup granulated sugar
3 tablespoons water
2 eggs
½ cup (1 stick) butter
2 squares semisweet chocolate, melted

1 bar (8 oz) milk chocolate
Golden rum
Confectioners' sugar

1. Make 3 (8-inch) Devil's-Food-Cake Layers as directed; cool.
2. Make Rum-Whipped-Cream Filling and Frosting: Combine heavy cream and 1 cup confectioners' sugar in medium bowl. Refrigerate, covered, 30 minutes.
3. With portable electric mixer at high speed, beat mixture until stiff. Gradually add 3 tablespoons rum, beating until stiff. Refrigerate.
4. Make Chocolate Buttercream: In small saucepan, combine granulated sugar and 3 tablespoons water. Bring to boiling, stirring with wooden spoon until sugar is dissolved.

5. Continue cooking, over medium heat, to 250F on a candy thermometer or until a little in cold water forms a soft ball.
6. Meanwhile, in small bowl, with electric mixer at high speed, beat eggs until thick and fluffy.
7. Gradually add sugar syrup to beaten eggs, beating until mixture is cool—2 to 3 minutes. Add butter and semisweet chocolate. Continue beating 5 minutes longer. Refrigerate 30 minutes before filling cake.
8. To shave chocolate: Warm milk-chocolate bar, still wrapped, in a warm spot just until soft, not melting. Then, with vegetable peeler, pressing lightly, pare along bar in short strokes.
9. To assemble cake: On plate, place a cake layer, top side down; brush with 1½ tablespoons rum; then spread with Chocolate Buttercream. Add second layer, top side down; brush with 1½ tablespoons rum; spread with 1½ cups whipped-cream filling. Add third layer, top side up; brush with 1½ tablespoons rum.
10. With spatula, frost cake with remaining whipped-cream filling.
11. Decorate side and top with shaved chocolate, as pictured. Sift confectioners' sugar over top. Refrigerate until ready to serve. *Makes 12 servings.*

Note: Use 1 package devil's-food-cake mix, making three 8-inch layers. Or make recipe for Three (8-inch) Devil's-Food-Cake Layers, page 197.

Chocolate-Mousse Cake
(pictured)

1 (8-inch) Fudge-Cake Layer, split in half (see Note)

Chocolate-Mousse Layer

2 cups heavy cream
1 cup sifted confectioners' sugar
½ cup unsweetened cocoa
1½ teaspoons unflavored gelatine
4 tablespoons cold water
1 teaspoon vanilla extract
Dash salt

1 bar (8 oz) milk chocolate, at room temperature

The Grandest Cakes of All

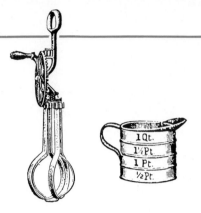

Chocolate-Sour-Cream Frosting

1 pkg (6 oz) semisweet chocolate pieces
½ cup sour cream
Dash salt

1. Prepare and bake Fudge-Cake Layer as directed; cool.
2. Make Chocolate-Mousse Layer: Refrigerate cream, confectioners' sugar and cocoa in medium bowl. In a small saucepan, sprinkle gelatine over 4 tablespoons cold water; let stand 5 minutes to soften. Heat, stirring, over hot water until dissolved; let cool. Line an 8-inch layer-cake pan with plastic wrap.
3. Add vanilla and salt to chilled cream mixture. Beat with portable electric mixer until stiff enough to hold its shape. Refrigerate ½ cup for decorating later. Stir cooled gelatine into remaining cream mixture.
4. Turn into prepared cake pan, spreading evenly. Refrigerate until firm—about 2 hours.
5. Make chocolate curls: Place chocolate bar in warm spot just until soft, not melting. With a vegetable peeler, pressing lightly, pare along bar in long strokes, forming large, thin curls. Refrigerate on tray until needed.
6. To assemble cake: Place a Fudge-Cake Layer, cut side up, on cake plate. Invert Chocolate-Mousse Layer on top. (Loosen with spatula.) Remove plastic wrap.
7. Place remaining cake layer on mousse layer, cut side down. Refrigerate.
8. Make Chocolate-Sour-Cream Frosting: In top of double boiler, over hot water, melt chocolate pieces. Remove top of double boiler from hot water.
9. Add sour cream and salt; using wooden spoon, beat frosting until of spreading consistency.
10. To frost: Remove cake from refrigerator. With spatula, frost entire cake smoothly.
11. Fill pastry bag, fitted with number-4 rose tip, with reserved chocolate mousse; pipe rosettes around edge of cake, as pictured.
12. Mound chocolate curls in center of cake. Refrigerate until ready to serve. *Makes 10 servings.*

Note: Use one package chocolate-cake mix; freeze one layer. Or make recipe for One (8-inch) Fudge-Cake Layer, this page.

One (8-inch) Fudge-Cake Layer

1 square unsweetened chocolate
1 cup sifted cake flour
¾ cup sugar
½ teaspoon baking soda
½ teaspoon salt
¼ cup shortening
½ cup sour cream
1 egg
½ teaspoon vanilla extract
2 tablespoons hot water

1. Preheat oven to 350F. Grease well and flour one 8-by-1½-inch layer-cake pan.
2. Melt chocolate over hot, not boiling, water; let cool.
3. Into large bowl, sift flour with sugar, soda and salt. Add shortening and sour cream. With portable electric mixer at medium speed, beat 2 minutes, occasionally scraping side of bowl and guiding mixture into beaters with rubber spatula.
4. Add egg, vanilla, melted chocolate and hot water; beat 2 minutes longer.
5. Pour batter into prepared pan; bake 30 to 35 minutes or until surface springs back when gently pressed with fingertip.
6. Cool in pan 10 minutes. Remove from pan. Cool thoroughly on wire rack. *Makes 1 (8-inch) cake layer.*

Crème-De-Menthe Chocolate Cake
(pictured)

3 (9-inch) Dark-Chocolate-Cake Layers (see Note)

Crème-De-Menthe Filling

6 tablespoons (¾ stick) butter, softened
3½ cups confectioners' sugar
6 tablespoons green crème-de-menthe

Dark-Chocolate Frosting

1 pkg (6 oz) semisweet chocolate pieces
½ cup light cream
1 cup (2 sticks) butter
2½ cups confectioners' sugar

1 box (6 oz) chocolate-coated square mints

The Grandest Cakes of All

1. Prepare Dark-Chocolate-Cake Layers; bake and cool.
2. Make Crème-De-Menthe Filling: In medium bowl, combine 6 tablespoons butter, 3½ cups confectioners' sugar and crème-de-menthe. Using a portable mixer or wooden spoon, beat until smooth and fluffy.
3. On cake stand, put layers together, using half of Crème-De-Menthe Filling between each two layers.
4. Make Dark-Chocolate Frosting: In medium saucepan, combine chocolate pieces, cream and butter; stir over medium heat until smooth. Remove from heat.
5. With wire whisk, blend in confectioners' sugar. Turn into bowl placed over ice; beat until it holds its shape.
6. With metal spatula, frost side of cake, as pictured; spread rest of frosting over top, swirling decoratively.
7. Cut mints in half, on diagonal; use to decorate cake, as pictured. Refrigerate cake about 1 hour before serving. *Makes 16 servings.*

Note: Use 1½ packages dark-chocolate-cake mix to make 3 (9-inch) layers. Or make recipe for Three (9-inch) Dark-Chocolate-Cake Layers, page 348.

Buttermilk Clove Cake

     3 **cups all-purpose flour**
  1½ **teaspoons baking soda**
     2 **teaspoons ground cloves**
     1 **teaspoon ground cinnamon**
   ½ **teaspoon ground nutmeg**
   ¼ **teaspoon ground allspice**
     1 **cup butter or margarine, softened**
  1½ **cups light-brown sugar, packed**
     2 **eggs**
     1 **egg yolk**
  1½ **cups buttermilk**

1. Preheat oven to 350F. Grease and flour 2 (9-by-1½-inch) round layer-cake pans.
2. Sift flour with baking soda, cloves, cinnamon, nutmeg and allspice; set aside.
3. In large bowl, with portable electric mixer at high speed, beat butter, brown sugar, eggs and egg yolk, occasionally scraping side of bowl with rubber spatula, until light and fluffy—about 5 minutes.
4. At low speed, beat in flour mixture (in fourths) alternately with buttermilk, beginning and ending with flour mixture. Beat just until smooth—about 1 minute.
5. Pour batter into prepared pans; bake 25 to 30 minutes or until surfaces spring back when gently pressed with fingertip.
6. Cool in pans 10 minutes. Remove from pans; cool completely on wire rack before filling and frosting. Frost as desired. *Makes 2 (9-inch) layers.*

Lemon-Strawberry Gâteau
(pictured)

Lemon Chiffon Cake
     1 **cup egg whites (7 or 8)**
  2¼ **cups sifted cake flour**
  1¾ **cups granulated sugar**
     3 **teaspoons baking powder**
     1 **teaspoon salt**
   ½ **cup salad oil**
     7 **egg yolks**
   ¾ **cup water**
     1 **tablespoon grated lemon peel**
     2 **teaspoons vanilla extract**
   ½ **teaspoon cream of tartar**

     3 **cups heavy cream, well chilled**
   ½ **cup confectioners' sugar**
   ½ **cup currant jelly**
     1 **tablespoon water**
     1 **pint medium-size fresh strawberries**

1. Make Lemon Chiffon Cake: Let egg whites warm to room temperature in large bowl—about 1 hour. Meanwhile, preheat oven to 325F.
2. Sift flour with granulated sugar, baking powder and salt into another large bowl. Make well in center.
3. Add, in order, the oil, egg yolks, ¾ cup water, the lemon peel and vanilla; beat with spoon until smooth.
4. Sprinkle cream of tartar over egg whites; with portable electric mixer at high speed, beat until very stiff peaks form when beaters are slowly raised. Do not underbeat.
5. Pour batter over egg whites; with rubber spatula or wire whisk, using an under-and-over motion, gently fold into egg whites just until blended.
6. Turn into an ungreased, 12-cup heart-shaped pan or 10-inch springform pan; bake 1 hour and 15 minutes or until cake springs back when gently pressed with fingertips.
7. Invert cake by hanging between two loaf pans; cool cake completely—about 2 hours.
8. With spatula, carefully loosen cake from pan; remove.
9. With mixer, beat cream with confectioners' sugar until stiff. Frost top and side of cake evenly, using 2 cups whipped cream.
10. With remaining whipped cream, in a pastry bag with a number-6 decorating tip, make lattice to cover top of cake. (Allow 1½ inches between diagonals.)
11. Melt currant jelly with 1 tablespoon water; cool. Dip strawberries with hulls into syrup. Remove to cake rack to set.
12. Place on top of cake, as shown. *Makes 12 servings.*

The Grandest Cakes of All

Chocolate-Sundae Cake

(pictured)

2 (9-inch) Devil's-Food-Cake Layers (see Note)

Whipped-Cream Filling

2 cups heavy cream, chilled
½ cup confectioners' sugar
1 teaspoon vanilla extract

Chocolate Frosting

4 squares unsweetened chocolate
¼ cup (½ stick) butter
3 cups sifted confectioners' sugar
⅓ cup warm water or coffee
1½ teaspoons vanilla extract

9 large maraschino cherries with stems, drained
½ cup coarsely chopped walnuts

1. Prepare Devil's-Food-Cake Layers; bake and cool.
2. Make Whipped-Cream Filling: In medium bowl, combine heavy cream, ½ cup confectioners' sugar and 1 teaspoon vanilla. Beat until stiff; refrigerate, covered.
3. Make Chocolate Frosting: In top of double boiler, over hot water, melt chocolate and butter. Remove from water; with wooden spoon, stir in confectioners' sugar, warm water and vanilla; beat with wooden spoon until smooth and creamy.
4. With long serrated knife, split cooled cake layers crosswise to make four layers. Place bottom layer, cut side up, on cake stand. Spread with one-third of filling; put rest of layers together with one-third filling between them.
5. Dip cherries (not stems) into frosting; sprinkle with a few chopped nuts, if desired. Set aside.
6. With metal spatula, frost side of cake. Pour rest of frosting on top. Decorate, partway up side, with chopped nuts. With cake comb, make lines around top half of cake. Place cherries evenly around edge of cake. Refrigerate if not serving at once. *Makes 12 servings.*

   Note: Use a packaged devil's-food-cake mix for two cake layers. Or make recipe for Three (8-inch) Devil's-Food-Cake Layers, page 197, but use two 9-by-1½-inch layer-cake pans.

Orange-Crème Chiffon Cake

Orange Chiffon Cake

1 cup egg whites (7 or 8)
2 cups sifted all-purpose flour
1½ cups granulated sugar
1 tablespoon baking powder
1 teaspoon salt
½ cup salad oil
5 egg yolks
¾ cup water
3 tablespoons grated orange peel
1 teaspoon vanilla extract
½ teaspoon cream of tartar

Orange Crème

1 cup heavy cream
½ cup confectioners' sugar
2 tablespoons grated orange peel
1 tablespoon shredded orange peel

1. Make Orange Chiffon Cake: Let egg whites warm to room temperature in large bowl—1 hour.
2. Preheat oven to 325F. Sift flour with 1½ cups granulated sugar, baking powder and salt into another large bowl. Make well in center.
3. Add oil, egg yolks, water, 3 tablespoons orange peel and the vanilla; beat with spoon until smooth.
4. In first bowl, with portable electric mixer at high speed, beat egg whites with cream of tartar until stiff peaks form when beaters are slowly raised.
5. Pour egg-yolk mixture gradually over egg whites; with rubber spatula or wire whisk, using an under-and-over motion, gently fold into egg whites just until blended.
6. Turn out into ungreased 10-inch tube pan; bake 60 minutes or until cake tester inserted in center comes out clean.
7. Invert and fit tube-pan opening over neck of bottle; let cake cool completely—1½ hours.
8. Carefully loosen cake from pan. Invert onto wire rack; then turn out, top side up, onto serving plate.
9. Make Orange Crème: In medium bowl, mix cream, confectioners' sugar and grated orange peel. Refrigerate until very cold—30 minutes. With portable electric mixer, beat just until stiff.
10. Frost top and side of cake with Orange Crème. Sprinkle with shredded orange peel. *Serves 12.*

The Grandest Cakes of All

Zuppa Inglese

Sponge Cake, recipe follows
Cream Filling, recipe follows
Custard Sauce, recipe follows
½ **cup light rum**
9 **tablespoons raspberry jam**
½ **cup heavy cream, whipped**
Toasted almonds (see Note)

1. Make Sponge Cake, Cream Filling and Custard Sauce as directed. Split cake layers to make four.
2. Sprinkle layers evenly with rum. Spread three layers with raspberry jam, using 3 tablespoons of jam for each layer.
3. In large serving bowl, put layers together with Cream Filling on three layers, using about a cup for each. Set plain layer on top.
4. Pour Custard Sauce over top. With pastry bag filled with whipped cream, using a number-6 decorating tip, pipe rosettes over top of cake. Insert toasted almonds in whipped cream. Refrigerate until serving time—several hours or overnight. *Makes 12 servings.*

Note: To toast almonds, preheat oven to 325F. Place almonds on cookie sheet. Bake until lightly browned—about 20 minutes. Let cool.

Sponge Cake

4 **eggs**
1 **cup sifted cake flour**
¾ **teaspoon baking powder**
¼ **teaspoon salt**
¼ **teaspoon cream of tartar**
1 **cup sugar**
¼ **cup water**
1 **teaspoon vanilla extract**
1 **teaspoon lemon juice**

1. Separate eggs, putting whites in large bowl, yolks in small bowl. Let the egg whites warm to room temperature—1 hour.
2. Preheat oven to 350F.
3. Sift flour, baking powder and salt onto a piece of waxed paper.
4. Add cream of tartar to egg whites. With portable electric mixer at medium speed, beat whites until foamy. Gradually beat in ½ cup sugar, a tablespoon at a time. Continue beating until stiff glossy peaks form when beaters are raised.
5. With same beaters, beat egg yolks until thick and lemon-colored. Gradually beat in remaining sugar, a tablespoonful at a time. Beat until thick and light—2 minutes.
6. In measuring cup, combine ¼ cup water, the vanilla and lemon juice.

7. At low speed, blend flour mixture, one-third at a time, into egg-yolk mixture, alternately with water mixture. Beat 1 minute.
8. With wire whisk or rubber spatula, fold into egg-white mixture.
9. Pour batter into two ungreased 8-inch layer-cake pans.
10. Bake 25 to 30 minutes or just until surfaces spring back when lightly pressed with fingertip.
11. Invert pans, setting rims on two other pans. Cool 1½ hours.
12. Loosen around edge. Tap inverted pans on counter top to loosen.

Cream Filling

⅓ **cup sugar**
1 **tablespoon cornstarch**
2 **cups milk**
2 **tablespoons butter or margarine**
6 **egg yolks**
½ **teaspoon vanilla extract**
¾ **cup mixed, candied fruit**

1. In medium saucepan, combine sugar and cornstarch. Gradually add milk; stir until smooth. Add butter.
2. Cook over medium heat, stirring constantly, until mixture is thickened and comes to boiling. Boil 1 minute. Remove from heat.
3. In medium bowl, slightly beat egg yolks. Gradually add a little hot mixture, beating well.
4. Stir into rest of hot mixture; cook over medium heat, stirring constantly, just until mixture boils. Remove from heat; stir in vanilla.
5. Strain custard immediately into bowl. Refrigerate, covered, until cool. Stir in candied fruit. Return to refrigerator until well chilled. *Makes about 2½ cups.*

Custard Sauce

½ **cup sugar**
1 **tablespoon cornstarch**
2 **cups milk**
½ **teaspoon grated lemon peel**
2 **egg yolks, slightly beaten**
¼ **teaspoon vanilla extract**
2 **tablespoons light rum**

1. In medium saucepan, combine sugar and cornstarch. Gradually add milk, stirring constantly. Add the lemon peel.
2. Bring to boiling, stirring constantly; boil 1 minute. Stir a little of hot mixture into egg yolks; return to saucepan, stirring. Bring to boiling; remove from heat and stir in vanilla.
3. Refrigerate, covered, until well chilled—at least 3 hours; stir in rum.

Ice Cream And Creamy Specialties

❦ ❦ ❦

Ice cream, plain and simple, is the all-time favorite treat. So it only stands to reason that desserts made with ice cream are fabulous favorites as well. In addition, we'd like to offer some creamy classics made with cream and other luscious ingredients. The first is this grand and glorious Diplomat Cake made with ladyfingers, orange marmalade, whipped cream and a flourish of chocolate curls. Recipes for this and other wonderful desserts begin on page 361.

Ice cream abounds in these frozen fantasy desserts that are unbelievably quick and easy to create. **In the center:** Cherry-vanilla ice cream and sherry-sprinkled jelly-roll slices are combined in this fabulous Ice-Cream Trifle With Custard Sauce crowned with whipped cream and maraschino cherries. Surrounding it, **clockwise from top:** Superbly simple yet sophisticated, Spumoni-Ice-Cream Cake consists of side-by-side bricks of spumoni ice cream decoratively frosted with whipped cream and served with juicy raspberries; a large brandy snifter catches this Rainbow Parfait with its pot-o'-gold stripes of fruited sherbets and coffee ice cream, all topped with a fluffy cloud of whipped cream and a solitary stemmed cherry; Ice-Cream Petits Fours are multicolored morsels of ice cream or sherbet daintily decorated with candied flowers and piped with whipped cream; crushed candies mix with vanilla ice cream for the bottom layer of this Lemon-Candy-Ice-Cream Pie, served à la mode with more scoops of vanilla and sprinkles of crumbs from the graham-cracker crust; and Pink-Pistachio Layer Cake stacks strawberry- and pistachio-ice-cream rounds inside a frosting of whipped cream garnished with pistachio nuts and strawberries. *Recipes begin on page 361.*

357

Clockwise from top: Della Robbia Ice-Cream Ring features marzipan fruits, assorted nuts and small leaves arranged artfully as a fanciful wreath that sits atop a ring of vanilla ice cream. Brandied chestnut sauce makes a delightful accompaniment. Bright stripes of chocolate, vanilla, mint and marshmallow build this Peppermint Parfait into a deluxe dessert that towers above the rest. Serve with long-handled spoons. A scoop of plain vanilla ice cream becomes a super-duper Caramel-Walnut Sundae when it's surrounded by vanilla wafers, accented with walnut halves and whipped cream and drenched with gooey, golden caramel sauce; and last but not least, simple vanilla ice cream assumes gourmet overtones when spiked with anise flavoring to become sophisticated Anise Ice Cream. *Recipes begin on page 363.*

358

At right: Strawberry-Ice-Cream Torte is so very simple, yet stunning, it's no wonder that it's a favorite with everyone. Strawberry ice cream, frozen in a round cake pan, becomes the colorful and creamy filling between a split layer of chocolate cake. A paper doily provides a decorative stencil for confectioners' sugar, and each slice is served with yummy chocolate syrup. Mix and match cake and ice-cream flavors to create your own terrific torte. *See recipe on page 366.*

Below is Lindy's Famous Cheesecake, one of the very best you'll ever have the pleasure of tasting. The recipe starts with a sweet home-made crust baked in a spring-form pan. The filling is an outrageously rich mix of cream cheese, heavy cream and eggs with a light accent of fresh lemon and orange. Glazed red cherries add the finishing flourish to this most fabulous of desserts. *See recipe on page 365.*

GEORGE RATKAI

GEORGE RATKAI/PAUL DOME

Ice Cream and Creamy Specialties

continued from page 355

Diplomat Cake
(pictured)

1⅓ cups orange marmalade
⅔ cup dark rum
3 pkg (3-oz size) ladyfingers
1 cup heavy cream, whipped
Chocolate curls (see Note)

1. Line a 1½-quart decorative mold with plastic wrap.
2. In small bowl, combine orange marmalade with ⅓ cup rum; mix well. Set aside ¼ cup of mixture and refrigerate for later use.
3. Split ladyfingers; brush cut sides with remaining ⅓ cup rum.
4. In bottom of mold, arrange two layers of split ladyfingers, cut side up. Spread with 2 tablespoons marmalade mixture.
5. Repeat Step 4.
6. Around side of mold, arrange a row of split ladyfingers vertically, rounded side against mold. Continue layering ladyfingers and marmalade mixture to fill center of mold, as in Step 4, ending with ladyfingers. Cover top with plastic wrap; refrigerate several hours or overnight.
7. To unmold, remove plastic wrap from top; invert mold onto serving plate; gently remove mold and wrap.
8. Spoon reserved ¼ cup marmalade-rum mixture over top of cake, letting it drizzle down sides.
9. Using pastry tube with number-5 star tip, make rosettes of whipped cream around base of cake and on top, as pictured. Arrange chocolate curls on top rosettes. Refrigerate. *Makes 8 servings.*

Note: To make chocolate curls: Put squares of unsweetened chocolate or a chocolate bar in a warm place to soften slightly but not melt. Pare with vegetable parer, forming curls.

Spumoni-Ice-Cream Cake
(pictured)

2 (½-gallon) bricks spumoni ice cream
3 cups heavy cream, whipped
2 pkg (10-oz size) frozen raspberries, thawed

1. Place serving dish in freezer to chill.
2. To assemble cake: Place firm ice-cream bricks side by side on chilled serving plate to form a square. Frost top and sides with some of whipped cream. Using remaining whipped cream in a pastry bag with rosette tip, decorate top and sides, as pictured.
3. Freeze until very firm—about 3 hours. If keeping more than one day, wrap with plastic wrap after cream has frozen.
4. To serve: Cut cake in slices. Let guests spoon raspberries over individual servings. *Makes 18 servings.*

Pink-Pistachio 'Layer Cake'
(pictured)

2 quarts strawberry ice cream
1 quart pistachio ice cream
1 cup strawberry jam
2 cups heavy cream, whipped
½ cup chopped pistachio nuts
1 pint box strawberries, washed, hulled and halved

1. Let ice cream soften slightly. Line 3 (8-inch) layer-cake pans with plastic wrap.
2. Press each quart ice cream firmly and evenly into a prepared layer-cake pan.
3. Freeze, covered, until very firm—several hours.
4. To assemble: Remove ice cream from pans; remove plastic wrap. Place a strawberry layer on serving plate; spread with half of jam. Add pistachio layer; spread with rest of jam. Top with remaining layer.
5. Frost top and side with the whipped cream. Sprinkle side with pistachio nuts. Freeze until very firm—about 3 hours. (For longer storing, wrap frozen cake in plastic wrap or foil.)
6. To serve: Decorate top of cake with strawberry halves. *Makes 12 to 15 servings.*

Ice Cream and Creamy Specialties

Ice-Cream Trifle
With Custard Sauce
(pictured)

Custard Sauce
- 3 **cups milk**
- 6 **egg yolks**
- ½ **cup sugar**
- **Dash salt**
- 1 **teaspoon vanilla extract**

Trifle
- **Baker's jelly roll (about 11 oz)**
- ½ **cup cream sherry**
- 3 **pints vanilla ice cream**
- 6 **tablespoons maraschino-cherry juice**
- 1 **cup heavy cream, whipped**
- 10 **maraschino cherries**
- **Angelica (optional)**

1. Make Custard Sauce: Heat milk in top of double boiler, over direct heat, until tiny bubbles appear around edge of pan.
2. In medium bowl, combine egg yolks, sugar and salt; beat until well mixed. Slowly add hot milk, beating constantly.
3. Return mixture to double-boiler top; cook over hot, not boiling, water, stirring constantly, until thin coating forms on metal spoon—12 to 15 minutes.
4. Stir in vanilla. Immediately strain into bowl; cover and refrigerate.
5. Make Trifle: Cut jelly roll into 10 slices. Use 6 slices to line side and bottom of a 2-quart glass serving bowl. Sprinkle with ¼ cup sherry. Set aside.
6. In large bowl of electric mixer, combine ice cream and cherry juice; let stand until ice cream has softened. Beat first at low speed, then at high speed until well combined and ice cream is evenly colored.
7. Spoon one-third into cake-lined dish; top with remaining cake slices, cutting to fit if necessary. Drizzle with remaining sherry. Spoon about 1 cup remaining ice cream over top—just enough to cover cake. Turn remaining ice cream into a 9-by-9-by-1¾-inch baking pan.
8. Freeze both, covered, until very firm—about 3 hours.
9. To serve: Make small balls from ice cream in square pan. Place on top of trifle in bowl. Decorate with

whipped cream; garnish with maraschino cherries and angelica, if desired. Pass Custard Sauce. *Makes 10 to 12 servings.*

Lemon-Candy-Ice-Cream Pie
(pictured)

Crust
- 1¼ **cups packaged graham-cracker crumbs**
- ¼ **cup sugar**
- ¼ **cup (½ stick) butter or margarine, softened**

Lemon-Candy Ice Cream
- 2 **quarts vanilla ice cream**
- 1 **cup (½ lb) lemon sour balls, crushed**
- ⅛ **teaspoon yellow food color**

1. Make Crust: In medium bowl, combine graham-cracker crumbs, sugar and butter; blend with fork. Measure ⅓ cup and set aside. Press remaining crumb mixture evenly on bottom and side of a 9-inch pie plate. Place in freezer until ready to fill.
2. Make Lemon-Candy Ice Cream: Let 1 quart ice cream soften slightly. Turn into medium bowl; add crushed lemon candy and food color. With wooden spoon, stir just until combined and ice cream is evenly colored.
3. Spoon into crust, mounding slighty in center. Freeze, covered, until firm—about 1 hour.
4. Top pie with medium scoops of ice cream, mounding in center. Sprinkle reserved crumb mixture on pie, as pictured. Cover and return to freezer until firm—about 1 hour.
5. To serve, cut into wedges. *Makes 8 to 10 servings.*

Ice-Cream Petits Fours
(pictured)

- 4 **(1-pint) bricks ice cream and/or sherbet (any desired flavors)**
- 1 **cup heavy cream, whipped**
  Crystallized violets, rose petals, lilac blossoms and/ or mint leaves

Ice Cream and Creamy Specialties

1. Line a shallow baking pan with waxed paper; place in freezer to chill well.
2. Remove very firm ice cream from freezer, one pint at a time; quickly unwrap and cut as follows: Using long, sharp knife, cut in half lengthwise; then cut each half crosswise into thirds. With spatula, arrange pieces in chilled prepared pan; return to freezer immediately.
3. Freeze until very firm—about 2 hours.
4. To decorate, place whipped cream in pastry bag with star, leaf or small writing tip, or use all three. Pipe whipped cream on each block of ice cream and add flowers as pictured. (To prevent excess melting, set pan over ice cubes in a roasting pan when decorating.)
5. Cover pan of petits fours with foil or plastic wrap. Freeze until very firm—about 2 hours.
6. To serve: Using a spatula, remove petits fours from pan. Place in white paper baking cups, if desired, and arrange on chilled dessert plates. *Makes 12 servings.*

Caramel-Walnut Sundaes
(pictured)

Caramel Sauce
- 1 cup sugar
- 2 tablespoons light corn syrup
- ¼ cup water
- 1 cup heavy cream

- 1 quart vanilla ice cream
- 18 vanilla wafers
- ¾ cup walnut halves
- ½ cup heavy cream, whipped

1. Make Caramel Sauce: Combine sugar, corn syrup and ¼ cup water in small, heavy skillet.
2. Heat, stirring constantly, just until sugar dissolves. Then cook over very low heat (mixture should just barely bubble), uncovered, 30 to 40 minutes or until a light-amber color. Do not stir. Syrup should not be dark.
3. Remove from heat. Let cool slightly—about 5 minutes. Slowly add 1 cup cream, stirring constantly until syrup is smooth. Let cool.

4. To make sundaes: Place a scoop of ice cream in each of 6 chilled sherbet glasses.
5. Cut wafers in half and press 6 halves into each scoop of ice cream. Place walnut halves between wafers, as pictured.
6. Spoon 1 or 2 tablespoons Caramel Sauce over each sundae.
7. Decorate each with whipped cream and top with a walnut half. Pass remaining sauce. *Makes 6 servings.*

Rainbow Parfait
(pictured)

- 1 pint raspberry sherbet
- 1 pint orange sherbet
- 1 pint lime or mint sherbet
- 1½ pints coffee ice cream
- 1 cup heavy cream
- ¼ cup confectioners' sugar
- 3 tablespoons curaçao (see Notes)
  Maraschino cherry, with stem

1. Let sherbet and ice cream soften slightly before making each layer as follows: For first layer, lay 2-quart brandy snifter on side and, using back of wooden spoon, press raspberry sherbet evenly over side of snifter. Lay snifter on side in freezer, propping it so it won't roll, and freeze until sherbet is firm—about 1 hour.
2. For second layer, press orange sherbet on top of raspberry sherbet and freeze.
3. For third layer, press lime sherbet on orange sherbet and freeze.
4. For fourth layer, stand snifter upright and fill with ice cream. Freeze, covered, in upright position until very firm—at least 4 hours.
5. To serve: In medium bowl, beat cream with sugar until stiff; beat in curaçao. Spoon some on parfait; garnish with cherry. Pass rest of whipped cream. *Makes 8 to 10 servings.*

   Notes: You may purchase a miniature bottle of curaçao (orange liqueur), if desired.

   The picture shows a 4½-quart brandy snifter filled with 4 pints raspberry sherbet, 2 pints orange sherbet, 2 pints lime sherbet and 1 quart coffee ice cream.

Ice Cream and Creamy Specialties

Peppermint Parfaits
(pictured)

    Chocolate Sauce, recipe follows
2 pints vanilla ice crem
¾ cup green mint jelly
1 pint pink-peppermint-stick ice cream
¾ cup prepared marshmallow sauce
1 cup heavy cream
2 tablespoons confectioners' sugar
    Maraschino cherries (optional)

1. Make Chocolate Sauce; let cool to room temperature. Spoon a tablespoon Chocolate Sauce into bottom of each of eight 8-ounce chilled parfait glasses (or use any tall glasses).
2. Add to each, in order, a rounded tablespoon vanilla ice cream, rounded tablespoon mint jelly, small scoop (¼ cup) peppermint ice cream and a tablespoon prepared marshmallow sauce.
3. Top each with a scoop of vanilla ice cream; then drizzle with remaining Chocolate Sauce. Place in freezer.
4. Whip cream with confectioners' sugar until stiff. Decorate each parfait with whipped cream and maraschino cherries. Freeze until firm. If keeping more than one day, cover with plastic wrap.
5. To serve: If parfaits are kept in freezer more than 24 hours, remove them from freezer 15 minutes before serving. *Makes 8 servings.*

Chocolate Sauce

½ cup sugar
¼ cup unsweetened cocoa
½ cup light cream or half-and-half
⅓ cup light corn syrup
¼ cup (½ stick) butter or margarine
2 squares unsweetened chocolate
    Dash salt
1½ teaspoons vanilla extract

1. In small saucepan, combine sugar and cocoa; mix well. Add cream, corn syrup, butter, chocolate and salt.

2. Cook over medium heat, stirring constantly, until sauce is smooth and comes to boiling. Remove from heat; stir in vanilla. *Makes 1½ cups.*

Anise Ice Cream
(pictured)

1 pint vanilla ice cream, softened
½ teaspoon anise flavoring

1. In medium bowl, combine ice cream and anise; quickly stir until well blended.
2. Return to ice-cream container, ice-cube tray or 3 or 4 Dixie cups. Freeze until firm. *Makes 3 or 4 servings.*

Della Robbia Ice-Cream Ring
(pictured)

4 pints vanilla ice cream
1 jar (9½ oz) marrons (chestnuts) in vanilla syrup
2 tablespoons brandy
1 pkg (8 oz) marzipan fruits
½ cup assorted nuts (walnuts, Brazil nuts, pecans, filberts, almonds)

1. Place a 1½-quart ring mold in freezer to chill well.
2. Press ice cream firmly and evenly into chilled mold. Freeze, covered with foil or plastic wrap, until very firm—several hours or overnight.
3. To unmold: Dip ring mold into warm water; invert onto chilled serving plate or cookie sheet. Return ice cream to freezer until top is firm.
4. Drain marrons, reserving syrup. Set aside 4 marrons for decorating ice-cream ring. Chop remaining marrons and add to reserved syrup with brandy; refrigerate.
5. To decorate ice cream: Arrange marzipan fruits, the 4 marrons and the nuts on top of firm ring. Return to freezer. If keeping more than one day, wrap with foil or plastic wrap.
6. To serve: Garnish wreath with small leaves, if desired. Pass marron sauce. *Makes 10 servings.*

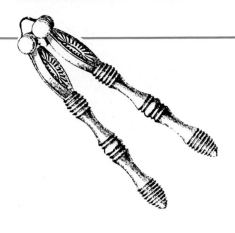

Ice Cream and Creamy Specialties

Lindy's Famous Cheesecake
(pictured)

1 **cup sifted all-purpose flour**
¼ **cup sugar**
1 **teaspoon grated lemon peel**
½ **teaspoon vanilla extract**
1 **egg yolk**
¼ **cup (½ stick) butter or margarine, softened**

Filling

5 **pkg (8-oz size) cream cheese, at room temperature**
1¾ **cups sugar**
3 **tablespoons all-purpose flour**
1½ **teaspoons grated lemon peel**
1½ **teaspoons grated orange peel**
¼ **teaspoon vanilla extract**
5 **eggs**
2 **egg yolks**
¼ **cup heavy cream**

Red-Cherry Glaze or Strawberry Glaze, recipes follow

1. In medium bowl, combine flour, sugar, lemon peel and vanilla. Make well in center; add egg yolk and butter. Mix with fingertips until dough cleans side of bowl.
2. Form into a ball and wrap in waxed paper. Refrigerate about 1 hour.
3. Preheat oven to 400F. Grease the bottom and side of a 9-inch springform pan. Remove the side from the pan.
4. Roll one-third of dough on bottom of springform pan; trim edge of dough.
5. Bake 8 to 10 minutes or until golden.
6. Meanwhile, divide rest of dough into 3 parts. Roll each part into a strip 2½ inches wide and about 10 inches long.
7. Put together springform pan, with the baked crust on bottom.
8. Fit dough strips to side of pan, joining ends to line inside completely. Trim dough so it comes only three-fourths way up side of pan. Refrigerate until ready to fill.
9. Preheat oven to 500F. Make Filling: In large bowl of electric mixer, combine cheese, sugar, flour, lemon and orange peels and vanilla. Beat, at high speed, just to blend.

10. Beat in eggs and egg yolks, one at a time. Add cream, beating just until well combined. Pour mixture into springform pan.
11. Bake 10 minutes. Reduce oven temperature to 250F and bake 1 hour longer.
12. Let cheesecake cool in pan on wire rack. Glaze top with Red-Cherry or Strawberry Glaze. Refrigerate 3 hours or overnight.
13. To serve: Loosen pastry from side of pan with spatula. Remove side of springform pan. Cut cheesecake into wedges. *Makes 16 to 20 servings.*

Red-Cherry Glaze

1 **can (1 lb) sour red cherries, packed in water**
¼ **cup sugar**
1 **tablespoon cornstarch**
1 **tablespoon lemon juice**

1. Drain cherries, reserving ½ cup liquid. Set cherries aside until ready to use.
2. In small saucepan, combine sugar and cornstarch. Add reserved cherry liquid, stirring until mixture is smooth.
3. Bring to boiling, stirring, over medium heat; boil 2 or 3 minutes. The mixture will be thickened and translucent.
4. Remove from heat; let cool slightly. Add lemon juice and cherries. Cool thoroughly before spooning over top of cooled cheesecake. *Makes 2 cups glaze.*

Strawberry Glaze

2 **pkg (10-oz size) frozen strawberry halves, thawed**
2 **tablespoons sugar**
1 **tablespoon cornstarch**

1. Drain strawberries, reserving ½ cup liquid.
2. In a small saucepan, combine sugar and cornstarch. Stir in reserved liquid.
3. Over medium heat, bring to boiling, stirring; boil 1 minute.
4. Remove from heat; cool slightly. Stir in strawberries; cool completely before spooning over top of cooled cheesecake. *Makes 2 cups.*

Ice Cream and Creamy Specialties

Strawberry-Ice-Cream Torte
(pictured)

8-inch chocolate-cake layer (see Note)
1 quart strawberry ice cream or ice milk
2 tablespoons strawberry preserves
Confectioners' sugar
Chocolate syrup

1. Split cake layer in half crosswise.
2. Line an 8-inch layer-cake pan with plastic wrap. Pack with ice cream; freeze until very firm.
3. Shortly before serving, place a cake layer, split side up, on cake plate. Unmold ice-cream layer on top, removing plastic wrap. Spread with preserves. Top with remaining cake layer, split side down.
4. Place paper doily with cutout pattern on top. Sift confectioners' sugar over top; carefully remove doily. Serve torte with chocolate syrup. *Makes 12 servings.*

Note: Make from packaged mix or favorite recipe. Freeze other layer for use another time.

Black-Bottom Ice-Cream Pie

Crust
1¼ cups chocolate wafer crumbs
¼ cup (½ stick) butter or margarine, melted

2 pints chocolate ice cream
2 squares semisweet chocolate, melted
1 cup heavy cream
¼ cup sugar
2 tablespoons golden rum
Semisweet chocolate curls

1. Make Crust: In medium bowl, combine cookie crumbs and melted butter; mix well. With fingers, press mixture evenly on bottom and side of a 9-inch pie plate. Place in freezer.
2. Let ice cream soften slightly. Turn into large bowl. With portable electric mixer at medium speed, beat just until smooth. Gradually add melted chocolate, beating constantly—chocolate will harden and form very fine pieces. Turn into crumb crust; return to freezer.

3. In small bowl, beat cream until thick. Gradually beat in sugar until mixture is stiff. Fold in rum.
4. Freeze until mixture mounds—about 2 hours. Spoon on pie, swirling top.
5. Freeze until very firm—at least 2 hours. If keeping more than 1 day, wrap with plastic wrap after cream has frozen.
6. To serve, garnish with chocolate curls. *Makes 8 servings.*

Pineapple Upside-Down Ice-Cream Cake

2 quarts pineapple ice cream
1 can (1 lb, 4½ oz) sliced pineapple, well drained
5 maraschino cherries
Whipped cream or whipped dessert topping
1 jar (6 oz) pecan-sundae topping

1. Let ice cream soften slightly. Line an 8-inch square baking pan with plastic wrap.
2. Press ice cream firmly and evenly into prepared pan. Freeze, covered, until very firm—several hours or overnight.
3. To serve: Invert ice cream onto serving plate; remove plastic wrap. Arrange a pineapple slice in each corner and one in center of ice-cream square. Cut 4 other slices in half; press 2 halves against each side of ice cream. Place a cherry in center of each whole pineapple slice.
4. Pipe rosettes of whipped cream on plate around ice cream. Decorate open space on top with some of pecan topping. Spoon rest of pecans on plate. Drizzle any remaining syrup from topping over all. *Makes 8 to 10 servings.*

Pistachio-Ice-Cream Surprise

4 pints pistachio ice cream
Chocolate Sauce, page 364
½ cup coarsely chopped pistachios
1 cup heavy cream
¼ cup confectioners' sugar
½ teaspoon vanilla extract

Ice Cream and Creamy Specialties

1. Line side and bottom of 9-inch tube pan with foil. Press 3 pints ice cream firmly and evenly into pan. Then, with back of spoon, make a 1-inch-deep and 1-inch-wide trench in ice cream ½ inch from outside edge. Freeze until firm—about 2 hours.
2. Meanwhile, make Chocolate Sauce. Let cool to room temperature. Spoon ½ cup sauce into trench in firm ice cream; return to freezer for 1 hour. Refrigerate remaining sauce.
3. Spoon remaining ice cream evenly over sauce in trench, covering completely. Freeze, covered, until very firm—at least overnight.
4. To assemble: With spatula, loosen around edge of pan and center tube. Invert onto serving platter; peel off foil. Press pistachio nuts around side. Place in freezer.
5. Whip cream with confectioners' sugar and vanilla. Place in pastry bag with number-6 star tip; decorate top of ice-cream ring. Freeze until firm. If keeping more than one day, wrap with plastic wrap.
6. To serve: Cut ring into wedges. Pass remaining Chocolate Sauce, reheated in double boiler. *Makes 10 to 12 servings.*

Mocha Gâteaux Glacés

 3 **pints coffee ice cream**
 3 **(1⅛-oz size) chocolate-covered toffee bars, chilled**
 1 **pkg (6 oz) semisweet chocolate pieces**
 2 **tablespoons butter or margarine**
 2 **tablespoons light corn syrup**
 2 **jars (1½-oz size) chocolate shot**
 ½ **cup heavy cream, whipped**

1. Let ice cream soften slightly. Pound toffee bars into small pieces; return to refrigerator. Line an 8-by-8-by-2-inch pan with plastic wrap.
2. Turn ice cream into large bowl; add pieces of toffee. With wooden spoon, stir just until combined. Turn into prepared pan; freeze, covered, until very firm—several hours.
3. Meanwhile, in top of double boiler, combine chocolate pieces, butter and corn syrup; cook over hot

water, covered, until melted and smooth. Remove from heat but leave top over hot water.
4. On sheet of waxed paper, draw an 8-inch square and, next to it, a 4½-inch square. Place on a cookie sheet. Spread squares evenly with chocolate mixture; freeze 1 hour.
5. About an hour before serving, remove ice cream from pan; remove plastic wrap. Cut into 9 equal portions. With fork, lift squares one at a time and dip sides in chocolate shot. Place on a cookie sheet and return to freezer.
6. Cut each chocolate square into 9 equal pieces. Halve each piece from smaller square diagonally. Return to refrigerator.
7. To serve: Place ice-cream pieces on chilled serving plates. Cover each with a chocolate square. Then top each with a swirl of whipped cream; decorate with two chocolate triangles, set in cream at desired angle to each other. *Makes 9 servings.*

Ice-Cream Bonbon

Chocolate Coating
 1 **cup semisweet chocolate pieces**
 2 **tablespoons butter or margarine**
 2 **tablespoons light corn syrup**

 2 **pints butter-pecan ice cream**
 2 **pints chocolate ice cream**
 ¼ **cup semisweet chocolate pieces**

1. Make Chocolate Coating: Draw a 9¼-by-8¾-inch rectangle on waxed paper placed on a cookie sheet. Also draw two 5-by-3-inch rectangles on the waxed paper.
2. In top of double boiler, combine 1 cup chocolate pieces, the butter and corn syrup. Cook over hot water, stirring, until melted and smooth. Remove from heat; keep double-boiler top in place over hot water.
3. Spread 1 tablespoon Chocolate Coating over each small rectangle on waxed paper; spread rest over large rectangle. Refrigerate until firm.

Ice Cream and Creamy Specialties

4. Line a 9-by-5-by-3-inch loaf pan with foil. Press butter-pecan ice cream firmly and evenly into pan. Freeze until firm.
5. Spread chocolate ice cream over firm layer in loaf pan. Freeze, covered, until firm.
6. To assemble: Remove chocolate-coated waxed paper from refrigerator. Let stand at room temperature 3 minutes or just until chocolate will peel off easily.
7. Turn ice cream out of pan onto a chilled cookie sheet; peel off foil. Press small chocolate rectangles against ends of ice cream and large chocolate rectangle over top and sides, trimming to fit. Return to freezer.
8. Place ¼ cup chocolate pieces in custard cup; set in hot water until melted. Put chocolate in pastry bag with number-6 plain writing tip and quickly decorate top of mold and close chocolate seams. Freeze until firm. If keeping more than a day, wrap with plastic wrap.
9. To serve: Let stand at room temperature several minutes before slicing. Cut into 8 thick slices; then cut each in half. *Makes 16 servings.*

Christmas Ice-Cream Torte

Meringue Layers

9 egg whites
1½ teaspoons cream of tartar
3 cups sugar
1 tablespoon white vinegar
1½ teaspoons vanilla extract

2 pints mint-chocolate-chip ice cream
2 pints pink-peppermint-stick ice cream
Chocolate Sauce, page 364

1. Make Meringue Layers: In large bowl, let egg whites warm to room temperature — about 1 hour.
2. With portable electric mixer at high speed, beat egg whites with cream of tartar just until soft peaks form when beaters are slowly raised.
3. Gradually beat in sugar, ¼ cup at a time, beating well

after each addition. Beat in vinegar and vanilla. Continue beating until very stiff — 12 minutes longer.
4. Meanwhile, using inverted 8-inch round layer-cake pan as guide, trace three 8-inch circles on three 10-inch squares of heavy brown wrapping paper. Place paper on cookie sheets.
5. Preheat oven to 200F. Spread 1½ cups meringue evenly on each circle on brown paper to within ½ inch of edge. With wooden pick, draw lines, ½ inch apart, on one layer; then draw lines at right angles, ½ inch apart.
6. Using remaining meringue in pastry bag with number-6 star tip, make decorative border around each layer. On layer with lines, make a double border of meringue — this will be top layer.
7. Bake meringues 3 hours. Turn off oven heat; let cool in oven several hours.
8. Meanwhile, line two 9-inch round layer-cake pans with foil. Press mint-chocolate-chip ice cream firmly and evenly into one pan, peppermint ice cream into other pan. Freeze, covered, until firm.
9. To serve: Peel paper very gently from meringue layers. Remove foil from ice cream. Layer meringues and ice cream on serving plate, topping with meringue layer with double border. Pass Chocolate Sauce. *Makes 12 servings.*

Valentine Cheesecake

1 pkg (8 oz) cream cheese, softened
½ lb creamed cottage cheese
¾ cup granulated sugar
2 eggs
1½ tablespoons cornstarch
1½ tablespoons flour
2 teaspoons lemon juice
½ teaspoon vanilla extract
¼ cup (½ stick) butter or margarine, melted
1 cup sour cream

Confectioners' sugar
Sour cream (optional)
1 pkg (10 oz) thawed, frozen strawberries (optional)

Ice Cream and Creamy Specialties

1. Preheat oven to 325F. Line bottom of a 9-inch, heart-shaped layer-cake pan with waxed paper. Grease bottom and side generously.
2. In large bowl, with portable electric mixer at high speed, beat cream cheese and cottage cheese until creamy and well combined. Gradually beat in granulated sugar; then beat in eggs until well combined.
3. At low speed, beat in cornstarch, flour, lemon juice and vanilla. Add melted butter and 1 cup sour cream; beat just until smooth.
4. Pour into prepared pan; bake 40 minutes or until firm around the edge. Turn off oven heat; let cake stand in oven 2 hours.
5. Remove cake from oven. Let cool completely in pan; then refrigerate until well chilled — several hours.
6. Remove cheesecake from pan: Run spatula around side of pan; then turn out cheesecake onto cookie sheet; invert onto serving plate so that browned side is up.
7. Refrigerate until serving time. To serve: Sprinkle lightly with confectioners' sugar. Serve with sour cream and thawed, frozen strawberries. *Makes 8 to 10 servings.*

Strawberries on Strawberry Bavarian Cream

4 pint boxes strawberries
1 tablespoon lemon juice
1 cup sugar
 Red food color
2 env unflavored gelatine
½ cup cold water
2 cups heavy cream
 Fresh mint sprigs

1. Gently wash strawberries under cold water; drain well. Hull.
2. Crush half the strawberries with potato masher or blend in electric blender 1 minute. You should have about 2 cups purée.
3. In large bowl, combine crushed strawberries, lemon juice, sugar and a few drops food color; stir until well blended.

4. In small saucepan, sprinkle gelatine over ½ cup cold water to soften. Heat over low heat, stirring constantly, until gelatine is dissolved. Stir gelatine into the strawberry mixture.
5. Place bowl in larger bowl of ice and water. Chill, stirring occasionally, until mixture thickens and mounds slightly.
6. Meanwhile, in large bowl with portable electric mixer, beat cream until stiff. Carefully fold chilled gelatine mixture into cream.
7. Turn mixture into a 2-quart, shallow glass serving bowl; cover and refrigerate at least 4 hours or until firm.
8. To serve: Mound remaining whole strawberries on Bavarian cream. Decorate with sprigs of fresh mint. *Makes 8 to 10 servings.*

Rum-Date Ice Cream

½ cup quartered, pitted dates
¼ cup coarsely chopped walnuts
 4 candied red cherries, quartered
 1 tablespoon dark rum
 1 pint vanilla ice cream, softened

1. In medium bowl, combine dates, walnuts, cherries and rum; let stand 30 minutes.
2. Add ice cream; quickly stir just until combined.
3. Turn into ice-cube tray. Freeze until firm. *Makes 3 or 4 servings.*

Plum-Pudding-Ice-Cream Bombe

 3 pints coffee ice cream
 Dark fruitcake
 1 pint cherry-vanilla ice cream

1. Line 2-quart round or oval mold with foil. Using back of wooden spoon, press 2 pints coffee ice cream over entire bottom and against side of mold to within 1 inch of top. Place in freezer until firm — about 1 hour.

Ice Cream and Creamy Specialties

2. Cut five or six ¾-inch-thick slices of fruitcake, 3 inches long and 1½ inches wide. Arrange vertically against ice cream around side of mold, overlapping if necessary. Pack cherry-vanilla ice cream into center of mold to within 1 inch of top; fill with remaining coffee ice cream, completely covering fruitcake and cherry-vanilla ice cream.
3. Place in freezer, covered, until very firm — at least overnight.
4. To serve: Loosen around edge of mold with spatula. Invert onto chilled serving plate; peel off foil. *Makes 10 to 12 servings.*

Pink-Champagne Sherbet

> 3 pints vanilla ice milk or ice cream
> 1¼ cups pink champagne
> ⅛ teaspoon red food color
>   Fruit for garnish (optional)

1. Turn ice milk into large bowl; beat just until smooth but not melted. Quickly stir in champagne and food color until well combined.
2. Turn into a 1½-quart heart-shaped mold. Freeze until firm — overnight, if possible.
3. To serve: Invert mold onto serving platter; place hot, damp cloth over mold and shake to release ice milk. Garnish with fruit, if desired. Serve at once. *Makes 6 to 8 servings.*

Cold Caramel Soufflé

> ¾ cup egg whites (about 6 eggs)
> 3¼ cups superfine granulated sugar
>   English Custard Sauce, recipe follows

1. In large bowl of electric mixer, let egg whites warm to room temperature—about 1 hour.
2. Meanwhile, place 1½ cups sugar in medium-size heavy skillet. To caramelize, cook over medium heat, stirring, until sugar is completely melted and begins to boil—syrup should be a medium brown.

3. Hold a 1½-quart ovenproof glass casserole with a pot holder, and pour in hot syrup all at once. Tilt and rotate casserole until bottom and side are thoroughly coated. Set on wire rack and let cool.
4. Beat egg whites at high speed until very stiff—about 5 minutes.
5. While continuing to beat, gradually pour in 1¼ cups sugar in continuous stream—takes about 3 minutes. Scrape side of bowl with rubber spatula. Beat 10 minutes.
6. Meanwhile, about 5 minutes before beating time is up, place ½ cup sugar in heavy medium skillet and caramelize as in Step 2. Remove from heat and immediately place skillet in pan of cold water for a few seconds or until syrup is thick; stir constantly.
7. With mixer at medium speed, gradually pour syrup into beaten egg-white mixture. Scrape side of bowl with rubber spatula. Return to high speed and continue beating 3 minutes longer.
8. Preheat oven to 250F.
9. Turn out egg-white mixture into prepared casserole, spreading evenly. Set in large baking pan; pour boiling water to 1-inch depth around casserole.
10. Bake 1 hour or until meringue seems firm when gently shaken and rises about ½ inch above casserole.
11. Meanwhile, make English Custard Sauce.
12. Remove casserole from water; place on wire rack to cool. Refrigerate until well chilled—6 hours or overnight.
13. To unmold: Run small spatula around edge of meringue to loosen. Hold casserole in pan of very hot water at least 1 minute. Invert onto serving dish.
14. Pour some of the sauce over meringue and pass the rest. *Makes 8 servings.*

English Custard Sauce

> ⅓ cup sugar
> 1 tablespoon cornstarch
> 2 cups milk
> 2 tablespoons butter or margarine
> 6 egg yolks
> 1½ teaspoons vanilla extract
> ½ cup heavy cream

Ice Cream and Creamy Specialties

1. In medium saucepan, combine sugar and cornstarch. Gradually add milk; stir until smooth. Then add butter.
2. Cook over medium heat, stirring constantly, until mixture is thickened and comes to boil. Boil 1 minute. Remove from heat.
3. In medium bowl, slightly beat egg yolks. Gradually add a little hot mixture, beating well.
4. Stir into rest of hot mixture; cook over medium heat, stirring constantly, just until mixture boils. Remove from heat; stir in vanilla.
5. Strain custard immediately into bowl. Refrigerate, covered, until cool. Stir in heavy cream. Return to refrigerator until well chilled. *Makes about 2½ cups.*

Danish Cherry-Rice Pudding

½ cup short-grain white rice
5 cups milk
  Sugar
½ teaspoon salt
1 tablespoon butter or margarine
3 env unflavored gelatine
½ cup cold water
1 tablespoon vanilla extract
1 teaspoon almond extract
½ pint heavy cream

Sour-Cherry Topping

1 can (1 lb) sour red cherries, packed in water
⅓ cup sugar
1 tablespoon cornstarch
2 drops red food color (optional)

¼ cup sliced, unblanched almonds

1. Lightly oil an 8-inch springform pan. In top of double boiler, combine rice, 4 cups milk, ½ cup sugar, the salt and butter. Cook, covered, stirring occasionally, over boiling water (add more boiling water as needed to bottom of double boiler) until rice is tender—about 1 hour to 1 hour and 10 minutes.
2. Meanwhile, sprinkle gelatine over ½ cup cold water to soften.

3. Add softened gelatine to rice mixture; stir to dissolve. Remove from water. Turn into medium mixing bowl. Add ½ cup sugar, the vanilla and almond extracts and remaining cup milk; mix well.
4. Set bowl in larger bowl of ice cubes to chill, stirring occasionally, until mixture is as thick as unbeaten egg white—15 minutes. Meanwhile, beat cream until stiff; refrigerate.
5. With wire whisk or wooden spoon, fold whipped cream into chilled rice mixture, mixing until well combined. Turn into prepared pan. Refrigerate until well chilled and firm—4 hours or overnight.
6. Make Sour-Cherry Topping: Drain canned cherries; reserve liquid. Set cherries aside.
7. In small saucepan, combine sugar and cornstarch; mix well. Add 1 cup reserved cherry liquid, stirring until mixture is smooth.
8. Bring to boiling, stirring, over medium heat; boil 2 to 3 minutes. The mixture will be thickened and translucent.
9. Remove from heat; let cool slightly. Add the cherries and the food color. Cool thoroughly before spooning over top of rice.
10. To serve: Loosen side of pan with spatula; remove. Spoon Sour-Cherry Topping over top. Garnish edge with almonds. Refrigerate until ready to serve. *Makes 12 servings.*

Butterscotch-Cornflake Ice-Cream Ring

1 cup light-brown sugar, packed
1½ tablespoons light corn syrup
⅓ cup milk
3 tablespoons butter or margarine
4 cups cornflakes

1 quart strawberry ice cream
  Strawberries (optional)
1 jar (12 oz) chocolate sauce

1. In small saucepan, combine brown sugar, corn syrup, milk and butter. Cook, stirring, over medium heat until sugar is dissolved. Continue cooking, without

Ice Cream and Creamy Specialties

stirring, until a little dropped in cold water forms a soft ball or until temperature on candy thermometer registers 238F. Remove from heat.

2. Meanwhile, grease a large bowl well with butter. Add syrup mixture; then add cornflakes; toss together until cornflakes are completely coated with syrup.

3. Pack cornflake mixture into a buttered 8- or 9-inch ring mold. Let stand at room temperature until serving.

4. Form ice cream into balls. Freeze until serving.

5. To serve: Turn ring out on serving platter. Fill with ice-cream balls. If desired, decorate with strawberries. Serve with chocolate sauce. *Makes 8 servings.*

Chocolate-Cinnamon Ice Cream

½ vanilla bean
2 cups light cream or half-and-half
2 egg yolks
½ cup sugar
1½ teaspoons cornstarch
⅛ teaspoon salt
3 squares (1-oz size) semisweet chocolate
1 tablespoon ground cinnamon
¾ cup heavy cream

1. Split vanilla bean; with tip of knife, scrape seeds into light cream in medium saucepan. Heat until bubbles appear around edge of pan.

2. In medium bowl, beat egg yolks with sugar, cornstarch and salt until well combined. Gradually stir in hot cream. Return to saucepan; cook over medium heat, stirring constantly, until mixture is thickened and just comes to boiling.

3. Add chocolate and cinnamon. Remove from heat; stir until chocolate is melted. Set aside until cool.

4. Stir in heavy cream.

5. Freeze in ice-cream maker according to manufacturer's instructions.

6. Serve immediately or spoon into freezer containers and place in freezer. Serve with prepared semisweet chocolate sauce. *Makes 6 servings (about 1 quart).*

Pontchartrain Ice-Cream Pie

1 pkg (11 oz) piecrust mix
1 quart strawberry ice cream
1 quart chocolate ice cream
5 egg whites
½ teaspoon vanilla extract
½ cup sugar
   Chocolate Sauce, page 364

1. Prepare and bake 10-inch pie shell according to package directions; cool thoroughly. Wrap and freeze remaining pastry for another use.

2. Let ice cream soften slightly. Spoon in alternate layers into baked pie shell. Wrap and freeze until very firm—several hours or overnight.

3. To serve: In large bowl, let egg whites warm to room temperature—about 1 hour. With portable electric mixer at high speed, beat egg whites and vanilla just until soft peaks form when beaters are slowly raised.

4. Add sugar, 2 tablespoons at a time, beating well after each addition. Continue beating until meringue is shiny and stiff peaks form.

5. Spread meringue over pie, covering ice cream and edge of crust completely. Make swirls on top.

6. Broil, 5 to 6 inches from heat, until meringue is lightly browned—about 3 minutes.

7. Serve at once. Pass Chocolate Sauce. *Makes 8 servings.*

Note: If ice-cream pie is frozen very hard, remove from freezer about 20 to 30 minutes before putting on meringue and broiling.

Ginger Ice Cream

1 pint vanilla ice cream, softened
2 tablespoons chopped, candied ginger
   Yellow food color (optional)

1. In medium bowl, combine ice cream, ginger and a few drops food color; quickly stir just until combined.

2. Return to ice-cream container or ice-cube tray. Freeze until firm. *Makes 3 or 4 servings.*

Index